HISTORY OF BRIGHAM YOUNG

1847 - 1867. *Berkeley, Calif.*

MassCal Associates
2855 Telegraph Avenue
Berkeley, California, 94705

CONTENTS

INTRODUCTION

This history is a copy of the three manuscripts

"Early Records of Utah" [P-F 22]
"Incidents in Utah History" [P-F 26]
"Utah Historical Incidents" [P-F 67]

in the Bancroft Library, University of California, Berkeley. A number of descriptions of these manuscripts have appeared in the literature, three of which follow:

History of Brigham Young. 1847-1867.
3 v. 32 cm.   HHB [P-F 22, 26, 67]
Abstracts from an official journal, kept in Brigham Young's name in the Church Historian's Office. Sent to H. H. Bancroft in three instalments, entitled "Early Records of Utah" [1847-1851] P-F 22: 164 p.; "Incidents in Utah History" [1852-1854] P-F 26: 63 p.; and "Utah Historical Incidents" [1855-1867] P-F 67: 324 p. (D. L. Morgan and G. P. Hammond (eds.), A Guide to the Manuscript Collections of the Bancroft Library (Berkeley: University of California Press, 1963), I, 98.)

EXCERPTS FROM THE MANUSCRIPT HISTORY OF BRIGHAM YOUNG
A journal of the early history of Utah, 1847-1867, abstracted from records in the Church Historian's Office, Salt Lake City, for H. H. Bancroft. 3 v. 31 cm. Bound and cataloged separately.
Under Brigham Young, the Church Historian's Office maintained the manuscript collection "History of Brigham Young," into which were copied, in journal fashion, letters, reports, official acts of ecclesiastical and civil government, newspaper items, diaries,

and otherwise original sources, detailing the
history of the church and territory. The ma-
terials abstracted from these records for
Bancroft were bound into three volumes, titled and cataloged in Bancroft Library as
follows:

"Early Records of Utah," [1847-51]. 164
p. 31 cm. Monthly journal, July 1847-Dec.
1851. [P-F 22]

"Incidents in Utah History," [1852-54]. 63
p. 31 cm. Monthly journal, Jan. 1852-Dec.
1854. [P-F 26]

"Utah historical incidents," [1855-67]. 324
p. 31 cm. Monthly journal, Jan. 1855-Dec.
1867. With letter, July 22, 1885, written
and signed for F. D. Richards by John
Jaques (between pp. 154-55).
In the hand writing of John Jaques. [P-F 67]
(Utah Hist. Quart. XXII (1954), 202.)

Early Records of Utah.
(This manuscript volume, comprising one
hundred and sixty four pages, is practically
an abridgment of the Manuscript History of
Brigham Young in the Mormon Church archives for the period 1847-1850. In many
paragraphs the wording is identical, excepting that the Bancroft manuscript is written in
the third person, whereas the original appears
in the first person. Another interesting variation consists in the explanatory clauses that
are inserted here and there in the Bancroft
compilation. The one is a faithful reproduc-
tion of essential facts as they occur in the
original, though of course not as complete.
(A. L. Neff, History of Utah (Salt Lake City:
Deseret News Press, 1940), 912.)

The importance of having this extract available is
best indicated by a comment of L. J. Arrington concerning the "History of Brigham Young" in the Church
Historian's Office, Salt Lake City. In a recital of the

basic material on Utah and Mormon history he refers
to the Historian's Office and describes its collection as .
embracing six major categories. The first of these,
"The 'History of Brigham Young,' a multi-volume
work kept by historians and clerks under the direction
of Brigham Young, for the years 1847-1877, contains
an account of affairs in the church and territory coming to the attention of church headquarters. This history is not available to scholars except for checking."
(L. J. Arrington, Great Basin Kingdom (Cambridge:
Harvard University Press, 1958), 415.)

It is the combination of these factors, i.e., that
this history contains the chronological record of the
Territory and Church, and that the original is not
available "except for checking," that impelled us to
seek permission of the Director of the Bancroft Library to copy their manuscripts and reproduce a limited
number of copies. This permission was readily
granted, and every assistance was rendered to make
the task of copying as easy as possible. It was soon
apparent that as basic a document as this needed an
index if its full usefulness was to be exploited, and the
compilation of an index was undertaken.

As indicated by the descriptions above, the manuscript was prepared in the Church Historian's Office
by clerks, and forwarded, as completed, to H. H.
Bancroft in San Francisco. There is an interesting
letter from Franklin D. Richards to Bancroft which
reads as follows:

Salt Lake City, Utah 22 July 1885

Mr. H. H. Bancroft
San Francisco
Dear Sir--
In "Incidents in History of Utah," for October
1858, one paragraph commences thus--
"On the 8th, D. B. Huntington reported that
Gov. Cumming had ordered Gen. Johnston,"
etc.
The "8th" should be changed to the "9th",
and the paragraph should read like that on the
enclosed slip.

Please correct manuscript and oblige
Yours Respectfully
F. D. Richards
Per J. J.

This evidence of the care with which the document
was prepared and reviewed prompted us to refrain
from editing or correcting the manuscript. We have
tried to render an exact copy. It was manifest, upon
a second proofreading, that our attempt failed; hence,
the errata sheet following. Spelling variations, and
errors in spelling, grammar, and punctuation have
been faithfully copied. In this regard, an exasperating
problem was encountered. In certain places in the
manuscript it was impossible to distinguish between
capital and lower case letters, particularly the letters
C, S, and M. Also, the pagination of the manuscripts
has been parenthetically indicated in the body of the
history and its peculiarities maintained.

A number of people have contributed to the pro-
duction of this history. Specifically, Miss Ann Reiche
spent many hours of a pleasant Berkeley summer typ-
ing in the Library. The staff of the Bancroft Library
were unanimously helpful and interested in the project.
We appreciate the help of those who read and re-read
early copies of this history and who pointed out the
errors in copying. We also want to acknowledge the
assistance of our spouses, Eunice Knecht and Donna
Crawley. They were not only patient with us and our
undertaking, but they rendered direct assistance in
its execution.

William L. Knecht
Peter L. Crawley

Berkeley, California, 1964

ERRATA SHEET

Please make the following corrections:

Page 6	line 33	Delete the word "formed"	
Page 10	line 42	Delete the word "and"	
Page 16	line 5	"Jebediah" should read "Jedediah"	
Page 18	line 20	"glows" should read "flows"	
Page 34	line 37	"institued" should read "instituted"	
Page 35	line 22	"Philps" should read "Phelps"	
Page 41	line 25	Delete the word "an"	
Page 61	line 21	"that" should read "than"	
Page 61	line 21	"mouth" should read "month"	
Page 68	line 34	"mounth" should read "month"	
Page 81	line 10	"tole" should read "toll"	
Page 88	line 2	"contrators" should read "contractors"	
Page 96	line 12	"that" should read "at"	
Page 101	line 30	"indicental" should read "incidental"	
Page 103	line 19	"unsuing" should read "ensuing"	
Page 110	line 10	"seditions" should read "seditious"	
Page 111	line 16	"resdidence" should read "residence"	
Page 117	line 21	"aggreeable" should read "agreeable"	
Page 118		Heading on page should read 1852	
Page 119	line 33	"Bernhsel" should read "Bernhisel"	
Page 126	line 14	"Diety" should read "Deity"	
Page 129	line 32	"Wahington" should read "Washington"	
Page 130	line 27	"Genl. Jas," should read "Genl. Jas."	
Page 133	line 25	"Summet" should read "Summit"	
Page 144	line 23	Omit comma after "Young"	
Page 153	line 7	"complement" should read "compliment"	
Page 163	line 3	"weights" should read "weighs"	
Page 167	line 5	should read "their talk was true"	
Page 167	line 7	"ture" should read "true"	
Page 169	line 5	should read "killed in"	
Page 173	line 35	"Mromons" should read "Mormons"	
Page 181	line 40	"Representatives" should read "Represen-	[tations
Page 197	line 16	"by" should read "be"	
Page 200	line 39	"him" should read "his"	
Page 205	line 33	"peices" should read "pieces"	
Page 216	line 8	"amoung" should read "among"	
Page 219	line 20	"as" should read "an"	

Page 224 line 38   "serveral" should read "several"
Page 234 line 3   "mear" should read "meat"
Page 234 line 26   "say" should read "saw"
Page 237 line 10   "were" should read "where"
Page 256 line 3   "packeages" should read "packages"
Page 257 line 7   "Legislatives" should read "Legislatures"
Page 259 line 35   "provo" should read "Provo"
Page 265 line 2   "theives" should read "thieves"
Page 266 line 42   "pervent" should read "prevent"
Page 272 line 39   "recieved" should read "received"
Page 281 line 6   "recieved" should read "received"
Page 283 line 26   "recieved" should read "received"
Page 284 line 7   "head" should read "heard"
Page 286 line 1   "finsh" should read "finish"
Page 288 line 13   "hundred" should read "hundreds"
Page 290 line 12   "Presdient" should read "President"
Page 290 line 14   "recieved" should read "received"
Page 293 line 26   "murchant" should read "merchant"
Page 294 line 17   "whithout" should read "without"
Page 295 line 4   "extinquishing" should read "extinguishing"
Page 295 line 31   "recieved" should read "received"
Page 297 line 1   "siad" should read "said"
Page 304 line 3   "recieved" should read "received"
Page 305 line 31   "settement" should read "settlement"
Page 320 line 24   "disconted" should read "discontented"
Page 325 line 1   "INDICENTS" should read "INCIDENTS"
Page 325 line 7   "Terriroty" should read "Territory"
Page 328 line 29   "at" should read "an"
Page 335 line 42   "forteited" should read "forfeited"
Page 339 line 34   "him" should read "his"
Page 353 line 25   "commemced" should read "commenced"
Page 364 line 1   "precession" should read "procession"
Page 368 line 19   "manufactruing" should read "manufacturing"

EARLY RECORDS OF UTAH
1847-1851

P-F 22

EARLY RECORDS OF UTAH

July

On the 21st of July, 1847, Orson Pratt and Erastus Snow, belonging to the van of the Mormon Pioneers, and having but one horse between them, entered the valley of the Great Salt Lake. They came through the Wasatch range of mountains and down Emigration Cañon, the mouth of which lies about five miles, south of east, from the Temple Block in Salt Lake City.

The bottom of the Cañon, for a short distance from the mouth, was thickly overgrown with brushwood, so as to make travelling very difficult, if not impossible, until a road was made through. Consequently Messrs. Pratt and Snow went over the foot of the mountain on the south side of the cañon into the valley. Mr. Snow having a small horse and Mr. Pratt walking. After travelling about three miles westward in the valley, Mr. Snow discovered that he had lost his coat off his horse, and he returned to look for it. Meanwhile Mr. Pratt went on by himself on foot and traversed the present site of the city and the Temple Block. He then returned to Mr. Snow at the mouth of the cañon, having made a circuit of about twelve miles in the valley. The two then retraced their way to their (2) company, finding it, about 9 o'clock p.m., encamped from one and a half to three miles up the cañon.

On the 22nd, Orson Pratt, George A. Smith, and seven others rode into the valley to explore, leaving their camp to follow and work the road. They went into the valley about five miles, and then turned northward or northwestward toward the Salt Lake. They found streams and springs of excellent water, green grass where the soil was damp, brown grass where the soil was dry. As they proceeded northward toward and into what is now Davis County, they found warm and hot springs at the base of the mountain spur, and the soil thereabout had a sterile appearance. When they returned toward their point of entrance of the valley, they found their advance company and the main company encamped in the valley, about five and a quarter miles from the mouth of the cañon, on Parley's Cañon Creek, as it is now termed.

On the 23rd the camp moved northward two or three miles and encamped on a small grove of cottonwood trees, on the bank of the south fork of a beautiful creek of pure cold water, now termed City Creek. Willows and other shrubs covered both sides of the stream. The camp was called together and Orson Pratt dedicated the land and themselves unto the Lord. Committees were appointed to attend to different branches of business. A patch 20 by 40 rods was (3) staked off, on which to plant potatoes, and another piece for beans, corn, and buckwheat. In two hours after arrival, some of the men began to plow, the first furrow being turned over by Wm. Carter about noon. Three plows and one harrow were at work most of the afternoon. At 2 p.m. a company started to build a dam across the creek and cut trenches to convey water to irrigate the soil, which was exceedingly dry. At three p.m. the thermometer was at 96°F. in the shade. At four p.m. a company commenced mowing the grass and preparing a turnip patch. At six a thunder shower passed over the camp, not quite enough rain to lay the dust.

On the 24th, about noon, the five acre potato patch having been plowed, the company commenced to plant potatoes, and some early corn was planted, after which the water of the creek was turned upon the soil until it was well soaked.

At two p.m. the remainder of the pioneers arrived, with Brigham Young the leader, who was sick of mountain fever, and who consequently had not been able to travel with the van or with the main body of the company from Bear River.

At five p.m. a light shower fell, accompanied with thunder and a stiff breeze.

On the 25th, which was Sunday, a meeting was held around the cannon, at 10 a.m., at which the audience was addressed by George Albert Smith, Heber

(4) Chase Kimball, and Ezra Taft Benson. In the afternoon another meeting was held, and the congregation was addressed by Wilford Woodruff, Orson Pratt, Willard Richards, and Brigham Young, and the Sacrament was partaken of.

On the 26th the company continued busy in plowing, planting corn, and irrigating. A party was appointed to make a road into City Creek Cañon, to facilitate the procuring of timber. About noon, Brigham Young, Heber C. Kimball, Willard Richards, George A. Smith, Wilford Woodruff, Ezra T. Benson, Albert Carrington, and Wm. Clayton ascended a prominent hill or mountain, a mile or two north of the encampment, and named it Ensign Peak.

John Brown and Joseph Matthews returned from a trip to the Western Mountains, which they reported about 16 miles distant, and that most of the land west of the Jordan River was covered with wild sage and destitute of fresh water.

On the 27th Burr Frost's blacksmith shop was put up, and plowing and planting were continued. Amasa Lyman, Rodney Badger, R. Stevens, and Samuel Brannan joined the camp, having left the members of the invalid detachment of the Mormon Battalion on the Weber River.

Brigham Young and several others (16 in all) went on an exploring expedition westward to Salt Lake. (5) All bathed in it near Black Rock. Some of the party went westward three or four miles further, to the entrance of what is now called Tooele Valley. The north end of the western mountains for several miles skirts the south end of Salt Lake.

A pine tree, 14 feet long and 20 inches in diameter, was taken into camp, to be sawn into boards, to make into a boat. Some wagons were driven upon the intended site of the city. Two Utah Indians visited the Camp to trade ponies and skins for guns and ammunition, and remained all night.

On the 28th Wilford Woodruff went west again about two miles, but, discovering about 20 Utah Indians, he returned to camp. One of the Utes over took him and went with him into camp. The exploring

party went southward about ten miles, along the eastern base of the western mountains, and Orson Pratt,
who went three miles further south, but passed no
water, saw from an eminence (locally known as the
Sand Ridge) the Utah Lake, in Utah Valley, and apparently about 20 miles south. He could also see the
several streams running from the Wasatch Mountains
on the east side of Salt Lake Valley, there being no
streams on the west side, except one or two small
ones further south, which run short distances and then
sink.

The party returned to the encampment. Some (6)
of the party wished to explore the country further, for
a site for a settlement. Brigham Young said he was
willing that the country should be explored until all
were satisfied, but he believed firmly, every time a
party went out, and returned, that they would agree
that the place already chosen was the place for them
to locate.

Joseph Hancock and Lewis Barney returned from
a two day's tour in the mountains east, and reported
an abundance of good timber, principally pine and bal-
sam fir, with a little cottonwood, but access to the
same was very difficult. A pit was dug for sawing.

About five p. m. Brigham Young, Heber C.
Kimball, Willard Richards, Orson Pratt, Wilford
Woodruff, Amasa Lyman, George A. Smith, Ezra T.
Benson, and Thomas Bullock walked to a point between
the two forks of City Creek, and Brigham Young struck
his stick on the site of the present Temple and said that
should be the site of the Temple Block. This was mid-
way between a cluster of trees on the South Fork and a
few trees on the North Fork. It was resolved that the
Temple should be built there, that the city blocks or
squares should be ten acres each, the city lots one and
a quarter acres each, the streets eight rods wide, the
sidewalks twenty feet wide, the houses to be built
twenty feet back from the sidewalk and fence. A public
meeting was also held about (7) eight p. m. on the
Temple Square, when it was voted to build the Temple
there, and lay out the city thence, and that the Twelve
Apostles be a committee to superintend the laying out

of the city.

Orson Pratt reported the latitude of the north line of the Temple Block to be 40° 45' 44" north, as ascertained by meridian observations of the sun; the longitude to be 111° 26' 34" west of Greenwich, as obtained by lunar distances taken by the sextant and circle; altitude 4,300 feet, as ascertained by calculations deduced from the mean of a number of barometrical observations, taken on successive days. It is usual in taking lunar distances for longitude to have four observers, but Mr. Pratt was under the necessity of getting the altitudes without any assistant. Consequently he expected that there might be found in his calculations some little variation from the true figures.

(Mr. Dean, of the Coast Survey, Sept 20, 1869, with the use of the transit instrument on the Temple Block, determined as follows--latitude 40° 46' 02"+2; longitude from Greenwich 111° 53' 30"; longitude from Washington 34° 50' 37".)

Report of War Department 1874-5--Salt Lake City, latitude 41° 10', longitude 112° 00'.

About nine a.m. of the 29th, Brigham Young, Heber C. Kimball, Willard Richards, George A. Smith, Amasa Lyman, Wilford Woodruff, Ezra T. Benson, and five others rode on horseback to Emigration Cañon, to meet a detachment of the Mormon Battalion, which detachment was composed of the sick, sent to (8) Pueblo, on the Arkansas to winter, and had come on in the summer to Salt Lake Valley, via Fort Laramie. At noon a thunder shower fell on the camp, and was very heavy in the mountains, Emigration Creek rising three or four feet very suddenly and washing away the bridges made by the pioneers. About three p.m., the detachment of the Mormon Battalion, about 150 in number, arrived in camp, led by Captains James Brown and Nelson Higgins and Lieut. Wesley Willis. They were accompanied by a small party of about 50 Latterday Saints who started from Mississippi in 1846, who had wintered at Pueblo, Arkansas. The Battalion company were caught by the storm in Emigration Cañon and the water rose up to their wagon beds. They had designed to proceed to

the bay of San Francisco, but, many of their wagons
being broken and their teams failing, they were under
the necessity of waiting for further orders.

On the 30th Orson Pratt took several observations of the sun's azimuths and altitudes, and by the
mean of seven calculations ascertained the variation
of the magnetic needle to be 15° 47' 23" east.

At 8 p.m. a meeting was held and Brigham
Young preached.

On the 31st a brush bowery, 40 by 28 feet, was
made by the Battalion men.

A number of Utah Indians with squaws (9) visited
the camp. One of the Indians had stolen a horse from
another Indian, and had traded it, with a man of the
camp, for a gun, but refused to give up either, whereupon the man took the gun from him and broke the
stock over his head. The Indian then stole another
horse and galloped away southward. He was pointed
out to another Indian, who chased, overtook, and
killed him a few miles away.

In the evening Colonel Stephen Markham reported
that thirteen plows and three harrows had been stocked
during the past week, 35 acres of land had been broken
up and planted in corn, oats, buckwheat, potatoes,
beans, and garden seeds. About three acres of corn
was up two inches above ground, and beans and potatoes were up and looking well.

August

At a meeting in the afternoon of the 1st of August
it was resolved that all the companies should be formed
formed into one, and that a stockade of houses should
be built.

On the 2nd the different companies moved their
wagons and formed as a corral between the forks of
City Creek.

Ezra T. Benson, accompanied by Orin P.
Rockwell and three men of the Battalion left camp
about noon to meet the Mormon companies coming
from Winter Quarters (now Florence, Neb.) They
met the advance companies at Deer Creek on the 15th.

There were nine companies in all, with (10) 566 wagons.

On the 3rd, Orson Pratt and H. G. Sherwood surveyed a base line, and commenced to survey the Temple Block, which, it was then designed, was to contain forty acres.

On the 4th it was determined to confine the Temple Block to ten acres, its present size.

Samuel Brannan, Wesley Willis, Jesse C. Little and another man went on an exploring trip to Utah Lake returning the next day.

Thomas Tanner and Burr Frost were building their blacksmith shop.

On the 5th, Messrs. Clark and Owens returned from an exploring trip to Tooele Valley.

On the 6th, Brigham Young and several others of the Twelve Apostles were rebaptized in City Creek, Many others were rebaptized the next two days.

On the 7th, lots and blocks near to Temple Block were apportioned to members of the Twelve Apostles.

On the 9th, Orson Pratt ascertained by barometrical observations that City Creek descended 251 feet in the first mile from and above the Temple Block, and 569 feet in two and a half miles.

A number of men were sent on various expeditions --Samuel Brannan and J. S. Fowler to San Francisco; Jesse C. Little, Wesley Willis, (11) Jos. Matthews, James Brown, and J. Buchanan to go with them to Bear River and explore the valley; Ebenezer Hanks, Thomas Williams, and Edward Dalton to Fort Hall for provisions for the Battalion men; James Brown, Jesse S. Brown, Wm. Squires, William Gribble, Lysander Woodworth, Gilbert Hunt, and --- Blackburn to California to get discharges for the Battalion men; Stephen H. Goddard, Chester Loveland, and Zebedee Coltrin to the Salt Lake to make or obtain Salt. Mr. Brannan arrived at San Francisco Sept. 17.

John Steele claims that a daughter of his was born on the Temple Block at four a.m. this day, and was the first white child born in the valley of the Great Salt Lake. She was married to James Stapley, at Toquerville, Washington, Kane County, Feb. 21st,

1864, by Bishop Joshua T. Willis.

On the 10th, the ground at the fort (known now as the Old Fort, or the Sixth Ward Square) was laid out for the erection of log houses, and some logs were laid. This Square (10 acres) is bounded by

Starling Driggs and Simeon Howd returned from an eight day's hunting expedition, having killed one hare, one badger, one white wolf, and three sage hens. Brigham Young said he was glad they did not find much game, as it would not encourage others to hunt. It would be better to have cattle.

On the 11th, the city survey ran fifteen blocks (12) north and south, and nine east and west.

The boat was finished in the afternoon, and launched into the creek about 4 p. m.

The first death in the valley occurred. Milton Howard Thirlkill, son of George W. Thirlkill and Martilla Jane, his wife, fell into the creek, southeast of the camp, and before assistance could be rendered was quite dead. He was between three and four years old and was buried next day, Orson Pratt preaching the funeral sermon.

Norton Jacobs and ten other persons, with four wagons, being short of provisions, started to return to the hunting grounds eastward.

A large number of Utah Indians in a body visited the camp, many of them entirely naked and all armed with bows and arrows.

Orson Pratt reported the altitude of the Temple Block to be 4309 feet above sea level.

On the 13th, Stephen H. Goddard and two others returned from the Salt Lake, having prepared 125 bushels of coarse white salt, and boiled down four barrels of salt water to one barrel of fine white table salt.

On the 14th, Wesley Willis and others returned from Cache Valley with a good report. At Miles Goodyear's garden (Ogden) there was corn in tassel, planted June 9, beans ripe, carrots a foot long, (13) cabbage, radishes, etc., looking well. Mr. Goodyear had a large flock of goats, which looked well, and some sheep that needed shearing. Mr. Wells was in charge of the place.

Albert Carrington and others returned from a fishing expedition to Utah Lake. They could not get their boat over the mountain spurr at the south end of Salt Lake Valley. They returned via the Utah Outlet (Jordan), which was there a rapid stream, thickly fringed with willows. They caught only four fish.

On the 16th it was decided to name the streets around the Temple Block East Temple Street, South Temple Street, West Temple Street, and North Temple Street. The other streets were to be named First East Street, second East Street, First South Street, Second South Street, First West Street, Second West Street, First North Street, Second North Street, and so on, as far as necessary; that the lots in the blocks be numbered from the South East Corner of each block, along the south, west, north, and east sides to place of beginning, eight lots in a block, each lot being 20 x 10 rods.

There was a heavy thunder shower in the night.

On the 17th, a company, numbering 24 pioneers and 46 Battalion men, with thirty-four (14) wagons, 92 yoke of oxen, 18 horses, and 14 mules, started for Winter Quarters (Florence, Neb.) The whole company was in charge of Shadrach Roundy and Tunis Rappelye. The Battalion men were in command of Lieut. Wesley Willis and went east for provisions for their part of the Battalion. As provisions were scarce in the valley, this company was to tarry on the way, to kill buffalo for its own members and for another company which was to follow.

On the 20th, H. G. Sherwood returned from an excursion to Cach Valley, bringing with him an Englishman, named Wells, from the Weber River (Ogden). Mr. Wells had formerly lived in New Mexico for some years.

At 8 1/2 p.m. Albert Carrington, J. Brown, W. W. Rust, G. Wilson, and A. Calkins left the city to go to the top of the Twin Peaks, a mountain lying about fifteen miles southeastward, and being the highest mountain in the Wasatch range, visible from the city. They reached the base of the mountain by mid-

night, and then rested till morning. At 8 a. m. on the
21st, leaving A. Calkins with the animals, A.
Carrington, J. Brown, W. W. Rust, and G. Wilson
began to ascend the mountain. After a while Rust gave
out and rested. The others pushed on, and reached
the summit of the western peak about 4 1/2 p. m. The
two peaks are about half a mile apart. At 5 p. m. (15)
the thermometer stood at 55 F. and the barometrical
height of the mountain was found to be 11,219 feet
above the sea. So far as known, these were the first
white men who had ever ascended the Twin Peaks. At
half past five the party started back down the mountain.
At 10 o'clock Carrington and Brown lay down on the
gravel to sleep. Wilson arrived at the foot of the
mountain at 2 a. m. Carrington and Brown at 7 a. m.
and Rust at 9 a. m. of the 22nd. As they were riding
to the city, which they reached at 2 1/2 p. m., some
sage hens frightened the animals, causing them to
start suddenly, which resulted in breaking one tube of
the barometer.

On the 21st, Brigham Young and Heber C.
Kimball took their wagons into the fort and moved into
their log houses.

On the 22nd, a Special Conference was held in the
Bowery on the Temple Block in the afternoon, at which
it was resolved that the city, or portions of it, should
be fenced in for cultivation; that the City should be
called Great Salt Lake City; that the creek should be
called City Creek; and that the Utah Outlet should be
called the Western Jordan. (The word "Western" was
afterwards dropped.) names were also given to other
streams in the valley.

On the 23rd, Thomas Williams, Ebenezer Hanks,
and Edward Dalton, returned from Fort Hall with some
flour at $ 20.00 per hundred pounds, (16) and beef cat-
tle at 10¢ per pound.

By this time twenty-nine log houses were built in
the fort, each eight or nine feet high, and about sixteen or seventeen feet long by fourteen feet wide, elev-
en of them roofed with poles and soil. The logs were
obtained in City Creek Cañon, as Salt Lake Valley was
a treeless valley, excepting a few Cottonwoods and

and possibly some other sorts of trees on the banks of
some of the streams.

The wolves made the night hideous by a continual
howling around the camp.

On the 26th, Brigham Young and a company of
pioneers and Battalion men, the whole company consisting of 107 men, 36 wagons, 71 horses, & 49 mules,
left Great Salt Lake City on their return to Winter
Quarters (Florence, Neb.), where they arrived October 31st, after having suffered many privations, living
much of the time on wild meat killed by the company
as they went along.

September

On the 19th of September, the first twenty wagons
of the Mormon immigration (after the pioneers, Battalion detachment, and Mississippi company) arrived
in the city, and within a few weeks subsequently all
the companies arrived, the rear companies having been
helped by teams sent from the city. All these companies were under (17) the general supervision of Parley
P. Pratt, who arrived in the city on the 25th, and
John Taylor. According to a schedule taken by
Thomas Bullock, early in September, on the upper
Sweetwater River, between 200 and 300 miles east of
this city, the companies numbered 1540 souls, with
580 wagons, 124 horses, 9 mules, 2213 oxen, 887
cows, 358 sheep, 35 hogs, and 716 chickens.

As more room than the ten acre fort was needed
to accommodate the people, two blocks were added to
it, on the south side, and called the New Fort, thus
making the whole fort to consist of a tier of three
blocks running north and south, each block being a
square of ten acres. An adobie wall was run around
the three open sides of these two additional blocks, and
another wall was run across, east and west, between
them, thus making three equal ten-acre inclosures in
one. On each side of the two interior walls, a row of
log houses was built, thus making two double rows
across the inclosure. Strictly speaking this combined
fort was larger than the three ten-acre blocks, because

it included eight rod streets across and between the
blocks.   Log or adobic houses were built all around
the whole fort, in fact constituting in large part the
walls of the fort.

The men cut a large quantity of hay and stacked it
within the fort.

The cattle and horses entirely destroyed the crops
sown, except the potatoes, the tops of which (18) they
ate smooth, with the ground.

Philemon C. Merrill and fifteen others of the
Battalion left Great Salt Lake City, Oct. 8, and arrived at Winter Quarters Dec. 11.   About 25 men,
with a mail of 144 letters, from Great Salt Lake City,
arrived at Winter Quarters Dec. 18.

On or about the 16th, in the midde of November,
A. T. Lathrop, O. P. Rockwell, and E. K. Fuller,
accompanied by others, were sent to Califomia to
buy cows, mules, mares, wheat & seeds of different
kinds.

During the Fall, two or three small parties of
Battalion men arrived in the city form California,
bringing with them some Spanish wheat for seed.

Archibald Gardiner and brother built a small saw-
mill on the Warm Springs stream, and a little lumber
was cut there, but the stream was small, and, as
there was not water to furnish sufficient power, the
mill was soon removed to Mill Creek, about five miles
south-east.

Charles Crismon built a small grist-mill on City
Creek, about half a mile up the cañon, having one run
of small stones, and no bolt, making Taos flour.
Soon removed.   Ira Eldrdge & Co. were to build a mill
there.

George B. Wallace, Levi Riter, and John (19)
Nebeker were to build a saw mill on a creek eight or
ten miles north of the city (Mill Creek North, Davis
County.)

In the forepart of December, Captain Grant, of
Fort Hall, visited the city, with the view of opening
up a trade with the Mormons.   After some discussion,
a letter was written to the board of management of the
Hudson's Bay Company, and sent by Captain Grant.

In the middle of December Captain James Brown returned from California. He soon after bought the Goodyear place (Ogden) for $1950 cash down, and moved to settle there, with Mr. Chilton, Mr. Myers, Mr. Thurlkill, and their families.

The High Council, a local ecclesiastical court, consisting of twelve members, presided over by the president of the stake and his two counselors, fifteen in all, besides the clerk, assumed provisional municipal powers by the common consent of the community. A stake is an ecclesiastical district, comprising several wards or branches of the church. In Utah a stake is now (1881) usually coextensive with a county, not necessarily so, but for convenience. (20)

January

In January the High Council decided that fencing be commenced, beginning at the fort, and fencing with poles; after leaving the city the fence to be pole and ditch. The farming lands to be selected as near together as possible, and to be immediately south of the city.

February

The High Council gave permission to Archibald and Robert Gardner (brothers) to build a sawmill on Mill Creek, about four miles south, provided that water for irrigation purposes be not interfered with. The Council also decided that no person should build with logs without permission, and made other stringent regulations for the preservation of the timber.

March

About the last of February or the first of March, five Battalion men started for Winter Quarters.

The particulars in the following paragraph are condensed from a letter of the High Council to Brigham Young, dated March 6—

C. Crismon had a small grist mill, with one run of small stones, on City Creek. (He had no bolting cloth.) He had the frame and gearing for a saw mill nearly ready to put up. Isaac (21) Chase had a saw mill in operation, a mile or so south-east of the city, on a spring. --- Nebeker, --- Riter, and G. B. Wallace were building a saw mill in (north) Mill Creek Cañon, ten miles north, of the city. Amasa Russell had leave to put up a frame for a carding mill near Gardner's saw mill. The land had been taken up from the north fork of City Creek to one mile south of (south) Mill Creek, and from the bench (about two and a half miles east of the fort) to the east line of the fort, including 5133 acres, of which 872 were sown with winter wheat, and the remainder was designed for spring and summer crops. The line of the fence

began at a steep point in the bluffs just south of the
Warm Springs, thence straight to the north-west corner of the fort, then from the south-east corner of
the fort, east of south, to some distance south of
Mill Creek, thence east to the bluffs (or bench) again.
Whole length of line of fence, besides the fort, 3638
rods. A part of the fence was up and people were
busy preparing to put the rest up. Jedediah M. Grant,
John Nebeker, and Stephen Chipman were appointed
a committee to build bridges over Mill Creek and the
Jordan, and Daniel Spencer to be roadmaster. The
bridges to be built and roads made by a polltax. The
weather had been remarkably mild and pleasant during the winter. All animals that ran loose were in
fine condition. But many cattle had been lost by mire
holes, springs, wolves, and Indians, and many had
been killed for beef. The population of the city was
(22) 1671, houses 423. P. P. Pratt was authorized to
raise a company of volunteers, with small or no families, and make a location in the Utah Valley, if he
could make a treaty with the Indians. The marshal
and forty-four men had just returned from visiting the
Indians on the east side of Utah Lake, who had driven
off and killed seventeen cattle and one horse. The
only compensation obtained was one gun. The chief
whipped several of the band, and they all promised
to do better. Levi W. Hancock and company carried
this letter to Winter Quarters.

The High Council wrote a letter to the Latter-day
Saints in California, on the 12th, which was sent by
the hand of Levi E. Riter.

Sometime in the Spring, William Gardner,
Samuel Lewis, Alva C. Calkins, William Garner,
Ami Jackman, David Stewart, Robert S. Bliss, and
Abner Blackman left the city for Winter Quarters,
carrying many letters.

April

The High Council appointed Tarleton Lewis and
Edward Hunter to act in behalf of the destitute, and
to receive donations, buy, sell, exchange, and dis-

tribute, according to circumstances, for that purpose.

"April 19th, Thomas J. Thurstin, Joseph Mount, Madison D. Hambleton, Albert (23) Carrington, Jebediah M. Grant and Wm. W. Potter started at 2 p.m., with a skiff on wheels, for the ford of Jordan, with a view of exploring the Great Salt Lake and its islands for two weeks. Got aboard and proceeded down Jordan till after dark and camped on its west bank, estimated distance by stream 15 miles; channel good, current strong.

"20th. --Killed a mud hen, from which circumstance we named our skiff the "Mud Hen" according to previous agreement. Rowed two miles, passing two outlets on the West and two inlets on the East side made by the waters of the North Kanyon and the Kanyons north of it. The Jordan suddenly spread out without leaving any channel that would float our boat. We stepped out and drew our boat four miles, water varying from one to four inches, bottom sandy, covered with two or three inches of slime or soft mud; we did not discover a living thing in the water; water fowl in great abundance. Got aboard and steered for the first island, (Antelope) hauled our boat over a bar one half mile, and when one and a half or two miles off the island the water again shoaled so that our boat struck bottom. There were several Indian ponies and three Indians in sight on the island. From Jordan to the Island the bottom was sandy; greatest depth of water four and a half feet, average ditto two feet. Bore into (24) deeper water and continued on North-West, and made for shore again but struck bottom about one hundred yards from the beach; took our loading and went ashore, near sunset, on the East side of the Island six miles from its north point; day's travel 25 miles.

"21st, Found the island covered with good grasses, bunch grass prevailing; abundance of starch root; many sunflowers and rose bushes; some sage; a few service-berry bushes, a few willows and some shrubbery in the ravines. A few antelope tracks, one antelope and two prairie hens seen. From the main shore to the beach in many places, there is a wide, slimy,

and oozy bed, caused by the issuing of a great number of brackish springs, good for stock. We named
this island Porpoise, now Antelope, from the large
fish, bro. Bainbridge said he saw at the south end of
the lake. Proceeded towards its northern extremity,
three by land and three in the boat, passed several
dikes of mica slate and several ledges of gneiss of
different degrees of fineness; when within two or more
miles of the North point the beach became narrow and
pebbly; boat came to shore by the crew getting out and
wading, and we filled our keg from a large flush
spring of cold mineral water, which we named the
Sulphur spring. Steered west by north for a small
island. (Fremont's) and run aground 400 (25) yards
before we reached the shore; waded over an extensive
bed of tufa, full of holes and short channels, and
reached dry land at a large ledge of redish mica slate.
thickly studed with cubes and pseudomorphous crys-
tals of compact red oxide of iron, strata highly in-
clined. Onions, starch root, and wild parsnips plenty;
some sage and grease brush, with much fine, rank
bunch grass; found the summit composed wholly of
micaceous pudding stone or mica schist, sprinkled
with red oxide of iron; this island is in the shape of a
triangle, its largest side some five miles; we named
it Castle island, (now Fremont's) from the shape of
its summit; it has a few brackish springs near low
water mark at the south-East point, --put 150 blue
heron and geese eggs aboard, passed on to the north
point of the island and landed about sunset on a narrow rocky beach with large ledges of gneiss, distance
from camp to camp twenty miles. Greatest depth of
water 1042 feet, average ditto 6 feet.
        "22nd. --Started west by north for a high point of
land, (now Promontory point) reached shore in about
eight miles near an extensive ledge of alum slate with
a slight incrustation of alum on the soil, in many
places; cleavage fine and regular, but with cross
seams so frequent in all we could see that is is of no
use for roofing, but might be if quarried. Greatest
depth of water 13 feet, average (26) ditto 12 feet, three
of us remained on the land to explore, the rest coasted

north; found larg ledges of basalt and towards the
summit basalt and trapp alternating; quite a number of
dwarf cedars, the largest we noticed was one foot in
diameter and eighteen inches to the first limb. On
returning to the shore passed two springs of good
pure water in a fine site for a vineyard; plenty of
brackish springs along the shore, bunch grass high and
plenty, starch roots and onions plenty in spots; waded
3/4 of a mile in mud and water to our knees to get to
our boat. Water freshened so much off the outlet of
Bear and Weber rivers that it answered tolerably
well to drink--sun getting low we turned west to land,
soon ran aground, jumped out and hauled our boat one
and a half miles, left it and walked one mile farther
and reached land at a long high ledge of basalt from
the base of which issued many small and some large
brakish springs, and is 23 miles.

"23rd. --Went on to the height of ground near our
camp with a good spy glass and found we were north
of the outlet of Weber river which glows into the lake
in a wide shallow channel; we also saw Malad valley
and discovered that we were on a high long promontory
running south into the lake from the high range west of
Malad valley, --saw that our boat was as far north as
we could (27) go in this bay, as the water shoaled
northward to an extensive mud beach, from the shal-
lowness of the water and the extensive mud flats on
the east, North and West sides of it, we named this
mud bay, (now Bear river bay). Hauled our boat
about three miles into eight inches water, got aboard
and bore south with a good breeze in our favor, when
about ten miles from all land, we had a speed of eight
miles per hour, with flaws of wind, the waves running
three feet high, passed the south East point of Castle
(Fremont's) island and steered for a high point on the
west side of Antelope at a distance of twelve miles,
wind increased almost to a gale, and when about half
way across the waves ran four feet high, an occasional
one five feet, we attained a speed, at times, of ten
miles per hour; bro. Potter steered our boat admir-
able and we landed, at one hour by sun, on the west
side of Antelope island, in a fine harbor which we

called Rock harbor, having sailed 42 miles in seven hours, without shipping one half pint of water. Rock harbor bears nearly north east from Dome island (now called Stanbury's), the next island west, which we so named from a fine dome near its centre. At this point are extensive ledges of gneiss, with dikes and blocks of hornblende.

"24th. -- Steered for the salt works, passed the south point of Antelope, and seeing no one at the Salt works, bore for the city, soon got into shoal (28) water and when within one and a half mile of land ran aground, each one took his gun and provision and walked to land, reached Jordan ford at dark, wet with perspiration from rapid walking, and though we had all been advocates for the erection of a bridge over Jordan, none of us had so personally and keenly felt the want of it before, but there was no alternative, so we started in with the night air high and cool, and the water cooler, channel between three and four feet deep and current strong; we came near losing our boots in the stiff mud of the East bank, --days travel 35 miles. Distance out 83 miles, ditto back 81 miles; average rate of travel for 5 1/2 days, a small fraction under 30 miles per day. We estimated Antelope island to be twenty miles long by three broad on an average, and considered it very well adapted to herding.

"We generally found drift wood sufficient for camp purposes. Bro Hambleton suggested, what we considered a very appropriate and characteristic name for the Lake, viz., "the briny shallow" in contradistinction to the "briny deep". We found our skiff, made of five fir planks, length 15 feet 4 inches and breadth 4 feet 4 in., to be sufficiently large for six persons with their baggage to explore, in perfect safety, any portion of the lake that we were over or any (29) part that we could see with our glass. We were highly fortunate in our expedition, with constant good feelings, which we attributed to our custom of attending to our prayers daily night and morning, having no disposition to shove prayer off the great checkerboard of duties in this probation."

The High Council granted a millsite to John Neff, on Mill Creek (south), decided to employ four horsemen to guard the fields, and instituted prohibitory regulations against trading guns and ammunition to Indians.

A. A. Lathrop and E. K. Fuller, with a company of nineteen persons, including five hired Indians, arrived from California by the Southern route, after a ninety day's journey. They had bought two hundred cows in California at six dollars per head, but lost forty on the Mohave, which went back toward California. The company also brought fruit cuttings of various kinds.

On the 26th Brigham Young started from Winter Quarters on his second trip to Great Salt Lake Valley, his and other companies rendezvousing on the Elk Horn.

Considerable rain fell, and the crops generally looked well. The health of the people was good.

Black crickets and other insects were very (30) destructive to the crops in some places during the Spring. Many of the vines, peas, and beans were destroyed by frost and crickets.

When the crickets came and ate up nursery trees, grain, etc., many were discouraged. John Young, (brother to Brigham Young) wanted an express sent to Brigham, telling him not to bring the people to Great Salt Lake Valley, for they would all starve to death. John Neff left off building his mill on Mill Creek for a while, as many expected there would be no grain to grind, and John Young told him the people would have to leave, and he might as well stop wasting his money. John Smith, president of the Stake, said there would be plenty, and told Mr. Neff to keep on building his mill and he would secure him against loss thereby. By and by the gulls from the lake came in large flocks and devoured multitudes of the crickets, sweeping them up as they went along.

June

In May or June, John Y. Greene, Joseph W. Young, Rufus Allen, and Isaac Burnham, with letters,

eighteen wagons and teams, left the City to meet and
assist the emigration, eight of the teams continuing on
to Winter Quarters.

Early in June O. P. Rockwell arrived from
Califor- (31) nia, also Captain Daniel C. Davis and
part of his company.

In the latter part of the month, O. P. Rockwell,
Quinson Scovil, D. C. Davis, and Jacob Earl left the
city to meet Brigham Young's company.

A few of the people began to have the California
gold fever.

July

In June and July, Parley P. Pratt and others made
two exploring excursions in the Wasatch Mountains
east and south-east of the city. In the last, among Mr.
Pratt's associates were Daniel Spencer and John Van
Cott. The excursions were undertaken partly with the
view of finding a shorter road to and from the Weber
and Bear Rivers. The party went through Parley's
Cañon and Park (named after Mr. Pratt) and the upper
valleys of the Weber and Provo Rivers. Before their
return, some of the company were without shoes, and
almost without pants, the former having been worn out
by the journey, and the latter having been torn to
shreds by the brushwood in the cañons. Nor did the
flesh of their nether limbs escape without severe lac-
eration.

In the first week of the month some wheat was
harvested.

On the 9th, William and Nathan Hawks, Sanford
Jacobs, and Richard Slater, from California, left the
(32) city, to meet Brigham Young and the emigration.

August

A letter from P. P. Pratt, John Taylor and John
Smith to Brigham Young on the 9th of August said that
there were 450 buildings in the fort, besides a number
of temporary farm buildings outside. Three sawmills
were in operation, and another was partly finished,

also one temporary grist-mill, and an excellent one
nearly finished by John Neff, who was having two four
feet blocks dressed for millstones. They were of native vesicular basalt from the West Mountains, the
runner to weigh 4,000 lbs. Mr. Leffingwell had put up
a water-power thrashing machine on City Creek, that
would thrash and clean 200 bushels a day. The population was not far from 1800, and was enjoying excellent
health. About 5000 acres had been plowed and planted
or sown. The wheat crop had done very well, far exceeding expectations, and grain was selling at two dollars a bushel. The people had eaten green peas until
they were tired of them. The main fence of the Big
Field was twelve miles long, not quite finished. Ten
U. S. Troops, under Captain Hensley, had recently
arrived, on their way to California. Much more rain
had fallen during the latter part of July and the beginning of August than in the same time the year pre-
(33) vious.

On the 10th, several hundreds of the people met
under a large awning, to celebrate the first harvest in
the Valley. They had prayer, thanksgiving, a feast,
music, dancing, firing of cannon, etc.

About the beginning of the month, Lorenzo Snow
and A. O. Smoot, with about 47 wagons and 124 yoke
of oxen, left the city to meet and assist the emigrants.

About the 28th, 48 men and boys, 59 wagons, 121
yoke of oxen, 44 mules and horses were sent back to
Winter Quarters, from the camps of Brigham Young
and others on the Sweetwater, in charge of Allen
Taylor.

September

On the fifth of September, Parley P. Pratt wrote
to his brother Orson, in England, saying that a few
weeks previously, the Indian Chief, Walker, accompanied by Soweite, chief of all the Utah nations, with
some hundreds of Indians, men, women and children,
visited the city. They had several hundred horses for
sale. They were much pleased with what they saw in
the city, and expressed a desire to become one people

with the Mormons and learn to cultivate the earth, and
live as the Mormons did. They would like some
Mormons to go and commence farming with them in the
valleys southward. The Indians were enjoined to live
at peace with each other and with all people, and cease
to war. They had agreed to do so, and (34) had sent a
deputation to their old enemies, the Shoshones, whose
principal chiefs were encamped with the Utes, making
a treaty of peace with them. Spaniards, Indians, and
others had supplied the market with horses and mules
in abundance. There had been no prevalent sickness
and few deaths. The people generally were strong,
healthy and active. Light rains had fallen every few
days. The following is an extract from Mr. Pratt's
letter--

"I have now resided almost one year in this lone
retreat, where civilized man has not made his home
for the last thousand years, and where the ripening
harvest has not been enjoyed for ages, until this present season. During all this period, the sound of war,
the rise and fall of empires, the revolution of states
and kingdoms--the news of any kind has scarcely
reached my ears. It is but a few days since we heard
of the revolutions and convulsions which are agitating
Europe. All is quiet--stillness. No elections, no police reports, no murders, no wars in our little world.
How quiet, how still, how peaceful, how happy, how
lonesome, how free from excitement we live. The legislation of our High Council, the decision of some judge
or court of the church, a meeting, a dance, a visit, an
exploring tour, an arrival of a party of trappers and
traders, a Mexican caravan, a party arrived from the
Pacific, from the States; from Fort Hall, or Fort
Bridger, a visit of Indians, or, perhaps, a mail from
the distant world, once or twice a year, is all that
break up the monotony of our busy and peaceful life.
Our old fire- (35) locks have not been rubbed up, or
our swords unsheathed because of any alarm. No policemen or watchmen of any kind have been on duty to
guard us from external or internal danger. The drum
has beat to be sure, but it was mingled with merry
making, or its marshal sound was rather to remind us

that war had once been known among the nations, than
to arouse us to tread the martial and measured step of
those who muster for the war, or march to the battle
field. Oh, what a life we live! It is the dream of the
poets actually fulfilled in real life."

Brigham Young arrived on the 20th with his company, or part of it. Heber C. Kimball and company
arrived a few days after.

On the 24th, Brigham Young preached at the
Bowery, in the centre of the fort.

The same day the High Council appointed Brigham
Young and Heber C. Kimball to apportion city lots to
applicants. Leave was granted to build on said lots
that fall. It was voted that the houses be set at least
20 feet back from the sidewalk. An order was made
for the removal of Crismon's Mill and machinery from
City Creek.

On the 28th, Addison Pratt arrived from the
Society Islands, accompanied by a number of the Battalion men from San Francisco, with 13 wagons. Some
days behind him was a company with 15 wagons, being
part of the company which went from New York to San
Francisco in the ship "Brooklyn."

(36) On the 30th the High Council, on petition
headed by Brigham Young, gave liberty to cut down any
trees, green or dry, within thirty miles of the valley,
except the timber in City Creek cañon. It was voted
that a land record be kept, and that $1.50 be paid for
each lot, $1.00 of it to the surveyor, and fifty cents to
the clerk for recording. Thomas Bullock was the recording clerk. It was voted that the farm land be apportioned by lot, also that Crismon's toll for grinding
grain be increased from one sixteenth to one-tenth.
Brigham Young proposed to bring the waters of Big
Cottonwood along the east of the farming land, called
the Big Field, to the City by canal, which would make
one line of fence.

In those early days, writing paper was so scarce
that deeds of property were written on bits about three
by two inches, or less than that.

October

At a meeting, Oct. 1st, it was voted to build a
Council House by <u>Tithing</u>, and that Daniel H. Wells
superintend the building of it.

The Conference of the Church of Jesus Christ of
Latter-day Saints commenced on the 6th, but was postponed till the 8th, to allow the Battalion men to have a
dinner and a celebration, which had been postponed
from the 5th on account of the unfavorable state of the
weather.

(37) In Conference on the 8th, John Smith was released from the presidency of the Stake, and Charles
C. Rich was appointed his successor, with John Young
and Erastus Snow as his Counsellors. Arrangements
were entered into for building a Council House.

The Conference met again on the 15th, when it was
voted that Addison Pratt should return with some other
missionaries to the Society Islands, also that missionaries should be sent to New Holland, East Indies, China,
and all the world as soon as they could be spared.
Newell K. Whitney, Edward Hunter, and Tarleton
Lewis were appointed to draw lots for the applicants
for land in the five-acre plot. It was voted that a mile
square should be reserved for a church farm in the
Big Field.

The Conference also met on the 22nd and the 29th.
Among the subjects considered were cañon and other
roads, management of a church farm, employment of
such mechanics <u>wholly</u> at their trade as were wanted,
etc. Joseph L. Heywood was appointed supervisor of
roads.

Howard Egan and company left Salt Lake City on
the 13th for Council Bluffs.

Amasa Lyman's company of emigrants from
Winter Quarters began to arrive on the 10th. Soon after, 15 wagons arrived, with a portion of the company
that went from New York to San Francisco in the ship
"Brooklyn." Willard Richards' company arrived on the
19th. Heber C. Kimball's company arrived on the 24th.

(38) Early in the month there were 863 applications for lots in the Big Field, taking up 11,005 acres

of land. It was designed to have the five acre lots
nearest the city, the ten acre lots next, then the 20
acre lots, followed by the 40 and 80 acre lots, on
which last the farmers could build and live. All the
farming land was to be enclosed in one common fence,
which would be 17 miles and 53 rods long, the land to
be distributed by lot. The city plot was already allot-
ted, and many families were still unprovided with lots,
so that an addition to the city on the east side was surveyed. It was also proposed to lay off a city ten miles
to the north, and another ten miles to the south.

November

At a meeting on the 5th, Brigham Young advised
the people to take up their farms on the east side of the
Jordan for the present, and to fence the city in blocks;
also that the mechanics let the farmers have the five
and ten acre lots.

On the 7th a number of Masons commenced laying
the foundation of the Council House.

On the 13th fifteen Battalion men arrived from
California. During the month several other small
companies arrived. Some of them brought considerable gold dust with them.

(39) About the middle of the month Brigham
Young and Heber C. Kimball, in building their houses,
attended or served the masons, carrying them adobies,
mortar, etc.

On the 19th Captain Grant, from Fort Hall, arrived with some pack horses, laden with skins, grocer-
ies and other goods, and opened a store in the morning
on the south side of the Old Fort.

Preparation was made to make coin of the gold
dust brought from California.

On the 25th, Brigham Young, John Taylor, and
John Kay made out an inscription for the gold currency
--on one side "Holiness to the Lord," with an emblem
of the Priesthood. On the reverse the words "Pure
Gold," and the value of the coin, surrounding two
hands clasped, representing friendship.

On the 26th, about 20 men were called to go on a

mission to San Francisco and vicinity.

On the 30th, Allen Compton, Ezekiel Lee, William Casto, and John Smith arrived from Winter Quarters with a mail of 227 letters and many papers.

Wintry weather, snow and frost commenced the latter part of the month. (40)

December

There was severe cold and snow this month.

A few of the people caught the gold fever. Brigham Young advised all to remain at Salt Lake, make improvements, build comfortable houses and raise grain.

On the 20th, Thomas Williams started east with a petition to Congress for a Territorial government, but returned in a few days because of the deep snow.

The residents of Great Salt Lake City suffered so much annoyance from the wolves howling at night, and from depredations committed by foxes, cata-mounts, and other animals, that two rival companies were organized to have a grand hunt to destroy the pests, the company securing the least game to treat the other company to a dinner. John D. Lee and John Pack were appointed Captains, each to choose his company of 100 men. Shooting commenced on the 25th.

As there was considerable gold dust in the pos-session of various persons in the city, and there were no more crucibles in which to melt any more of it, and a currency of some sort was greatly needed, it was resolved in a public meeting on the 28th that Brigham Young should issue notes for circulation on dust deposited with him, the notes to be redeemed when the dust was coined.

The same day Brigham Young accompanied by three or four friends, took a sleigh ride to Chase's (41) Mill, south east of and just outside the city, to locate a site for a carding machine.

In the latter part of the month, a number of one, three, and five dollar bills were prepared and signed.

The following is given as a statement of the "Mormon" emigration from Winter Quarters to Great

Salt Lake City during the year--2393 souls (whites),
24 negroes, 792 wagons, 181 horses, 64 mules, 2527
oxen, 1743 cows and loose cattle, 1023 sheep, 300
pigs, 59 cats, 178 dogs, 1074 chickens, 4 turkeys, 12
ducks, 16 doves, 6 goats, 10 geese, 5 hives of bees.
(42)

January, 1849

A "Prophetic Almanac for 1849, being the First after Bissextile or Leap Year, calculated for the Eastern, Middle, and Western States and Territories, and also for the Great Interior Basin of Upper California; By Orson Pratt, Sen., A. M.," was circulated in manuscript among the people in the valley.

On the first of January the first bill (one dollar) of local paper currency was issued. The Bills were signed by Brigham Young, Heber C. Kimball, and Thomas Bullock, clerk.

In a council held on the 6th it was resolved that the High Council should be relieved from municipal duties; that Amasa Lyman, O. P. Rockwell, George D. Grant, Jedediah M. Grant, David Fullmer, Lewis Robison, Dimic B. Huntington, William Crosby, and George Boyd go to Utah Valley, to learn its capabilities for a stock range; that the fort buildings be removed; that Isaac Higbee, John M. Higbee and, and William Wadsworth be a committee to seek out suitable fishing places in the Utah Lake, establish fisheries, and supply the market; that Alanson and Ira Eldredge engage in the business of tanning and manufacturing leather, and that the Council exert its influence to sustain them therein; that the Council approbate Joel Johnson in his journey to the States to buy sheep; that Brigham Young and Heber C. Kimball have the privilege of fencing in as much of the table (bench) lands and (43) the spurs of the mountains east of the city as they want for pasturage; that the Kirtland (Ohio) Safety Bank bills be put into circulation for the accommodation of the people.

Amasa Lyman and party started for Utah Valley on the evening of the 7th.

In a council of prominent citizens on the 20th, Amasa Lyman reported that several of the cattle committee had been to Utah Valley and had found from two and a half to four inches of snow, and they concluded that Great Salt Lake Valley was the best place to keep the cattle. Thomas Farmer was appointed public armorer. The Council resolved that a building

for an armory should be erected forthwith, for which
$30 was subscribed by the Council.

On the 22nd, Brigham H. Young and Thomas
Bullock were engaged in setting type for the 50 cent
bills, paper currency, the first type-setting in the
Great Basin.

The winter so far, was much more severe than
that of 1847-8, and was consequently hard on cattle,
the ground having been completely covered with snow
the two months past. The length and severity of the
cold season, compared with that of the preceding year,
made some of the people discontented, and rumors
were strong that many people would leave the valley in
the spring. (44)

February

On the first of February the following, signed by
many citizens was made public--

"Notice is hereby given to all the citizens of that
portion of Upper California, lying East of the Sierra
Nevada Mountains, that a Convention will be held at
the Great Salt Lake City, in said Territory, on Monday, the fifth day of March next, for the purpose of
taking into consideration the propriety of organizing
a Territorial or State government.

"Dated at the Great Salt Lake City, Great Basin,
North America, this first day of February, 1849."

In a council on the 3rd it was resolved that a
bridge be built across the Jordan; that a standard be
established of the following weights for grain--wheat
60 lbs. and corn 56 lbs. per bushel; that Albert
Carrington, Joseph L. Heywood, and Philip B. Lewis
be a committee on weights and measures, and that
P. B. Lewis be sealer thereof. Daniel Spencer,
Edward Hunter, John Vance, and William M. Lemon
were appointed to superintend and apportion the fencing to be made in the different districts. The winter
having proved severer than that of 1847-8 had led the
people to expect, more sustenance was required by
men and animals than was anticipated, and much of
the last season's crops was destroyed by crickets and

grasshoppers. The immigrants who arrived from
Winter Quarters in the fall were instructed to bring
with them (45) eighteen months' provisions, but they
brought much less, and their limited stock was reduced faster than expected because of the great appe-
tite induced by the toilsome journey and the keen
mountain air. So that by this time many families were
destitute of provisions, and it was evident that something must be done for their relief. It was therefore
resolved that no corn should be made into whisky, and
that if any man was preparing to distil corn into whisky
or alcohol, the corn should be taken and given to the
poor; that the bishops should ascertain the true situation of the people in relation to bread-stuffs, and what
amount each family had per head.

On the 8th Thos. S. Williams returned from
Parley's Cañon and reported it impossible to continue
his journey to the merchant train of Williams & Co.,
encamped near Fort Bridger, the snow being as high
as the horses' necks.

In a council on the 9th, the committee on breadstuffs reported that there was in the valley 78/100 of
a pound of bread-stuffs per head per day for the next
five months, corn and wheat being rated at only 50 lbs.
per bushel. The cost of a bridge across the Jordan
was estimated at $700 to $800, mechanics' wages
being reckoned at $1.50 to $2.00 per day. It was resolved that a tax of one per cent. per annum be assessed on property, to repair the public highways,
bridges, and other works; that Albert Carrington be
assessor, collector and treasurer, with certain dis-
cretionary powers in collecting from the poor and
widows, that the supervisor (46) draw on him for funds,
and that one or two auditors be appointed to audit his
accounts. The clerks of the Council were instructed
to write eight notices containing the laws made by the
Council, for posting up in different places for the
information of the public.

On the 13th Daniel Spencer was set apart as (ecclesiastical) President of the Stake, with David Fulmer
and Willard Snow as his Counsellors. Newel K.
Whitney, Brigham Young, Heber C. Kimball, Parley

P. Pratt, John Taylor, Amasa Lyman, and Thomas
Bullock were appointed a committee to lay the City
off into Wards.

On the 14th the committee divided the city into
nineteen Bishop's Wards of nine (ten-acre) blocks
each.

On the 16th, the ecclesiastical High Council was
organized, or rather re-organized, as follows--
Isaac Morley (President), Eleazer Miller, Titus
Billings, Levi Jackman, Shadrach Roundy, John
Vance, Ira Eldredge, Henry G. Sherwood, Phinehas
Richards, Edwin D. Woolley, Wm. W. Major, and
Elisha H. Groves. The following division of the valley
into wards was decided upon--south of the city and
east of the Jordan into four Wards--Cañon (Parley's)
Creek Ward, embracing the five-acre survey and all
east of it; Mill Creek Ward, embracing the ten-acre
survey and all east of it; a third Ward, embracing the
country between the ten-acre survey and the Big
Cottonwood Creek; and a fourth Ward, embracing all
south of Big Cottonwood. West of the Jordan, Canaan
Ward; north of the City and east of the Jordan and the
Lake; three Wards--first, all north of (47) the City,
so far as to include Sessions Settlement; second, the
country between Sessions' and the settlements on the
Weber River; third, the Brown Settlement. (Ogden.)

In a Council on the 17th the committee on fencing
the Big Field reported that the fence would include
291 ten-acre lots, 460 five-acre lots, the Church farm
of 800 acres, and 17 acres of fractional lots, the whole
requiring 5,240 rods of fencing, of which 3216 were
recommended to be built of adobies, 663 of adobies or
stone, and 1361 of ditch and posts and rails. Committees were appointed to locate the site of the Jordan
bridge, to direct the locating of streets through the
city and the fencing of the survey south of the Big
Field, to erect a public bath-house at the Warm
Springs, and to select a suitable place for a burying
ground. Permission was given to Brigham Young to
build a mill in the ravine east of Chase's Mill, and to
take the water out of (Parley's) Cañon Creek to run
the mill, except when needed for irrigation.

On the 18th the people began to move out of the fort to their city lots.

In a council on the 22nd the following men were set apart as bishops of the city wards--

David Fairbanks, 1st Ward; John Lawry, 2nd; Christopher Williams, 3rd; William Hickenlooper, 6th; William J. Perkins, 7th; Addison Everett, 8th; Seth Taft, 9th; David Pettigrew, 10th; Benjamin Covey, 12th; Edward Hunter, 13th; John Murdock, 14th; Abraham O. Smoot, 15th; Isaac Higbee, 16th; (48) Joseph L. Heywood, 17th; James Hendrix, 19th.

Brigham Young advised to first fence the city by Wards. He wished the bishops to gather up the poor and look after them, and each bishop to provide for the poor of his own Ward, and not depend upon the bishops of other Wards.

In a council on the 24th, fines were instituted for driving animals from the range, or using them without the consent of the owner. Privilege was granted to Amasa Lyman to fence in some land south of his survey and near the cottonwood Creeks, and to James B. Porter to remove his saw-mill two or three miles up Cottonwood Cañon. Horace S. Eldredge was appointed marshal of the valley. The road supervisor was instructed to build bridges across the Cottonwood Creeks and other streams, as the convenience of the people might require. Owing to the absence of small change, the tax-collector was instructed to give due-bills for sums less than a dollar, and redeem them when presented in sufficient amount.

On the 25th a number of adobie houses in the fort fell down from the effects of the thaw.

On the 26th, work was re-commenced on the Council House.

On the 27th a report was received that Indians had stolen fourteen horses from Orr's herd and several cattle out of Tooele Valley, and had taken them to Utah Valley.

On the 28th a company of thirty or forty men under Captain John Scott, started south, in pursuit of some Indians who had been stealing and killing cattle and (49) running off horses from Willow Creek and

other places.   The company proceeded to Utah Valley,
and found Little Chief and his band of Timpany Utes on
the Provo, who told where the thieving Indians were.
The company left the Provo in the night, taking with
them Little Chief's son, as guide, who led them over
the Provo Bench towards the Creek north and the base
of the mountains, whence from an eminence they discovered the fires of the Indians, who were encamped
on the creek, which ran in the midst of willows and
dense brush wood in a deep ravine.   The company were
divided into four smaller bodies and posted north,
south, east, and west of the Indians, who, when they
awoke, found themselves beseiged.   So they immediately packed up their baggage, and ineffectually
tried every way to escape.   They then commenced to
fight--by shooting arrows and firing guns.   This small
predatory band of Indians consisted of two lodges under
Cone and Blue Shirt, and numbered seventeen souls in
all, including four men.   The squaws and children
were got out and fed and warmed.   After a desultory
fight of three or four hours, the four men, who took
every advantage of the brush for cover, were killed.
None of the brethren were injured.   The skins of fifteen cattle which the Indians had killed, were found
near.   During the fight, Stick-in-the-head and his band
of Timpany Utes came up, ready for a fight, and took
a position on an elevation, whence they vainly called
to the besieged and urged them to call that way.   The
company returned to the city March 6th.   The squaws
and children (50) of the slain followed the company to
the city, and after being fed went to their friends
among the Snake Indians.   The creek on which the
fight took place was afterwards named Battle Creek,
from the above circumstances.

    This winter the Federal Government established
a post office at Great Salt Lake City, and appointed
Joseph L. Heywood postmaster, and also instituted a
bimonthly mail between Kanesville (Council Bluffs) and
Great Salt Lake City.   Almon W. Babbitt engaged to
carry the mail at his own expense and charges for the
net proceeds.

March

In a council on the 3rd a committee was appointed to superintend the organization, into different companies, of all the able-bodied men, over 14 and under 75 years of age, in the valley, the whole to form a military organization of the entire people, under the name of the Nauvoo Legion. Parley P. Pratt was appointed to take charge of a company to go to Green River ferry, and Orin Porter Rockwell, Charles Shunnway, and Edmund Ellsworth were appointed to go to the ferry on the north fork of the Platte. It was resolved that Allen Compton should take charge of a mail for Winter Quarters on the 20th of March, or as soon thereafter as practicable.

In a council on Monday, the 4th, a committee (51) was appointed to apportion the digging required, on the irrigating canal, of each owner of land in the Big Field and the city.

On the same day a large number of the inhabitants of that portion of Upper California lying east of the Sierra Nevada Mountains, met in convention in Great Salt Lake City, and appointed Albert Carrington, Joseph L. Heywood, Wm. W. Philps, David Fulmer, John L. Fulmer, Charles C. Rich, John Taylor, Parley P. Pratt, John M. Bernhisel, and Erastus Snow a committee to draft and report to the convention a constitution under which the inhabitants of said Territory might organize and govern themselves, until the Congress of the United States should otherwise provide by law.

The same day the hunting companies, organized in December 1848, under John D. Lee and John Pack, met and counted their game, when it appeared that John D. Lee's company of 37 persons had killed 516 wolves, 238 foxes, 20 minx, 4 eagles, 173 magpies, and 439 ravens, which were considered equivalent to 8455 ravens; and that John Pack's company of 47 persons had killed 2 bears, 2 wolverines, 2 wild cats, 267 wolves, 171 foxes, 11 minx, 5 eagles, 357 magpies, hawks and owls, and 587 ravens, equivalent to 5912 ravens; thus Lee's company claiming a count of 2543

majority.   Total killed by both companies, 2 bears,
2 wolverines, 2 wild cats, 783 wolves, 409 foxes,
31 minx, 9 eagles, 530 magpies, hawks, and owls,
(52) and 1026 ravens. This hunt proved of great benefit to the settlers, in the destruction of so many predatory animals, and also in furnishing quills for the
clerks.

On the 8th the men in and near Sessions settlement commenced to get timber out of the cañons for
the Council House at Salt Lake City.

The Convention met again on the 8th, 9th and 10th
and adopted the following Preamble and Constitution--
(*) "Whereas, by reason of said treaty, all civil organization, originating from the Republic of Mexico
became abrogated; and

"Whereas, the Congress of the United States has
failed to provide a form of civil government for the
Territory so acquired, or any portion thereof; and

"Whereas, civil government and laws are necessary for the security, peace, and prosperity of society; and

"Whereas, it is a fundamental principle in all
Republican Governments, that all political power is
inherent in the people; and governments instituted for
their protection, security, and benefit, should emanate from the (53) same.

"Therefore, your Committee beg leave to recommend the adoption of the following Constitution until
the Congress of the United States shall otherwise provide for the Government of the Territory hereinafter
named and described.

"We, the People, grateful to the Supreme Being
for the blessings hither to enjoyed, and feeling our
dependence on Him for a continuation of those blessings,
do ordain, and establish a free and independent Government, by the name of the State of Deseret: including all the Territory of the United States within the
following boundaries, to wit: commencing at the 33°
N. latitude were it crosses the 108° longitude, west of
Greenwich, thence running south and west to the northern boundary of Mexico, thence west to, and down the
main channel of the Gila river, on the northern line of

[The following paragraph should be inserted in page 36, opposite, as the paragraph preceeding the (*).]

"Whereas, a large number of citizens of the United States, before, and since the treaty of Peace with the republic of Mexico, emigrated to, and settled in that portion of the Territory of the United States, lying West of the Rocky Mountains, and in the Great Interior Basin of Upper California; and

Mexico, and on the northern boundary of Lower
California to the Pacific Ocean; thence along the coast
northwesterly to the 118° 30' of west longitude; thence
north to where said line intersects the dividing ridge
of the Sierra Nevada Mountains, thence north along
the summit of the Sierra Nevada mountains to the dividing range of mountains, that separate the waters
flowing into the Columbia river, from the waters
running into the Great Basin; thence easterly along the
dividing range of mountains that separate said waters
flowing into the Columbia river on the north, from the
waters flowing into the Great Basin on the South, to
the summit of the Wind river chain of mountains;
thence south-east and south by the dividing range of
mountains that separate the waters flowing into the
Gulf of (54) Mexico, from the waters flowing into the
Gulf of California; to the place of beginning, as set
forth in a map drawn by Charles Prenss, and published
by order of the Senate of the United States, in 1848.

"Article 1.

"The powers of Government of the State of
Deseret shall be divided into three distinct departments; viz., Legislative, Executive and Judiciary.

"Article 2.

"Of the Legislative.

"Sec. 1.   The Legislative authority of this State
shall be vested in a General Assembly, consisting of
a Senate and House of Representatives, both to be
elected by the People.

"Sect. 2.   The session of the General Assembly
shall be annual; and the first session be held on the
first Monday of July next; and, thereafter on the first
Monday of December; unless the Governor of the State
shall convene the Assembly, in the interim, by Proclamation.

"Sec. 3.   The members of the House of Representatives shall be chosen biennially, by the qualified
electors of their respective districts, on the first
Monday in August; whose term of office shall continue
two years from the day of the General Election.

"Sect. 4.   No person shall be a member of the
House of Representatives, who has not attained the

age of 25 years; the same to be a free white male
citizen of the United States, and an inhabitant of this
State, one year preceding the time of his election,
and a resident of the District or County 30 days next
preceding his election; and have, at his election, an
actual residence in the district he may be chosen to
represent.

(55) "Sec. 5. Senators shall be chosen for the
term of four years, at the same time and place of
representatives; they shall be thirty years of age, and
possess the qualifications of representatives, as to
residence and citizenship.

"Sec. 6. The number of senators shall not be
less than one-third, nor more than one-half of the
Representatives; and at the first session of the
General Assembly, after this Constitution takes effect,
the senate shall be divided by lot, as equal as may be,
into two classes; the seats of the senators of the first
class shall be vacated at the expiration of two years,
so that one half of the senate shall be elected biennially.

"Sec. 7. Each house shall choose its own officers;
and judge of the qualification, election, and return of
its own members; and contested elections shall be
Determined in such manner as shall hereafter be directed by law.

"Sec. 8. A majority, in each house, shall constitute a quorum to do business; but a smaller number
may adjourn from day to day, and compel the attendance of absent members, in such manner and under
such penalty as each house may provide.

"Sec. 9. Each house shall have all powers necessary for a branch of the General Assembly of a free
and independent Government.

"Sec. 10. Each member of the Assembly shall be
privileged from civil arrest, during any session, and
in going to and returning from the same.

"Sec. 11. Neither house shall, without the consent (56) of the other, adjourn for more than three
days, nor to any other place, than that in which they
may be sitting.

"Sec. 12. The Assembly shall, at its first session, provide for an enumeration of the white inhab-

itants, and an apportionment for the Senators and
Representatives.

"Sec. 13. Each member of the Assembly shall
take an oath or affirmation to support the Constitution
of the United States, and of this State; and members
shall, and are hereby empowered to, administer said
oath, or affirmation, to each other.

"Sec. 14. The veto power of the Governor, shall
be allowed by the Assembly, except on bills, which,
when reconsidered, shall be again passed by a majority of two-thirds of those present; and any bill vetoed
by the Governor, shall be returned within ten days,
(Sundays excepted,) with his objections; otherwise it
shall become a law; unless the Assembly, by adjournment, prevent its return.

"Sec. 15. Every law passed by the Assembly,
shall take effect from and after due publication, by
authority.

"Sec. 16. The voters of this State, may elect, at
the first election, not exceeding seventeen Senators
and thirty-five Representatives.

"Article 3.
"Of the Executive.

"Sec. 1. The Executive power shall be vested in
a Governor, who shall hold his office for four years.
A Lieutenant Governor shall be elected at the same
time, and for (57) the same term, who shall be President of the Senate.

"Sec. 2. No person shall be eligible to the office
of Governor, or Lieutenant Governor, who has not
been a citizen of the United States, and a resident of
this State, two years next preceding his election, and
attained the age of thirty-five years, at the time of
his election.

"Sec. 3. The Governor shall be Commander-in-
Chief of the Militia, Navy, and all the Armies of this
State.

"Sec. 4. He shall transact all executive business
with the officers of government, civil and military;
and may require information in writing from the officers of the executive department, upon any subject

relating to the duties of their respective offices.

"Sec. 5. He shall see that the laws are faithfully executed.

"Sec. 6. When any office shall, from any cause, become vacant, and no mode is prescribed by the Constitution and laws for filling such vacancy, the Governor shall have power to fill such vacancy by granting a commission, which shall expire when such vacancy shall be filled by due course of law.

"Sec. 7. He shall also have power to convene the General Assembly, by proclamation, when in his opinion the interests of the State require it.

"Sec. 8. He shall communicate by message to the General Assembly, at every session, the condition of the State, and recommend such matters as he shall deem expedient.

"Sec. 9. In case of Disagreement in the General Assembly, with regard to the time of adjournment, the Governor shall have power to dissolve the session by Proclamation.

(58) "Sec. 10. No person shall, by holding any lucrative office under the United States, or this State, execute the office of Governor, except as shall be prescribed by law.

"Sec. 11. The Governor shall have power to grant reprieves and pardons, and commute punishments after the conviction; except in cases of impeachment.

"Sec. 12. The Governor shall receive, for his services, such compensation as shall hereafter be provided by law.

"Sec. 13. There shall be a seal of this State, which shall be kept by the Governor, and used by him officially; and shall be called the Great seal of the State of Deseret.

"Sec. 14. All grants and commissions shall be in the name and by the authority of the people of the State of Deseret; sealed with the Great seal of this State, signed by the Governor, and countersigned by the Secretary of State.

"Sec. 15. A Secretary of State, Auditor of Public Accounts, and Treasurer, shall be elected by the

qualified electors, who shall continue in office for the
term of four years. The Secretary of State shall
keep a fair registry of all the official Acts of the
Governor, and shall, when required, lay the same,
together with all papers, minutes, and vouchers relative thereto, before either branch of the General
Assembly, and shall perform such other duties as
shall be assigned by law.

"Sec. 16. In case of the impeachment of the
Governor, his removal from office, death, resigna-
tion, or absence from the State, the powers and duties
of the office shall devolve upon (59) the Lieutenant
Governor, until such disability shall cease, or the
vacancy be filled.

"Article 4.
"Of the Judiciary.

"Sec. 1. The Judicial power shall be vested in a
Supreme Court, and such inferior courts as the General Assembly shall from time to time establish.

"Sec. 2. The Supreme Court shall consist of a
Chief Justice, and two Associates, either two of whom
shall be a quorum to hold courts.

"Sec. 3. The Judges of the Supreme Court shall
be elected by joint vote of both houses of the General
Assembly, and shall hold their courts at such time an
and place as the General Assembly shall direct; and
hold their office for the term of four years, and until
their successors are elected and qualified. The judges
of the Supreme Court shall be conservators of the
peace throughout the State, and shall exercise such
other jurisdictions and appellate powers as shall be
prescribed by law.

"Sec. 4. The style of all process shall be the
State of Deseret, and all prosecutions shall be in the
name and by the authority of the State.

"Article 5.
"Of Elections.

"Sec. 1. The Governor, Lieutenant Governor,
Auditor of Accounts, Treasurer and Secretary of
State, shall be elected by the qualified electors, as
provided for members of the General Assembly, and
at the time and place appointed for (60) holding the

same.

"Sec. 2.   The returns of every election for Governor, Lieutenant Governor, Auditor, Treasurer,
and Secretary of State, shall be sealed up and transmitted forthwith to the seat of Government, directed
to the Speaker of the House of Representatives; who
shall during the first week of the Session, open and
publish them in the presence of both houses of the
General Assembly; and the persons receiving a majority of all the legal votes cast for their respective
offices, shall be declared duly elected.

"Sec. 3.   The Governor, Lieutenant Governor,
Auditor, Treasurer and Secretary of State, shall,
before entering upon the duties of their respective
offices take an oath, or affirmation, to support the
Constitution of the United States, and of this State,
which oath, or affirmation, shall be administered by
the Speaker of the House of Representatives.

"Sec. 4.   The first election for members of the
General Assembly, and other officers under this Constitution, shall be held on the first Monday of May
next, at the usual places of holding public meetings in
the different districts and settlements; at which time
and place the qualified voters shall vote for or against
the adoption of this Constitution; and, if a majority of
all the legal votes shall be in favor of its adoption,
the same shall take effect from and after said election.

"Sec. 5.   At the time and place of holding the
elections, the qualified electors shall organize the
polls by appointing two Judges, who shall be authorized
to qualify each other, and appoint two suitable persons,
as clerks; and said (61) Judges shall, at the close of
said election, seal up the number of votes so cast,
and forthwith transmit them to the President of this
Convention.

"Sec. 6.   The returns of the first election herein
provided for, shall be made to the Chairman of this
Convention, who, together with the two Secretaries,
shall proceed immediately to open said returns, and
count the votes, upon ascertaining the persons receiving a majority of votes they shall forthwith notify
them of their election.

"Sec. 7. The General Assembly shall, at its first session, provide, by law, a general system of election for officers under this Constitution; and such other officers as may be hereafter created by law.

"Sec. 8. The manner of voting shall be by ballot.

"Sec. 9. The General Assembly shall meet at Great Salt Lake City; which place shall be the seat of government, until otherwise provided by law.

"Sec. 10. All white male residents of this State, over the age of twenty-one years, shall have the privilege of voting at the first election, and at the adoption of this Constitution; Provided, that no person in the military, naval, or marine, service of the United States, shall be considered a resident of this State, by being stationed in any garrison, barrack, military, or naval place or station within this State; unless otherwise provided for by law.

"Article 6.

"Of Militia.

"Sec. 1. The militia of this State shall be com-
(62) posed of all able bodied white male citizens; between the ages of 18 and 45 years, except such as are, or may hereafter be exempt, by the laws of the United States, or of this State, and shall be armed, equipped, and trained as the General Assembly may provide by law.

"Sec. 2. All commissioned officers of the militia, (staff officers excepted) shall be elected by the persons liable to perform military duty in their respective divisions; and all commissioned officers shall be commissioned by the Governor.

"Article 7.

"Amendments of the Constitution.

"Sec. 1. If at any time the General Assembly shall deem it necessary, and for the best interest of the State, that this Constitution should be revised, altered, or amended, the Assembly shall cause such revisions, alterations, or amendments to be published in the same manner as shall be provided for the publication of the statutes, and appoint a day, not less than thirty days thereafter, for the electors of the commonwealth to assemble in their several precincts, and

vote for or against said revisions, alterations, or
amendments; and if a majority of said electors shall
vote in favor of said revisions, alterations, or amendments; the same shall thereafter become parts and
parcels of this Constitution; otherwise, this Constitution shall remain unaltered.   (63)

"Article 8.

"Declaration of Rights.

"Sec. 1.   In republican governments, all men
should be born equally free and independent, and possess certain natural, essential, and inalienable rights,
among which are those of enjoying and defending their
life and liberty; acquiring, possessing, and protecting
property, and of seeking and obtaining their safety and
happiness.

"Sec. 2.   All political power is inherent in the
people; and all free governments are founded in their
authority, and instituted for their benefit; therefore,
they have an inalienable and indefeasible right to institute government; and to alter, reform, and totally
change the same, when their safety, happiness, and
the public good shall require it.

Sec. 3.   All men shall have a natural and inalienable right to worship God, according to the dictates of
their own consciences; and the General Assembly shall
make no law respecting an establishment of religion,
or of prohibiting the free exercise thereof, or disturb
any person in his religious worship or sentiments;
provided he does not disturb the public peace, nor obstruct others in their religious worship; and all persons demeaning themselves peaceably, as good members of the State, shall be equally under the protection
of the laws; and no subordination or preference of any
one sect or denomination to another, shall ever be
established by law; nor shall any religious test be ever
required for any office of trust under this State.

(64) "Sec. 4.   Any citizen of this State, who may
hereafter be engaged, either directly or indirectly, in
a duel, either as principal, or accessory before the
fact, shall be disqualified from holding any office under the Constitution and laws of this State.

"Sec. 5.   Every person may speak, write, and

publish his sentiments on all subjects, being responsible for the abuse of that right; and no law shall be
passed to abridge the liberty of speech or of the press.

"Sec. 6. The people shall be secure in their persons, houses, papers, and possessions from unrea-
sonable searches and seizures.

"Sec. 7. The right of trial by jury shall remain
inviolate, and all criminals shall be heard by self, or
council, at their own election.

"Sec. 8. All penalties and punishments shall be
in proportion to the offence; and all offences, before
conviction, shall be bailable; except capital offences
where the proof is evident, or the presumption great.

"Sec. 9. The writ of Habeas Corpus shall not be
suspended, unless, in cases of rebellion or invasion,
the public safety shall require it.

"Sec. 10. Treason against this State, shall consist only in levying war against it, or adhering to its
enemies, or giving them aid and comfort.

"Sec. 11. The General Assembly shall pass no
bill of attainder, or ex-post facto law, or law im-
pairing the (65) obligation of contracts to hinder the
execution of Justice.

"Sec. 12. The laws shall not be suspended, but
by the Legislative or Executive authority.

"Sec. 13. The right of petition, by the people,
shall be preserved inviolate.

"Sec. 14. The right of citizens to keep and bear
arms for common defence shall not be questioned.

"Sec. 15. Private property shall not be taken for
public use, without just compensation.

"Sec. 16. No standing army shall be kept up in
time of peace, and the military at all times, and in
all places, be in strict subordination to the civil power.

"Sec. 17. The enumeration of certain rights shall
not be construed to impair nor deny others retained by
the people.

In a council, on the 10th, Joseph Mount, Samuel
Thompson, and Wm. W. Willis were given a grant of
land on Mill Creek, provided that the land be held
open for all necessary public roads. It was resolved

that a colony of 30 men should settle in Utah Valley
that spring, for the purpose of farming and fishing and
of instructing the Indians in cultivating the earth and
of teaching them civilization.

A general election was held in the Bowery, on the
12th, the first held in the Great Basin, for the election
of the requisite officers for a provisional state government. Six hundred and twenty-four votes were polled
(66) in favor of the following ticket--

For Governor,	Brigham Young.
Secretary,	Willard Richards.
Chief Justice,	Heber C. Kimball.
Associate Justices,	Newell K. Whitney & John Taylor.
Marshal,	Horace S. Eldridge.
Attorney General,	Daniel H. Wells.
Assessor and Collector,	Albert Carrington.
Treasurer,	Newel K. Whitney.
Supervisor of Roads,	Josep L. Heywood.

Magistrates.

For 1st	Ward,	David Fairbanks.
2nd	"	John Lowry.
3rd	"	Christopher Williams.
4th	"	Benjamin Brown.
6th	"	William Hickenlooper.
7th	"	William G. Perkins.
8th	"	Addison Everett.
9th	"	Seth Taft.
10th	"	David Pettigrew.
11th	"	Daniel Carn.
12th	"	Benjamin Covey.
13th	"	Edward Hunter.
14th	"	John Murdock.
15th	"	Abraham O. Smoot.
16th	"	Iraac Higbee.
17th	"	Joseph L. Heywood.
(67) 19th	Ward,	James Hendrix.
Weber River Precinct,		James Brown.
North Cottonwood	"	Joseph L. Robinson.
North Mill Kanyon	"	Orvil S. Cox.
South Cottonwood	"	William Crosby.
Big Cottonwood	"	John Holliday.

Mill Creek   "   Joel H. Johnson.

On the 15th, John Van Cott sold a peck of potatoes for $5.00, which was considered cheap.

In a Council on the 17th, the names of a company of thirty-three were read, who were going to settle in Utah Valley. This company, a few days previously, had chosen John S. Higbee for president and bishop, Isaac Higbee for first counsellor, and Dimick B. Huntington for Second counsellor.

In a public meeting on Sunday, 18th, Amasa Lyman called on the men to organize the military companies, Daniel Spencer called on the people to build a bowery on the Temple square, and wished them not to withhold the beeves to feed the poor and help out the breadstuffs.

About this time a council of health was instituted and an expedition proposed to the large island in Great Salt Lake, for the purpose of learning the botanical, mineralogical, and geological character of the island, and securing for medicinal purposes such saline plants and roots as were much needed.

(68) The first public meeting on the Temple Block was held on the 25th.

On the same day at a meeting of the bishops, the subject of providing for the poor was considered, as there were many calls for assistance. It was resolved to support the poor, as last year, by donations given into the hands of the bishops, for them to deal out, holding the receivers responsible for the pay when they were able. James Brown was ordained bishop of Weber River Ward, and Joseph L. Robinson, bishop of North Cottonwood Ward. (Farmington.)

On the 26th, men commenced building the Council House by removing adobies and hauling stone.

In a Council on that day it was resolved to send Amasa Lyman and Orin Porter Rockwell to Western California, to preach, look after the interests of the Church and return with such members as came in the fall.

On the 30th, President Zachary Taylor appointed John Wilson of Missouri, Indian Agent at Great Salt

Lake.

In a Council on the 31st, it was reported that a survey had been made for a canal from Parley's Cañon Creek to the City, and that part of a burying ground, northeast of the city had been laid out.

Willard Richards was appointed post-master for Great Salt Lake City. It was resolved that Am- (69) asa Lyman and O. P. Rockwell should start with a mail for the Pacific Coast immediately. George D. Grant was appointed to raise a company of fifty mounted men to preserve the city and vicinity from Indian depredations.

It was reported that, during the month, about a dozen wagons and families moved, or prepared to move, off to the California gold mines.

April

In Council on the 5th, William Clayton and Thomas Bullock were appointed Auditors of Public Accounts.

The General Conference of the Church of Jesus Christ of Latter-day Saints was held on the Temple Block, on the 6th, 7th, and 8th, when much good instruction was given and the usual votes were taken to sustain the General Authorities of the Church.

On the 8th, Benjamin Brown was set apart as Bishop of the 4th Ward. Orville S. Cox as bishop of the North Mill Creek (Sessions) Ward, and Joel H. Johnson as bishop of the South Mill Creek Ward. Charles C. Rich was appointed to go and establish a settlement on or near the Bay of San Francisco.

The following is from the "First General Epistle of the First Presidency of the Church of Jesus Christ of Latter-day Saints from the Great Salt Lake (70) Valley to the Saints scattered throughout the earth, which was written about this time and signed by Brigham Young, Heber C. Kimball, and Willard Richards, --

"On our arrival in this Valley, we found the brethren had erected four forts, composed mostly of houses, including an area of about 47 acres, and numbering about 5,000 souls, including our camp. The brethren had succeeded in sowing and planting an extensive variety of seeds, at all seasons, from January to July, on a farm about 12 miles in length and from one to six in width, including the city plot.   Most of their early crops were destroyed in the month of May by crickets, and frost, which continued occasionally till June; while the latter harvest was injured more or less by drouth, by frost, which commenced its injuries about the 10th October, and by the outbreaking of cattle; the brethren were not sufficiently numerous to fight the crickets, irrigate the crops, and fence the farm of their extensive planting, consequently they suffered heavy losses; though the experiment of the past year is sufficient to prove that valuable crops may be raised in this Valley, by an attentive and judicious management.

   "The winter of 1847-8 was very mild, grass abundant, flocks and herds thriving thereon, and the earth tillable most of the time during each month, but the winter of 1848-9 has been very different, more like a severe New England winter.   Excessive cold commenced on the first day of December, and continued till the latter (71) part of February.   Snow storms were frequent, and though there were several thaws, the earth was not without snow during that period, varying from one to three feet in depth, both in time and places. The coldest day the past winter was the 5th of February, the mercury falling 33 degrees below freezing point, and the warmest day was Sunday, the 25th of February, mercury rising to 21 degrees above freezing point, Fahrenheit.   Violent and contrary winds have been frequent.   The snow on the surrounding mountains has been much deeper, which has made the wood very difficult of access; while the cattle have become so poor, through fasting and scanty fare, that it has been difficult to draw the necessary fuel, and many have had to suffer, more or less from the want thereof.   The winter commenced at an unusual and unexpected moment, and found many of the brethren without houses or fuel, and although there has been considerable suffering, there has been no death by the frost.   Three attempts have been made by the brethren with pack animals or snow shoes to visit Fort Bridger, since the snow fell,

but have failed; yet it is expected that Compton will be
able to take the mail east soon after April Conference.

"In the former part of February, the Bishops took
an inventory of the breadstuff in the Valley, when was
reported a little more than three-fourths of a pound per
day for each soul, until the 9th of July; and considerable was known to exist which was not reported. As a
natural consequence some were nearly destitute while
others had an ab- (72) undance; the common price of
corn since harvest has been two dollars; some have
sold for three; at present there is none in market at
any price. Wheat had ranged from four to five dollars,
and potatoes from six to twenty dollars per bushel, and
though not to be bought at present, it is expected that
there will be a good supply, for seed, by another year.

"Our public works are prosperous, consisting of a
Council House, 45 feet square, two stories, building
by tithing; also a bridge across the Western Jordan at
an expense of $700, and six or seven bridges across
minor streams, to be paid by a one per cent. property
tax; also a bath house at the Warm Springs.

"A field of about 8000 acres has been surveyed
south of and bordering on the City, and plotted in five
and ten acre lots, and a Church farm of about 800
acres. The five and ten acre lots were distributed to
the brethren by casting the lots, and every man is to
help build a poll, ditch, or a stone fence, as shall be
most convenient, around the whole field, in proportion
to the land he draws, also a canal on the east side, for
the purpose of irrigation. There are three grist-mills,
and five or six saw-mills in operation, and several
more in contemplation. Mill stone equal to French
burr has been found here.

"The location of a tannery and foundry is contemplated, as soon as the snows leave the mountains.

"The forts are rapidly breaking up, by the removal of the houses on to the city lots; and the city is (73)
already assuming the appearance of years, for any ordinary country, such is the industry and perseverance
of the Saints.

"A winter's hunt by rival parties of one hundred
men each, has destroyed about 700 wolves and foxes,

2 wolverines, 20 minx and pole cats, 500 hawks, owls
and magpies, and 1000 ravens, in this Valley and vicinity.

"On the return of a portion of the 'Mormon Battalion,' through the northern part of Western California,
they discovered an extensive gold mine, which enabled
them, by a few days' delay, to bring sufficient of the
dust to make money plenty in this place, for all ordinary purposes of public convenience, in the exchange
the brethren deposited the gold dust with the Presidency, who issued bills, or a paper currency; and the
'Kirtland Safety Fund' resigned, is on par with gold.

"The Valley is settled for twenty miles south and
40 north of the City. The City is divided into 19
Wards; the country south into three Wards, and north
three Wards, and over each is ordained a Bishop,
with his Counsellors, with Newel K. Whitney, President of the Bishop's Quorum, presiding; who has been
instructed to set in order all the lesser offices.

"About thirty of the brethren have recently gone
to the Utah Valley, about 60 miles south, to establish
a small colony for agricultural purposes and fishing,
hoping thereby to lessen the call for beef, which at the
present time is rather scarce at an average of 7 and 8
cents per pound, but will improve with the vegetation.

(74) "The Wards of the City, generally, consist
of nine blocks, each three blocks square, and each
Ward will be fenced by itself this season, on the plan
of a big field, for the purpose of saving time for cultivation.

"In consequence of Indian depredations on our
horses, cattle, and other property, and the wicked
conduct of a few base fellows who came among the
Saints, the inhabitants of this Valley, as is common
in new countries, generally, have organized a temporary government, to exist during its necessity, or
until we can obtain a charter, for a Territorial Gov-
vernment, a petition for which is already in progress.

"There have been a large number of schools the
past winter, in which the Hebrew, Greek, Latin,
French, German, Tahitian, and English languages
have been taught successfully.

"Last fall the brethren had liberty to cut all the timber within thirty miles of the city, provided they would haul it into the city in the course of the winter. They have been diligent and done the best they could, but have made but a small beginning towards securing what there is within fifteen miles.

"The month of March, and April to the 4th, was very mild and pleasant, and many small crickets have made their appearance, but large flocks of plover have already come among them and are making heavy inroads in their ranks.

(75) On the 12th, Amasa Lyman and O. P. Rockwell and others started for the Western Coast.

In a Council on the 14th, George B. Wallace was appointed Sexton, to take charge of the public burying ground. Shadrach Roundy was ordained Bishop of the 16th Ward.

The same day, Allen Compton and nine others, named Casto, Hawkins, Woodards, Johnson, Preese, Huntington, Haskell, Brown, and Study, started for the States, carrying a mail of 502 letters.

On the 16th, Thomas S. Williams returned from Fort Bridger. He reported that the winter had been unusually severe there, and the traders at that place had suffered almost starvation, having lived on their cattle, which had perished. The snow was 50 feet deep at Yellow Creek, and 15 feet on the plain at Cache Cave.

In Council on the 28th, the Canal Committee, reported that they had surveyed a route for a canal from Mill Creek to the North-east corner of the city, and found it practicable. William Waterman Phelps was appointed surveyor-general and chief engineer.

On the 30th, Brigham Young signed the following Memorial, to which 2270 signatures were appended--

Memorial.

To the Honorable the Senate and House of Representatives of the United States of America, in Con-(76) gress assembled.

"Preamble.

"Whereas, your memorialists are residents of that portion of North America commonly called

Eastern California, or are emigrating thither, and,

"Whereas, we are so far removed from all civilized society and organized government, (say about
one thousand miles equi-distant on the four points of
the compass,) and also by natural barriers of track-
less deserts, everlasting mountains of snow, and
savages more bloody than either, so that we can never
be united with any other portion of the country, in
Territorial or State Legislature, with advantage to
ourselves or others; and

"Whereas, the soil is so sterile, that it is with
the utmost exertion the laborer can procure a subsis-
tance; and the markets so distant, that merchandize
is obtained at the greatest expense; and

"Whereas, with all the difficulties of a new,
interior, desert country, the straggling Indians have
already commenced their depredations on our flocks
and herds; and

"Whereas, we have done more, by our arms and
influence, than any other equal number of citizens to
obtain and secure this country to the Government of
the United States; and

"Whereas, a large portion of this Territory has
recently been ceded to the United States;

(77) "Therefore, we respectfully petition your
honorable body, to charter for your Memorialists, a
Territorial Government of the most liberal construction authorized by our excellent Federal Constitution,
with the least possible delay, to be known by the name
of Deseret; including and covering all lands and waters,
with all privileges, - - - - immunities and advantages
thereunto belonging, lying between Oregon and Mexico,
and between the Sierra Nevada and the 27° W. L., or
more particularly bounded and described as follows,
to wit, commencing at the Rio Grande del Norte, at
its crossing of the 32° N. L., (or the northern line of
Mexico,) thence running west on the 32° (or the Northern line of Mexico) to the Pacific Ocean; thence along
the coast northward to the 42° W. L., thence on said
42° to the Sierra Nevada; thence continuing along the
summit of the Sierra Nevada, or Snowy Mountains, to
the 42° N. L.; thence running east by the southern

boundary of Oregon to Green River; thence northerly
up the main channel of Green River to the 43° N. L.;
thence east on said degree to the 27° longitude, west
of Washington; thence south along said degree to 38°
N. L.; thence west on said degree to the Rio Grande
del Norte; thence southerly down the main channel of
said river, to the place of beginning.

"And your Memorialists will ever pray."

The Bishops of the several Wards reported that
there were at this time in the city about 450 houses,
in North Mill Creek 47, and in South Cottonwood 53.

(78) On the 4th of May, Dr. John M. Bernhisel
and Lorenzo D. Young, Brother of Brigham Young,
started for the States. Dr. Bernhisel had in his care
a mail of thirty-one letters. He also went as delegate
of the citizens of Great Salt Lake Valley, bearing their
petition to Congress for a Territorial government, and
had letters of introduction to Col. Thomas L. Kane
and Hon. Stephen A. Douglas.

On the 5th the Nauvoo Legion, six companies of
foot and three of horse, met on the Temple Block to
train.

On the 7th, George D. Grant and company started
out after the Indians, who had stolen some horses.

In a Council on the 12th it was resolved that a
company of men be appointed, to start as early as convenient, to explore the region near the north point of
the (Oquirrh) mountains west of the valley, to ascertain its adaptability to farming purposes, and also the
most suitable point to establish a manufactory of salt.

In a Council on the 26th, Parley P. Pratt reported
that he had not found men to go to Green River ferry.
Charles C. Rich and Daniel H. Wells, of the Committee on Military Affairs, made the following Report to
the Council, which, was adopted:--

They have organized the Nauvoo Legion, as follows:
--To consist of--men, divided into two Cohorts, four
Regiments in a Cohort, two Battalions in a Regiment,
and five Companies in a Battalion, and commanded by
a Major General.

The first Cohort consists of mounted men, (79)

and is commanded by a Brigadier General.

The Second Cohort consists of footmen, and is also commanded by a Brigaider-General.

At an election, held at the Stand in accordance with previous notice, on the 28th day of April last, --

Daniel H. Wells was elected Major-General of the Legion.

Jedediah M. Grant was elected Brigadier-General of the first Cohort.

Horace S. Eldredge was elected Brigadier-General of the second Cohort.

They have organized eleven companies, six of horse and five of foot; which are organized into four Battalions for present purposes, composing two Regiments.

The six horse Companies constitute the first Regiment of the first Cohort.

John S. Fullmer has been elected Col. of the first Regiment, first Cohort, and Willard Snow Mayor of the first Battalion of said Regiment.

George D. Grant, captain of the First Company of said Battalion.

William H. Kimball,	First Lieut.	"
James Ferguson,	Second "	"
Ephraim Green,	Third "	"

This is a company of Life Guards, designed to protect the City and vicinity from Indian depredations, and consists of--selected men.

(80) Daniel C. Davis, Captain of the Second Company of said Battalion.

Nelson Higgins,	First Lieut.	"
Joseph W. Young,	Second "	"
Anson Call,	Third "	"

This is a company of mounted Dragoons.

Samuel Thompson, Captain of the Third Company of said Battalion.

-----------	First Lieut.	"
-----------	Second "	"
-----------	Third "	"

This is a Company of mounted Dragoons.

Ira Eldredge, Major of the Second Battalion.

Benjamin F. Johnson, Captain of the First Company of Said Battalion.

Hosea Stout,	First Lieut.	"
John Alger,	Second "	"
J. C. L. Smith,	Third "	"

Company of mounted men.

James T. S. Allred, Captain of the Second Company of said Battalion.

P. R. Wright,	First Lieut.	"
Erastus Bingham,	Second "	"
John Steele,	Third "	"

Mounted Company.

John Brown, Captain of the Third Company of said Battalion.

(81) Albert Carrington, First Lieut. of the Third Company of said Battalion.

Joseph Mathews,	Second "	"
John D. Holliday,	Third "	"

Pioneer and Exploring Company.

John Scott, Colonel of the First Regiment of the Second Cohort.

Andrew Lytle, Major of the first Battalion of said Regiment.

Jesse P. Harmon, Captain of the first Company of said Battalion.

Shadrach Roundy,	First Lieut.	"
Isaac Morley,	Second "	"
Phineas Richards,	Third "	"

This Company consists of Men, who are Silver Greys over fifty years of age.

Daniel Tyler, Captain of the Second Company of said Battalion.

------------	First Lieut.	"
Dorr P. Curtis,	Second "	"
Charles Shumway,	Third "	"

This is the First Artillery Company.

Daniel Carn, Captain of the Third Company of said Battalion.

Truman O. Angel,	First Lieut.	"
Wm. M. Lemon,	Second "	"
James Beck,	Third "	"

(82) This is the Second Artillery Company.

Henry Harriman, Major of the Second Battalion of said Regiment.

George B. Wallace, Captain of the First Company of said Battalion.

J. A. Stratton,	First Lieut.	"
Jacob Gates,	Second "	"
Jonathan H. Holmes,	Third "	"

This is a Company of Infantry.

Edmund Ellsworth, Captain of the Second Company of said Battalion.

Henry P. Richards,	First Lieut.	"
Joseph A. Young,	Second "	"
Lyman L. Rockwood,	Third "	"

This is the Juvenile Rifle Company, and consists of young men under eighteen years of age.

Charles C. Rich,

Daniel H. Wells, Committee.

In a Council on the 27th, Alexander Williams presented the subject of trading with the Indians. He said Walker, the Indian Chief, said he looked upon the "Mormons" as his fathers, mothers, brothers, and sisters, and that none of his people should meddle with their cattle. Mr. Bridger had told Walker that the "Mormons" had killed a Utah Indian, but the Indians were satisfied that Bridger had lied. The Council resolved that Alexander Williams and Dimick B. Huntington should do the trading (83) with the Indians for the community, that all other persons should be prohibited under fine, and that the traders should be paid double wages when so engaged. It was resolved that Charles C. Rich, Addison Pratt, and George Langley should prepare to start for the western coast by the first of July if possible, Mr. Pratt, on his way to the Pacific Islands; that George Pitkin, Jonathan Crosby, Joseph Busby, John L. Smith, and John Eldredge go to the Pacific Islands on Missions. Parley P. Pratt was to go to the Islands after a while, and also visit Chili. Brigham Young said he wanted to settle a colony in Walker's valley (Sanpete) next season; and send another down to the Gila River to raise cotton and sugar cane.

June

On the 2nd of June, D. B. Huntington (interpreter)
visited Brigham Young, with three Indians, whose
names were Grosapene and Tobiob, brothers to
Walker, and Antaro, Delegate from Big White Eye,
Chief of all the Utes from Uintah to Taos, and had a
peaceable and friendly talk.

In a Council, Archibald and Robert Gardner, were
granted the privilege of building a sawmill near the
forks of Mill Creek, about seven miles south-east, the
right of way being reserved for all persons and teams
into and out of the canon.

(84) The Council resolved that John Barnard, sen.,
S. Willis, J. C. Sly, Dr. Morse, and Dr. Ezekiel Lee
should go to the South Pass, to examine for gold.

In Council on the 10th it was voted that Chauncey
W. West, James S. Brown, John Egar, and Sidney
Alva Hanks go on a mission with Addison Pratt to the
Pacific Islands, and that --- Tomkins, Benjamin F.
Johnson, and Francis M. Pomeroy go to the Pacific
Coast with C. C. Rich, making the two companies, in
all, as follows--with C. C. Rich, George Langley, B.
F. Johnson, F. M. Pomeroy, and --- Tomkins; with
A. Pratt, Geo. Pitkin, Jonathan Crosby, Joseph Busby,
John L. Smith, John Eldredge, Chauncey W. West,
James S. Brown, John Egar, and S. Alva Hanks.
Some of these appointments were afterwards cancelled,
owing to the heavy emigration of gold diggers to
California.

On the 12th a company of nine men, with wagon-
makers and blacksmiths, under A. L. Lamoreaux left
the City for Green River to trade, and to ferry the
California and Oregon emigrants over that stream.

A Council was held on the 14th, with Walker, the
Utah Indian Chief, and twelve of his tribe, D. B.
Huntington interpreter. The pipe of peace was smoked.
Walker said he had never killed a white man. He wanted
the "Mormons" to go and settle at his place, south-
ward, Sanpete valley, also Iron County. Brigham
Young said in six moons they would send a company to
teach the (85) Indians to farm, build, etc. Brigham

Young gave the Indians half an ox, and then trading commenced between them and the people.

At a meeting on the 24th, Brigham Young proposed that a shade of boards be built to protect the congregation from the weather, that it be ready by July 24th, and that a celebration and a dinner be then had.

"G. S. L. City,
June 25, 1849.

This is to certify that we, the undersigned members of the Delaware Mining Company, from Ohio, when passing by the south side of the Platte River, met Jaques Rouvel Brunette, a resident of Fort Laramie, about 180 miles east of his said fort, who informed us that the Mormons had instigated the Indians to be unfriendly to all emigrants on the south side of said river, and that they were bad men. But we found the Indians friendly, and we firmly believe his statement to be false; and as he said he should report it to Government, we sign this in favor of the Mormons in the Salt Lake Valley, from whom we have received universal kind treatment.

Andrew McIlvain	P. Knight Gault,
L. B. Harris	A. C. Moses,
Daniel Plotmer	E. L. Coldren
A. G. Hinton	E. R. Moses
James A. Barnes	James Hinkle
Simpson Laid	James Edelman (86)
Joshua D. Breyfogle	Evan Evans
Josephus McClead	Jedh Allen
John C. Murphey	John F. Stimmel
Simeon Badley	Daniel A. High
Israel Breyfogel	Irwin Boynton
R. Cadwalader	Robert Cunningham

Samuel High."

In consequence of the scanty harvest of 1848, breadstuffs and other provisions became very scarce and many of the people were necessitated to eat rawhides, and to dig sego and thistle roots for months to subsist upon. The Thistle Roots proved highly diuretic. Those persons who had provisions imparted measurably to those who had not, so that all extremity of suffering from hunger was avoided.

July

At a meeting on the first it was voted to build a
shade or bowery of posts and boarding 100 by 60 feet,
which would require upwards of 7,000 ft. of lumber to
cover it once.

The General Assembly of the provisional State of
Deseret met in Great Salt Lake City on the 2nd, 3rd,
and 5th. The House also sat on the 6th, and the
Senate on the 9th. Willard Snow was elected Speaker
of the House.

(87) In the House, on the 3rd, the Speaker admin-
istered the oath of office to the Governor, Lieutenant-
Governor, Secretary of State, Auditor of Public
Accounts, and Treasurer.

On the 5th, in joint session, Almon W. Babbitt
was elected Delegate and representative to Congress.

The House on the 6th, adopted the following
Memorial, in which the Senate concurred on the 9th--

"To the Honorable Senate and House of Representatives in Congress assembled:

"Your Memorialists, members of the General
Assembly of the State of 'Deseret,' would respectfully
lay before your honorable body the wishes and interests of our constituents, together with the reasons and
design of our early organization as a civil government;
to which the consideration of your honorable body is
most earnestly solicited.

"Whereas the history of all ages proves that civil
governments, combining in their administration the
protection of person, property, character, and religion,
encouraging the science of agriculture, manufactures,
and literature, are productive of the highest, happiest,
and purest state of society; and

"Whereas all political power is inherent in the
people, and governments, to be permanent and satisfactory, should emanate from the same; and

(88) "Whereas the inhabitants of all newly-settled
countries and Territories, who have become acquainted
with their climate, cultivated their soil, tested their
mineral productions, and investigated their commercial advantages, are the best judges of the kinds of

government and laws necessary for their growth and
prosperity; and

"Whereas Congress have failed to provide, by law,
a form of civil government for this or any other portion
of Territory ceded to the United States by the Republic
of Mexico in the late treaty of peace; and

"Whereas, since the expiration of the Mexican
civil authority, however weak and imbecile, anarchy to
an alarming extent has prevailed; the revolver and
bowie-knife have been the highest law of the land; the
strong have prevailed against the weak; while person,
property, character and religion have been unaided and
virtue unprotected; and

"Whereas, from the discovery of the valuable gold
mines west of the Sierra Nevada mountains, many thousands of able-bodied men are emigrating to the Section, armed with all the implements and munitions of
war; and

"Whereas strong fears have been, and still are,
entertained, from the failure of Congress to provide
legal civil authorities, that political aspirants may
subject the government of the United States to the sacrifice (89) of much blood and treasure in extending
jurisdiction over that valuable property; and

"Whereas the inhabitants of the State of Deseret,
in view of their own security, and for the preservation
of the constitutional right of the United States to hold
jurisdiction there, have organized a provisional State
Government, under which the civil policy of the nation
is duly maintained; and

"Whereas there are so many natural barriers to
prevent communication with any other State or Territory belonging to the United States during a great portion of the year, such as snow-capped mountains, sandy
deserts, sage plains, saleratus lakes, and swamps,
over which it is very difficult to effect a passage; and

"Whereas it is important, in meting out the boundaries of the States and Territories, so to establish
them that the heads of departments may be able to communicate with all branches of their government with
the least possible delay; and

"Whereas there are comparatively no navigable

rivers, lakes, or other natural channels of commerce;
and whereas, no valuable mines of gold, silver, iron,
copper, or lead having as yet been discovered within
the boundaries of this State, commerce must necessarily be limited to few branches of trade and manufactures; and whereas, the laws of all States and Territories should be adopted to their geographical location, protecting and regulating those (90) branches of
trade only which the country is capable of sustaining,
thereby relieving the government from the expense of
those complicated and voluminous statutes which a
more commercial State requires; and whereas there is
now a sufficient number of individuals residing within
the State of Deseret to support a State Government,
thereby relieving the general government from the expense of a Territorial Government in that section, and
in evidence of which the inhabitants have already
erected a legislative hall equal to most, and surpassed
by few, in the older States:

"Your Memorialists, therefore, ask your honorable body to favorably consider their interests; and, if
consistent with the Constitution and usages of the
Federal Government, that the constitution accompanying this memorial be ratified, and that the State of
Deseret be admitted into the Union on an equal footing
with other States; or such other form of civil Government as your wisdom and magnanimity may award to
the people of Deseret; and, upon the adoption of any
form of government here, that their delegate be received, and their interests properly and faithfully represented in the Congress of the United States. And
your memorialists, as in duty bound, will ever pray."

The Assembly resolved that 2000 copies of the
Memorial, together with the Constitution and an ab-
stract of all records, journals, and other documents
pertaining to the organization of the State should be
printed, and that the President of the United States,
the Senate, and (91) the House of Representatives be
furnished with copies thereof.

On the 17th, Brigham Young, Daniel H. Wells,
Charles C. Rich, and about a dozen others went to
Salt Lake and Tooele Valley, visiting the cave at the

point of the mountains on the south shore of the lake,
and returning on the 18th. Antelope, cranes, snipe,
gulls and Mosquitoes abounded in that Valley, and
there were some Indians on the west side.

On the 23rd, Walker, the Utah Indian Chief, and
several other Indians, with D. B. Huntington interpreter, called on Brigham Young and it was agreed that a
company of settlers should be sent southward in a
month.

The same day, tables and seats were put up in in
the Bowery, and a liberty pole was erected. Some
emigrants for California furnished seventy-five pounds
of powder for firing salutes, Captain Tyler and the ar-
tillerists made cartridges for the cannon. In the evening the flag that used to fly on the Nauvoo Temple was
hoisted at the east side of the Bowery.

The 24th, the anniversary of the arrival of the
Pioneers in the Valley, was observed with great enthusiasm. The Fourth and Twenty-fourth were celebrated
together on the latter date because bread and vegetables
were more plentiful in the end of the mouth that in the
beginning. In the programme of observances for the
day were nine rounds of artillery with martial music at
dawn, followed by brass and (92) martial bands in two
carriages playing through the city. At half-past seven
o'clock the national flag, 65 feet long, was unfurled at
the top of the liberty pole, 104 feet high, which was saluted with the firing of six guns, the ringing of the
Nauvoo bell, and music from the bands. At eight
o'clock the people were called together at the bowery
by firing of six guns and music by the bands. The bishops and people of the several Wards, with banners and
mottoes, ranged themselves in order in the bowery,
which was 100 by 60 feet, built on 104 posts, and roofed
with boards. On each side of the bowery an awning 100
feet wide was extended, to increase the shelter and accommodation for the day. A procession or escort, with
banners, singing, band music, firing of cannon and mus-
ketry, pealing of the Nauvoo bell, marched from
Brigham Young's house, with prominent citizens, to the
Bowery, when the assembly was called to order, and
there followed prayer, speeches, reading of

Declaration of Independence and odes, singing of songs,
for the occasion, speeches by R. Ballantyne, Phineas
Young, Joseph Young, Charles C. Rich, Heber C.
Kimball, and Brigham Young. The audience then went
to dinner in the annex several thousands of people, including several hundreds of emigrants on the way to
California, all such as were in the Valley, and two or
three score of Indians. Company of emigrants who arrived during the meal were stopped, dismounted, and
placed at one of the tables. They were astonished at
the warmth of their reception. At 3 p.m. the audience
reassembled in the Bowery, when toasts, songs, in-
(93) strumental music, speeches by Parley P. Pratt,
Brigham Young, and Horace S. Eldredge were indulged
in. Not an oath was uttered, not a man was intoxicated,
not a disturbance nor a jar occurred to mar the union,
peace and harmony of the day."

On the 27th, Almon W. Babbitt started for
Washington, as Delegate to Congress, carrying with
him the Constitution of the State of Deseret and the
Memorial to Congress. R. L. Campbell, Oliver G.
Workman, and Edgar G. Blodgett started with him
from the City.

At a public meeting on the 29th the congregation
voted that no man bringing whisky into the settlements
should retail it, but that it should be delivered to some
persons authorized to sell.

August

At a meeting on the 12th of August, it was agreed
to furnish 52 teams with wagons to send back on the
plains to assist the Mormon emigrants to Salt Lake.

At a meeting on the 26th, it was reported that 27
wagons and 206 yoke of cattle with drivers were ready
to start to meet the emigrants. David Fullmer was
chosen Captain of the Company which was to rendez-
vouse for organization the next day.

On the 28th, Captain Howard Stansbury, U. S.
Topographical Engineers, and command arrived in the
City.

(94) On the 30th, Gen. John Wilson arrived in the

City, on his way to California, as General Indian
Agent.

September

On the 1st of September, Brigham Young, Heber
C. Kimball, Willard Richards, Jedediah M. Grant, and
several others, including the band, went to Brown's
Fort, where preaching was held the next day, Sunday.
On the 3rd the party went on the bench, looked over the
country, and decided that a city (Ogden) should be laid
out on the south side of the Ogden River, at the point of
bench land between the forks of the Ogden and Weber
Rivers, so that water from both streams might be tak-
en out for irrigation and other purposes. A dance was
held in the evening. The party returned to the city on
the 4th.

On the 6th, Brigham Young, Heber C. Kimball,
Willard Richards and several others had an interview
with General John Wilson, Indian Agent, in relation to
the temporary amalgamation of the States of Deseret
and California, in accordance with the wish of President Zachary Taylor, as represented by Gen. Wilson,
in order to avoid possible difficulty on the question of
slavery. The following basis was agreed upon--A general constitution for two States, those of the provisional State of Deseret, the other boundaries to be defined
by the people on (95) the coast in general convention;
the two States to be consolidated in one and named as
the convention should think proper, but to be dissolved
at the commencement of the year 1851, each State having its own constitution, and each becoming a free,
sovereign, independent State, without any further action of Congress. Amasa Lyman and --- Pickett was
chosen in conjunction with Gen. Wilson, to act as delegate from the people of Salt Lake. Mr. Wilson was to
confer with Mr. King, who went by the southern route.

(The following winter, Gen. Wilson and Amasa
Lyman presented to the Legislature of California a
memorial, with a view to the calling of a convention of
the people to consider propositions in unison with the
above. Gov. Burnett in a message, spoke adversely

to the memorial, and the Legislature refused to receive it.)

Among the passing emigrants to California were
some preachers of different denominations. It was a
custom to ask such to address the congregation on
Sundays in the Bowery. On Sunday the 9th, the Revd.
Henry Kroh, a German, preached on the text, "Sancti-
fy them through thy truth; thy word is truth." John
XVII, 17. The same day the congregation voted that a
perpetual fund be instituted to gather the poor Latter-
day Saints, and that Willard Snow, John D. Lee,
Lorenzo Snow, Franklin D. Richards, and John S.
Fullmer, be a committee to collect and preserve said
fund.

(96) On the 14th, Brigham Young, Heber C.
Kimball, Willard Richards, Erastus Snow, Franklin D.
Richards, and several others started on a visit to Utah
County. They preached at the Cottonwood settlement
and at Utah Fort. About two miles southeast of the latter place they found an eligible site on which it was decided to build a city (Provo) a mile square, in blocks
of four acres each, divided into lots of half an acre
each, reserving the centre block of four acres for the
site of a chapel and four schoolhouses, the streets to
be five rods wide.

In the Bowery in the City on the 16th the Revd.
Perry B. Marple preached from the text, "The Righteous perisheth." Isaiah LXII, 1.

On the 23rd, Orson Spencer and company of
"Mormon" Emigrants from the States arrived.

On the 28th fourteen or fifteen "Mormons" arrived
from the Pacific Coast, mostly belonging to the
"Brooklyn" company.

While resting in the City, many of the emigrants
to California, in writing letters to their friends in the
States, gave flattering descriptions of the city and valley, and spoke in glowing terms of the kindness and
hospitality which they had met here. A number of these
letters, or extracts from them, were published, in various newspapers in the States. (97)

October

A General Conference of the Church of Jesus
Christ of Latter-Day Saints was held in the Bowery on
the 6th and 7th of October at which it was voted that a
Perpetual Emigration Fund be raised to gather (immi-
grate) the poor; that Willard Snow, John S. Fullmer,
Lorenzo Snow, John D. Lee, and Franklin D. Richards
be a committee to raise funds; that Edward Hunter carry the funds back to the States, buy cattle, take the
oversight of the property, and bring the poor; that
Amasa Lyman and Charles C. Rich be agents Fund in
California; that the business of the Fund be under the
direction of the First Presidency; that Isaac Morley,
Charles Shumway, and Seth Tuft have the presidency of
the settlement in Sanpete Valley; that Henry G.
Sherwood build a glass factory as soon as circumstances would permit; that a company be organized to
carry goods and merchandize from the Missouri River
to Great Salt Lake Valley, and that a passenger train
be started between the same points; that a city (Ogden)
be laid off in Captain Brown's neighborhood, or
Brownville, and one (Provo) in the Utah Valley, and
that a settlement be made and a city (Manti) be laid off
in Sanpete Valley; that the following persons go on
Church missions--Charles C. Rich to Western
California, to assist Amasa Lyman and to succeed him
after a while, Francis M. Pomeroy to accompany Mr.
Rich; Addison Pratt, James Brown, and Hyrum H.
Blackwell to the Society Islands. Lorenzo Snow and
Joseph Toronto to Italy; Erastus Snow (98) and Peter O.
Hanson to Denmark; John Taylor, Curtis E. Bolton,
and John Park to France; Franklin D. Richards Joseph
W. Johnson, Joseph W. Young, Job Smith, Haden W.
Church, George B. Wallace, John S. Higbee, and
Jacob Gates to England, John E. Forssgren to Sweden.
    Several hundred emigrants for California arrived
too late in the season to continue the journey by the
northern route, and many contemplated wintering at
Salt Lake. But so large an accession of mouths, in addition to the emigration proper to Salt Lake, threatened
a famine. Some of them concluded to pass the winter

at Salt Lake.   But on the 8th Jefferson Hunt started
with a company of about 100 wagons, by the southern
route, Charles C. Rich, Addison Pratt, and other missionaries going with them. When the company were
near Beaver Creek, an emigrant named Captain Smith,
with a company of packers, came up and urged the emigrants to go westward by Walker's cut off, to avoid the
desert. Captain Hunt insisted that the Westerly route
was not safe. However, Captain Smith and the packers
went that way and eventually, when near the rim of the
Basin, most of the emigrants followed him, leaving
Captain Hunt with only seven wagons, with which he arrived safely in California. Most of those who took the
cut-off wandered a while in the mountains with insufficient grass and water, and then turned back and followed Captain Hunt. Captain Smith and some others
struggled westward, and a few of (99) them, after much
suffering and disaster, arrived on foot in California.

The Second General Epistle of the Presidency of
the Church of Jesus Christ of Latter-day Saints, from
the Great Salt Lake Valley, to the Saints scattered
throughout the earth, dated the 12th, was issued on
the first sheet ever printed in the Valley, so far as
known.

On the 19th, John Taylor, Lorenzo Snow, Erastus
Snow, Franklin D. Richards, Edward Hunter, and
about 30 others left the city for the east, most of them
on missions to Europe.

Five companies of Latter-day Saint emigrants
came across the plains this season, led respectively
by Orson Spencer, Allen Taylor, Silas Richards, Geo.
A. Smith, and Ezra T. Benson. Total about 500 wagons and 1,400 souls.

In this mounth Isaac Morley, with a company of
about 30 men and 224 souls, started to form a settlement in Sanpete Valley.

November

Early in November an addition to the city, on the
west side and extending to the Jordan, was surveyed
and partly apportioned.

On the 19th nine "Mormons" arrived from California. Small companies had been arriving from there at intervals since the latter part of September. During the (100) summer several small companies went from Salt Lake to California.

In a council on the 20th it was decided that Parley P. Pratt with a company should go on an exploring expedition southward to the outside of the Rim of the Basin.

On the 21st Mr. Vasquez opened a store of merchandize in the city and soon sold all his sugar at three lbs. for two dollars.

On the 23rd the Southern Exploring Company numbering about fifty persons, met and organized on Cottonwood Creek as follows--Parley P. Pratt, President, William W. Phelps and David Fullmer, his Counsellors; John Brown, captain of fifty, William W. Phelps, topographical Engineer; Ephraim Green, chief engineer; Isaac C. Haight, Joseph Mathews, Joseph Horne, Ephraim Green, and Josiah Arnold, captains of tens; Robert L. Campbell, clerk. The company had 12 wagons, 1 carriage, 24 yoke of cattle, 38 horses and mules, an odometer to measure distances, a brass field piece, small arms, 7 beeves, also 150 lbs. of flour to each man, besides crackers, bread and meal.

December

On the 1st of December, 19 emigrant men, who started from the States Sept. 24, came into the city on (101) foot and destitute, having left their wagons on Echo Creek, and the last of their arrivals at Willow Springs, fast in the snow, which was six feet deep on the level. They were two days working over the Big Mountain, and had had very little to eat for four days. Several men from the city went over the mountains to hunt for the horses, but returned in a few days unsuccessful.

The same day the General Assembly of the provisional State of Deseret met in Heber C. Kimball's schoolroom.

On the 10th, Governor Brigham Young approved
an ordinance regulating the militia of the State of
Deseret.

On the evening of the 24th the city was enlivened
by the firing of cannon and of guns and pistols in every
direction, which continued most of the night.

On the 25th, 150 persons assembled at Brigham
Young's house to celebrate Christmas day. Feasting
and dancing continued till a late hour.

On the 26th the first beam of the roof of the
Council House was put in place.

Shadrach Roundy, Jedediah M. Grant, John S.
Fullmer, George D. Grant, and Russell Homer issued
a "Prospectus of the Great Salt Lake Valley Carrying
Company," proposing to run passenger and freight
trains from the Missouri River to the California Gold
regions via Great Salt Lake City. The prospectus set
forth the following advantages secured by travelling
in the Compa- (102)nie's carriages--

The company possess facilities that few at present
avail themselves of. Owing to their peculiar situation
or location, living, as most of them do, in the Valley
of the Great Salt Lake, they can (by active exertion)
obtain fresh supplies of animals to aid in the enterprise,
they trust, to the full and entire satisfaction of all concerned. Two or more of the firm will remain in the
valley, to see that suitable horses or mules are on
hand to aid the line, when it shall require their assistance from the Valley to Sutter's Fort. Emigrants
last year, from inexperience and other causes, sacri-
ficed hundreds and even thousands of dollars, and most
generally broke down their teams before or by the time
they arrived in the valley." Terms -- For passengers
to Sutter's Fort, $300--$200 in advance, and $100 in
Great Salt Lake City. For hauling goods to Great Salt
Lake Valley $12.50 per hundred pounds, or $250 per
ton, two-thirds to be paid in advance. (103)

January 1850

A letter was received from Alexander Williams
and other settlers in Utah Valley, stating that the
Indians were hostile and threatened to make war upon
the settlers. Brigham Young answered it, recommending careful judicious, peaceable conduct on the part
of the settlers, and discountenanced killing Indians for
stealing. He proposed for the consideration of the
settlers the following question--"Why should men have
a disposition to kill a destitute, naked Indian who may
steal a shirt or a horse, and think it no harm, when
they never think of meting out a like retribution to a
white man who steals, --although he has been taught
better from infancy?"

At a public meeting in the Bowery, Brigham Young
recommended the construction of a dam across the
Jordan River, that the water might be used to irrigate
the land and propel machinery. Shortly afterward, the
General Assembly of the Provisional State of Deseret
by ordinance appropriated $3000 for the construction of
such a dam, and appointed George A. Smith and E. T.
Benson a committee to build the same.

On the 5th, Captain Howard Stansbury sent an express to Fort Hall, which accomplished the task and
returned, after a tedious journey, with the paymaster
and some other officers of the U. S. army, from the
command at Fort Hall. An express, despatched in
December failed, owing to the deep snow.

(104) In a Council on the 24th, the following
Church appointments were made--Newel K. Whitney,
to receive and disburse the public works funds,
Truman O. Angell, architect; Norton Jacobs, foreman
of the joiners and carpenters; Samuel Ensign, foreman
of the Carpenters; Alonzo H. Raleigh, foreman of the
masons; Reynolds Cahoon, foreman of the Tithing
hands. It was agreed to pay mechanics two dollars
and a half a day, and the architect three dollars a day.

On the 30th, four men arrived from Fort Bridger,
having left their goods and pack animals in Weber
Cañon. This was their second attempt to get from
Bridger to the Valley during the winter.

February

Some unruly Indians in Utah Valley, having killed or stolen 50 or 60 head of cattle and horses, and having become very saucy and threatening, the settlers at Utah Fort (Provo) became very anxious to defend themselves and chastise the depredating Indians. On the a meeting on the subject was held in the Council House, after consultation with Captain Howard Stansbury and Lieut. Gunnison. U. S. A. Brigham Young reluctantly advised the settlers to take measures to compel the Indians to desist from committing depredations, which advice Captain Stansbury, who was present, (105) approved. Gen. Daniel H. Wells called for volunteers of the militia to go to Utah Fort.

On the 4th, Captain George D. Grant started with a company of volunteers for Utah Valley. Major Andrew Lytle overtook the command at Cottonwood. By direction of Captain Stansbury, Dr. Blake and Lieut. Howland, U. S. A., accompanied the expedition. Several fights were had with the Indians at Provo and other places in Utah Valley, resulting in the killing or wounding of 20 or 30 Indians, the killing of one white man and the wounding of several others. Old Elk, the Utah Chief, who had sworn never to live in peace with the white man, was found dead in Rock Cañon, a few miles from Provo. On the 10th, General Daniel H. Wells started for Utah Valley. The volunteers returned on the 19th. The squaws and children of the slain Indians were fed, clothed, and taught to work.

On the   Governor Brigham Young approved the ordinance incorporating the University of the State of Deseret.

The provisional General Assembly held an adjourned session at intervals during the winter, divided the State into Counties and precincts, and established County Courts with Judges, clerks, sheriffs, justices, constables, also a supreme Court, with annual sessions at Great Salt Lake City. (106)

March

On the 13th, the chancellor and regents of the University of the State of Deseret held their first meeting, at which a committee of three was appointed, in connection with Governor Brigham Young, to select a site for University buildings, and also locations for buildings for primary schools.

April

At a General Conference of the Church of Jesus Christ of Latter-day Saints on the 6th, 7th, and 8th, it was voted that eight missionaries go to the Society Islands, nine to England, two to California, and two to the States. At a meeting of mechanics, Brigham Young proposed that the wages of carpenters and joiners be $2.00 per day, and of masons $2.50 per day.

On the 17th, Orson Spencer, Chancellor of the University of Deseret, issued a circular to the patrons of learning throughout the world, asking them to contribute to the establishment and sustenance of the institution.

On the 20th, the last of the missionaries for England left the City.

On the 30th, Brigham Young, Heber C. Kimball, Geo. A. Smith, E. T. Benson, and Wm. M. Lemon, Surveyor, went on the other side of Jordan, , with leveling instruments, to examine the river and its (107) banks with the view of deciding upon a site for a dam with which to take out the waters for irrigation.

May

On the 1st, Brigham Young and party returned from the other side of Jordan. They had been up the river about 25 miles without finding a very favorable site for a dam, the river having a slow current. The committee appointed by the Legislature to build a dam across the river decided that the sum appropriated was insufficient.

On the 13th, at a meeting, it was agreed to send

ten teams with grain to help the Sanpete settlement.

The same day a farm, two miles by one, was located near Jordan Bridge, for the poor. It was designed to build houses for the accommodation of all such as were not able to build for themselves, but on investigation it was discovered that there were but two persons of that description in the valley. So the farm was used for a pasture.

On the 27th, the first company of the season's emigrants, from Chicago, for California, arrived. They reported that they had left on the road thirty wagons laden with grain.

During this month, Brigham Young, in different meetings, advised the people to feed the Indians (108) more or less until they could raise grain or provide for themselves, and to set them an example worthy of civilized men.

June

On the 8th, Thos. Williams arrived with the mail from Kanesville (Council Bluffs).

On the 15th, the first number of the "Deseret News" was published, Willard Richards Editor. It was an eight page quarto weekly. Eack page of print was eight and three-eighths by six and three-eighths inches, in three columns, without column rules. This was the first newspaper issued in the Rocky Mountains.

The same evening the band gave a concert in the Bowery, the first concert in the Rocky Mountains.

In the night of the 17th and morning of the 18th a severe frost greatly injured tender vegetation.

July

The following letter was published in the "Deseret News" of the 6th:-- (109)

For the Deseret News.

G. S. L. City, July 1, 1850.

Mr. Editor, --

I ask a small space in your paper, to correct an error, which, to my surprise, I have been informed,

exists on the eastern side of the mountains, with regard to the reception here of the party under my command. An impression, I find, has gone abroad, not
only that we were received with coldness and suspicion, but that the survey of the Great Salt Lake, which
was the object of the expedition, had been forcibly
opposed by the inhabitants of the Valley. How this
rumor became prevalent, I am ignorant, as my official reports to the War Department, gave ground for
no such impression. Let that be as it may, I take
pleasure in declaring that nothing can be further from
the truth. We were received by the President and
Public Authorities with the greatest courtesy, both
officially and personally; and will remember with
gratitude the many tokens of kindness and regard we
have received from them, and the citizens of the
place.

Every facility has been studiously afforded us for
the prosecution of our duties; instruments of science
frankly and gratuitously loaned, and the able and faithful assistance obtained, from their commencement
here, of a gentleman, well known as a fearless advocate of your doctrines, and a prominent and influential member of your community. (110)

I have deemed it not improper to say thus much,
to counteract an erroneous impression against a
people, already burthened with too much undeserved
reproach.

> Very Respectfully,
> Your ob't servant,
> Howard Stansbury.
> Captain Corps Topographical Engineer,
> in charge of Survey of the Great Salt Lake.

The General Assembly met in the Bowery in the
afternoon of the 4th, and the Nauvoo Legion, which
had been having a public parade, marched in, when
Gov. Brigham Young made a public address, after
which the Assembly continued its sitting and appropriated $2,000 to repair the road to Black Rock and
the bridge over the Jordan, and Ezra T. Benson being
appointed a committee to see that the work was pro-

perly done and to draw the pay for it.

On the 20th, John Y. Greene, started to meet the emigration for Salt Lake and report on the condition of the same.

The 24th was celebrated by the firing of cannon and muskets, music by the brass and martial bands, the brass band parading the city in its new carriage, which was 29 by 9 feet, and drawn by 14 (111) horses. There was also a procession, assemblage in the Bowery, morning and afternoon, speeches by Brigham Young, H. G. Sherwood, John Dilworth, Willard Snow, Parley P. Pratt, Heber C. Kimball, and Geo. A. Smith; orations by Willard Richards and Orson Spencer; songs, anthems, odes, toasts, etc.

On the 31st, Brigham Young, Heber C. Kimball, Newel K. Whitney, and others left the City for Sanpete.

In consequence of the great amount of snow in the mountains this season, the Jordan and other streams overflowed their banks, destroying considerable grain and other crops. The Jordan rose several feet higher than previously known. An unusual amount of summer rain fell, so that comparatively little irrigation was needed, and an abundant harvest was secured, notwithstanding the loss by floods.

August

Brigham Young and party arrived at the Sanpete settlement on the 4th, and on the 5th selected a site for a city (Manti). Wm. M. Lemon commenced to survey the plot, which subsequently showed 110 blocks, each 26 rods square, with eight lots in a block, streets six rods wide. In the Schoolhouse, a sawed log building, 26 by 20 feet, a picnic party or feast was held, followed by preaching. The party left Sanpete on the 8th, and arrived in Great Salt Lake City on the 12th.

Orson Hyde arrived on the 15th from Kanes-(112) ville, with a mail.

On the 21st an express arrived from the States, with letters. Brigham Young received information of his appointment as census agent or marshal for Deseret.

On the 28th, Captain Howard Stansbury and suite left for the States. The day previous the Captain, Lieut. Gunnison, prominent citizens, merchants, members of the Legislature were entertained at dinner by Heber C. Kimball.

The same day Brigham Young, Heber C. Kimball, Orson Hyde, Newel K. Whitney, Daniel H. Wells, and others, with the band, went to Weber County, returning on the 31st. While there, the site for Ogden City was located, and a plan given for the city. Brigham Young advised the settlers not to scatter in the country, but to move to the city lots, build good houses, with school-houses, meeting-house, and other public buildings, fence their gardens, and plant out fruit trees, so that Ogden might be a permanent city and a suitable head quarters for the northern country.

Peaches were raised this year, the first raised in the Great Basin, though they were destroyed by the children before they were ripe.

The emigration across the Continent for California, more numerous this year than ever, caused provisions to be very high. Flour ran up to a dollar a pound. After harvest, which commenced on the first of July, it fell to twenty-five dollars a hundred. The (113) flour mills were crowded with work, grinding for the emigrants, who hung around, begging for enough to feed them to the gold mines. Beef was ten cents a pound. Horses, harness, carriages, wagons, etc., were bought of eager emigrants at one-fifth of their cost in the States.

September

A General Conference of the Church of Jesus Christ of Latter-day Saints was held on the 6th, 7th, and 8th, in the Bowery, and was addressed by Brigham Young, Isaac Morley, Parley P. Pratt, Orson Hyde, Heber C. Kimball, Geo. A. Smith, and Newel K. Whitney. The subjects treated upon were strengthening the Sanpete settlement, sending missionaries abroad, tithing, education, cleanliness, temperance, emigrating the poor from a distance and

making settlements and improvements, rather than
running off to California to dig gold.

On the 10th, the U. S. Mail arrived from the East.

The same day John P. Barnard and a few others
arrived from California.

On the 11th the Perpetual Emigrating Fund Company incorporation ordinance was passed by the General Assembly.

At a public meeting on the 15th, Brigham Young
was chosen president of the Perpetual Emigrating
(114) Fund Company, with a number of assistants.
Subsequently Willard Richards was chosen Secretary,
Newel K. Whitney Treasurer, and Thomas Bullock
Recorder.

On the 23rd Newel K. Whitney died, aged 55 years,
7 months, and 18 days, after an illness of 48 hours of
bilious pleurisy. He had been for many years the presiding Bishop of the Church of Jesus Christ of Latter-
day Saints. He was a straightforward, upright man,
and universally esteemed in the community.

On the 25th it was voted that Daniel Spencer be
treasurer of the Perpetual Emigrating Fund Company,
in place of Newel K. Whitney deceased.

On the 29th, Amasa Lyman, with 34 others, arrived from California, via Carson Valley.

October

On the 1st, Orson Hyde started on his return to
Kanesville.

On the 5th, Ira Eldredge finished surveying the
State Road from Great Salt Lake City to the Provo river, Utah County.

The General Assembly met on the same day and
passed a bill for the organization of Davis County,
which was approved.

On the 14th, Wilford Woodruff arrived from the
States.

(115) The eastern mail arrived on the 15th, with
news of the passage by Congress of the bill to establish a Territorial government for Utah.

At a meeting on the 27th it was resolved to build a

"Seventies Hall of Science," in shares of $25 each, and $5,200 was immediately subscribed.

This season the following buildings were raised--State House (Council House), stores for Williams and Blair, Reese and Clawson, Livingston and Kinkead, Mr. Thomas and Holladay & Warner, also the Tithing Office, and public bathhouse a one story adobe building, (since known as the Old Bath House) situate on a small rise of ground a few rods immediately south of the present Bath House. It was used of late years as a residence, and was pulled down in 1881. Schoolhouses were built in most of the Wards.

November

On the 3rd, Geo. A. Smith was appointed to make a settlement in Little Salt Lake Valley (now Iron County).

A parent school for the qualification of district or Ward schoolteachers was commenced under the auspices of the Chancellor and Board of Regents of the University, who had engaged Dr. Lyons Collins as teacher.

On the 9th the eastern mail arrived, bringing a copy of the act incorporating the Territory of Utah, also confirmation (116) of the report that Brigham Young had been appointed census agent for Deseret or Utah, and Willard Richards postmaster of Great Salt Lake City. The mail had passed through snow from one to three feet deep for 17 days.

In the evening the band gave a grand concert in the Bowery.

On the 12th Charles C. Rich, Orin Porter Rockwell, and about fifty others arrived from California, via Carson Valley.

On the 22nd the mail for the east left the city. Brigham Young sent four men to break the road over the second mountain.

On the 27th the Warm Springs Bath House was dedicated and opened with prayer, festival, and dance.

December

On the 2nd the General Assembly of the State of
Deseret met in the new State House (Council House)
which was sufficiently near completion for the purpose.
The Senate organized in the northeast room, second
story, Lieut. Governor Heber C. Kimball presiding,
William Clayton Secretary. Jedediah M. Grant
Speaker of the House, Thomas Bullock Clerk. Governor Brigham Young delivered his message, which was
read in joint session. The following are extracts--

"In this State no expense has been incurred (117)
by any of the departments of the government for services rendered."

"All the Indians, with whom we have had difficulties are detached or broken off bands from the main
tribes, with them (the latter) our peaceful relations
have never been interrupted."

"Not a solitary case was reported for trial before
the regular sessions of either the county or the supreme courts during the past year, and no offence beyond the control of a justice of the peace seems to have
been committed."

On the 7th, Geo. A. Smith's Company, partly selected and partly volunteers to make a settlement in
Little Salt Lake Valley left the City, and on the 16th,
after organization, left Utah Fort (Provo), numbering
163 souls, of which 30 were women over 14 years of
age, with 101 wagons, 2 carriages, 100 horses, 12
mules, 368 oxen, 166 head of loose cattle, seed grain,
etc.

On the evening of the 24th, the explosion of fireworks and firing of guns and pistols were indulged in.

On the 25th the band promenaded the city and
played at the houses of principal residents.

On the evening of the 27th a concert was given by
the band and a play was performed in the Bowery, after
which there was a grand display of fireworks opposite
the Bowery.

Word was received this month, by letter from
Dr. J. M. Bernhisel, that Brigham Young had been ap-
(118) pointed Governor of Utah, also of the establish-

ment of the following post routes--between Great Salt
Lake City and Utah Lake and Sanpete Valley, between
Great Salt Lake City and Brownsville (Ogden) and San
Francisco, and between Great Salt Lake City and Santa
Fe.

The General Assembly continued its sittings at intervals during the month, passing various ordinances,
one granting to Brigham Young the control of City
Creek Cañon, and another authorizing the State
Commissioner to contract for building a tole bridge
across Jordan River.   (119)

January 1851

On the 9th, the ordinance incorporating Great Salt Lake City was passed by the General Assembly and the following officers were appointed--Jedediah M. Grant, Mayor; Nathaniel H. Felt, William Snow, Jesse P. Harmon, and N. V. Jones, Aldermen; Vincent Shurtliff, Benjamin L. Clapp, Zera Pulsipher, William G. Perkins, Lewis Robison, Harrison Burgess, Jeter Clinton, John L. Dunyon, and Samuel W. Richards, councillors.

On the 11th the members of the City Council took the oath of office before Thomas Bullock, Clerk of the County Court, and elected Robert Campbell, recorder; Thomas Rhodes, treasurer; and Elam Luddington, marshall, who were also sworn in. The Council also divided the City into four municipal Wards, bounded as follows--first Ward, by the eastern and southern limits of the City, west by East Temple Street, north by Third South Street; Second Ward, east by East Temple Street, south by southern limits, west by west bank of Jordan, north by South Temple Street; Third Ward, east by East Temple Street, south by South Temple Street, west by west bank of Jordan, north by northern limits; Fourth Ward, east by eastern limits, south by Third South Street, west by East Temple Street, north by northern limits.

In a public meeting on the 12th, it was unanimously voted to put down swearing and the profane use (120) of the name of Jehovah.

On the 13th the City Council passed an ordinance to have the Old Fort removed by the first of April.

On the 20th, Brigham Young, Heber C. Kimball, Amasa M. Lyman, Jedediah M. Grant, and several others, went on a preaching tour as far as Ogden, returning on the 28th. On their return they were met at Judson Stoddart's (Farmington) by Major-General D. H. Wells and a large company of mounted men and the band, and escorted to the city, with firing of cannon and other demonstrations of rejoicing, which was occasioned by the arrival of Jefferson Hunt and company of eight persons in all from California by the southern

route, with letters, papers, and copies of the New
York "Tribune" containing the appointment of government officers for Utah, by President Millard Fillmore.

The Deseret Almanac, by W. W. Phelps, was
published this month.

February

On the 3rd, Brigham Young took the oath of office
as Governor of Utah before Daniel H. Wells, Chief
Justice of the State of Deseret.

On the 4th an ordinance was passed by the Legislative Assembly incorporating the Church of Jesus
Christ of Latter-day Saints.

(121) On the 19th a company under Mayor Geo. D.
Grant started for Tooele Valley in pursuit of Indian
and other cattle thieves. Twenty more men started the
next day for Utah Valley, to meet those gone to Tooele.
The company returned on the 25th and 27th, after a
hard trip, in consequence of the severity of the weather.

In the latter end of the month a company under
William Taylor was sent to guard the pass of Black
Rock, south end of Great Salt Lake.

March

On the 9th in a public meeting, Brigham Young
urged the people not to sell their beef and butter to the
emigrants and go without themselves, and Ezra T.
Benson presented the subject of fencing the University
grounds (now covered by Fort Douglas reservation),
with a stone wall.

On the 12th Wm. H. Arnolds arrived with the
January mail from Independence, Mo. At this time the
mail contract required ten mails per annum, each way.

On the 16th Parley P. Pratt and others started on
preaching missions to the Pacific Coast and Islands.

On the 17th Brigham Young, Heber C. Kimball,
and others started on a preaching trip to Utah County,
returning on the 27th.

Amasa M. Lyman and Charles C. Rich, with about

20 others, were going to Southern California, to (122)
form a settlement near the Cajon Pass, and also for
missionary purposes. This company rendezvoused at
Payson, Utah County, where it was addressed and organized by Brigham Young's party on the 23rd, but it
was found to have swelled to 520 persons with 157 wagons, some intending to locate in Iron County and a few
others being missionaries to the Pacific Islands, but
the company consisted mostly of persons enamored
with reports of the California paradise, though it was
contrary to Brigham Young's wishes that so many
should go.

On the 28th, in consequence of the passage of an
act by Congress for the organization of the Territory
of Utah, the appropriations made for public buildings,
and the extension of the Constitution of the United
States over said Territory, information of which by the
mail having been received but recently, the Legislature
of the Provisional State of Deseret, in joint session,
unanimously resolved that they cheerfully and cordially
accepted of the Legislation of Congress in the act to
establish a Territorial Government for Utah, that they
welcomed the extension of the Constitution of the United
States over the Territory; that all provisional state officers be requested to furnish their Territorial successors every facility in their power by turning over public documents, etc.; that Union (16th Ward) Square,
Great Salt Lake City, be devoted for the use of public
buildings of said Territory; that Governor Brigham
Young be their agent to make drafts upon the treasury
of the United States (123) for the amount appropriated
for said buildings, and to take such measures as he
should deem proper for their immediate erection; that
Truman O. Angell be architect of said buildings, and
Daniel H. Wells a committee of one to superintend
their erection, and that they proceed immediately to
design and erect them, that the General Assembly of
the Provisional State of Deseret finally dissolve on the
5th day of April following.

About this time the Deseret Pottery, under the
superintendence of Messrs. Tomkinson & Ralphs, two
experienced Staffordshire potters, was ready to burn

saggars.

A number of the emigrants who started from the States for California, after their arrival at Salt Lake, were baptized into the Church, and most of such remained in Utah. About 300 others of the emigrants wintered in the Valley, and in the spring resumed their journey to California.

About this time the city was being fenced into blocks instead of into Wards.

During its session the General Assembly appropriated $2,000 towards establishing a woollen-manufactory in the valley.

April

The first impannelment of a grand jury, and the first jury trial in the Provisional State of Deseret, was at a special session of the Great Salt Lake County court, on the (124) 3rd, when several emigrants were convicted of stealing, and were sentenced to hard labor for various terms. After serving a portion of their time, they were pardoned by the executive, and went on their way to California.

On the 5th, according to a joint resolution of that body, the General Assembly of the Provisional State of Deseret dissolved.

On the 6th a General Conference of the Church of Jesus Christ of Latter-day Saints commenced in the Bowery, on the Temple Block, but in consequence of heavy rains it was adjourned till the 7th, when it was voted that Edward Hunter succeed Newel K. Whitney as presiding bishop in the Church, that a Temple to the name of the Lord be built in Great Salt Lake City, and that Daniel H. Wells be a committee of one to superintend the building of the same, and the public works. A number of persons were called to go to Iron County, and thirty-seven agreed to go. Brigham Young was too sick to attend Conference, which was addressed by Heber C. Kimball, Ezra T. Benson, Jedediah M. Grant, and Anson Call.

The same day a municipal election was held, when the previous incumbents were elected, excepting that

John L. Dunyon and Benjamin L. Clapp resigned, and
Enoch Reese and Robert Purce were chosen to fill
their places.

The Fifth General Epistle of the Presiden- (125)
cy of the Church of Jesus Christ of Latter-day Saints,
to the members of the Church, is dated the 7th, with
an addenda dated the 16th.

On the 10th Col. Reese sent 10 or 12 wagon loads,
of flour to Carson Valley to trade to the emigrants.

In a public meeting on the 13th, Brigham Young
proposed and the congregation voted that a tabernacle
for religious worship be built, 120 by 60 feet.

On the 17th a small party, in search of provisions
and Indian goods, arrived from Fort Hall, and reported
deep snow on the route.

On the 22nd, Brigham Young, Heber C. Kimball,
Willard Richards, Ezra T. Benson, and a number of
others, started with a company on a visit to the southern settlements. The company included several families to strengthen the Iron County settlement.

The Indians in Tooele Valley having been very
annoying in stealing and killing live stock, Orin P.
Rockwell, with a company of men, went to Tooele
Valley and captured about 30 marauding Indians. At
night, on the 22nd, the Indians attempted to escape,
all but four getting away, in the scuffle an emigrant
was shot and killed by them. A reinforcement of 25
men was sent to Rockwell's command.

On the 30th, the ground was broken for a railway
between Great Salt Lake City and the mountains east,
for the conveyance of rock for the building of the Tem-
(126) ple. The intention was to build the whole track
of wood. It was known as the Red Butte railroad,
from a cañon and creek where red sandstone is obtained.

About the same time a raft of lumber rails for the
railroad came down the Jordan, from Gardener's Mill,
a few miles south, and was landed in the city.

Several swarms of bees, brought from the States,
were doing well at this time.

Messrs. Beach (of St. Louis) and Blair (of Texas)
opened a molasses and vinegar manufacturing esta-

blishment in the city this spring.

May

May Day (the first of May) was observed by several parties of young ladies attired in white, and
others, among the scholars of the parent school of the
University, visiting the cañons, after which the evening was spent at Mrs. Pack's Assembly Room in a
social entertainment, with collation, songs, prayer,
speeches, dancing, etc.

On the same day, O. P. Rockwell's posse returned
from pursuit of the Indians, having killed six, and followed the remainder of the body to their stronghold in
the mountains, on the west side of Tooele Valley, but
not attacked it considering the numbers of the posse
insufficient for that purpose.

(127) On the 7th the first train of merchandize
for the season arrived, consisting of four or five wagons loaded with bacon, hams, sugar, coffee, and
calicoes.

On the 18th, a meeting was held in the Council
House to get up subscriptions for building a Tabernacle
on Temple Block.

On the 21st the Tabernacle was commenced near
the S. W. Corner of the Temple Block.

On the 24th the officers of the Nauvoo Legion and
the band went south two or three miles to Chase's
Mill, and met Gov. Brigham Young and company,
and thence escorted them into the city, where they
were saluted with firing of cannon and other demonstrations of welcome.

In public meeting on the 25th, Brigham Young advised the people to embark in home manufactures and
develop the resources of the Territory.

On the 31st, the Nauvoo Legion, numbering about
700, had drill and parade. A new regiment was organized. A flag was presented to the band by Major
General Daniel H. Wells.

June

On the 5th the California mail arrived in care of Mr. Chorpenning, one of the contrators, with seven men. They left Sacramento May 3, and were 14 days getting their (128) mules over the Nevada Mountains. They were also hindered by snow on the Goose Creek Mountains.

On the 4th, men commenced plowing for the foundation of the Tabernacle.

On the 7th, Lemuel G. Brandenbury, Chief Justice of the Territory, with Ben Holladay, arrived from the States.

On the 9th, Brigham Young, Heber C. Kimball, Willard Richards, and others had a friendly interview with the Indian Chiefs Walker, Sowiette, Arrapene, and Unhoquitch. Elijah Ward Interpreter.

On the 10th the Wolverine (Michigan) train of emigrants to California, 13 wagons and 40 men, arrived, the first company of the season.

On the 12th a company with a few wagons started for Little Salt Lake Valley.

The Indians having driven of cattle at Black Rock, a company left the City on the 14th to recover the stolen stock. The company pursued the Indians to their stronghold in the mountains on the west side of Tooele Valley, but were not strong enough to dislodge them. So on the 20th, a company of 35 men, under Wm. H. Kimball, were sent to the assistance of McBride's company.

On the 27th the first wheat of the season was harvested on Cottonwood Creek.

The same day E. Tompkinson burned the first kiln of yellow pottery ware, in Deseret Pottery, (129) near the east end of Third South Street, also known as emigration Street.

The same day Major Geo. D. Grant and company returned from Tooele Valley and reported having killed 11 Indians and burned up tons of beef which they had killed and laid out to dry, an acre or more of it.

July

On the 1st, Governor Brigham Young issued a proclamation embodying an apportionment of the members of the Council and House of Representatives, in accordance with the ratio of population in each county of the Territory, and directing the holding of an election in the respective precincts on the first Monday in August for the election of 13 Councillors and 26 Representatives for the Legislative Assembly, also for the election of a delegate to the House of Representatives of the United States, to represent said Territory.

The 4th of July was celebrated at Black Rock. The company left this city at 9 a.m., in about 130 carriages, with the Nauvoo Brass Band in its large band carriage drawn by 16 mules, four abreast. The company enjoyed themselves in picnicing, bathing, scaling the mountains, and various other recreations, and were addressed in the evening by Governor Brigham Young, Heber C. Kimball, Orson Spencer, Jedediah M. Grant, Willard (130) Snow, James Ferguson, and John Kay. The addresses were interspersed with toasts and instrumental and vocal music. The company returned to the city the next day.

The Buffalo "Courier" and other papers having published charges against Governor Brigham Young of wholesale abuse of the United States and the institutions thereof, of leaguing with the Indians to harrass travellers on the road to California, of openly abusing the democracy, and other things, and having furthermore charged President Millard Fillmore with a knowledge of the same, President Fillmore wrote to Col. Thomas L. Kane, asking him to state whether or not the charges preferred against Governor Young were true. Col. Kane replied by letter, exonerating Gov. Young from all those charges and unreservedly reiterating his previous oral recommendation of Governor Young's capacity, energy, and integrity.

On the 18th Feramorz Little and Alva Hanks contracted to carry a monthly mail to and from Salt Lake City and Fort Laramie for $8,000 a year.

On the 19th Dr. John M. Bernhisel, Hon. A. W.
Babbitt, Judge Zerubbabel Snow, Secretary B. D.
Harris, and sub-Indian agents Stephen B. Rose and
Henry R. Day, arrived from the States. Dr. Bernhisel
had been intrusted with the selection of 4000 or 5,000
volumes of books for the Utah Library, which were on
the way. Mr. Babbitt brought $20,000 appropriated by
Congress to build a State House (131) for the Territory.
Secretary Harris was intrusted with $24,000 for the
expenses of the Legislature.

On the 21st, Gov. B. Young, by proclamation,
divided the Territory into three Indian agencies and
assigned sub-agents Henry R. Day and Stephen B.
Rose to two of them.

The 24th was celebrated by procession through
several streets to the Bowery and entertained, morning and afternoon, with orations by Daniel H. Wells
and Willard Richards, addresses by Governor Brigham
Young, Heber C. Kimball, Wm. W. Phelps,
Zerubbabel Snow, Ezra T. Benson, John Banks,
Henry G. Sherwood, Seth M. Blair, James Ferguson,
and Hon. John M. Bernhisel, and with songs, music,
and toasts. There was also a ball given to the bands
and public hands in the new storehouse.

On the 26th a political meeting was held in the
Bowery, at which addresses were made by Gov.
Brigham Young, Daniel H. Wells, Jedediah M. Grant,
Seth M. Blair, George D. Grant, and Willard Snow.
A Delegate to Congress, Councillors and Representa-
tives to the Territorial Legislature, and County officers
were nominated.

August

On the 4th a general election was held.

On the 8th Gov. B. Young issued a proclamation,
temporarily defining the judicial districts and as- (132)
signing the judges thereto. Great Salt Lake City was
in the first district, with Lemuel G. Brandenbury
Judge. Each district to hold semi-annual terms of
court, extending to one week if necessary.

On the 14th, Gov. B. Young, Heber C. Kimball,

and Phineas Young visited Weber County, returning
on the 16th.

On the 17th, Orson Hyde, Albert Carrington, and
Associate Justice Perry E. Brocchus arrived from
the States.

On the 19th, Gov. B. Young, Heber C. Kimball,
and others visited Call's settlement (afterwards
Bountiful) Davis County, as a watermelon party.

On the 31st, Governor B. Young received the following note--

"Sunday morning, Aug. 31st, 1851.

"Judge Brocchus tenders his compliments to
Gov. Young, and begs leave to say that he would be
glad to accompany his Excellency to Church this morning.

"Judge B. is still in feeble health, and could not
with propriety venture to walk to Church."

Gov. B. Young went on foot to meeting in the
Bowery. When he arrived at the stand, Judge
Brocchus was already there. (133)

September

On the 1st the foundation for a State House on
Union (16th Ward) Square was commenced.

The same day Hon. John M. Bernhisel, delegate
elect to Congress, left for the States.

On the 3rd, seven wagons started eastward from
the city with provisions for the "Mormon" emigrants.

On the 5th, a ball was given at the Bath House to
Orson Hyde, Almon W. Babbitt, Ezra T. Benson,
and Jedediah M. Grant.

On the 7th, 8th, 9th, and 10th a General Conference of the Church of Jesus Christ of Latter-day
Saints was held in the Bowery. The Hon. Perry E.
Brocchus, Associate Justice for the Territory, requested the privilege of addressing the Assembly. On
being asked what would be his subject, he replied that
he did not know. The privilege was granted, and on
the second day of the Conference he appeared in company with Judge Brandenbury, Indian Superintendent
Day, and several others of his friends, and addressed

the congregation. He expressed his everlasting gratitude for the kindness and hospitality of the people to
him when sick and a stranger. He bore testimony to
the peacefulness of the inhabitants of the Territory
and their submission to tribunals of their own choice,
and prayed to God that all the United States might
soon have such tribunals as were in this Territory,
and then it would always bring peace to the hearts of
those who had to be judged. He hoped there (134)
would be no litigation. He denied that he came to
Great Salt Lake with the view of being elected delegate
to Congress, but he had expressed his willingness to
accept that office, if elected, and that he thought he
could do the Utah people good in that way. He wanted
the respect of the people. He was an honorable man,
or he would not have been appointed to office in the
Territory. President Fillmore, who appointed him,
was an honorable and virtuous man. He appeared before his audience, under a commission by the board
of managers of the national Washington monument, to
ask the Territory to contribute a block of marble
towards the erection of that building. He cursorily
reviewed the career and character of George
Washington. He objected to some portions of the oration of Hon. D. H. Wells on the 24th of July. The
government was not responsible for the persecutions
of the "Mormons" in Missouri and Illinois. President
Polk expressed decided disapprobation of those deeds.
He (Brocchus) felt indignant about them, and he believed the mass of the people at the time boiled with
rage towards the perpetrators. The Federal Government had not injured the "Mormons." To those per-
secuting States the "Mormons" should look for redress.
If the people of Utah could not offer a block of marble
in full fellowship with the United States, it were better
to leave it unquarried in the bosom of its native mountain. He directed a portion of his discourse to the
ladies, and, though he was well understood to be a
boastful libertine himself, he strongly rec- (135)
ommended them to become virtuous.

At the close of Judge Brocchus' speech, Gov.
Brigham Young arose and said that Judge Brocchus

was either profoundly ignorant or wilfully wicked.
Several gentlemen were present who would be glad to
prove, then and there, certain statements concerning
Judge Brocchus, if they were permitted to do so, and
discussions were allowed at that meeting which was
convened specially for religious worship. It was well
known to every man in the community, and had become
a matter of history throughout the enlightened world,
that the Government of the United States looked on the
scenes of robbing, driving, and murdering of the
Latter-day Saints and said nothing about the matter,
but by silence gave sanction to the lawless proceedings.
Hundreds of women and children had been laid in the
tomb prematurely in consequence thereof, and their
blood cried to Heaven for vengeance against those who
had caused or consented to their death. George
Washington was not dandled in the cradle of ease, but
schooled to a life of hardship in exploring and surveying the mountains and defending the frontier settlers,
even in his early youth, from the tomahawk and the
scalping knife. God inspired him and enabled him to
assert and maintain the independence of the country.
The same God led the Latter-day Saints. He (Gov.
Young) loved the Government and the Constitution of
the United States, but he did not love corrupt ministers
of the Government. He was indignant at such corrupt
fellows as Judge Brocchus coming there to lecture the
people on mor- (136) ality and virtue. He could buy a
thousand of such men and put them into a bandbox. It
was an insult to that Congregation to throw out such
insinuations as Judge Brocchus had. He said it was
an insult, and he would say no more. ..

    Judge Brocchus appears to have been ambitious
and presumptuous, full of self importance, with a
talent for political and social intrigue, and withal
somewhat corrupt, hypocritical, and revengeful.
During the progress and at the end of his speech the
audience was greatly incensed at his offensive remarks,
not only because of their inherent offensiveness, but
also because of his introducing them at a public religious Conference and thereby inexcusably doing violence to the purpose of the meeting as well as to the

feelings of the audience.   Nothing would have better
pleased some persons present than to have been permitted to tell what they knew about him, or had been
informed concerning him, thereby making some revelations damaging to him.   Among other things it
had been reported, on good authority, that on his
journey to Salt Lake he had unburthened himself substantially as follows-- "If the citizens of Utah do not
send me as their Delegate to Washington, by God,
I'll use all my influence against them and will crush
them.   I have the influence and power to do it, and I
will accomplish it if they do not make me their Delegate."   Before he arrived at Great Salt Lake City, he
learned of the election of Dr. John (137) M. Bernhisel as
Delegate to Congress, and thenceforth Judge Brocchus
appears to have set himself to work mischief in and
against the community.

At the Conference about a dozen missionaries
were called to go to the States and Europe to preach.
Brigham Young proposed to inaugurate foot companies
of poor Latter-day Saint emigrants, to cross the plains,
and invited the women to save their rags for the manu-
facture of paper.   The Conference was addressed by
Brigham Young, Heber C. Kimball, Willard Richards,
Ezra T. Benson, Orson Hyde, Geo. A. Smith, Wilford
Woodruff, Levi W. Hancock ----- Kempton, Henry G.
Sherwood, Levi Gifford, John Young, John Smith,
Edward Hunter, William W. Phelps, Isaac Chase,
Zera Pulsipher, Noah Packard, Edwin D. Woolley,
and Lorenzo D. Young.

On the 18th, Gov. Brigham Young issued a proclamation, declaring the council and representatives
elect to the Territorial Legislature, and appointing a
meeting of the Assembly on the 22nd of the month at
10 a.m.

On the 19th, Gov. Brigham Young by letter invited
Judge Brocchus to meet with the public assembly at
the Bowery on the 21st to explain or apologize to the
ladies who heard his address on the 8th.   He was assured that no gentleman would be permitted to make
any reply to him.

In answer to the above, the same day, Judge

Brocchus declined the invitation, but stated that his
speech of (138) the 8th, in all its parts, was the result
of deliberation and care. He intended to say what he
did say, to vindicate the government, but he did not design to insult or offer indignity or disrespect to anybody,
particularly the ladies. He still believed his speech
was undeserving of censure.

On the 20th, 25th, and 30th, Governor Brigham
Young answered, at some length, the letter of Judge
Brocchus of the 19th:

Brigham Young to P. E. Brocchus.

G. S. L. City, Sept. 20, 1851.

Dear Sir--The perusal of your note of the 19th inst.,
has been the source of some sober reflections in my
mind, which I beg leave to communicate in the same
freedom with which my soul has been inspired in the
contemplation.

With a war of words on party politics, factions, religious schisms, current controversy of creeds, policy
of clans or State clipper cliques, I have nothing to do;
but when the eternal principles of truth are falsified,
and light is turned into darkness, by mystification of
language or a false delineation of facts, so that the just
indignation of the true, virtuous, upright, peaceful citizens of the commonwealth is aroused into vigilance for
the dear bought liberties of themselves and fathers, and
that spirit of intolerance and persecution, which has
driven this people time and times again from their
peaceful homes, manifests itself in the flippancy of
rhetoric for female insult and (139) desecration it is
time that I forbear to hold my peace, lest the thunder-
ing anathemas of nations born and unborn should rest
upon my head, when the marrow of my bones shall be
illy prepared to sustain the threatened blow.

It has been said that a wise man forseeth evil, and
hideth himself. The evil of your course I forsee, and
shall hide myself. --not by attempting to screen my conduct, or the conduct of this people, from the gaze of an
assembled universe, but by exposing some of your
movements, designs, plans, and purposes, so that the
injury which you have designed for this people may fall
upon your own head, unless you shall choose to accept

the proffered boon--the friendship which I extended to
you yesterday--by inviting you to make satisfaction to
the ladies of this valley, who felt themselves insulted
and abused by your address of the 8th inst., and which
you have declined to do in your note, to which this is a
reply.

In your note, you remark--"If, at the proper time,
the privilege of explaining had been allowed me, I
should promptly and gladly have relieved myself from
any erroneous impressions that my auditors might have
derived from the substance and tone of my remarks;
but as that privilege was denied me, that the peril of
having my hair pulled or my throat cut, I must be permitted to decline appearing again in public on the subject."

Sir, when was the "proper time" to which you
refer? Was it when you had exhausted the patience of
your (140) audience on the 8th, after having given a personal challenge to any one who would accept? Was it a
proper time to challenge for single combat, before a
general assembly of the people, convened especially
for religious worship?

How could you, then, have "promptly and gladly
relieved yourself from any erroneous impression your
auditors might have derived from the substance and
tone of your remarks," when you knew not from what
source your auditors derived those impressions? And
was it your boasted privilege, your proper time to fire
and "fight your battles o'er again," as quick as you had
given a challenge, without waiting to see if any one accepted it? If so, who would you have been likely to hit
--ladies or gentlemen?

It was true, sir, what I said, at the close of your
speech, and I repeat it here, that my expressions may
not be mistaken--I said in reference to your speech,
Judge Brocchus is either profoundly ignorant, or wilfully wicked--one of the two. There are several gentlemen who would be very glad to prove the statements
that have been made about Judge Brocchus, and which
he has attempted to repel; but I will hear nothing more
on either side at this Conference.

And why did I say it? To quell the excitement

which your remarks had caused in that audience; not to
give or accept a challenge, but to prevent any one (of
which there were many present wishing the opportunity),
and every one, from accepting your challenge, and
thereby bringing down (141) upon your head the indignation of an outraged people, in the midst of a Conference
convened for religious instruction and business, and
which, your remarks continued, must have continued
the excitement, until there would have been danger "of
pulling of hair and cutting of throats," perhaps, on both
sides, if parties had proved equal--for there are points
in human actions and events, beyond which men and women cannot be controlled. Starvation will revolutionize
any people, and lead them to acts of atrocity that human
power cannot control; and will not a mother's feelings,
in view of her murdered offspring, her bleeding husband, and her dying sire, by hands of mobocratic violence, be equally strong and uncontrollable, and especially when tantalized to the highest pitch by those who
stand, or ought to stand or sit, with dignity on the
judgment seat, and impart justice alike to all?

Sir, what confidence can this persecuted, murdered, outcast people have in your decisions from the
bench, after you have tantalized their feelings from the
stand, by informing them there is yet hope in their case,
if they will apply to Missouri and Illinois. I ask you,
sir, if you did not know, when you was thus making
your plea, that this people have plead with the authorities of those States, which are doomed to irretrievable
ruin by their own acts, from their lowest magistrate to
their highest Judge, and from their halls of legislature
to their governors, times and times, and times again,
until they, with force of arms, have driven us from
their midst, and utterly refused the possibility of the
(142) cries of murdered innocence from reaching their
polluted ears? I ask, sir, did you know this? If not,
you are profoundly ignorant; you were possessed with
ignorance not to be tolerated in children of ten years,
in these United States. But, on the other hand, if you
were in possession of the facts, you were wilfully
wicked in presuming to tantalize, and rouse in anger
dire, those feelings of frail humanity on one hand and

offended justice on the other, which it is our object to
bury in forgetfulness, and leave the issue to the decision of a just God.

Your motive, action, or design, you wholly con-
cealed, or you could never have gained a hearing on
such an occasion.

As presiding officer in said Conference, did I permit any man to accept your challenge? No, sir, you
know I did not; and could you, as a gentleman, ask the
privilege to defend your challenge before it was accepted? Don Quixotie should not be named in such a
farce. No, sir, out of mercy to you I prohibited any
man from accepting your challenge. --And until the
challenge was accepted you had nothing to reply to.
When, then, was the proper time, you refer to, when
you would have replied, and the privilege was denied
you? No such time as you had supposed existed.

And now, sir, as it appears from the whole face of
the subject, that to-morrow might have been the first
"proper time" that might have given you the "priv-
(143) ilege of explaining," and as this courtesy you
have utterly refused, and thereby manifest a choice to
leave an incensed public, in incense still, against your
(as they now view it) dishonorable course, I shall take
the liberty of doing my duty, by advertising still further
to your reply of yesterday. Charity would have induced
me to hope, at least, that your speech, in part, was
prompted by the impulse of the moment; but I am forbid
this pleasing reflection, by your note, wherein you
state that "my speech in all its parts, was the result of
deliberation and care, not proceeding from a heated
imagination or a maddened impulse." "I intended to
say what I did say." Now, if you did actually "intend
to say what you did say", it is pretty strong presump-
tive testimony that you were not ignorant, for if you
had been ignorant, from whence arose your intentions?
And if you were not ignorant, you must have been wilfully wicked; and I cannot conceive of a more charitable
construction to put upon your conduct on that occasion
than to believe you designedly and deliberately planned
a speech to excite the indignation of your hearers to an
extent that would cause them to break the bands of pro-

priety, by pulling your hair or cutting your throat,
willing, no doubt, in the utmost of your benevolence to
die a martyr's death, if you could only get occasion to
raise the hue and cry, and re-murder a virtuous people, as Missouri and Illinois has so often done before
you. --Glorious philanthropy this; and corresponds
most fully with the declaration which, it is reported,
on pretty good authority, that Judge Brocchus made
while on his (144) journey to the valley, substantially
as follows: "If the citizens of Utah do not send me as
their delegate to Washington, by God, I'll use all my
influence against them, and will crush them. I have
the influence and the power to do it, and I will accomplish it if they do not make me their delegate."

Now sir, I will not stop to argue the point whether
your honor made those observations that rumor says
you did; but I will leave it to an intelligent world, or
so much of that world as are acquainted with the facts
in the case, to decide whether your conduct has not
fully proved that you harbored those malicious feelings
in your heart, when you deliberately planned a speech
calculated in its nature to rouse this community to violence, and that, too, on a day consecrated to religious
duties, your declaration to the contrary notwithstanding,
that you "did not design to offer indignity and insult."
When a man's words are set in direct opposition to his
acts, which will men believe? His acts all the time.
Where, then, is the force of your denial?

One item more from your note, reads thus--"My
sole design in the branch of my remarks which seems
to be the source of offence, was to vindicate the government of the United States from those feelings of prejudice; and that spirit of defection which seemed to per-
vade the public sentiment." &c. Let me inquire what
"public sentiment" you referred to? Was it the sentiments of the States at large? If so, your honor missed
his aim, (145) most widely, when he left the City of
Washington to become the author of such remarks.
You left home when you left Washington. If such "prejudice and defection" as you represent there existed,
there you should have thundered your anathemas, and
made the people feel your "patriotic allegiance; but, if

ever you believed for a moment--if ever an idea entered your soul that the citizens of Utah, the people
generally whom you addressed on the 8th, were possessed of a spirit of defection towards the general government, or that they harbored prejudices against it
unjustly, so far you proved yourself "profoundly ignorant" of the subject in which you was engaged, and of
the views and feelings of the people whom you addressed; and this ignorance alone might have been sufficient to lead you into all the errors and fooleries you
were guilty of on that occasion. But had you known
your hearers, you would have known, and understood,
and felt that you was addressing the most enlightened
and patriotic assembly, and the one furthest removed
from "prejudice and defection" to the general government that you had ever seen, that you had ever addressed, or that would be possible for you or any other
being to find on the face of the whole earth. Then, sir,
how would it have been possible for you to have offered
your hearers on that occasion a greater insult than you
did? The most refined and delicate ladies were justly
incensed to wrath against you for intimating that their
husbands were ever (146) capable of being guilty of such
baseness as you represented, in "prejudice and defection" towards a constitution which they firmly believe
emanated from the Heavens, and was given by revelation, to lay the foundation of religious and political
freedom in this age--a constitution and union which
this people love as they do the gospel of salvation; and
when you, sir, shall attempt to fasten the false and
odious appellation of treason to this community, you
will find plenty, even among the ladies, to hurl falsehood back to its dark origin, in tones of thunder, even,
as we have supposed, you have done it ignorantly; but
if, as you say, you know (or else how could the whole
have been "the result of deliberation and care,") the
plea of ignorance ceases again to shield you, and you
stand before the people in all the naked deformity of
"wilful wickedness," and who can plead your excuse?
Who under such circumstances, can make an apology?
I wonder not that you should excuse yourself from the
attempt, or "decline appearing again in public on the

subject."

Permit me, sir, to subscribe myself, as ever, most respectfully, your servant,

Brigham Young.

On the 22nd the Legislature convened and organized pro tem.

(147) The sixth General Epistle of the Church of Jesus Christ of Latter-day Saints was dated the 22nd.

Judge Zerubbable Snow wrote to President Millard Fillmore, informing him that Judges Brandenbury and Brocchus and Secretary Harris were about to leave the Territory for the States, that he had used all his influence unavailingly to bring about a reconciliation, and that he should not return to the States unless the President and Congress considered that he ought to do so.

On the 23rd, Orson Hyde started back on his return to Kanesville.

On the 24th, Almon W. Babbitt, who had started for the States the day previous, drew his pistol on Rodney Badger, an officer sent to arrest Joseph L. Babbitt, for debt. On the 25th, a posse took Almon W. Babbitt into custody and brought him back to the city, but the Supreme Court judges released him on writ of habeas corpus.

Secretary Harris having neglected his duty in furnishing the usual conveniences for the Legislative Assembly, that body passed a resolution directing the drawing of an order on the Secretary for the sum of $500 towards defraying the indicental expenses of the Assembly. On presentation, Secretary Harris declined to pay the order, under the plea that the Assembly was not legally elected.

The Assembly, learning that the Secretary was (148) about to run from the Territory and carry away, or otherwise dispose of, the Territorial seal and records, with papers, documents, and other property pertaining to his office, including $24,000 appropriated by Congress for compensation and mileage and other expenses, legislative and territorial, passed a joint resolution that it should be the duty of the U. S. Marshal for the Territory to take possession of said money, documents, and other property, and, if the Secretary would not give them up, to arrest him, and keep him in custody until he should comply with those conditions.

On the 27th, the Supreme Court issued an injunction, restraining the Marshal from arresting the Secretary or seizing upon the federal or Territorial property in his possession.

On the 28th, Secretary Harris and Judges Brandenbury and Brocchus deserted their posts and set out on their return to Washington.

The following letter was forwarded to Washington--
        "Great Salt Lake City, Sept. 29th, 1851.
"To his Excellency Millard Fillmore, President of the United States of North America:

"Sir: It is now over one year since "An Act to establish a Territorial Government for Utah" became a law of Congress: Information of this fact reached this place in November following: and about the first of (149) January authentic information was received of the appointments of the Territorial officers by the President, this news being confirmed on the 3rd day of February. I took the oath of office as Governor of this Territory in accordance with the provisions of the organic act. Owing to the great distance from this place to the seat of the General Government, I considered of the first importance that the preliminary arrangements for the organization of the Territory should be accomplished as soon as possible, in order that a delegate might be legally returned to the Congress of the United States before the lateness of the season should render the (at any time) long and arduous journey dangerous, if not impracticable; Hence my anxiety to proceed with as little delay as possible in obtaining the enumeration of the inhabitants preparatory to appointing the election districts, and apportioning the members of Council and House of Representatives to be elected from each.

"Having been appointed Census Agent to take the Census of Deseret, and owing to the total mis-carriage of instructions and blanks, which had not, neither indeed have yet, arrived, the taking of that census has been delayed for a season; but now being required to

cause the enumeration to be taken for the use of the
Territory, and despairing of the blanks coming on, I
proceeded to take the census, and appointed my assistants to make out two sets of returns, one for the
United States, as census agent for Deseret, and one
for Utah, which required not the full census, but
merely the enumeration of the inhabitants. This was
sufficiently accomplished (150) to enable me to make
out the apportionment about the first of July, which I
did, and issued my proclamation declaring the same.
This being previous to the arrival of the Secretary, of
course his seal and signature were not attached. The
reason inducing this order has been recited alone that
the election might come off in time that whoever should
be elected as Delegate to Congress might be enabled to
go before the inclement season should set in.

"Although the appointments were made early in the
fall, yet no new resident officer made his appearance
until the unsuing summer, and some of them not until
about the first of August.

"Upon the arrival of a majority of the Supreme
Court, I again issued my proclamation districting the
Territory into three Judicial districts, and assigning
the Judges to their several districts. This proclamation bears the impress of the seal of the Territory and
signature of Mr. Harris.

"Learning, to my very great regret, that the Secretary, (Mr. Harris,) and Judge Brandenbury and
Associate Judge Brocchus intended to return to the
United States this fall, I called upon them personally to
ascertain the fact, and, if possible, induce them to remain. They, however, assured me it was their intention to leave, and Mr. Harris also declaring that he
should carry with him all the funds in his hands for the
payment of the Legislative expenses of the Territory,
as also the seal, records, doc- (151) uments, &c.,
pertaining to his office--plainly indicating that it was
his intention to essentially vacate said office, so far as
Utah was concerned, and anticipate, by leaving with the
funds, the nonpayment of the Legislative Assembly.

"I considered this course illegal, wholly unauthorized, and uncalled for by any pretext whatever. I

therefore concluded that I would use all legal efforts
that should seem practicable for the retention of the
property and money belonging to the United States in
the Secretary's hands, designed for the use of this
Territory. I therefore issued my proclamation declaring the result of the election, and convening the
Legislative Assembly on the 22nd of the present month.
This proclamation was dated on the 18th instant, thus
showing but a hurried notice; but notices had been sent
previously to the members elect, and when the day
arrived, all of the Council were present, and only one
member of the House absent. It is but due to myself
to say, that this proclamation was delayed from the
fact of a misunderstanding with the Secretary that he
would make out the declaration of the members elect,
and prepare the proclamation; which, failing to do, I
caused it to be done, and sent it to him for his signature and impress of the seal of the Territory--intend-
ing for him to keep the manuscript thus furnished and
return a copy suitable for publication. Much to my
astonishment, he placed the seal and signature to the
manuscript thus furnished, not even filing a copy for
record. It was published, however.

(152) "The Legislature convened in accordance
therewith, with the exception of one member of the
House, from Iron County. The Secretary did not attend
to furnish a roll of the members. I therefore had this
duty to perform, when they were called and qualified
by His Honor Judge Snow.

"My message was the next document in order.

"On the 24th inst., the Legislative Assembly
passed a joint resolution, making it the duty of the
United States Marshal to proceed forthwith and take
into his custody all of the aforesaid funds, property,
&c. This resolution was presented to Mr. Harris, as
also an order for five hundred dollars to defray the
incidental expenses of the Legislative Assembly. He
refused to comply with the requirements of each.

"At this time, September 26th, I addressed a note
to the Supreme Court, who I understood were then in
session, asking their opinion in regard to my duty,
having reference to the organic act, which requires

the Governor to see that the laws are faithfully executed,
and requiring the said Secretary to reside in said
Territory, &c.

"After awaiting a reply to this note until the day
fixed for their departure had far advanced, I directed
the United States District Attorney to file a petition
which would cause them to give their opinion, having
determined to abide the decision of the Judges. (153)
I accordingly stayed all further proceedings, and on
yesterday, the 28th, I understand the Secretary,
Mr. Harris, and the two Judges, Mr. Brandenbury
and Mr. Brocchus, left this City on their return to the
United States.

"For a reply to Mr. Harris's decision, I refer
you to file, No. 12.

"Thus, sir, I have given you a plain, unvarnished
tale of all our proceedings pertaining to governmental
affairs, with the exception of report upon Indian affairs,
which will be made to the proper Department.

"If your Excellency will indulge me in a few remarks, I will proceed and make them.

"Mr. Harris informed me, in a conversation
which I had with him, that he had <u>private instructions
designed for no eye but his own,</u> to watch every movement, and not pay out any funds unless the same should
be <u>strictly legal, according to his own judgment.</u>

"The Supreme Court organized and held a session,
as will appear by reference to the certified copy of
proceedings, without waiting for the Legislative authority fixing the time; and apparently having no other
object than to shield and protect Mr. Harris in leaving,
with the funds and property designed for the use and
benefit of this Territory.

"It has been and is said of myself and the people
over whom I have the honor to preside, that they frequently indulge in strictures upon the acts of men who
are intrusted with governmental affairs, and that the
gov- (154) ernment itself sometimes does not wholly
escape... Now, sir, I will simply state what I know
to be true, that no people exist who are more friendly
to the Government of the United States than the people
of this Territory.

"The Constitution they revere, the laws they seek
to honor, but the nonexecution of those laws in times
past, for our protection, and the abuse of power in
the hands of those intrusted therewith, even in the
hands of those whom we have supported for office, even
betraying us in the hour of our greatest peril and extremity, by withholding the due execution of laws designed for the protection of all the citizens of the
United States: it is for this we have cause of complaint,
not the want of good and wholesome laws, but the execution of the same, in the true meaning and spirit of
the Constitution.

"The foregoing is a case in point. What good and
substantial reason can be given, that the people of this
Territory should be deprived, for probably near a year
to come, of a Supreme Court, of the official seal of a
Secretary of State, of the official publication of the
laws, and other matters pertaining to the office of
Secretary?

"Is it true that officers coming here by virtue of
any appointment by the President, have private instructions that so far control their actions as to induce the
belief that their main object is not the strict and legal
performance of their respective duties, but rather to
watch for iniquity, to catch at shadows, and make (155)
a man "an offender for a word," to spy out our liberties, and, by manifold misrepresentations, seek to
prejudice the minds of the people against us? If such
is the case, better, far better would it be for us, to
live under the organization of our Provisional Government, and entirely depending upon our own resources,
as we have hitherto done, until such time as we can be
admitted as a State, than thus to be tantalized with the
expectation of having a legal government, which will
extend her fostering care over all her offspring. In
infancy, if ever, it is necessary to assist the rising
State.

"If it be true that no legal authority can be exercised over a co-ordinate, and even a subordinate
branch of the government, by the Legislature thereof,
then indeed we may expect the harmony of Government
to be interrupted, to hear the discordant sounds of ir-

responsible and law-defying agents, desecrating, by
their acts, the very name of American liberty.

"In the appointment of new officers, if you will
pardon me for making a suggestion, I would propose
that such men be selected as will reside within the
Territory, or have a general and extended knowledge
of men and things as well as of the elementary and
fundamental principles of law and legislation; men who
have lived and practiced outside, as well as indoors,
and whose information extends to the duties of a justice of the peace, as well as the well known passages
and districts of the court room. In relation to our
present unfortunate position, pertaining to the Supreme
Court, I can only hope that early the ensuing season
we may (156) be favored with a quorum.

"As regards the funds, if an arrangement could be
made authorizing Mr. Livingston, a merchant in this
place, to receive the money appropriated to meet the
Legislative expenses, he would most probably make
such advances as might be necessary, after being advised of the privilege of so doing.

"The Legislative Assembly are yet in session.
Of their acts and doings I shall take the liberty of making report, the same as would have been the duty of
the Secretary, had he remained. I cannot conceive
that it can or ought to be in the power of any subordinate officer to subvert, or even retard, for any length
of time, the ordinary motion of the wheels of government, although I am equally satisfied that it was and
is the intention of a portion of those aforesaid officers
to utterly subvert and overthrow the Government of
Utah, But of this I have no fears, as I know they can
have no good and sufficient apology for the course they
have and are pursuing.

"The money that was appropriated for the year
ending the 30th of June 1851, should have been used to
defray the expenses of the Legislature of '50 and '51,
and the government might have been organized, had the
officers been as efficient in coming here, as they are
now in going away. The Legislature can now, as heretofore, do without their compensation and mileage,
and find themselves; they were all unanimously elected,

(with one exception,) as (157) was our Delegate to Congress, the Hon. John M. Bernhisel.

"We have sought to obtain an authorized government, and the people have been well satisfied with the government, in regard to all their acts in relation thereto, so far as I am acquainted; and if the men appointed had endeavored to be active in the discharge of their duties, all would have been well.

"Mr. Harris takes exceptions to everything that has been done; did he take hold, upon his arrival at this place, and endeavor to assist in the organization of this government as a Secretary should do? Not at all! Never was he the man to do the first thing, either by suggestion or otherwise, unless perhaps it was occasionally to set his hand and seal of the Territory to some document that had been prepared for him. Has either of the Judges who are returning ever done anything towards the organization of the Territory? They organized the Supreme Court chiefly, as I think, to assist Mr. Harris in leaving with the funds; and I believe Judge Brandenbury appointed a clerk of the district. Judge Brocchus had determined on returning this fall, previous to his arrival, as I am credibly informed, and they both leaving at this time, just when the time has arrived for them to act, postpones indefinitely all courts in their respective districts. Judge Brocchus has never been in his district, that I know of. Thus, so far as the public interests are concerned, it would have been quite as well if neither of these gentlemen or Mr. Harris (158) had ever troubled himself to cross the plains.

"Whatever may be your decision upon all these matters, be assured that it is and has been my intention to discharge faithfully every duty pertaining to my office; and that I shall receive very gratefully any instructions that you will please to give.

"Awaiting most anxiously to hear from you, I have the honor to be, your Excellency, very respectfully and truly yours,

                   Brigham Young."

On the same day the Legislative Assembly signed

a memorial to the president of the United States,
showing that two of the justices of the Supreme Court
of the United States for the Territory, and the Secretary had removed from the Territory and vacated
their offices. The Memorialists prayed the chief executive to fill the vacancies as speedily as possible
with residents of the Territory.

About this time there were four grain mills, five
saw mills, one carding machine, and one small
woollen mill in operation in Great Salt Lake County; a
portion of the cobble stone wall around the University
lands on the bench South-east of the city was completed; a farm for the benefit of the poor on the west
side of the Jordan was laid out and partly fenced; and
common schoolhouses had been erected in most of the
Wards in the City. (159)

October

On the 1st, the Legislature adjourned to the first
Monday in January, 1852.

On the 4th, Orson Pratt arrived from England.

A General Conference of the Church of Jesus
Christ of Latter-day Saints, adjourned from September 7th, was held in the Bowery on the 6th. The Conference was addressed by Brigham Young, Heber C.
Kimball, George A. Smith, Zerubbabel Snow, and
Orson Spencer. It was voted that three companies
piloted respectively by Peter Shirts, John A. Woolf,
and Andrew Love, should start within about two weeks,
to make or strengthen settlements in the Southern
parts of the Territory. It was also proposed to bring
Big Cottonwood Creek, Mill Creek, and Parley's
Cañon Creek toward the city for irrigation purposes.

About this time Judge Zerubbabel Snow delivered
an opinion to the effect that Gov. Brigham Young's acts
in getting up and calling together the Legislative Assembly were strictly legal.

On the 15th, to prevent further derangement of
local governmental affairs, and for the safekeeping of
the Territorial records, Governor Brigham Young appointed Willard Richards Secretary pro tem.

On the 17th, in the U. S. District Court for the
Territory, First District, Judge Zerubbable Snow presiding. Howard Egan was on trial on charge of murdering James Monroe, Mr. Egan having shot
Mr. Monroe at Yellow (160) Creek (east), Sept. 19th,
for crim. con. with Mrs. Egan during Mr. Egan's absence in California. The jury returned a verdict of
"not guilty."

On the 21st, Gov. Brigham Young, left the city
on a trip to Pauvan Valley. He was accompanied on
the trip by the Board of Commissioners for locating
the seat of Government for Utah--Orson Pratt, Albert
Carrington, Jesse W. Fox, and William C. Staines,
also by Heber C. Kimball, George A. Smith, and
Daniel H. Wells, Judge Zerubbabel Snow, Sub-Indian
Agent S. B. Rose, and several other citizens, fifteen
in all.

On the 29th Fillmore City, Millard County, was
located as the Capital of the Territory, being situated
on Chalk Creek, in Pauvan Valley, about 150 miles
southward from Great Salt Lake City.

November

On the 7th, Gov. Brigham Young and party returned from their trip to Pauvan Valley.

On the 15th, the "Deseret News" resumed issue,
enlarged to a super-royal sheet, of four pages, each
20 by 15 inches. Willard Richards Editor. The "News"
had been suspended for three months for want of paper.

(161) On the 25th in consequence of threatened
Indian hostilities at San Bernardino, the people there
built a stockade fort, inclosing ten acres.

December

On the 15th, Indian Agent, Stephen B. Rose,
Marshal J. L. Heywood and others started for San Pete
Valley, to arrest certain Mexicans, who were trading
for Indian children to take to Mexico to sell for slaves.

On the 17th, Gov. Brigham Young issued a proclamation proclaiming Thursday, the first day of

January, 1852, a day of Praise and Thanksgiving.

On the 19th Lemuel G. Brandenbury, Chief Justice, Perry E. Brocchus, Associate Justice, of the Supreme Court of the Ter'y. of Utah, and B. D. Harris, Secretary of the Ter'y., issued a report, dated Washington City, Dec. 19, to His Excellency President Fillmore, in which they stated that they had been compelled to withdraw from the Territory and their official duties, in consequence of the lawless acts and the hostile and seditions feelings and sentiments manifested by Brig. Young, the Governor of Utah Ter'y, and the great body of the residents there, to- (162) ward the government and officers of the United States, in aspersions and denunciations so violent and offensive as to render the discharge of official duties impracticable, and a longer resdidence in the Territory incompatible with self-respect and the high regard due the United States. That almost the entire population consisted of a people called Mormons, and the Mormon church overshadowed and controlled the opinions, actions, property, and lives of its members, usurping and exercising the functions of the Legislature and the judiciary, organizing and commanding the military, disposing of the public lands upon its own terms coining money and issuing it on a forced circulation, openly sanctioning and defending polygamy, exacting tithes from members and onorous taxes from non-members, penetrating and supervising social and business circles, and inculcating and requiring as an article of religious faith, implicit obedience to the council of the church, as paramount to all the obligations of morality society allegiance and law. That Brigham Young, the Governor, stood at the head of this formidable obligation, claiming and represented to be the Prophet (163) of God, and his sayings as direct revelations from heaven, and thereby commanding unlimited sway over the ignorant and credulous, ruling without a rival or opposition, for no man dared question his authority. His sympathies were entirely with the church and against the government, being jealous of his power as head of the church, and hostile to a division of it, even with the United States.

The whole report was an amplification and ela-
boration of the above charges. After presenting it to
the government, the authors withdrew and revised
their report. Eventually three or four varying editions
were presented to the public.

On the 29th, Judge Z. Snow opened court to try
some Mexican slave dealers.

During the year the settlers at Parowan built a
fort, the houses being on the lines and the intervening
spaces being filled with pickets, ten feet high. On the
southeast corner of the fort a meeting house, in the
form of a St. Andrew's Cross, was built of hewed logs,
which projected sixteen feet over the lines, so as to
form a bastion, and completely commands two sides
of the fort. On the opposite or northwestern corner a
pentagon bastion was erected of logs, so as (164) to
hold a cannon, and thus command the other two lines.
The stockade of the public corral was built two feet in
the ground and six feet above. On Centre Creek
George A. Smith built a grist mill with one run of
stone, and a saw mill. A handbolt was also but into
operation.

In the City of Nephi, Juab Valley, which was re-
gularly laid out into lots, twenty-three cabins were
built, mostly of willows and mud, some were dug two
feet into the ground.

INCIDENTS IN UTAH HISTORY

1852 - 1854

P -F 26

INCIDENTS IN HISTORY OF UTAH

January, 1852

The Legislative Assembly of the Territory of Utah met on January 5th and organized. Willard Richards was chosen President of the Council, and William W. Phelps speaker of the House. Hon. David Evans, member from Utah County, appeared in the Representatives Hall, clad in homespun. Gov. Young's message was read (See Des. News of January 10, 1852), after which the Governor remarked to the Assembly that he was opposed to the system of slavery;--its cruelties and abuses were obnoxious to humanity. The negro, however, should serve the "seed of Abraham"; he should not be a ruler, nor vote for the rulers of the people. The Constitution of Deseret was purposely silent upon this. "The seed of Canaan," he continued, "cannot hold any office, civil or ecclesiastical. They have not wisdom to act like white men. The decree of God that Canaan should be a servant of servants unto his brethren (i. e. Shem and Japhet) is in full force. The day will come when the seed of Canaan will be redeemed and have all the blessings their brethren enjoy. Any person that mingles his seed with the seed of Canaan forfeits the right to rule and all the blessings of the Priesthood of God." The Territorial Auditor's report showed a total of property assessed, amounting to $1,160,883, on which a tax of two per cent was (2) levied, securing a territorial revenue of upwards of $23,000, including merchants' licenses; liquor was taxed fifty per cent.

Wm. C. Staines and Thos. Bullock arranged the books of the Utah Library, numbering 3,023 volumes, in the northeast room of the State House (Council House), thenceforth used as the Library room. (This house was burned down about midnight between June 20th and 21st, 1883.)

February

Amasa M. Lyman and Chas, C. Rich obtained a warrantee deed for the Rancho de San Bernardino, California, having paid the second payment of $25,000, and for the remaining $52,500 given their notes payable in two years.

On the 22nd the mail arrived from the East. Letters from Dr. John M. Bernhisel, Washington, D. C., were received, giving information about the reported difficulties in Utah, between the returned U. S. officials, and the Governor and inhabitants of Utah.

On the 28th Brigham Young wrote to Dr. Bernhisel that the people in Utah did not feel anywise alarmed as to the final issue of the matter. The Government might, if it saw proper, be so influenced by the returned officers as to take strong (3) ground against them, sending troops to overawe them, and governors and judges to rule over them. But the people of Utah would certainly protest against such proceedings, if any such were contemplated. They had dug their way into the mountains, where none but the destitute Mormons would think of settling; but they, being instructed by their past experience of the danger of seeking a location on the rich and fertile lands of the United States, sought out and had settled (in the language of Capt. Stansbury) that "God forsaken country in which none but a Mormon could live;" and even preferred these wild and barren wastes to the rich vales of California or the sunny south, for the boon of quietness and peace.

Prest. Young says: "I reminded the Doctor that we had lived before the Territorial Charter was extended to us, and that we could do so again, though we would like to have it continued, if it could, upon righteous principles; but if not, the people would readopt the Provisional Government, and apply again for admission as a free and sovereign state and recall their Delegate.

As for my own feelings I was perfectly assured that all would be right, when matters were explained

and considered; but suppose the reverse (4) should
happen and we again were compelled to seek another
location to free ourselves from bondage and oppression,
and though many of us might fall into our graves, vic-
tims to exposure and hardships thereby encountered,
if our work is accomplished and it is the Lord's will,
all right; to die is nothing. I should a thousand times
rather encounter the grim 'monster' than to have my
religion, and the love and adoration which I feel towards
God, become of secondary consideration with me.
And I wished all men, whether Presidents or Kings,
Congressmen or Noblemen, to know, that I sought
first the mind and will of God, and all my acts had to
become subservient thereto.

"I also reminded Dr. Bernhisel that all the rights
and immunities we sought might be enjoyed under the
wise and faithful administration of the laws and glorious
Constitution of the United States, which was designed
to shield the sincere worshipper of every religion, and
also guaranteed the free expression of sentiment and
opinions upon any subject, whether religious or political, that might arise for the consideration of any
person. These were privileges of which I was not
willing to be denied, and for the enjoyment of which I
would seek a shelter in some far distant corner of the
(5) earth's surface, where the bleak, barren and in-
hospitable features should be so apparent, as to cause
the cupidity of the most eager aspirant to revolt, and
leave this so recently and so ardently sought asylum
to its wonted desolation, without an inhabitant to sing
the requiem of departed liberty.

"I exhorted the Doctor not to be afraid to tell the
President, or any other person, whether in or out of
Congress, of our rights as a free people, who are not
indifferent to the majesty and glory of our common
country, and who are and ever have been its true
supporters; and that now to be accused of defection
and required to send a block of marble to the Washington
monument as a test of our loyalty was an insult not to
be borne nor easily forgotten.

"I also wrote as follows to Dr. Bernhisel:

"The Legislature located the seat of Government

at Fillmore city and have purchased the Council House,
so called, which you know was built for a State House
in Great Salt Lake City. It was considered best to
purchase it for the accommodation of the Territorial
Government, until suitable public buildings could be
erected at the seat of Government, arrangements for
which have been made and entered into with the Architect and Superintendent of Public works. It was accordingly purchased with the under- (6) standing that
when those buildings should be erected the Church
should have the privilege of re-purchasing as it is
worth considerably more than the amount sold for, it
having cost a little over $45,000.

"A catalogue of the Library is nearly finished.
It is a splendid library, and will always reflect great
credit upon him who made such an able selection. * * *

"The Legislature is yet in session; will probably
adjourn in a few days. In other Territories the time
of the session has been prolonged from forty to ninety
days. It should be in this; that should have been the
length of the first term, for it is then, if ever, that
we might reasonably expect a protracted session. * * *

"The public works are steadily progressing. The
Tabernacle is being plastered, and the digging for the
foundation of the wall around the Temple Block is progressing. The winter has been very mild, so much
so, that for the past three weeks the people have been
sowing wheat and planting their gardens. I contem-
plate taking a trip south soon after conference, to
seek a location for a settlement over the rim of the
basin, where it is considered that cotton if not sugar-
cane will flourish; the cotton is the most important
for us, as the sugar can (7) be produced from beets
as the experience of the past season, although but partially made, yet sufficiently demonstrates.

"We are going in for home manufacture pretty
extensively. My own family alone have this season
manufactured over five hundred yards of cloth, and
the home made frequently makes its appearance in
our streets and gatherings. This I consider a new
element in the history of our prosperity, more than
ever balancing the inconvenience caused by the scarcity

of money.   This will indeed prove a blessing to the best
and truest interests of the Territory, if it will prove
an inducement to the people to depend and rely upon
their own resources for their own supplies.   * * * Tan-
neries sufficient for the manufacture of our own leather
are now going into operation.   A pottery at Provo is
producing a good article of common ware, in addition
to the one here.   A paper mill has also been commenced,
but it is suspended for the present for the want of means.

"So little confidence have we in the present mail
arrangements that we feel considerable dubiety of your
receiving this or any other communication from us."(8)

March

On the 6th of March the Legislature adjourned
sine die.   There was not a member of the Assembly
that had ever been a member of any Legislature before,
except the Legislature of Deseret.   The session was
remarkable for the industry, unity and strict attention
to business matters.   The most aggreeable concord
existed between the Assembly and the Governor, who
gave all the bills passed a careful and attentive perusal and approved of them all.   The absence of lawyers
presented an anomalous feature, notwithstanding
which it is questionable whether any of the sister
Territories had a code of laws on their statute books
which had been digested by their own Legislators
that would have compared favorably with those enacted
during this--Utah's first session.

Conformable to the 6th section of the organic act,
which provides that all laws passed by the Assembly
and Governor shall be submitted to Congress, and if
disapproved should be null and void, Gov. Young forwarded copies of the laws to the President of the
Senate and Speaker of the House of Representative, at
Washington.   On their presentation in the House of
Representatives they were referred to the committee
on Territories, and by them to a sub-committee who
examined them and re- (9) ported that the laws in
general were excellent, and that the code of practice
was better than that of any of the States.

On the 25th the mail arrived from the east.
Dr. John M. Bernhisel wrote from Washington,
Jan. 10th, of the establishment by the Postmaster
General of post offices at Springville, Salt Creek
(Nephi) Corn Creek and American Fork. The Doctor
also wrote that a resolution had passed the House of
Representatives requesting President Fillmore to
communicate all such information as might be in his
possession, calculated to show the actual condition of
things in Utah Territory, and especially to enable the
House to ascertain whether the due execution of the
laws of the United States had been resisted or ob-
structed; whether there had been any misappropriation
of the public funds; and whether the personal rights of
citizens had been interfered with in any manner.

Accompanied by J. M. Grant, Doctor Bernhisel
called at the Executive mansion, and asked the President to defer transmitting the report of the U. S.
officers from Utah to Congress, until an answer could
be prepared, and further intelligence received from
Utah. They also called on the Secretary of State,
Daniel Webster, who had apprized the Doctor by note,
that a report from the officers lately from (10) Utah,
in relation to the differences which had occured between them and the Governor of that Territory, had
been received at the department of State and would be
submitted to his perusal if it should suit his convenience
to call. Mr. Webster furnished Dr. Bernhisel with a
copy of said report.

The Doctor wrote to President Fillmore, that as
to so much of the charges of the late officers of Utah
Territory against the Governor and council thereof,
as could be matter of public concern, he should esteem
it his duty at the earliest moment to ask for them the
closest scrutiny of a congressional committee; meanwhile he took leave to place among the Executive
Archives his prompt, unqualified and peremptory ne-
gation of their truth.

The report of the fugitive officers had raised
such a tempest during the latter part of autumn and
the first month of the session of Congress, and caused
the tide of public sentiment to set so strongly against

the people in Utah, that at one time it threatened to
prostrate every thing before it. In a subsequent communication, however, the Doctor stated that the returned officers had withdrawn their report for the purpose of making some alterations, and that two newspaper versions had appeared, each differing from the
copy (11) he received from the Department of State,
and that he had protested in the House against the alteration of an official report, and that he would hold
that furnished the department of State to be the true
copy of the indictment.

On the presentation of the report to the House
Doctor Bernhisel insisted upon a thorough investigation of the allegations preferred against the Governor
and people of Utah; and that the committee, to whom
the reference was made should have power to send for
persons and papers, and to send a commissioner to
Utah under authority and with instructions to take testimony in writing to be laid before the committee.

The Doctor added that public sentiment was turning in favor of the people of Utah, and that the New
York "Herald"'s version of the report had caused much
amusement. Chief Justice Brandebury had said he
could not go anywhere without being laughed at.

Mr. Briggs, of New York, at the instance of the
fugitive officers, introduced a resolution in the House,
instructing the Committee on Election to inquire whether Delegate Bernhisel's election was held according
to law, and whether any bribery, corruption or other
illegal means were made use of by said Bernhisel with
Brigham Young or any other persons to secure said
election and return.

(12) The day following Dr. Bernhsel made a short
speech on the subject and produced his certificate of
election. A spirited debate issued. The whole House,
apparently with but two exceptions, were in favor of
sustaining the Doctor. Mr. Briggs withdrew the resolution and informed the Doctor, that he had been mis-
informed, and that he should have nothing more to do
with it. The Doctor added: "This proved to be a very
fortunate move for our cause and myself."

Mr. Kennedy, Supt. of the 7th census, having on

two different occasions expressed himself much
pleased with the manner and accuracy with which
Gov. Young had taken the census of Utah Territory,
and the returned officers having denied in their report
that the census was taken at all, Mr. Kennedy wrote
Delegate Bernhisel a very satisfactory letter upon the
subject.

By virtue of Gov. Young's proclamation an election was held on the 27th in each military district
throughout the Territory to fill the office of Lieutenant-
General, created by act of the Legislature, to which
office D. H. Wells was duly elected.

April

On the 6th of April the 32nd annual conference of
the Church of Jesus Christ of Latter-day Saints (13)
commenced in the Tabernacle, on the southwest corner
of the Temple Block. About 2,500 persons attended.
Upon this occasion the Tabernacle was dedicated.
This building, which afterwards was known as the Old
Tabernacle, was torn down in 1877 to give room for the
present Assembly Hall. The dimensions were 126 feet
in length and 64 in breadth, with three feet walls, the
whole in one entire arch sprung from the base. The
pulpit was situated near the center of the west wall, to
be entered by an ante-court or vestry; the seats were
ascending on three sides from the pulpit, so that the
prospect for all was equal; and about 2,200 could be
pleasantly accommodated.

Lieut. Gen. D. H. Wells upon taking command of
the Nauvoo Legion issued general orders No. 1, an-
nouncing the names of the general officers of the Legion and appointing inspections of the Sanpete, Pauvan
and Iron military districts. (Des. News of April 17th.)

For a minute description of the general condition
of the Territory--See the Seventh General Epistle from
the First Presidency in Mill. Star, Vol. 14, pp. 321-
326.

In consequence of the hostile disposition of the
Indians on Mary's river, and their frequent interrup-
tions of the mail and travellers when passing over that

route to California, as ex-officio Supt. of Indian affairs Gov. Young instructed Major Holman, Indian
Agent, (14) to repair thither and endeavor to concili-
ate the Indians; also to learn their numbers, situation,
usual haunts, disposition to make treaties, and obtain
their consent, if possible, for a settlement upon such
location as shall be most desirable for an agency and
farming operations.

On the 29th John Y. Greene arrived from the East
with the U. S. mail. Dr. W. Richards, in Gov.
Young's absence, replied to Delegate Bernhisel's
letters, assuring him, notwithstanding the statement
of the judges and the U. S. officials who had deserted
their posts and absconded from the Territory that
Utah was loyal to the interest of the U. S. and patriotic towards the same, as the noblest Spartans that
ever lifted an arm to defend their invaded country.
And that Prest. Fillmore's declining to act in the Utah
question until he heard both sides was but another of
the many proofs the people had that he was worthy of
the dignified station he occupied.

May

On the 21st of May Gov. Young (who had left the
city on April 22nd, together with H. C. Kimball,
Orson Pratt, Geo. A. Smith, W. Woodruff and others)
returned with the exploring party, having visited many
Indian tribes and preached in all the settle- (15) ments
of the southern part of the Territory. The energy and
industry displayed by the settlers generally were com-
mendable. At Coal Creek, Iron Co., they had erected
dwelling houses and corrals and had just organized
into an Iron Manufacturing Company, for the purpose
of carrying on that business. Orson Pratt determined
by observation that Parowan was 1,271 feet higher
than G. S. L. City.

On the 22nd Gov. Young wrote to Delegate
Bernhisel and enclosed petition of 3,488 persons to
Prest. Fillmore for the appointment of resident citi-
zens to the Federal offices in Utah.

On the 30th the first company of immigrants with

one hundred wagons crossed the Missouri river en
route for Utah. Jno. S. Higbee, Capt.
        Delegate Bernhisel wrote from Washington, D. C.,
May 8th, that he had had an interview with Prest.
Fillmore relative to Utah affairs, at which the Doctor
had urged the nomination of Messrs. H. C. Kimball,
W. Richards and O. Hyde to offices vacated by the
returned officers. Prest. Fillmore repeated his for-
mal avowal, that he had no prejudices against Utah,
and that he wished to pursue that policy which was
right towards her people.
        Amasa M. Lyman's letter in "Mill. Star", Vol. 14,
p. 491, contains some interesting San Bernardino (16)
(Cal.) facts.

July

        On Monday the 5th of July the celebration of
Independence Day took place with much spirit and
ceremony. (See Des. News of July 10, 1852.)
        Prest. Fillmore nominated to the Senate Benj. F.
Ferris, of Ithaca, N. Y., for U. S. Secretary, and
Orson Hyde, of Iowa, for U. S. Associate Justice of
Utah.
        Dr. Bernhisel wrote from Washington, "that al-
though the returned officers had been beaten on every
point, and their libellous report was not even noticed
by Congress, Utah did not stand so favorable in the
eyes of the nation as before the explosion, and this
the Doctor regretted the more as it would seriously
affect the people in obtaining needful and desirable
appropriations for the distant and dependent Territory.
        The Historian writes: "On the 27th the thermo-
meter ranged at 127°; on the 28th and 29th 114° in the
sun, and in our coolest room at 94°; and yet the refreshing breezes from the mountains and G. S. Lake
enable the husbandman to continue his labors; and the
meteoric appearances in the Heavens have added a
beauty and sublimity (17) to life in the mountains."
        On the 24th, the fifth anniversary of the entrance
of the Pioneers into the valley was celebrated with
much enthusiasm at G. S. L. City, Provo and

Parowan. (See Des. News of Aug. 7th and 21st.)

On the 26th a political caucus was held in the Bowery, G. S. L. City, at which the Delegate to Congress, Councillors and representatives for the Territorial Legislature, also county and precinct officers, were nominated; there was not a dissenting vote, although the number of citizens present was estimated at fourteen hundred.

August

E. T. Benson estimated the immigrant companies en route for Utah at 1200 wagons and 6,000 souls, and the entire season's immigration at about 10,000 souls.

Dr. Bernhisel wrote from Washington, Aug. 13th, that Orson Hyde's nomination by the President as Associate Justice for Utah was not confirmed by the Senate, because he was not a "regular bred lawyer." Dr. Bernhisel regarded the nomination of Mr. Hyde by Prest. Fillmore as a great trimuph because it showed that the President discredited the report of the fugitive officers, and by that act had placed the seal of his (18) condemnation on the same.

Prest. Fillmore had nominated Lazarus H. Read, Esq., of Bath, Steuben Co., N. Y., for Chief Justice and Leonidas Shaver, of Virginia, later of Lexington, Mo., for Associate Justice. These gentlemen were highly recommended for integrity and high moral character, and as being unprejudiced. Dr. Bernhisel added that Prest. Fillmore was a friend to the people of Utah and had done all he could for the interest of the Territory.

At a special conference of the Church, held in the Tabernacle, G. S. L. City, on the 28th and 29th of August, the principle of plural marriage was first made public. (Des. News of Sept. 18, 1852.)

September

On the 3rd of Sept. Abraham O. Smoot arrived in G. S. L. City with the first company of European emigrants assisted by the Perpetual Emigrating Fund.

(See Des. News of Sept. 18, 1852.)

On the 15th of Sept. the first snow fell this fall on the highest mountains; and the first frost to injure vines in the City was on Sept. 26th.

October

The eighth General Epistle from the First Presi-(19) dency, dated Oct. 13th, gives interesting details. (See Mill. Star, Vol. 15, p. 113.)

On the 16th of October Eli B. Kelsey's emigrant train arrived in G. S. L. City. Among the immigrants were 28 souls from Scandinavia (mostly Danes). These were the forerunners of the many thousands who since have emigrated to Utah from Denmark, Sweden and Norway.

December

On the 8th Ephraim Hanks returned with the Eastern mail, with which he started on the 1st; the snow was so deep that he was unable to proceed. The day after, the mail for California returned, being unable to proceed past Deep Creek; and on the 12th, the mail from Oregon arrived, having lost six horses and mules in the snow.

On the 13th the Legislative Assembly met in the State House (Council House). Willard Richards was elected President of the Council, and James Ferguson Secretary, Jedediah M. Grant, Speaker of the House, and Thomas Bullock Chief Clerk. Gov. Young's message was read. (See Des. News of Dec. 25, 1852.)

The Auditor of Public Accounts reported to the Legislature of Utah that the taxable property in the Territory amounted to $932,586, and the revenue thereof (20) assessed at one percent $9,325$\frac{86}{100}$. There had been collected from ferry and merchant licenses $1,859$\frac{55}{100}$, and for fines and docket fees $610. The account of disbursements showed the principal amounts expended on roads and bridges; for assessing and collecting, for Librarian and Library, bounty on wolf pates, and public printing. The law expenses, including fees of attorneys, marshal, clerk, jurors, and witnesses amounted to $110.

For important information about the settlements in Southern Utah, see "Mill. Star," Vol. 15, p. 286, letter from Geo. A. Smith. See also Des. News of Dec. 11, 1852. (21)

January 1853

On the 15th Brigham Young received an epistle by express from Fillmore, with the news that the Indians had stolen some powder and stabbed Peter Robinson.

On the 21st, the Legislative Assembly adjourned, after passing many important bills, amongst which were acts regulating the mode of procedure in civil and criminal cases; an act regulating Elections; Acts of Incorporation to several companies, and to the cities of Springville, Payson, Palmyra and Tooele, all of which Gov. Young approved. He congratulated the members on the pleasant and harmonious feelings manifested during the session; spoke of the impropriety of making light of any person's religion or using the name of the Diety in vain, and remarked that it grieved and hurt his feelings when present on any occasion where such things were allowed.

Speaker Grant said he had not had occasion to call a member to order, neither had any member been under the necessity of calling another member to order.

The Eastern mail, which left Independence Nov. 1st, arrived at Laramie on the 30th of that month, the day it was due in Great Salt Lake City.

Mr. Feramorz Little "received the mail at Laramie Dec. 1st, and making his way partly through (22) an unknown country, the snow being so deep at the South Pass he could not pursue the usual route, there being snow, generally, in his path from eighteen inches to four feet, in an unceasing storm of snow from the Platte river to Fort Bridger, so that he could discern no mountains or beacons to direct his course, and so cold that sometimes he dare not close his eyes during the night, being lost for two days, and during that time without fire, food, sleep or grazing; finally he arrived at Fort Bridger and was informed he could go no further on account of the snow; but nothing daunted, Mr. Little procured some of the best horses, known as the Flat-Head breed, which are famous for good stock, and broke his way to the Weber, and although several gentlemen accompanied him, his flat-head horses had to break the track almost the entire distance, notwithstanding one or two other noble animals died, in consequence of a short attempt to lead.

"Leaving his horses at Weber, as any further attempt to get them through would be useless, Mr. Little commenced drawing the mail bags of one hundred and fifty pounds on the snow, in par flesh, but after a few miles hauling found it impossible, cached the news bag, and continuing with the letter bag arrived on the 25th, having dragged the mail (23) by hand nearly forty miles, over snow in the Wasatch, from ten to twenty feet in depth, in many places. We will add that Mr. Little broke his ancle, about one week before he left Laramie, and when he started, and for some days after was so lame he could not put his foot in the stirrup, but was obliged to walk in the soft snow and broke the path much of the way, and that was quite a relief to him."

February

Advices from San-Bernardino, Cal., about this time, said that there had been nearly 1800 acres added to the fields of that settlement for cultivation, the ensuing year. Arrangements had been made to secure reapers and threshers for harvesting, and three saw mill companies had been organized. The average daily attendance at their school was over one hundred pupils.

On the 14th, ground was broken, preparatory to excavating for the Temple foundation in Salt Lake City. (Mill. Star Vol 15, p 391, also Des. News Feb. 19, 1853) (24)

March

George A. Smith wrote from Provo that after a severe winter of four months' duration the inhabitants of Utah County had commenced making extensive preparations for farming.

A company of men were employed in rebuilding a bridge across Provo river, that had been destroyed by the flood of last year. Another company is turning the

Provo river into its former channel to prevent the
overflow of farming lands as several hundred acres of
grain had been destroyed the previous summer by the
flood.

April

On the 6th, the corner stones of the Temple in
Great Salt Lake City, were laid. (See Deseret News of
March 19, 1853.)

For important historical information see Ninth
General Epistle of the First Presidency of the Church
in Deseret News, April 16, 1853.

On the 20th, Brigham Young, accompanied by H. C.
Kimball, John Taylor, E. T. Benson, Erastus Snow,
Ed. Hunter, U. S. Atty. S. M. Blair, and others, left
G. S. L. City, intending to go to Iron Co., and were
joined at Provo by George A. Smith. While there
Gov. Young was accosted in a very abrupt manner by
a stranger, who wanted to have a little private conversation with him. (25) The Governor told him he did
not hold private interviews with strangers, that if he
had anything to communicate he could do so in writing.
Subsequently it was learned that the stranger was from
New York, had lived in Mexico for several years, and
had come into the Territory to buy Indian children to
trade to the Mexicans. On being informed that such
traffic was contrary to law, he made some threats and
boasted that he had 400 Mexicans on the Sevier River
waiting his orders.

On the 23rd Brigham Young as Governor and ex-
officio Superintendent of Indian affairs, issued a Proclamation at Provo, forbidding traffic with the Indians
in arms, ammunition, etc., and directed the Com-
mandant of the Nauvoo Legion to send a detachment of
thirty men to proceed south, through the settlements,
warning the settlers to be on their guard against
Indians who might be incited to war by Mexicans or
others.

Afterwards it was learned that offense was taken
by the Indians at Gov. Young's Proclamation, which
also forbade the traffic in Indian children, and that

Batteez, (Baptiste?) an Indian chief, had ordered all
his Indians to flee to the mountains.

The Utes were in the habit of stealing children
from the Piedes, and other weak tribes, and trading
(26) them to the Mexicans. When the parents of the
stolen children resisted, the Utes would kill the parents rather than relinquish the children. Batteez had
been accustomed to this traffic.

May

On the 29th, the Independence (Mo.) letter mail
arrived in G. S. L. City. The newspaper mail had not
arrived at Laramie when the Carrier left. Such had
been the state of travelling for the preceeding eight
months between G. S. L. City and Independence, from
snow, rain and high water that it was impossible to
get the heavy mails through, and from the best information that could be obtained it was supposed there
were twenty-four heavy bags of mail matter cached en-
route for G. S. L. City. The letters were generally
brought through the diligence of the carriers, who frequently swam rivers with mail bags on their heads,
formed floats of Indian Rubber bed sacks and incurred
such like life risks. "We understand" says the Deseret
News "that trains are now in motion, gathering up all
the mails, and that some are not far distant from this
place, but no matter how near or far off, if only forty
miles distant, they must wait till the waters abate"
(From Des. News, June 18, 1853.)

Delegate John M. Bernhisel arrived from
Wahington in good health and spirits. He had been
successful in (27) obtaining compensation from the
General Government for Willard Richards, whom
Gov. Young appointed Acting Secretary of State upon
the withdrawal of B. D. Harris from the Territory.

On the 31st, Wm. M. Wall, Commander of detachment, sent to reconnoitre the southern part of the
Territory, reported that he had visited the southern
settlements and given the settlers the instructions contained in Gov. Young's Proclamation. The detachment
was entertained with great cordiality at the settlements.

Capt. Wall had several talks with the chiefs of the
Pauvante and Piede Indians, who said their hearts
were good towards the Mormons and they wished to
live in peace with them.   They were afraid of Walker,
(Utah Chief) and the Utah warriors, because they stole
their children, and sold them to the Mexicans, and to
accomplish this they did not scruple at killing the parents when they opposed them in their nefarious designs.

June

On the 1st, the Legislative Assembly met, agreeable to adjournment.   A majority of members were
present, although the high waters rendered it impossible for some districts to be represented.   After a session of three days, and the passage of ten bills, including a charter for Lake City, the assembly adjourned.
(28) On the 5th, Chief Justice Lazarus H. Reid
arrived in the City, to whom Gov. Young administered
the oath of office the following day.   (See Reid's letter
in Mill. Star Vol. 15, p. 641.)

July

The 4th was celebrated at the principal settlements
in the Territory.   At G. S. L. City, after the reading
of the Declaration of Independence, Genl. Jas,
Ferguson delivered an oration, and Chief Justice
Lazarus H. Reid, Hon. Orson Hyde, John M. Bernhisel
and Parley P. Pratt and Associate Justice Shaver delivered speeches.

August

On the 15th Amasa M. Lyman and C. C. Rich
arrived at San Bernardino, Cal.   The Saints generally
were healthy.   Crops looked well.   The title of the
brethren to their land had been confirmed by the commissioner.
On the 23rd, the Bishops of all the wards in G. S.
L. City met with the City Council in the State House
and reported all their wards unanimous for walling in

the whole of the City, with a good ditch upon the outside of the wall; whereupon the City Council appointed Albert Carrington, P. P. Pratt and F. D. Richards a commitee to locate the line of said wall and report thereon on the 27th, from which day it was intended to labor upon the wall and ditch with all (29) diligence until completed. The wall was to be built of mud taken from the ditch, and mixed with straw or hay and gravel, and laid up in courses as deep as the consistency of the mud would allow, to be repeated when the previous course was dried, until the wall was finished. This was deemed to be the cheapest and in the end most durable method that could be adopted at that time.

On the 27th, the committee above named reported on the line of said wall and recommended that it be made twelve feet high and six feet thick at the bottom, carried up with an equal slope on each face, so as to be two and a half feet thick at the height of six feet, then carried up the remaining six feet two and a half feet thick and rounded on the top.

On the 29th, the City Council passed an ordinance that such a wall and ditch should be constructed and for that purpose assessed ten dollars on each lot; also five per cent on each lot and improvements, and on all taxable property in the city.

"The following account of the Indian difficulties is extracted from the Deseret News and the Journal of the Southern campaign kept by Lt. Col. Kimball's adjutant, John L. Smith: (July 17th) On the 17th, Indian hostilities commenced (30) by a menace on Springville, Utah County. Next day, Walker (Utah Indian Chief) and his two brothers, Arrowpeen and Ammon were encamped on the Peteetneet, above Payson. While Arrowpeen and another Indian were riding from town to camp, one of them shot Alexander Keele, (who was standing guard) dead. The Indians then moved up Peteetneet Canyon, the rear firing heavilly as they passed, upon some half dozen families in the canyon, injuring no one, but leaving quite a quantity of balls in the buildings.

(19th) "Col. Peter W. Conover started from Provo City with one hundred and fifty men, to assist the weak settlements on the route, reconnoitre, rendez-

vous and await further orders at Manti in San Pete
Valley, which place he reached on the evening of the
20th. The Indians, however, were neither idle nor
dismayed by the force sent out, but on the night of the
19th undertook to surprize the post at Pleasant Creek
in San Pete County, and on the same evening stole
several head of cattle from Manti, three horses from
Nephi City and wounded William Jolly in the arm while
on picket guard near Springville; thus demonstrating
that they were in some force and acting in concert.

(21st) "As Governor and ex officio Superintendent
of Indian affairs in conjunction with the Lieu. General
of the Nauvoo Legion, Daniel H. Wells, I issued General orders (31) No. 1, directing that the policy of con-
structing forts and occupying them be adopted and
rigidly enforced--that the commandants of the various
military districts in the Territory cause all of the
forces under their commands respectively to repair
immediately to their posts in their various settlements
putting the same in a state of effecient defence, keeping their arms and ammunition in readiness, construc-
ting corrals for stock and stack yards for the grain and
taking all possible care of the grain, hay and vegetables
--that Col. Conover, Majors Markham and Boyce bring
their present expedition against the Indians to a close,
and return to their several posts in their respective
districts, with the forces under their commands--that
citizens repair to their various locations and remain
at home in order to enable officers to carry into effect
the instructions issued; and that all stock be strongly
herded by armed herdsmen; also, forbidding the settlers to retaliate on the Indians or threaten retaliation
but to act on the defensive until further orders, and to
be particular in ascertaining the name and tribe of
every depredating Indian.

(22nd) "A detachment of volunteers was ordered
South under Lt. Col. W. H. Kimball to assist the inhabitants in the Southern settlements in defending themselves, preserving peace, securing their grain and
stock, (32) and if hostilities continued to advise the
owners of stock to send them north, and if need be,
also to send north, under a safe escort, the women

[The following paragraph should be inserted in
page 133, opposite, as the paragraph preceeding the (*).]

(29th) "The company arrived at Fillmore, which
was found to be in a poor state of defence.   Lieut. S.
F. Attwood and fifteen men were detailed to assist the
settlers in securing their fort and grain.

and children.

(23rd) Col. Conover sent out a scouting party from Manti, San Pete, under Lt. Col. Jabez Nowlin who fell in with a company of twenty or thirty Indians about ten miles east of the Pleasant Creek settlement, who were addressed by the interpreter of the party; the Indians in reply said they were enemies and commenced firing; Col. Nowlin charged upon them and killed six, the rest scattering and escaping.

"The company ordered for service on the expedition south to suppress Indian hostilities and assist the Southern settlements left G. S. L. City and traveled to Dry Creek.

(24th) "Lt. Col. Kimball and Dr. Andrews joined the company, which was organized by the appointment of the following officers: Thomas Callister Captain, H. M. Alexander, John Alger and Hosea Cushing Lieutenants, and Lt. John L. Smith Adjutant; the company proceeded to Provo bench and camped. Next day, the company proceeded to Spanish Fork bench and camped, and the following day, proceeded to and camped at Spring Creek, where the company was augmented by seventeen men and boys from G. S. L. City.

"Bro. Clark Roberts was shot in the shoulder and bro. John W. Berry in the wrist by Indians secreted (33) in the vacated houses at Summet Creek. These brethren were bringing an express, and within twenty minutes after they reached Provo City twenty mounted men were out in pursuit of the aggressors.

(25th) "General orders No. 2 were issued, assigning Col. Geo. A. Smith to the command of all the Military districts south of Great Salt Lake County, with instructions to enforce General orders No. 1, and to see that all surplus stock were driven to Great Salt Lake City.

(27th) "Col. George A. Smith and guard overtook and joined the company at Summit Creek. The Colonel appointed Evan M. Greene his adjutant. The company passed on to Salt Creek, (Nephi) and camped; they found the settlers on guard; ten men were detailed to assist the people in securing their fort and grain.

(*) (Aug. 2nd) "Col. Geo. A. Smith and guard ar-

rived and camped at Parowan; Col. Kimball remained
at Red Creek and detached Captn. Callister and company to guard the stock while the settlers removed to
Parowan. A surveying party en-route for California,
including Dr. E. F. Beal, G. W. Heap Esq., and
seven others arrived and stayed with Col. Geo. A.
Smith. (34) At every settlement General orders No. 1,
were read, the arms and ammunition of the settlers
inspected and such instructions given as were necessary.

(3rd) "The company proceeded to Cedar City and
found that the settlers at Johnson's Springs had moved
thither, Mr. F. D. Richards, being at this point,
aided the command in carrying out the instructions.

(4th) "Twelve teams were sent from Cedar to
move in the houses and effects at Shirts' settlement
and twenty teams to move the houses from Johnson's
settlement. The Piede Indians at these settlements
were very friendly; the settlers left their grain;
chickens, &c., in their care.

"Cols. Smith and Kimball located a fort for the
settlers at Cedar, and selected sites for the erection
of barricades to protect the miners working at the
coal beds, also the hands at the mill.

"Col. Kimball, accompanied by Elder F. D.
Richards, Surgeon Andrews and company, with twenty-
six teams, proceeded to Harmony, took down and
loaded up the logs of eight houses and returned to
Cedar; the Piede Indians there were very friendly but
afraid of the Utahs--they were willing to remain and
take charge of the grain of John D. Lee and others.

(35) (9th) "Captn. Callister reported at Cedar,
that himself and detachment had assisted the settlers
at Red Creek to take down their houses and thirty five
rods of picketing preparatory to removing the same to
Parowan.

"Col. Kimball's command moved their camp to
the vicinity of the new plot at Cedar sending detachments to herd and thus affording the settlers every
opportunity to remove their houses on to the fort plot.

(10th) "Shortly after ten P.M., the Indians commenced firing on a party of ten men, under command of

Lieut. R. Burns, who were driving surplus stock to G.
S. L. City and were encamped on Clover Creek, Jual
Valley, and continued firing for an hour and twenty minutes, slightly wounding Isaac Duffin in the knee, killing
two horses and wounding one horse and several calves.

(12th) "Col. Geo. A. Smith and guard removed
from Cedar to Parowan, and sent orders for
Col. Kimball and command to join him and proceed to
Salt Lake City with the surplus stock which had been
gathered up.

(16th) "Col. Kimball and command left Red Creek
with two hundred and seventy-one head of cattle and
four horses.

(17th) "As four men were hauling lumber from
Snyder's (36) mill, near Parley's Park, and had arrived just east of the summit of the second or big
mountain, a party of Indians fired upon them from an
ambush, and instantly killed John Dixon and John
Quayle, and wounded John Hoagland through the fleshy
part of his arm, between the shoulder and elbow.
Hoagland and Knight then loosed and mounted two
horses, and escaped to G. S. L. City, leaving the dead
and four horses and two mules in possession of the
Indians. A detachment was immediately sent out,
which brought in the dead bodies unmutilated; a portion
of the detachment proceeded to Snyder's mill, dis-
mantled it, and all returned in safety, and without
being able to find any Indians.

(19th) "As Governor and Superintendent of Indian
affairs I issued a Proclamation, directing that all the
Militia beheld in readiness to march to any point at a
moment's notice, recapitulating former instructions
as to securing crops and hay and keeping strict guard
upon stock and counselling the completion of the forts
and defences throughout the settlements with all possible speed; also strictly forbidding every person, resident or non-resident, from giving away or traffick-
ing to the Indians arms and ammunition, and revoking
every license issued to trade with the Indians; likewise
advising all parties going into the canyons or other unprotected places to go together, well armed and be on
the alert; and (37) requiring all officers to keep an

account of all services performed and expenses incurred by their commands.

"Cols. Smith and Kimball returned to Salt Lake
City, the former on the 22nd, the latter on the 24th,
and reported all the settlements south of Salt Lake
County, either in excellent condition for defence, or
rapidly urging on the completion of their fortifications;
and that the inhabitants were using all exertions to secure their crops and preserve their stock and other
property. Col. Kimball's party were closely watched
by the Indians until they reached Punjun Spring in Juab
Valley, when the Indians were discovered retreating
into the mountains without making any demonstration.

"Col. Smith reported that he had given special
orders to every settlement to gather into a fort, and
directed all isolated buildings to be removed. In Iron
County he had directed the removal of Old Cedar fort
on to the city plot and made plans to inclose the city;
he had also directed the removal of the people from
Paragoonah to Parowan, and had given plans of forts
to many of the settlements; held several interviews
with Onwonup, Piede chief, who was very friendly,
some of his tribe having learned to work and were baptized. Col. Smith had travelled nine hundred miles in
about one month; during (38) all of this time he had
suffered from the excruciating torment of a nervous
headache."

September

On the 1st A. M. Lyman and C. C. Rich wrote
from San Bernardino that the sickness that had prevailed there had begun to subside. A small accession
had been made to their numbers by the arrival of a
company from Australia.

On the 13th, Wm Hatton was killed by Indians while
standing guard at Fillmore.

October

On the 1st, Jas. Nelson, Wm Luke, Wm Reed and
Thos. Clark were killed by Indians and dreadfully

mutilated at Uinta Springs, just east of Salt Creek
Canyon, while on their way from Fountain Green, San
Pete Valley, to G. S. L. City, hauling wheat.

On the 2nd, in a skirmish at Nephi, Juab Valley,
eight Indians were killed and one squaw and two boys
taken prisoners.

On the 4th, John E. Warner and Wm Mills were
killed by Indians a few hundred yards above the grist
mill, near Manti, San Pete Valley.

On the 7th, G. A. Smith, E. Snow and F. D.
Richards were appointed to gather up fifty families to
(39) strengthen the settlements of Iron Co. , and a like
number for Fillmore. W. Woodruff and E. T. Benson
were appointed to gather up fifty families to strengthen
Tooele. Lyman Stevens and Reuben W. Allred were
appointed to gather up a like number of families for
each of the settlements in San Pete; L. Snow a like
number of families for Box Elder, and Jos. L.
Heywood to take a like number to Nephi in Juab Co.
O. Hyde was appointed to raise a company to make a
permanent settlement at Green River.

The bishops' reports of the various wards in the
Territory, given at the October Conference, showed
that there were at that time 18, 206 persons, belonging to the Church, in the Territory, namely: 5979 in
G. S. L. City, and 2273 in the county, outside the city
(Total in County 8252), 4064 in Utah, 229 in Juab, 765
in San Pete, 304 in Millard, 847 in Iron, 215 in Tooele,
1598 in Davis and 1932 in Weber County.

For important historical information see Tenth
General Epistle from First Presidency, in Deseret
News, Oct. 15th.

On the 14th, twenty-five or thirty Indians attacked
a few men who were securing their crops at Summit
Creek, Utah Co; they killed and scalped Farney F.
Tindrel, drove off six head of cattle and killed two.

(40) On the 26th, Capt. J. W. Gunnison, U. S.
Topographical Engineer, with six members of his sur-
veying party and Wm Potter, a citizen of Manti, and
guide to the party, were surprised and killed by the
Pauvante Indians on the Sevier River, near the lake.
Several of the party escaped, leaving those killed, also

surveying implements, notes, &c., at the mercy of the
savages, but returned the same day with reinforcements and recovered what the Indians had left; the remainder was subsequently obtained and the remains of
the dead collected and buried by D. B. Huntington and
party, whom Gov. Young sent thither with instructions
and presents for that purpose. This massacre was the
direct result of the conduct of a party of emigrants
from the States on their way to California, who killed
a Pauvante Indian and wounded two others at Corn
Creek a short time previously; hence, according to the
Indian rule of revenge, the massacre of the next white
men found on their grounds.

November

On the 12th, the company of thirty-nine men selected by Orson Hyde to form a settlement near Green
River, arrived at Fort Bridger on their way thither.
Another company of fifty-three men for the same mission were organized on the 16th, and started (41) on
the way to join the former, all well equipped and in
good spirits. John Nebeker was captain of the former
company, and Isaac Bullock of the latter.

On the 28th, Ammon, brother to Walker, the Utah
Chief, visited Erastus Snow and F. D. Richards at
Parowan, to sue for peace in behalf of Walker and his
band.

An order was issued by the Commander of the
Nauvoo Legion, directing the further organization of
the Militia and requiring a company of minute men to
be attached to regiments and battalions throughout the
Territory, equipped for active service.

December

On the 1st, a slight shock of earthquake was felt
at Nephi, Juab Valley; the roofs of the houses moved
visibly in some places, insomuch that the inmates of
houses left them in fear. At Provo City the shock was
also felt.

The hands on the Grist Mill of Messrs. Smith and

Higbee, Provo, were attacked and fired upon by a party
of Indians, but none were injured. The Indians succeeded, however, in mortally wounding four horses.

Geo. A. Smith reported that in conformity with his
appointment at last conference he had (42) succeeded in
getting one hundred and twenty families under way
south-ward, amongst whom were Chas. Hopkins, President at Lehi, Geo. S. Clark, Bishop of Pleasant Grove,
and Wm Miller, late Bishop at Winter Quarters.
These brethren would locate in Iron County, and W^{m}
M. Wall, Bishop in Provo, in Millard Co.

At Fillmore and Payson numbers of Indians who
had listened to D. B. Huntington's counsel were
friendly.

The fort at Nephi was completed; those in Utah
County settlements nearly so. Commodious schoolhouses in most of the settlements were being erected.
At Provo, the adobe work of a seminary thirty by sixty
feet, two stories, was completed.

On the 6th, Erastus Snow and F. D. Richards
wrote of their journey to Iron Co. that they had
preached in the settlements intervening, as they had
opportunity; they had urged the execution of the general orders, instilled charity towards the Lamanites,
and checked the spirit of retaliation and revenge,
which, in some instances, had obtained among the
brethren.

On the 28th, of Oct. , near Cedar Springs, in
Millard Co. , they picked up four men of Capt. Morris'
command, who had escaped the massacre (43) of Capt.
Gunnison and party on the 26th, and who had travelled
without food and water until they were nearly exhausted.
They had also, the same day, with a plug of tobacco
and biscuit, captured two Pabowat Indians on the mountain near the Sevier River, one of whom accompanied
them to Fillmore, the other returned to their wick-a-
up (lodge or tent,) and brought in the squaws and ponies
the next day, all very friendly.

They spent the 29th counselling as to the best
means of recovering the instruments, papers, and lost
property of the topographical party and succeeded in
enlisting Kanosh and two of his tribe, who were suc-

cessful in obtaining them.

The massacre of Capt. Gunnison and party was the result of the unprincipled conduct of Hildrath's company of emigrants, who passed through about three weeks previously, and who undertook to disarm a party of friendly Indians that came into their camp, which ended in the death of an Indian, whose brother stirred up the Queon band of Pauvantes to the perpetration of the bloody deed to avenge his brother's death.

In Iron Co., about thirty souls had left for California. The flood in Coal Creek Canyon occasioned by the bursting of a cloud in the mountains, (44) had swept off all the bridges and dams on the stream, moving in terrific career rocks of many tons weight, inundating the present site of the Iron Works, to the depth of three feet, carrying off several hundred bushels of charcoal, also lumber, etc.

Messrs Snow and Richards found that the Piede Indians had mostly gathered in, and were living adjacent to, both the Parowan and Cedar Forts.

At the suggestion of these men the inhabitants of Cedar concentrated their efforts and erected a good adobe meeting-house twenty-eight by sixty feet, which, although unfinished, was dedicated at a conference held there.

Joel H. Johnson and sons were appointed to carry on farming and to teach the Piedes to cultivate the earth for their support; his son, Nephi, having a good aquaintance with the Indian tongue. Messrs. Snow and Richards returned to G. S. L. City, Dec. 6th.

On the 12th, the Legislative Assembly met in the State House, G. S. L. City, and organized by appointing Willard Richards Prest. of the Council, Jas. Ferguson Secretary, Jedediah M. Grant Speaker of the House and Thos, Bullock Chief Clerk. The Governor's message was read to the Assembly in joint session.

The Governor's Message, containing important historical points is published in Deseret News, Dec., 1853. (45)

During the year 1853 400 persons were assisted to emigrate from England by the Perpetual Emigration Fund. (47)

January 1854

On the 10th, A. M. Lyman and C. C. Rich wrote from San Bernardino, that considerable sickness had prevailed there, though it had not been attended with fatal results. Hyrum Clark had committed suicide by cutting his throat.

Gov. Young met with the Regents of the Deseret University this winter for the purpose of reforming the orthography of the English language. After many attempts to render the common Alphabet subservient, it was considered necessary to introduce a new set of characters, more simple in their structure, from which every superfluous mark should be excluded and in which every letter should have a fixed and unalterable sound, excluding the use of silent letters.

On the 20th, after the usual session of forty days, the Legislative Assembly adjourned, having transacted the business necessary and passed several acts, Resolutions and Memorials; which Governor Brigham Young approved.

On the 21st, the thermometer stood nineteen degrees below zero in G. S. L. City; the coldest day of the season.

On the 31st a mass meeting was held in the Tabernacle, G. S. L. City, for the purpose of memoralizing Congress to construct a national railroad from the Missouri River, via the South Pass and G. S. L. City, to the Pacific. Several thousand persons attended. The (48) subject was enthusiastically canvassed and the Legislative Memorial with spirited resolutions were adopted and ordered to be forwarded to Congress. The Legislative Assembly also memoralized Congress for the passage of an act authorizing the inhabitants of the Territory to call a Convention and form a Constitution and State Government, preparatory to the admission of Utah into the Union.

February

At Provo, Utah Valley, several buildings had been erected during the winter. Holdoway's Woolen Cloth

Factory had commenced operations. The Provo
Dramatic Association were playing to crowded houses.

On the 20th, Col. John C. Fremont, with nine
white men and twelve Delaware Indians, arrived in
Parowan, Iron Co., in a state of starvation; one of his
men had fallen dead from his horse the day previous,
and several more must inevitably have shared the same
fate had they not received succour that day. They reported that they had eaten twenty-seven broken down
animals; that when a horse or mule could go no further,
it was killed and divided out, one half given to the
Delawares and the other half to the Colonel and his
men; the hide was cut in pieces and lots cast for it.
After the bones had been made into soup, they were
burned and carried along by the men for luncheon. (49)
The entrails were shaken and then made into soup together with the feet and eyes. They stated that they
had travelled forty-five days living on this kind of fare.
Although Col. Fremont was considered by the people   .
an enemy to the Saints, being without money he was
kindly treated and supplied with provisions for himself
and men while at Parowan and fitted out with animals
and provisions to pursue his journey. The Colonel
believed he had found the best route for the great
national railway. He borrowed from John Steele,
County recorder, the plots and surveys of Iron County,
and carried them away with him, notwithstanding his
promise to return them. The Colonel took an observation by which he determined the latitude of Parowan
to be 37° 50; thus corroborating the observation taken
previously by Prof. Orson Pratt.

On the 28th, Geo. A. Smith wrote an historical
letter which was published in Mill. Star, Vol. 16, p. 397.

March

On the 11th, Dr. Willard Richards died at his
residence in G. S. L. City of dropsy. He had been
confined to his room since Jan. 20th, the last day of
the session of the Legislative Assembly, previous to
attending which, he said, "I will go and perform this
last duty, if, like John Q. Adams, I die in the attempt."

At the same time he remarked, "No one knows the
aggravated extent of my bodily malady. Death stares
me in the face, (50) waiting for his prey." He was the
first Apostle of this latter dispensation that died a
natural death. His biography was published in the Des.
News, Vol. 8th, Nos. 16 and 17, and in the Mill. Star,
Vol. 16, p. 360 etc.

On the 20th, E. T. Benson and E. Snow visited
Fillmore and remained several days, holding meetings and preaching to the Saints. John A. Ray was
appointed Prest. of the settlement. E. T. Benson and
E. Snow with others from Fillmore, went to Corn
Creek and had forty acres of land surveyed to Walker
and Kanosh, Indian Chiefs.

April

On the 10th, the Eleventh General Epistle to the
Church was written--(See Des. News of April 13, 1854)

On the 19th, P. P. Pratt, accompanied by about
fifteen brethren, had started from G. S. L. City for
the purpose of building a new fort at Harmony, Iron
Co.

Walker, Indian Chief, had been driven by the
Snake Indians into the neighborhood of the settlements
and was "very friendly."

On the 25th, B. Young, H. C. Kimball, J. M.
Grant & Geo. A. Smith, visited and preached to the
brethren in Stoker's Ward (Bountiful) and selected a
site for a city.

On the 29th, Brigham Young wrote to Hon.
Stephen A. Douglass, that it was rumored that Jas.
Bridger, from (51) Black's Fork of Green River, had
become the oracle in Congress, in all matters pertaining to Utah; that he had informed Congress (as
well as the Missouri Democrat) that Utah had dared to
assess and collect taxes; that the Mormons must have
killed Capt. Gunnison, because the Pauvantes had no
guns--that the Mormons were an outrageous set, with
no redeeming qualities. Gov. Young expressed his
astonishment that Bridger should be sought after for
information on any point, when a gentleman like

Delegate Bernhisel was accessible, and forwarded the
depositions of two strangers who had voluntarily given
the same, relative to the uncivilized conversation and
conduct of Mr. Bridger.

May

On the 19th, T. D. Brown, at the request of
P. P. Pratt, wrote from Harmony, Washington Co.,
that the missionaries to the Indians south, twelve in
number, arrived there May 2nd, in good health. They
had sown about 64 acres in grain and were then cutting
a ditch, eight feet wide, two feet deep and eight miles
long, for irrigation purposes. Some ten Piede Indian
warriors had arrived on their way south to steal children from a part of their own nation, but, through the
influence and teachings of the brethren, they had left
soon after with better feelings. An Indian child was
administered to and (52) restored to health by the
prayer of faith. Elder Brown appealed to the citizens
of G. S. L. City for clothing to cover the nakedness of
the Indians, especially the females.

On the 30th, Brigham Young, returned from visiting the settlements south, with H. C. Kimball and
others, in good health and spirits. Geo. A. Smith accompanied them from Provo. The trip was highly op-
portune, as their red neighbors were thawing out of
their winter retreats and had come into the valleys
and were undecided on the course they would pursue.
Their Summer haunts being within easy proximity to
the settlements Gov. Young as Superintendent of Indian
affairs was enabled to hold talks with the great majority of the Indians concerned in the difficulties of the
past year, among whom were Walker, Arrowpeen
(Arapene), and Washear. All the Saints were favorable
to a good peace, and the Indians were much pleased
and gratified with the presents of beef, cattle, blankets,
shirts, tobacco, &c.

June

On Friday 16th, the workmen began at the South

East corner to lay the foundation of the Temple in
G. S. L. City. The foundation was fifteen feet thick
at the bottom. The rock used was a reddish silicious
conglomerate, firmly cemented, weighing one hundred
and forty-eight pounds to the cubic foot.

On the 22nd T. D. Brown wrote from Harmony,
Iron Co., that he and seven others had been on a tour
south, visiting the Indians on Ash Creek. The Indians
(53) were clearing small patches of land. They had
corn, beans, potatoes, watermelons, and squashes.
They had made an irrigation canal, several feet deep
and over half a mile in length without any tools, except
wooden paddles.

Farther down the creek the brethren found the
Indians cultivating the soil, but they were almost
naked and destitute of ploughs, hoes, etc. On the
Santa Clara there was some good land cultivated, five
acres of good wheat all headed, and some of it ripe,
also corn, beans, &c.; ripe gooseberries, black,
white and red currants were plentiful on this stream.
Several miles further up, the Indians were more
numerous and the land more extensively cultivated,
and crops much better. These Indians lived in caves,
holes, and dens of the earth, and on the tops of almost
inaccessible mountains.

The brethren explored the Santa Cara from its
mouth to its source. Saw some 200 Indians and camped
among them unmolested. They were very industrious,
ignorant and poor, owned but few guns or horses, and
were destitute of agricultural implements.

July

About the celebration of the 4th in G. S. L. City
see Mill. Star Vol 16, p. 666 (54)

On the 13th, the south track of the Jordan Bridge
west of G. S. L. City, was planked and teams and
herds crossed it for the first time.

Richd. Robinson wrote from Harmony, Iron Co.,
that a company of six, under Capt. Lewis, visited the
Indians on the Santa Clara and preached to them
through interpreters, telling them of the Book of

Mormon, of the Great Spirit talking with the prophet, and counselling them to be good and not steal or fight, to learn to build houses and raise grain like the whites, which pleased them, and 119 of them were baptized, and they brought their sick to the Elders to have hands laid on them, manifesting great faith and confidence in the healing power of God.

Having learned that the principal chief of the Shoshones had invited Jas. S. Brown to go into his lodge and remain and identify himself with them, Gov. Young wrote to Mr. Brown on the 18th and counselling him by all means to do so, for it was what was needed and the very purpose for which the mission had been established. The object was to gain influence with the tribe in order to induce them to be peaceable and do them good.

The 24th, the seventh anniversary of the entrance of the pioneers into the Valley of the Great Salt Lake, was celebrated throughout the settlements of the Territory, (55) in G. S. L. City by a grand procession with banners, firing of cannon, music and feasting. Leo Hawkins read an interesting address on behalf of the young men. Also Misses Alice Young and Laura Hyde read addresses on behalf of the young ladies.

Lieut. Genl. Wells, Col. G. A. Smith and Gov. Young delivered addresses appropriate to the occasion.

On the 26th, Brigham Young wrote to the settlers at Harmony, Iron Co., counselling them to go on with their fort and improvements and endeavor to secure the good will of the Indians, so that they might be brought to an understanding of Gospel principles, which would require time and perseverance and a thorough knowledge of them in every particular, that the missionaries might have influence over and control them for good.

August

On the 8th, Hon. J. M. Bernhisel wrote from Washington, giving important historical information.

See Mill. Star Vol. 16, p. 687.

On the same day William and Warren, sons of Bishop Allen Weeks, left the fort in Cedar Valley, thirty miles south west of G. S. L. City, to get a load of wood, and a short time after were found dead, both being shot through the body, scalped and otherwise mutilated. Some moccasin tracks were found near (56) the scene of the murder. It was therefore thought that the deed had been committed by a few reckless savages without the consent or knowledge of the tribe, as nearly all the Indians were friendly.

Gov. B. Young wrote to Bp. Allen Weeks sympathizing with him in the death of his two sons by Indians and counselling the brethren to be friendly with the Indians, to seek out the guilty ones and deliver them up to justice, but not to have feelings against those who were not guilty.

On the 14th, in answer to a letter, Gov. Young wrote to Wm D. Huntington instructing him to tell the Indians not to be afraid, for no harm should befall them in consequence of the conduct of bad Indians, to counsel the brethren to treat the Indians as though nothing had happened. The friendly Indians would then probably bring in those who were guilty, and we would give up to the Indians those whites who committed outrages against the Indians.

On the 15th, a feast was made at Provo for the Indians, of which over 200 partook. Three beeves were killed, four barrels of biscuits furnished, together with a large quantity of vegetables. A large amount of clothing was distributed among them under the direction of George Bean, Indian interpreter, the whole being contributed by the inhabitants of Provo.

(57) On the 15th, the adobie work of the wall around the Temple Block was finished and much of the stone for coping was already cut.

Immense swarms of grass-hoppers had visited nearly all the farming districts of Utah County, doing considerable damage to corn, oats, and late vegetables.

On the 18th Gov. Young wrote to I. C. Haight and settlers in Iron Co., counselling them to persuade the Indians to work for the clothing donated by the citizens

of G. S. L. City for the naked Indian women and children
in their vicinity, as it would be much better than to be-
stow it upon them in idleness. They would then learn to
work and depend on their own exertions for a subsistence.

On the 19th at Sarpy's point, eight miles east of
Laramie, while a company of Saints was passing, a
camp of Indians about 1000 strong, a lame cow, belonging to the company, became frightened and ran
into the Indian camp, where she was left; some of
them killed and ate her, which circumstance was reported at Fort Laramie.

Lieut. Gratton with twenty-seven soldiers and an
interpreter repaired to Sarpy's point, to arrest the
Indian who killed the cow, but he refused to give himself up. The Lieut. then ordered his men (58) to fire
upon the Indians, which they did. The Indians then
charged and routed the soldiers, who were all killed
but one, who was dangerously wounded.

The Indians, highly excited, demanded of Jas.
Bordeaux, living there, what stores he had, which to
save life, he surrendered to the amount of $2,000.
They then went to the post of the American Fur Company and pillaged it of nearly $50,000 worth of goods.

On the 29th, the Indians who murdered Wm. and
Allen Weeks in Cedar Valley were captured by the
peaceable Indians and delivered over to the civil authorities, and their trial was then proceeding before
a special session of the U. S. Dist. Court.

Chief Justice Kinney and Mr. Holman, U. S.
Prosecuting Atty. for Utah Territory, and Col. Steptoe
with his command, numbering 200 men, arrived.

Washear (alias Squash Head) a Utah Chief, told
the people at Provo, that his brother was dead and
unless they would give him some cattle to offer as a
sacrifice (as is their custom on the death of a relative)
he would have to kill some big captain.

The authorities at Provo thought it best to humor
him, and accordingly gave him about $75⁰⁰ worth of
cattle and property, and he appeared satisfied. It is
a custom with the Utah Indians when (59) a relative
dies, to kill some other person; they prefer an enemy.

The following is a list of merchants and storekeepers, who resided in G. S. L. City, Aug. 1854, all doing a good business:

J. M. Horner and Co.;   J. and J. M. Hockaday, Livingston, Kinkead and Bell;   J. and E. Reese, Wm Mac;   Wm Nixon;   Branham and Norris; L. Stewart and Bros.;   George Goddard; C. H. and E. H. Perry;   Zerubbabel Snow; Abraham Taylor;   J. L. Mason; Middleton and Riley;   F. D. Clift; H. S. Southworth;   J. F. Kinney; Dustin Amy;   Orson Hyde; Wm C. Staines;   Rogers and Co.; Mrs Brooks.

September

On the 4th, Gov. B. Young returned from an official visit to a large number of Shoshone Indians, who had sent a deputation of chiefs and braves to request an interview with the Supt. of Indian Affairs, to be held five miles north of Ogden City, where they had assembled for that purpose. There were present seven chiefs, with nearly all their bands. After a mutually gratifying talk, a few appropriate presents were distributed, (60) but, through lack of means, not so many as desired. The Indians said they felt well and desired a continuation of peace and professed to be perfectly friendly.

On the 30th, G. A. Smith recorded that the U. S. officers had rented several large buildings in G. S. L. City, including W. Woodruff's house and P. H. and B. H. Young's store. Their horses with a portion of their troops were in Rush Valley.

The Shoshones and Utah Indians were at war, two battles had recently been fought, one near Provo, the other near Pleasant Grove; four Utes had been killed and four wounded; the Chief Squash among the latter, and three Shoshones wounded. The Utes lost eight horses and were much incensed because the whites would not interfere, and assist them against the Shoshones, and in revenge killed about thirty head of cattle belonging to the people.

October

On the 6th, the Semi-Annual Conference convened
in the Tabernacle, G. S. L. City. See Mill. Star
Vol 17. p. 58.

On Sept. 29th and 31st and Oct. 1st and 8th
Conference was held in the Bowery, San Bernardino,
Cal. Mill Star Vol. 17, p. 505.

On the 9th, Gov. B. Young wrote to W^m. D.
Huntington and Co., counselling them to be exceedingly careful and wise in their conduct towards, and
(61) their dealings with the Navajoe Indians. They
were not a people who roamed in idleness and lived by
hunting and stealing, but by tilling the earth. The
brethren were therefore to take implements of agriculture and teach the Indians the use of them, and
inculcate principles of industry, virtue and morality
by precept and by example; to deal honestly with them,
in all cases giving an equivalent for that received,
that the brethren might gain an influence over them
for good, and not, as was too often the case with white
people, sow among them the seeds of dissatisfaction,
hatred and deception, as well as disease, misery and
final extinction. In short the brethren should observe
the "Golden rule" to do unto the Indians as they would
that others should do unto them.

On the 10th, Gov. Young, accompanied by H. C.
Kimball, J. M. Grant, O. Hyde, G. A. Smith, L.
Snow and a few others, left G. S. L. City to counsel
the citizens in Utah, Juab, and Sanpete counties and
have a talk with the Indians, who were raising dis-
turbances. We found that, with a few exceptions, the
Indians manifested friendly feelings and a strong desire for a continuation of peace. Gov. Young and company returned to the city on the 18th.

(62) A Court House 35 x 45 feet, two stories high,
and about sixty adobe houses were erected during the
year in Farmington, Davis Co. The people of Parowan
were building a City Wall, a large portion of which was
already completed; it was to be twelve feet high, six
feet thick at the bottom and 2 1/2 feet thick at the top.
Nephi City, Juab Co., was enclosed with a wall nine

feet high. The people of Union Ward, Salt Lake Co., had gathered into Union Fort, where they had built a commodious school house and many good two story dwelling houses.

On the 30th, Gov. B. Young met with the Regents of the Deseret University, when resolutions were passed to extend the teaching of the new Alphabet. The Regents were directed to lecture in different parts of the country in favor of getting up schools.

During this month Gov. B. Young wrote to Washakee and Katat, two Shoshone Chiefs, advising them to not let their people divide into small parties as their enemies would have more power to injure them; also advising them to not depend on hunting for a living, but to settle in good localities, where they could raise grain, and the Governor would send men to teach them the art of husbandry.

On the 14, accompanied by H. C. Kimball J. M. Grant, Surveyor Genl. Jesse W. Fox, and others, (63) Gov. B. Young travelled up the west side of Jordan River to the head of the upper rapids, where they dedicated and broke the ground, preparatory to digging a canal to lead out the water of the Jordan, on the west side for irrigation and other purposes.

December

On the 11th, the Legislative Assembly of Utah convened in the Council House, G. S. L. City, and organized as follows: H. C. Kimball, Prest of the Councl; Wm Clayton, Secretary; Jedediah M. Grant, Speaker of the House; Thos. Bullock Chief Clerk. (See Des. News of Dec. 14, 1854.)

On the 25th, the Seventies' Council Hall was dedicated. The Hall was 25 feet wide, by 53 feet long, and cost $3,500.

A Petition was sent to Franklin Pierce, President of the United States, praying for the reappointment of Brigham Young to the Governorship of the Territory. (See Millennial Star, Vol. 17, page 268.)

UTAH HISTORICAL INCIDENTS

1855-1867

P-F 67

UTAH HISTORICAL INCIDENTS

January, 1855

On the 1st a party was given at the Social Hall, G. S. L. City, by the Governor and Legislative Assembly, in complement to Judge John F. Kinney, his associates, other United States Officers of the Territory, Lieut. Col. Steptoe, of the U. S. Army and the officers of his command. (See "Deseret News" of Jan. 4 and 11, 1855.)

On the 4th, Hon. J. M. Bernhisel wrote from Washington, D. C., to F. D. Richards as follows: "I regret to inform you, that Prest. Pierce finally declined to re-appoint Gov. Young. Lieut. Col. Steptoe is the appointee, etc" (See "Mill. Star," Vol. 17, p. 110.)

On the 19th, Secretary A. W. Babbitt gave the Legislative Assembly a collation. The time was agreeably passed in toasts, anecdotes, and speeches by Associate Justice G. P. Styles, Hon. Orson Hyde, Secretary Babbitt, and Gov. Young. Chief Justice Kinney made some remarks, for which see "Deseret News" of Feb. 8, 1855.

On the 29th, the Utah Indian Chief, Walker, died, at Meadow Creek, of lung fever. His brother, Arapene, was made Chief of the Utahs. When Walker was very sick he told his band to kill Pah-Utes and horses, thinking that would alleviate his sufferings; but when they had killed two Pah-Ute children he was not relieved. When nearly dead he told his people not to kill any horses or Pah-Utes at his decease. After ten days' illness he died, and the Indians killed two Pah-Ute squaws and three children, (2) and buried an Indian boy, of twelve years, in the same mound with Walker, telling him he was to watch Walker. He was a brave and shrewd man, equalled by few and excelled by none of his race west of the Rocky Mountains. His principal achievements had been the stealing of large bands of horses from Chihuahua and California.

February

On the 4th, Arapene, brother of Walker, Utah Chief, reported to the settlers in San Pete Valley that he had had a vision, in which Walker appeared to him and told him not to fight the Mormons, but cultivate peace with them. The Lord had revealed to Arapene that the land was His and did not belong to the Indians, nor the Mormons; that Walker had taken sick and died a natural death; that the Indians who stole should be whipped and have a ball and chain put on them, but it was not good to kill them and spill their blood on the land; that Arapene was to relate what was communicated to him to Welcome Chapman and Mr. Higgins and Mr. Dowry, and they would write it.

Arapene was also informed that it was not good for the Mormons to trade guns and ammunition to the Indians at present. The Lord said that by and by, when all people were good and at peace, He would live on the earth with them. Arapene saw three personages (3) whose garments were as white as snow and as brilliant as the Sun, and he was informed that all good people would eventually appear as these personages did.

On the 6th and 7th, the Mormon Battalion held a party in the Social Hall. Full particulars were published in a pamphlet form entitled, "First General Festival of the Mormon Battalion."

For important historical points see "Mill. Star," Vol. 17, p. 269, Also others of G. A. Smith's letters in the same volume.

On the 27th, Geo. A. Smith and E. T. Benson visited Session's settlement, Davis Co., lectured at the lyceum, and preached in the school house, a building twenty by thirty feet; the settlement was named Bountiful. A city plot had been surveyed and 150 families located there, who had raised 20,000 bushels of wheat the past year.

Messrs. Smith and Benson proceeded to Centerville, where there were forty families, and preached in the recently erected school-house, twenty-four by thirty feet. The erection of walls around those settlements was progressing.

The Deseret Typographical Association, the Battalion of Life Guards, the S. L. City Police, and other Associations and Quorums had parties, mostly in the Social Hall, at some of which good instruction was interspersed with music (4) and dancing.

March

On the 29th, Geo. A. Smith chronicled the following: "The Indians who murdered Capt. Gunnison and party were tried last week by Judge Kinney, in the 2nd Judicial Dist., at Nephi. The jury brought in a verdict of manslaughter against three of the Indians, who were sentenced to three years' imprisonment in the penitentiary. Col. Steptoe, with a company of his command, attended, and I understand, from the Indians, that some of the officers, civil and military, did some trading with the squaws, though not in buck "skin"; report says it was an effort at improving their morals, or introducing 'civilization.'

"The health of the inhabitants of the Territory is good.

"The Sugar Works have stopped for a season, having ground over 22,000 bushels of beets into molasses, during the seven weeks they were operating.

"In Iron Co. they have made some good bar iron out of the ore, using the puddling furnace, and drawing out some bars sufficiently malleable for horse nails, which they are manufacturing and using. The greatest difficulty is to get clay of consistency that will stand the fire, with which to build their furnaces.

"Prest. Young has been feeble this winter; his lack of health has generally prevented him from attending (5) the Tabernacle.

"Geo. A. Smith has just returned from a trip to Provo, and finds that an excellent bridge is being erected across that river by Col. Steptoe, 120 feet long, and the bank above the bridge is secured with rock and brush for 180 feet.

"At Cedar the brethren are building a Seventies' Hall, sixty-four by thirty feet.

For Dr. Wm France's Letter to Geo. A. Smith
see "Deseret News," Vol. 5, p. 36.

April

On the 6th, the Annual Conference convened at
10 A.M. (See "Deseret News," Vol. 5, p. 36.)

The Steuben (N.Y.) "Advocate" announced the
death of the late Chief Justice of Utah, Lazarus Reid,
at his residence in Bath, in the 40th year of his age.
Judge Reid was highly esteemed by the people of Utah
for his upright, unpredjudiced, frank and manly
course, pursued in his official capacity, and his cour-
teous bearing as a citizen of the Territory, and also
for the candor with which he expressed himself, in
publishing his sentiments concerning them, being in
fact a complete refutation of the many slanderous reports in circulation against the people over whose
judiciary he so honorably presided.

(6) For important historical information, see
Twelfth General Epistle in "Mill. Star", Vol. 17,
p. 497, or "Des. News" of April 25, 1855; also "Mill.
Star," Vol. 17, p. 507 for Geo. A. Smith's letter.

The most important feature in the emigration
from Europe this season was the change of the route
from Liverpool to St. Louis via New Orleans, to the
northern ports of Philadelphia and New York, thence
to Pittsburg by railway, thence to St. Louis by river
steamers, via Louisville and Cincinnati. From the
experience of the past season it was evident that the
new route was preferable to the old one, on account of
the climate being better adapted to the constitutions of
people from northern latitudes. The emigration generally was greatly favored with health, and that via
Philadelphia and New York peculiarly so. The number
of deaths, so far as ascertained, was far less among
the emigration this year by the northern than by the
southern route.

On the 20th, the Salmon River Lamanite mission
encamped at Bear River north. They had started from
G. S. L. and Davies Counties on the 15th. Col. Thos.
L. Smith, having been appointed President organized

his company, which consisted of himself and twenty-
six other brethren, with eleven wagons, forty-six
oxen, twenty one cows, and seven horses. At this
point, (Bear River) Orson Hyde, Marshall Jos. L.
Heywood, Judge Geo. (7) P. Styles, Enoch Reese and
several other missionaries en route for Carson Co.,
also encamped that night.

On the 25th, the Arsenal on the hill north of the
Temple Block was finished. The building was forty-
six by seventy-eight feet; built of adobies.

On the 27th, Gov. Brigham Young and company
returned to G. S. L. City. On their journey forth they
held meetings at Provo and Payson in Utah Co., and
Fort Ephraim in Sanpete Valley. They visited the coal
bed in San Pete Co., and on trial, found the coal to be
of excellent quality for blacksmithing and in abundance.
Visited the Pahvante Indians near Meadow Creek.
Kanosh, the Chief, accompanied them on their tour,
driving his own team.

On May the 19th, the company proceeded to Cedar
City and visited the Deseret Iron Works, and found the
operatives casting hot air pipes to expedite the heating
of the large furnace. Next day they organized Cedar
City and Harmony as a stake of Zion, with Isaac C.
Haight as President. Twelve High Councillors were
chosen and ordained. Brigham Young advised that a
new city be laid out at the foot of the Mountains, a mile
above the old survey.

On the 21st, the company returned to Parowan,
which was organized as a stake; J. C. L. Smith
President. Forty-seven baptized Piede Indians met in
the school-(8) house at Parowan, to whom Dimick B.
Huntington preached in their own tongue. Brigham
Young selected a site for a fort at Paragoonah and held
meeting at Fillmore. Met the missionaries bound for
Los Vegas, between Dog and Beaver Valleys, and those
destined for the White Mountains in Lake Valley.

In a communication from H. C. Kimball, dated
G. S. L. City, May 29th, will be found historical items
of interest. (See "Mill. Star," Vol. 17, p. 518.)

On the 30th, the Salmon River missionaries encountered the Bannock Indians on Snake River, to whom

G. W. Hill showed the Book of Mormon and preached
about the Latter Day Work of God. At their request
the Indians were baptized and confirmed.

On the 31st, the Historian wrote to the Editors of
the New York "Mormon" and St. Louis "Luminary"
and the "Millennial Star" the following items:

"The Eastern Mail arrived on the 12th inst, etc"
(See "Mill. Star", Vol. 17, p. 532.)

June

On the 11th, E. G. Williams wrote to Heber C.
Kimball a lengthy account of the travels of the missionaries to the White Mountain; the difficulties encountered in getting water for themselves and animals,
the same being found in out of the way places, known
to the Indian (9) guides who accompanied them; the
fearfulness of the Indians at their approach, and the
exertions of the missionaries to instil confidence into
them. Mr. Williams claims to be the first white man
that ascended the White Mountains.

On the 12th, Geo. A. Smith wrote the following
items: "On Friday last Mr. Huntington and Major G.
W. Armstrong, the Indian Sub-Agent, visited the
Indians, who were camped in the Old Fort Field at
Provo. There were 40 lodges of them, and they had
thrown down the fence, & turned their own horses and
the cattle of the inhabitants into the wheat; this was the
more aggravating as that was the only field where the
grasshoppers had not made a successful conquest, and
there were several hundred acres of grain. The
Indians had been requiring the people to throw open the
Old Fort Field, and also 400 acres of grass land adjoining, for their horses to feed, and had prohibited
the people from fishing in the Provo River.

"Mr. Huntington succeeded in pacifying the
Indians, and getting them to move out of the field, by
the agent engaging to fence in a pasture on the lower
part of the fort field, and to open a road on the banks
of the Provo from the City to said pasture, by the time
the Indians want to come again to fish.

"Major Armstrong called the citizens of Provo

together, (10) and he and Mr. Huntington addressed
them, explaining the provisions of the reconciliation
with the Indians; the people unanimously voted to sustain Major Armstrong in carrying out these proceedings, after which Geo. A. Smith addressed the settlers
on the necessity of preserving peace with the Indians,
and continuing measures to do them good.

"The Indians having requested the whites to fish
for them, Mr. Huntington accompanied A. P. Winsor
and a fishing company to the mouth of the Provo on
Saturday, when they caught a large amount of fish,
which was divided among the Indians. At one haul they
caught a thousand suckers, any one of which would
make a white man a good meal, and the Indians loaded
up four horses with them."

David Evans wrote from Fillmore: "I arrived
here from the desert country, with a portion of my company, all in good health and spirits. We were gone
fifteen days across the desert; had a first rate time;
none of us suffered any; our animals stood the trip
well, and we lost none. Saw Indians that had never
before seen a white man, and when they saw us it
alarmed them as much as it would the whites to see a
negro, if they had never seen or heard of one before.
They are not a war like people, never having had war
among themselves nor with any of the tribes.

(11) "Our guide said they did not know how to
fight, as they never had fought. They wear no clothing
and have no shelters only such as are made of sage
brush and willows, and sometimes cane, which will
neither turn snow nor rain. These Indians know nothing only what they know naturally; their food is
snakes, roots, locusts, and reptiles of every kind, in
short every and anything that hogs will eat. We killed
a large wild cat, and gave to them, and they ate it in-
sides and all. They have become very friendly with us
since they have got over their fright."

On the 17th, Delegate J. M. Bernhisel gave an
epitome of his labors in Congress, at the meeting in
the Tabernacle. He returned from Washington on the
5th inst.; he had succeeded in obtaining several appropriations. Senator Chase of Ohio, said that no Gov-

ernor had ever done so well by the Indians, since
W<u>m</u>. Penn, as Gov. Young had done.

Brigham Young expressed his entire satisfaction
with the course and labors of Dr. Bernhisel; said he
was a man of sterling integrity, firm to his faith,
punctual, fervent, industrious, and so kind and gentle-
manly that no man presumed to insult him.

About this time the missionaries to the Indians,
under the presidency of Col. Thos. J. Smith, had travelled in a north-westerly direction three hundred and
eighty miles and located a fort on Salmon River, (now
in Idaho,) called Fort Limhi.

(12) On the 19th, Orson Hyde wrote from Carson
as follows: (See "Deseret News", Vol. 5, p. 167.)

On the 25th, Brigham Young, H. C. Kimball, and
J. M. Grant, Orson Pratt, Albert Carrington and
Jesse W. Fox and others, returned from Malad Valley,
where they had been to determine the Utah and Oregon
boundary line.

On the afternoon of the 21st, while encamped
twenty-four and three fourth miles beyond the lower
ferry, on Bear River, on the Fort Hall road, Prof.
Pratt obtained an excellent observation for time, and
in the evening took eight observations of the Polar
Star, the mean of which determined the encampment
to be in north latitude 42° 6' 27". 2. On the 22nd he
measured the distance back to lat. 42°, where a stone
slab with "O.," (meaning Oregon) chiselled upon one
side and "U.", (meaning Utah) on the other, was
erected 108 miles north of G. S. L. City.

On the 29th, Leonidas Shaver, Associate Justice
of the Supreme Court and Judge of the 3rd Judicial
District, was found dead in his bed, and was enterred
with marked honors. He died of disease in the ear
and head. Judge Kinney, in dilivering a eulogy on the
deceased, said: ("Des. News", Vol. 5, pp. 132.-)

On the 30th, the Historian wrote as follows:
"The grasshoppers are still continuing their ravages
through- (13) out the Territory; young broods of them
continually hatching out on every bench. Large crickets are also making their appearance, and the sound
of the locusts is continually in the ears of the husband-

men.

"The weather has been oppressively hot and until
the 28th inst., there has been no rain of any amount,
so that the drouth was uncommonly great, and the
streams very low. There is not as much snow on the
mountains now, as there was last August, and the
common house flies are as thick as they were in
August and September. On the 28th, the weather
turned a little cooler, and there was a refreshing
shower in Davis County, and a little rain in this (G.
S. L. County).

"Some of the brethren, because of the water
failing at Parowan, have gone to the Rio Virgin to plant
corn, and a number of hands have gone lumbering for
the Iron Works. They have also organized a company
to go and fish at Pangwich Lake, at the head of the
Sevier River, where there is beautiful trout in great
abundance.

"At Cedar City the brethren are quite busy casting machinery for the Iron Works.

"At Fillmore the wheat is entirely destroyed,
Chalk Creek being very low. The finishing of the
State House is progressing rapidly.

"The fields in Juab County present the appearance
of a desert. (14)

"About two-thirds of the grain in Utah County is
destroyed, and a large black bug is devouring the
potatoes.

"All the farms south of this City are nearly a
desert; the northern counties and Tooele have fared
considerably better, but within the last few days the
latter have had a visit from the enemy, and the result
is that wheat stalks have lost their heads; and more-
over, as the farms have been located on small streams,
a large quantity of wheat has been burned up for the
want of water. This is rather a dark picture, but I
regret to say it is not overdrawn. Myriads of grasshoppers, like snow flakes in a storm, occasionally fill
the air over this city, as far as the eye can reach, and
they are liable to alight wherever they can distinquish
good feed. A great portion of them, however, alight
in the Great Salt Lake, which appears green at a dis-

tance, and the shore is lined with their dead, from
one inch to two feet thick, and which smell exactly
like fish.

"Wherever their is a chance for water the brethren are still planting corn.

"Ezra T. Benson has got the frame up for a large
flouring mill at Richville in Tooele."

July

On the   4th, the anniversary of American Independence was celebrated with much zeal and (15) spirit in
G. S. L. City and many other places in the Territory.
The assemblage at G. S. L. City was very large.   The
Nauvoo Legion was out.   The manoeuvring of the troops
indicated a marked improvement in drill, and throughout the day no fight or even quarrel was manifested;
neither was there any drunkenness or disorder.

Genl. D. H. Wells read Resolutions, adopting
the spirit of the Declaration of Independence and Constitution of the United States.   Hon. Geo. A. Smith,
Chief Justice Kinney and Dr. Garland Hurt delivered
speeches.

On the 8th, Associate Justice Drummond (and
lady!) arrived in G. S. L. City.

On the 17th, O. B. Huntington wrote that the persons appointed to make a settlement in the Elk mountain region left Manti, May 21, and arrived at the point
they had chosen for a location, on the left bank of
Grand River, June 15.   There are 41 men in this company under the presidency of Elder Alfred N. Billings.
They have located in a valley some ten miles long by
two and a half wide, within about thirty miles of the
Elk Mountains.   Elk Mountain and Pack-saddle Creeks
unite near the centre of the Valley and empty into
Grand River.   They have built a strong corral 130 by
64 feet, and a stone fort 64 feet square.

About this time the massive foundation of the
Temple was finished and the workmen were engaged
on the basement story.   (16)

Subsequently A. H. Raleigh measured the
quantity of rock in the foundation up to the commence-

ment of the basin and found it to be as follows:
101,056 cubic feet, making $789\frac{76}{128}$ cords, or $6.127\frac{11}{16}\frac{1}{2}$
perches; the rock work weights 148 lbs. per cubic foot,
making 14,956,288 lbs., or 7,478$^{28}/_{2000}$ tons.

Orson Hyde had arrived at Carson Valley and
wrote that all was right in that quarter, although there
was a feeling with some few in regard to coming into
an organization under Utah. The Indians on the route
were generally friendly.

The grasshoppers had done their work in G. S. L.
Valley and left; they had caused very much destruction
in many places, entirely destroying, not only the first,
but second and third sowings, also some corn and even
buckwheat. The grass had also dried up on the ben-
ches, so that cattle had to be driven high upon the mountains or to new and distant locations for grass.

August

On the 14th, the United States surveryors commenced operations at the Temple Block at 10 a.m.

On the 15th, Dr. John Riggs and Edson Whipple of
Provo brought to the Tithing Office 210 lbs. of manna
sugar, which was obtained by boiling down a saccha-
rine gelatinous substance found on the leaves of the
trees. (17)

September

On the 3rd, Erastus Snow arrived at Salt Lake
City safely from his mission to St. Louis. He reported that the season's emigration from Europe was
unusually large. Many of the emigrants were obliged
to tarry in the States. A place half way between
Weston and St. Joseph was selected for rendezvous
and outfitting, named "Mormon Grove." Eight immigrant companies were organized which were now en
route hither. There were 2046 persons, 344 wagons
and carriages, 1967 oxen, 341 cows and young stock,
95 horses and mules, 430 guns and pistols and 1460 lbs
of ammunition. Traders along the road were frightened
because of the hostility of the Indians. U. S. troops

were preparing for an expedition against the Sioux Indians.

On Sunday the 23rd, the Utah Indians treacherously killed Jas. W. Hunt, Wm. Behunin and Edward Edwards at the Elk Mountain mission. The Indians also burned the hay and turned off the water that supplied the Fort erected by the brethren on that mission.

At daylight on the 24th, the Indians began to gather around in great numbers, and there being no prospect of a speedy reconciliation the remaining thirteen brethren, by the advice of a few friendly Indians, took their horses and started for Manti, leaving their enemies quarreling over the spoils in the Fort, and the cattle.

Soon after crossing Grand River, and a short distance from the fort, they met an old chief and two of his sons, who told them (18) they should have their cattle. After they were about 15 miles on their way the old chief overtook them with eight cows (the other cattle having been killed or badly wounded) and some beef for their journey, and said he would see to burying the three brethren who were killed. The company were not molested on their way to Manti, San Pete County, where they arrived on the 30th.

The exhibition of fine peaches by the Deseret State Horticultural Society was a great stimulant to fruit raising, and opened the eyes of many as to its feasibility and advantages. Some very fine specimens of cotton were raised on the Santa Clara River.

October

On the 6th, the Semi-annual Conference convened. (See "Des. News," Vol. 5, pp 244-.)

For the General Epistle see "Des. News," Vol. 5, pp. 268- or "Mill. Star," Vol. 18, p. 49.

December

On the 3rd, with some of the members of the Legislative Assembly, Governor Brigham Young started for Fillmore.

On the 10th, the Legislative Assembly, met at Fillmore and organized. H. C. Kimball was elected President of the Council and J. M. Grant Speaker of the House. (19)

Gov. Brigham Young, presented his annual message to the Assembly on the 11th. (See "Deseret News," Vol. 5, p 325.)

During this year a number of Societies were organized, among them the Deseret Theological Institute, Deseret Typographical Association, Universal Scientific Society, and Deseret Horticultural Society, Polysophical, and Deseret Philharmonic. (21)

INCIDENTS IN THE HISTORY OF UTAH, 1856

January 1856

On the 4th, an act, granting to Brigham Young and Joseph Young the right to establish and control ferries on Bear River and also a bridge on the Malad, was approved, having been passed by both Houses of the Legislature. (See "Des. News," Vol. 6, p. 47.)

On the 5th, an act, creating Humboldt, St. Mary's, Greasewood, Malad, Cache, Box Elder, Cedar and Beaver counties, was approved, and on the 12th another act was approved, creating and defining the boundaries of Shambip County. (For further details see "Des. News," Vol. 5, p. 360.)

On the 6th, the California mail arrived in Fillmore from G. S. L. City, also the express. They brought generally good news, but spoke of the excessive cold weather in Salt Lake Valley, and of the immense amount of snow, in the mountains.

On the 9th, a meeting was held in Fillmore, at which the First Presidency, the Twelve, Secy. Babbitt, Judge Drummond, &c, were present, to take into consideration the establishment of a daily mail and carrying company to and from the States and the Territory of Utah. The meeting adjourned to G. S. L. City, for Saturday the 26th, when a large mass meeting convened in the Tabernacle. (See "Des. News," Vol. 5, p. 372.)

On the 18th, the Legislature, which had held an important session in Fillmore, adjourned till the second Monday in December following. Before the adjournment (22) Kanosh, Chief of the Pauvan Indians, delivered a speech, of which the following gives a general idea of the feelings among that Indian tribe at the time:

"I am just beginning to get my eyes open. I know that President Young's talk is good--what he says is so. I am like the Sun just rising in the East, and so with my people. We have been in the night. I have had eyes, but I could not see, and ears but I could not hear,

and this has been the case with my people. Our hearts
could not understand; but now our eyes see, our ears
hear, and our hearts understand. All that Brigham
and Heber have said is straight; but when I talked to
Colonel Steptoe and his men, their talk was not
straight; I could not believe one tenth part of their
talk; it is not ture; and so with the Spaniards, and all
white people, till I saw the Mormons. They are the
first to tell me the truth. You are here to make laws.
I hope you will make good laws, to punish the guilty
and spare the innocent. I wish to do right, and have
my people do right. I do not want them to steal or kill.
I want to plant and raise wheat, and learn to plough; to
do as the white people do. This I am going to do in the
Spring. I want to learn to read and write, and also my
children, so we can understand what you say to us,
that is good. "

February

On the 4th, the Regency of the University met (23)
in Governor Young's room, at candle light and held
till ten o'clock. The main subject dwelt upon was the
getting up of first and second Readers, for the children
in Utah Territory. A committee of three were appointed to get up those books, and present them to the
Board, for acceptance. The committee were G. D.
Watt, Saml. W. Richards, and W. Woodruff.

On the 9th, the first house in Beaver was finished

On the 10th, a heavy snow storm visited the
Territory and great numbers of cattle died. The snow
was two feet deep in Davis and Weber Counties.

On the 11th, the Regency of the County met and
the work of the committee was read and accepted. The
committee of Revision or examination was appointed to
assist those appointed as the first committee.

Prest. Young, for some time had his mind deeply
exercised upon the getting up of the "Deseret Alphabet"
and carrying it into practical use. The committee
were now making books under his direction, to be published in that Alphabet. They had to get new type made,
as the letters were entirely different from any others

in use at that time.

The committee last appointed were Albert Carrington, D. H. Wells and W^m. Willes.

On the same day (the 11th) a settlement was organized on the Beaver by Geo. A. Smith, and Jesse N. Smith, (24) who appointed Simeon Howd President.

On the 12th, the Seventies' Hall on First East Street, between First and Second South, was dedicated a second time, having undergone quite an improvement since the preceeding winter. (See "Des. News," Vol. 5, p. 408)

On account of the destruction of crops by the grasshoppers the year previous, breadstuff began to be very scarce in Utah. The First Presidency of the Church, therefore issued a printed circular to the Saints throughout the Territory, giving them some timely advice. (See "Deseret News," Vol. 5, p. 389.)

On the 21st, while G. A. Smith was travelling from Provo to American Fork, a posse, led by Thos. S. Johnson, passed him. This Johnson had writs for the arrest of Tintic, Squash, Cotton Logs, and several other Indians who were accused of transgressing the laws of the United States. In the evening he went to G. A. Smith for advice how to proceed. G. A. Smith advised him not to break peace with the Indians, nor kick up a war without the counsel of the Superintendent of Indian affairs.

On the 24th, word came that the Indians had again commenced war and had killed three boys, and driven off horses and cattle. Several Indians had been killed and wounded.

D. H. Wells drafted a Proclamation of the Governor to suppress Indian aggressions.

(25) On the 26th, Kanosh, the Indian chief, arrived in G. S. L. City.

During this month a number of missionaries were called to settle in Green River County, and others to strengthen the northern settlements. ("Des. News," Vol. 5, p. 405.)

On the 27th, the San Pete mail arrived with letters confirming the reports of Indian difficulties.

On the 28th, the news reached G. S. L. City that

Couzens and another man had been killed, and another wounded by the Indians on the west of Utah Lake;
also that the Indians had driven off 150 head of cattle
and 20 horses. This was done in the night.

On the 29th, Geo. Carson was killed in South Fort,
Cedar Valley; Hunsaker, a herdsman was also killed
at another place; his body was subsequently found.
Mr. Couzens and John Cathin were killed while sear-
ching for the others. Geo. Winn was wounded slightly.

Edward Hunter reported, that a great many cattle,
especially cows, had died in the north, and the people
had to drive the remainder of their stock from mountain to mountain in order to get a little feed to keep
them alive.

H. C. Kimball stated, at the Historian's Office,
that according to reports, their had been six men
killed by the Indians up to that time.

(26) On the 29th, H. C. Kimball wrote a lengthy
historical letter to his son William, which is found in
"Mill. Star," Vol. 18, p. 395.

March

On the 1st, G. A. Smith wrote to F. D. Richards
giving an interesting account of the Indian difficulties,
etc. (See "Mill. Star", Vol. 18, p. 379.)

At 4 P.M. Judge Kinney, Garland, Hurt, and
Judge Drummond came to the Presidents' office and
had an interview with the First Presidency, about the
Indian aggression. Kanosh, Indian Chief was also with
them. He reported that Squash Head, Indian Chief had
been put in irons some days.

On the 17th, the Delegates of the Convention from
the various counties, except Green River, met in the
Council House. The event was announced by the firing
of cannon, and music by Capt. Ballos' band.

Throughout the day flags floated from the cupolas
of the Governor's Mansion and Council House, also
from the tall flag poles on the Temple Block, and in
front of the Deseret and Livingston, Kinkead and Cos.
stores; from flag staffs on the roof of Gilbert and
Gerrish's store, and from those on the roofs of many

other public buildings.

At an early hour a large concourse of citizens had assembled, anxiously awaiting the commencement (27) of those deliberations and acts, which had for their object the addition of another star to the brilliant and thickly spangled constellation styled "E Pluribus Unum."

The Convention organized by unanimously electing J. M. Grant, President; T. Bullock, Secretary; J. Grimshaw, Assistant Secretary; R. T. Burton, Sergeant-at-arms; W. C. Staines, Messenger; T. Hall, Doorkeeper; and G. D. Watt and J. V. Long, Reporters.

In the afternoon, the freedom of the Convention was unanimously tendered to His Excellency, the Governor, the U. S. Officers of the Territory, H. C. Kimball, the members of the Legislative Assembly, Hons. E. Snow, A. Lyman, and E. Hunter, and Elias Smith, Probate Judge of G. S. L. County, and the Aldermen of G. S. L. City.

After a remarkably short, effective and harmonious session, the convention dissolved on Thursday, March 27th.

Hon. George A. Smith, and Hon. John Taylor, Editor of the "Mormon," were unanimously elected delegates, to proceed to Washington, and lay before Congress, Utah's request for admission into the Union.

The Constitution of the State of Deseret was signed by every member of the convention, though they were from various climes, and of diverse creeds, government officials, merchants, &c., &c., thus indicating beyond controversy the represented feelings of all classes of the Territorial population.   (28)

For further particulars about the convention and Constitution. (See "Des. News," Vol. 5, pp. 29-- 30.)

April

On the 22nd, O. Pratt, G. A. Smith, Ezra T. Benson, and E. Snow, Chief Justice J. F. Kinney, and family, Jos. L. Heywood, U. S. Marshall; Secy. Babbitt, Judge Appleby; A. O. Smoot, Phineas H.

Young, Ira Eldridge, Truman O. Angel, and many
others left for the States and other parts of the earth.

Prof. Pratt went to Liverpool to relieve Prest.
F. D. Richards, Hon. G. A. Smith, Delegate from
Utah, went to Washington, where he, in connection
with Hon. John Taylor, Editor of the New York
"Mormon," urged Utah's claim to be numbered with
the States. (See "Des. News," Vol. 6, p. 53)

May

On the 6th, Gov. B. Young, Jos. Young, L. D.
Young, Feramorz Little and Isaas Chase, with several others, left G. S. L. City on a short excursion to
the north. They returned on the 16th, having highly
enjoyed their drive through the flourishing settlements
north as far as Cache Valley, and left them rapidly
and peacefully progressing in the scale of faith and
good works. A large breadth of grain was being sown
for the first time in Cache Co.

On the 7th, a company of settlers left G. S. L.
City for Carson.

(29) On the 10th, the U. S. Mail came into the
Valley from the East, (the first news by way of the
South Pass since November) loaded with about one half
of the letters and papers that had left Independence
since last October; the remainder, Mr. McGaw, the
conductor, or his agent, had very considerately cached
by the way, or perhaps left at Fort Laramie, for the
soldiers to read through the long winter nights, when
tired talking about their victory over a few semi-sav-
ages, and half starved ignorant remnants of Indian
tribes, and they would also naturally be anxious to
read the correspondence of a people who believed in
polygamy.

W. Woodruff wrote: "We learn from a reliable
source that Mr. McGaw told his agent that when he
came with the mail from Salt Lake, if he came to any
stream that was deep, not to attempt to cross it, but
return to Salt Lake again, and stay until the waters
are down, for it would be all right, as the Government
had reimbursed Mr. McGaw $17,000 this trip and

$35,000 for last contract. When the Mormon boys,
Decker, Young, Hanks, Little and Co., carried the
mail to Laramie, we got the bags, but they have not
got their pay for it. The difficulties of crossing the
river are really awful, for a very respectable lady,
over 70 years of age, has started with oxen to go to
the Missouri River; Mr. M^C. Gaw is sadly to blame in
not engaging her to carry the mail, and then paying
her for the odd trip.

Genl. Harvey has been ordered by the Government (30) to march his troops to the scene of the
Indian wars in Oregon, and he expects to replenish his
supplies when passing through the northern part of this
Territory; if this be true, he is bound to be disappointed, for the severe winter has killed four out of
every five head of cattle in the northern counties; the
desolation is deplorable. Many persons are nearly
ruined. The Church had lost, last October, over 2600
head in Weber and Cache Counties; now they can count
nearly 500. Gilbert and Gerrish had nearly 700 head
when they started from the Missouri River; now they
have 95. Mess and Kerr lost their entire herd, valued
at $60,000, and all the citizens in proportion. Hun-
dreds of persons have lived on dead cattle when they
could not be got at for snow, and now it has disappeared;
they are living on weeds, roots, and greens. Although
we have had the grasshoppers' plague, and the excessive drouth of last summer, and the unparalleled severe winter, now they have disappeared; every face is
beaming with gladness, because the hand of the Lord
has been seen in His mercifully sending the rains once
a week this spring, which causes the wheat to rise
from the ground as a harbinger of 'the good time coming, boys'. Many are anxiously expecting to cut wheat
by the 20th of June, and then we'll have a jubilee.

"The potatoes, corn, squash, pease and other
vegetables look well, and we expect to reap a bountiful
harvest to feed those who are here, and those who are
wheeling their barrows over the plains." (31)

On the 19th, Prest. Young had an interview
with Indian Spoods, in the afternoon, several Indians
being with him. The President signed a paper privi-

leging any person to trade beaver traps with him.

June

On the 2nd, in the evening an Indignation Mass Meeting was held at the Council House. A committee was ordered to draft resolutions, expressive of the sense of the people in regard to the management and delivery of the Eastern Mail, under the contractor, Mr. McGaw and his conductors, who had lain over four days with the mail, within forty miles, under pretence that they could not cross the Weber, a stream that a farmer boy can cross with impunity at its present stage.

On the 14th, another mass meeting was held at the Council House at 6 P. M. Resolutions were read and ordered to be printed in the "Deseret News," N. Y. "Herald," the St. Louis "Luminary," & the S. F. "Western Standard."

About Military affairs see "Deseret News" Vol. 6, pp 112. -

On the 7th, one of the missing mail sacks came to hand at 3-15 P. M., containing papers.

On the 28th, Warren E. Snow of Manti, reported that Arapene was living twelve miles south of Manti, and felt well, but had a hard time to keep his people right. While trying to get a number of them to give back stolen (32) horses and cattle, some made an attack upon him and injured his breast, which made him sick for two weeks. He had delivered up 17 head of horses, which Tintic had stolen. This Tintic, who had stolen so many horses and cattle, and killed so many men, had sent word that he wanted to come and give up what he had left; he wished to know if the Mromons were angry with him. Gov. Young would make him no promises, but thought he deserved to die. Kanosh, who had been kicked by a vicious horse, had three ribs broken; he shot the horse dead.

July

For the celebration of the 4th, and Grand Military

Review, see "Deseret News," Vol. 6, p. 140.

The continued drought, the failure of the streams, the destruction by insects, and by cattle allowed to run at random, or badly herded, required the most strenuous efforts of the people in Utah to secure sustenance. (See "Deseret News," Vol. 6, p. 141.)

Thomas Bullock reported that the people at Cottonwood and the Big Field were making superior molasses out of milk weed and stink weed.

On the 11th, another one of the missing mail bags arrived; it was found by Indians, about five miles below the crossing of the Weber.

On the 24th, a grand celebration in commem- (33) oration of the entrance of the Pioneers into Salt Lake Valley was held at the Head Waters of Big Cottonwood, near the tops of the mountains. Dancing, singing, swinging, fishing, sailing on a raft, etc., etc., were indulged in. (See "Deseret News," Vol. 6, p. 164.)

August

During this month a stone wall was being erected in front of Gov. Young's offices.

September

About this time Gov. Young sent out teams with a large amount of flour to meet the hand cart companies of emigrants.

On the 1st, Seth M. Blair and company started to explore a new route to Carson County, by way of Ruby Valley; he was afterwards joined by Col. Reese, who reported to Gov. Young on the 22nd, that he and Blair had not been able to find a better road to Carson than the old one.

On the 9th and 10th of Sept., a company of U. S. troops shot down fifteen or sixteen Indians, of the Cheyenne tribe, while they were eating corn in the road near Fort Kearney, Nebraska. The Cheyennes, in a few days, retaliated and killed A. W. Babbitt, Thos. Margetts, and his wife, ----- Condy and his wife, four (34) of Mr. Babbitt's teamsters, who had

been continually cursing and swearing at the "Mormons"
when they were at prayers, a Mrs Wilson and her
child and four or five persons from California, who
passed through G. S. L. City, and swore considerably
because they could not get flour from the Mormons for
their journey, at a time when thousands were living on
half a pound of bread a day, and some hundreds had
none at all.   The Indians also took two women and one
boy prisoners, and killed one of the women because she
could not travel fast enough for them.   They were
willing to give up the other woman and child to the U.
S. officers in exchange for an Indian they had in their
possession. (See "Deseret News," Vol. 6, p. 245.)
       On the 26th, the first Hand Cart company of emi-
grants, under Capt. E. Ellsworth, arrived in G. S. L.
City. Gov. Young and a number of leading citizens
met the emigrants within about a mile and a half of the
Little Mountain. (See "Deseret News," Vol. 6, p. 236).
Also Edmund Ellsworth's report about hand cart travelling in "Deseret News," Vol. 6, p. 243.   Several
other hand cart companies arrived this, and the following months.

October

       On the 2nd, 3rd, and 4th, the First Deseret State
Fair, was held. (See "Deseret News," Vol. 6, pp. 245.-)
       The first annual address of the President of (35)
the Deseret Agricultural and Manufacturing Society
contains important historical facts (See "Deseret News,"
Vol. 6, p. 260.)
       On the 4th, Gov. Young and other leading men of
the Church, together with F. D. Richards and a number of other missionaries, who had just returned from
the East, held a meeting at the Historian's Office for
the purpose of devising plans towards aiding the emigrant companies, which were reported to be in a suffering condition in the mountains, especially the hand
cart companies.
       The following day a call was made upon the people,
who responded by donating liberally towards the relief
of the sufferers.

On the 7th, a number of teams, loaded with provisions, and clothing, started east to meet the emigrant companies.

On the 25th, Rev. C. R. Van Emmons, a missionary from the Bible Society, arrived with about a
ton and a half of Bibles for sale and distribution.

On the 31st Gideon H. Gibbs and Horace Newell,
(Express from Capt. Willie's company of hand carts)
arrived in G. S. L. City, and reported that the company was on Sweet Water on the 26th, and more teams
were immediately sent east to help Capt. Willie's and
other companies in. (36)

November

On the 9th, the fourth Hand Cart company arrived in G. S. L. City, under Capt. James G. Willie.

On the 30th, the fifth and last Hand Cart company
this season, under Capt. Edward Martin, arrived in
G. S. L. City.

During the season five companies of emigrants
came across the plains with hand carts, starting from
the general rendezvous at Iowa City. The three first
companies started early in the season and arrived at
G. S. L. City in good condition. Owing to various hin-
dering circumstances the two last companies did not
start until late in the season, and an early and unusually severe winter coming on, more time was necessarily consumed on the journey and consequently
considerable suffering was endured by them. But
through the very liberal and spirited assistance sent
to meet them from G. S. L. Valley, the companies
were eventually brought in, the last arriving on the
30th of this month.

Two companies of emigrants with wagons also
started late in the season, the members of which, after considerable privation also were brought in within
about a fortnight after the last hand cart company arrived. (37)

December

On the 1st, Jedediah M. Grant, second Counselor to President B. Young, died in G. S. L. City. (See "Des. News", Vol. 6, P. 317.) He was buried on the 4th.

On the 8th, the Legislative Assembly met in the State House in Fillmore, organized, met in joint session and passed a resolution, changing the seat of government of Utah Territory and adjourned to meet in the Social Hall, G. S. L. City, on Thursday the 18th, where the remainder of the session was held. H. C. Kimball was chosen President of the Council and Hosea Stout Speaker of the House.

(For Governor Young's Message, etc., see "Des. News," Vol. 6, P. 333.)

On the 9th, Orson Hyde arrived from his visit to Carson Valley. The following is an account of his mission--

"O. Hyde was elected Probate Judge of Carson Co., by the Legislature of Utah Territory in 1854, and was appointed a commissioner on the part of Utah to act with the California commission to determine the eastern boundary of California and the western boundary of Utah. He was accompanied by Joseph L. Heywood, U. S. Marshall of Utah; George P. Styles, Associate Justice of the U. S. Supreme Court and ex-officio Judge of the 3rd Judicial district for Utah and a formidable escort of 35 men. Elder Hyde started for Carson May 17th, 1855, and learning that part of the people contended (38) that they were situated in California, he proceeded to San Francisco, and induced Gov. John Bigler to appoint a commission, which proceeded to the spot and determined the boundary. He then proceeded to organize the county. He was appointed clerk of the 3rd Judicial district by Judge Styles. During the winter of 1855-6, he attempted to cross the Sierra Nevada on foot, in company with Mr. -- Willis, who froze to death. Elder Hyde came near perishing, his feet being severely frozen. He was confined for several months. In the spring of 1856, he commenced a saw-mill, and spent the sum-

mer in erecting it, costing $10,000. The settlement
was increased during the summer. He returned to
this City the 9th December 1856, having explored a
new route from Carson to this place. After his arrival he was elected to the Legislature in place of
Jedediah M. Grant."

On the 10th, the Fourteenth General Epistle from
the First Presidency, giving a general description of
affairs in the Territory, hand cart travelling, etc,
was written. (See Mill. Star, Vol. 19, P. 241 and
"Des. News," Vol. 6, P. 313.)

On the 18th, the Legislative Assembly met in the
Social Hall, G. S. L. City, having adjourned from
Fillmore, because there were better accommodations
in the City, and the message of Gov. B. Young was presented and read, and 500 copies were ordered printed.
(41)

INCIDENTS IN THE HISTORY OF UTAH, 1857

January 1857

On the 5th, the usual officers made elective by the joint vote of the Legislative Assembly, were elected in joint session.

On the 27th, Genl. Wells issued Genl. Orders No. 1, appointing certain officers to aid him. (See "Des. News," Vol. 6, p 384.)

February

On the 22nd, 99 names were read, of persons selected to accompany Prest. Young on his trip to Salmon River.

March

On the 2nd, Governor Brigham Young issued a proclamation for an election of a Lieut. Genl. (See "Des. News," Vol. 6, p. 413.)

On the 22nd, 34 names were selected for raising cotton on the Rio Virgin, from Salt Lake City, Fort Herriman, Ogden, Grantsville, Fillmore, Lehi, and South Cottonwood.

On the 27th, Genl. Wells issued Genl. Orders No. 2, with system of regulations for the Militia. (See "Des. News," Vol. 7, pp. 37.)

On the 28th, Howard Egan arrived from the west about sundown, bringing news that a large mail was on the way from California, having passed it at Mountain Springs. (42)

April

On the 6th, the Election for Mayor and City Council, took place at the Council house; Edward Hunter, Cols. L. W. Hardy; and J. C. Little were Moderators of the Election.

On the 6th, the General Conference was held in the Bowery, adjoining the north end of the Tabernacle on the Temple Block, G. S. L. City. (See "Des. News," Vol. 7, pp. 43-)

On the 11th, Lieut. Genl. D. H. Wells issued Genl. Orders, No. 1, ordering that the Territory be divided into Military districts, &c. (See "Des. News," Vol. 7, pp. 48-)

On the 16th, N. V. Jones gave an account of his mission to the Lead Mines of Los Vegas, in which he stated that owing to the difficulties attending the working of the mines, together with the hostile feelings of the Indians, he did not consider it judicious to remain there any longer.

On the 17th Prest. Young and others visited the Big Cottonwood canal.

On the 19th, B. F. Matthews wrote to Geo. Q. Cannon from San Bernardino, in which he referred to the introduction of Small Pox into the Territory. (See "Des. News," Vol. 7, pp. 160.)

On Monday, the 20th, a District Muster was held in Salt Lake City, and an election of officers to command the first division of the Legion, and the (43) several corps to be organized in G. S. L. Military District, according to the new system of regulations. See "Des. News," Vol. 7, pp. 61-)

On the 22nd, Hamilton H. Carns, in company with 18 others, mounted and armed, started as an express for Devil's Gate.

One of the Chiefs of the Bannock nation arrived in Salt Lake City with some of his band. He stated that he had been 36 days in travelling from Salmon River.

On the 24th, Brigham Young H. C. Kimball, and D. H. Wells, with a large company, started north with the intention of visiting Salmon River. They took with them two light boats, made at the public works, each 16 feet long, 3 feet, 7 inches broad at midships, 3 feet broad at stem and stern, and 15 inches deep, calked and painted; they were very light, being made of 1/2 inch lumber.

May

On the 14th, Parley P. Pratt was assassinated in Arkansas. (For particulars, see "Mill. Star" Vol. 19 pp. 417. -)

On the 19th, Judge W. I. Appleby, of Salt Lake City, wrote a letter to the "Mormon," New York, concerning the malignant and immoral conduct of Judge Drummond, a Federal Officer of Utah. (See "Mill. Star" Vol. 19, pp 401-)

(44) On the 26th, Brigham Young and the principal men of his company, returned from their northern trip, arriving in the City at 6-30 P.M. (For account of the excursion to Fort Limhi, see "Des. News", Vol. 7, pp. 108-.)

On the 29th, the Eastern mail arrived. (See "Des. News," Vol. 7, pp. 101-.)

June

On the 4th, Amasa Lyman arrived from San Bernardino, Cal.

On the 23rd, the Eastern mail arrived. Eight sacks of mail matter came through in twenty-three days.

On the 30th, Genl. Wells issued General Orders No. 3, ordering the organization of a Regiment of Infantry in each of the Lehi, Provo, Iron, Davis and Weber Military Districts, &c. (See "Des. News," Vol. 7, pp. 136. -)

Report from the General Land Office, Utah:-- The surveys of the public lands had rapidly progressed before the Surveyor General had abandoned his position, owing to reported hostilities on the part of the Mormon authorities at G. S. L. City. This happened early last spring, since which time we are advised of the forcible disbanding of the clerks, in the Surveyor General's office, but are uninformed as to the safety of the archives of that office

(45) Representatives have been made unfavorable to the surveys, which have been executed in that Territory, but we have no means of judging of the correct-

ness of these statements without actual examination on the ground.

The extent of the surveys since the beginning of the operations in Utah exhibits a sphere of field work embracing 2,000,000 acres, and the work executed at a cost of $90,000.

July

The 4th was celebrated in Salt Lake City. (See "Des. News," Vol. 7, pp. 141-).

On the 24th, the anniversary of the Pioneers entering G. S. L. Valley was celebrated at the mouth of Big Cottonwood Canyon (See "Des. News," Vol. 7, pp. 165.)

August

On the 2nd, the California mail arrived.

On the 3rd, Geo. A. Smith started at day break for Iron Co., with Samuel Lewis.

A company of emigrants arrived from the east, with a large herd of young cattle.

George A. Smith spent several hours at Lehi, and travelled to Provo in the evening. He delivered Genl. Orders from Genl. Wells to Col. Pace.

On the 4th, Another emigrant train, with a large drove of cattle, arrived from the East.

(46) George A. Smith left Provo at noon and delivered General orders to Genl. Aaron Johnson, at Springville.

On the 5th, another very large company of emigrants arrived, en route for California.

George A. Smith arrived at Nephi, and delivered Genl. orders to Major Bradley. On the 6th, he arrived at Fillmore, delivered Genl. orders to Major McCullough and camped in the evening at Cove Creek.

On the 7th, the St. Louis "Republican" contained the following:--

"Fort Kearney, Nebraska Tery.
August 7, 1857
"The 10th infantry and Phelp's battery of the Utah

army reached here today. The other regiment of infantry, the 5th I believe, is expected in a few days.
These troops do not appear to be very much delighted
with the service on which they are ordered. The season is so late that they anticipate a great deal of suffering during the approaching winter in the Rocky
Mountains, as they will have only their canvass to protect them from its rigors. The consequence is, that
the number of desertions has been unparalleled. The
fifth and tenth infantries have lost nearly five hundred
men since they first received orders for Utah. It is
very difficult to see why this expedition was not put off
till next spring, instead of being pushed on at the
eleventh hour at such an immense sacrifice of men (47)
and money. For the last six or seven years the Mormons have been conducting themselves the same as at
the present moment, and it is fair to presume that next
spring would have found them no worse. The secret
is, however, that the Utah movement was popular, and
every politician feels it his duty to mount the highest
wave of popularity at once, for fear some one else
might get there before him. *****.

"The merchants in Salt Lake, who wished to turn
an honest penny from the government and the troops,
have also had a hand in this business, as they represented to the authorities at Washington that the season
was not too late for moving troops across the Plains to
Utah..... Our army swore some in Flanders, it is
said, and it must be confessed that a listener might
now and then hear curses, not loud but deep, from our
army to Utah.

"The road is lined between here and the mountains
with contractors' trains loaded with stores for Salt
Lake.

"The Mormon emigration this year is truly formidable. It is confined almost exclusively to the road
along the north of the Platte. Some of the trains contain very nearly a thousand souls."

On the 8th, another company of emigrants for
California arrived.

George A. Smith arrived at Parowan at 5 P. M.,
found first battalion on parade, and delivered General

orders to Col. Dame, and at their request made a
speech.

(48) On the 11th, Geo. A. Smith went to Paragoonah and preached in the afternoon. The people
there had prospects of four or five thousand bushels of
wheat which they were engaged in harvesting.

On the 14th, many of the brethren were preparing
to go into the mountains to help the emigration and to
meet the enemy.

On the 15th, instruction was sent to Peter W.
Conover to go to Carson Valley and to take with him
some ten or twelve men, to gather the brethren home
from that place, to G. S. L. City.

There were many emigrants on their way to Carson Valley and California. Many of those Gentile emigrants shot the Indians wherever they met with them.
The Indians felt to retaliate and, if not watched would
kill innocent people. One woman who had fitted out to
come here to investigate "Mormonism" was killed,
and all her teamsters, and all this through the mur-
derous spirit manifested by emigrants.

On the 31st, George A. Smith returned to G. S. L.
City, having travelled about seven hundred miles, and
preached in all the settlements in Iron, Washington
and Beaver Counties.

At Parowan, Iron Co., at 9 a. m., a flood came
down the canyon, bringing with it all the bridges for
seven miles up, broke the saw mill dam, tore out the
ox frame dam, (49) at Cricket Fork; down Cricket
Fork it took the grist mill dam at the head of the
flume some 12 feet deep, blocked the culvert, ran
north outside the wall to the bastion by the east gate,
tore it all to flinders, and buried some of the fields.

September

On the 1st, Jacob Hamlin arrived from the Santa
Clara mission with some twelve Indian chiefs, who had
come to see Gov. B. Young. One was the head chief,
his name is Tutsegabot, the chief of the Piedes, of the
Desert, and Santa Clara, and Rio Virgin. He had a
chief with him of the Indians of Harmony; Kanosh the

chief of the Pahvants, and Ammon, Walker's brother.

On the 2nd at 10 P. M., the California mail arrived.

On the 4th, Mr. Ashby and others came in from
the East, bringing news that General Johnson's army
were a hundred and eighteen miles below Laramie.
They counted from 200 to 250 tents, a great quantity of
cattle, seven or eight trains of oxen with baggage, and
a great number of carriages, altogether rather formidable.

On the 5th, in the evening, J. R. Murdock arrived
from the States; he reports all our emigrating companies as far as Devil's Gate.

He stated that there were but sixteen hundred (50)
men started for Utah as an invading force, Gen. Harney
having been called to remain at Kansas, with part of
his force to fight the border ruffians and to assist the
Government to collect taxes from the abolitionists. It
was rumored that 500 of the troops had deserted, thirty
in one night. Col. Sumner had followed the Cheyennes
and found a village; he was discovered when seven miles
off. They tried to parley with him, but he would not
accede to their wishes, but pitched into the village.
Most of the women and children escaped. Sumner reported he had killed nineteen Indians. The Indians say
he killed only four. Sumner had two men killed, and
nine wounded. He sent Capt. Foote with sixty men to
guard the wounded into Fort Kearney. There was much
opposition in the States against the administration for-
cing its troops into Utah. All the way from the States
to Laramie, it was "God damn the Mormons"; at
Laramie the officers tipped their hats and said, "How
do you do, Mr. Murdock," and from there everybody
was very respectful. 850 head of beef cattle had been
stolen, and they had started back with the balance to
the States. A party of men came in Murdock's company and complained of the cattle being stolen and accused the Mormons of being in with the Indians, in the
stealing. Murdock replied, "This company are all
Mormons, you had (51) better mind what you say. After this they were very respectful.

Murdock's party went through to Independence in
16 days, to St. Louis in 18 1/2 days. On the way down

they were surrounded by a war party of Cheyennes;
they shook hands; he gave them tobacco and something
to eat. They said, "How do," and passed on. It is
reported that Col. Johnson will take command of the
army against Utah.

On the 8th Capt. Van Vliet, from Col. Johnston's
army, arrived in G. S. L. City.

On the 9th, Gov. B. Young and other citizens had
an interview with Capt. Van Vliet, Asst. Quarter
Master and Commissary of U. S. Army, repecting the
furnishing of lumber and supplies for the troops who
were coming from the States.

On the 12th, an express arrived in the morning,
stating that there were some 900 troops on the way
this side of Laramie and some twelve government baggage trains.

Capt Van Vliet came into the office and Gov. B.
Young had quite a long conversation with him.

On the 13th, 42 names were selected for the
Black Foot Fork mission.

Capt. Van Vliet was preparing to leave and Gov.
B. Young had his last interview with him. The
Governor talked to him in a plain manner. He wished
that Capt. Van Vliet would report at Washington (52)
just as things were in Utah. He said "I have seen the
sufferings of this people through the persecutions of the
people of the United States for the last twenty-five
years, and I will not bear it any longer. We have always treated the United States officers well, but they
have constantly lied about us, and tried to destroy us
all the time. We would still have received their Governors and officers if they had sent them here without
an army; but inasmuch as they are disposed to send one
to hold us still, while others run their red hot irons
into us, we will now say that we will defend ourselves."
Capt. Van Vliet said that if our Government pushed
forward this thing any more and made war upon the
Mormons, he should withdraw from the army; for he
would not have a hand in shedding the blood of
American citizens. At the close of the remarks, Gov.
Young said to Capt. Van Vliet, "As citizens, we are
friends," and shook hands in a friendly manner.

On the 14th, about six a.m., Hon. J. M. Bernhisel and Capt. Van Vliet started East.

On the 15th, Gov. B. Young issued a proclamation proclaiming a martial law in the Territory. (See "Mill. Star," Vol. 19, p. 822.)

A delegation of the Bannocks called to see Gov. B. Young. This was the first time these Indians had been in settlements.

(53) For Capt. Van Vliet's official account of his visit to Utah, (see "Des. News," Vol. 7 P. 392.)

On the 18th, between 7 and 8 P.M., Chas. Decker and Jesse Earl arrived, bringing an express, stating that the brethren were in want of clothing and meat. They brought a letter dated the 15th, written at Willow Creek, stating that 750 men were at Deer Creek--50 of them cavalry. They were travelling 15 miles a day. It was rumored that another detachment of the same size was below. 126 freight wagons were above Devil's Gate-- Their teams not in very good condition. These brethren disguised as California emigrants, went in among the soldiers and enquired what they were going to do-- "Scalp old Brigham, have you seen him?" "Yes" "How does he feel?" "Rather scary."

Gov. B. Young sent out an express by Van Ettan and Alma Williams to the relief guard.

On the 19th, orders were issued for a number of wagons to be fitted out to go with provisions to the brethren in the mountains. Col. Harman's regiment went today with all their baggage wagons.

A company from Deer Creek of about forty wagons and teams arrived about one P.M. in the city bringing the remainder of the goods left at Devil's Gate last fall.

On the 21st, in the afternoon and evening, the (54) St. Louis company of emigrants arrived.

On the 25th, N. V. Jones arrived from the invading U.S. Army. He visited, with Capt. Van Vliet both regiments. The first was the tenth regiment, being a full regiment. The officers were young and full of fire, and they swore they would come into our settlements any how, for they could whip out Utah. Capt. Van Vliet advised them not to come, for they

could get nothing, and they would have to fight their
way; but they swore they would fight their way through.
After Van Vliet left them, they marched thirty miles
instead of fifteen the next day. The second regiment
he met with had older officers over them. They considered the matter over more, and thought it an imposition to be sent out here as a political movement,
to kill innocent people or to get killed. They will be at
the Pacific Springs tonight when it is expected that our
brethren will commence operations upon them.

    Cyrus Wheelock took an express to Farmington,
to tell some of the officers to go to the Relief Guard.
Jesse Earle and Thos. Abbott left at 1 P. M., with an
express for Robt. Burton, Col. of the Relief Guard.

    At six P. M. a detachment of Lancers started east.

    On the 26th, Gov. B. Young, Supt. of Indian af-
fairs (55) wrote the following letter, to Dr. Garland
Hurt, U. S. Agent for Ty. of Utah:--

Office Superintendent Indian Affairs,
Great Salt Lake City, Utah Territory
September 26, 1857.

Sir:-- I am informed that you propose going to the
States by some unfrequented route, and in company
with some Indians as pilots and travelling companions.
Such a course is very unsafe, and highly improper in
an officer of the Government. I, therefore, respectfully advise you, when you are ready to start upon your
journey to the East, to call upon me, in my office in
Great Salt Lake City; and I hereby pledge you a sufficient escort and a comfortable carriage for your
speedy and safe transportation to the protection of the
United States troops en route for this Territory.

    Trusting that this advice will meet with a cheer-
ful compliance on your part,

I am

Brigham Young,

Governor and Ex-Officio Superintendent of Indian
Affairs. (See "Mil. Star Vol. 20 P. 109.).

    On the 27th, Gov. B. Young dictated a letter to
Garland Hurt, requesting him to deliver the property
in his charge over to Aaron Johnson, also informing
him he was discharged from his official duties.

D. H. Wells and staff and company left G. S. L.
(56) City at one P. M. , to join the relief guard in the
mountains, all armed and equipped for service.

At 7 P. M. , an express arrived from Springville,
informing Gov. B. Young that Dr Hurt was about
starting for the east, with the Government property
this evening, with return express.

On the 28th, an express arrived from an army in
the mountains, saying that our enemies were marching strongly toward us. N. V. Jones said that Capt.
Van Vliet tried to persuade the invading army to stay
on Ham's Fork or in that region to winter, but the
Tenth Regiment swore that they had started for Salt
Lake and they would go there. Capt. Van Vliet told
them that the people would not permit them to go thus
far, and that they would find a different warfare from
any they had met with.

On the 29th, another express arrived in the morning, saying that the invading army were rapidly marching toward us and would soon be at Fort Bridger. Our
guard in the mountains wished men immediately sent
out.

On the 28th, John D'Lee arrived from Harmony,
with an express and an awful tale of blood. He said
that a company of California emigrants of about 150
men, women and children, many of them belonging to
the mob in Missouri and Illinois and having many (57)
cattle and horses with them, as they travelled along
South went damning Brigham Young, Heber C. Kimball
and the heads of the Church, saying that Joseph Smith
ought to have been shot a long time before he was.
They wanted to do all the evil they could, so they poisoned the springs of water and several of the Saints
died. They also poisoned beef and gave it to the Indians
and some of them died. The Indians became enraged
at their conduct and they surrounded them on a prairie,
and the emigrants formed a bulwark of their wagons
and dug an entrenchment up to the hubs of their wagons,
but the Indians fought them five days until they killed
all their men, about 60 in number; they then rushed
into their corral and cut the throats of their women
and children, except some eight or ten children whom

they brought and sold to the whites. They stripped
the men and women naked and left them stinking in the
boiling sun. When Lee found it out, to took some men
and went and buried their bodies. It was a horrid
awful job; the whole air was filled with an awful stench;
many of the men and women were rotten with the bad
disorder before they were hurt by the Indians. The
Indians obtained all their cattle, horses and property,
guns &c. There was another large company of emigrants, who had 1000 head of cattle, who were also
damning both Indians and Mormons (58) They were
afraid of sharing the same fate, and Lee had to send
interpreters with them to the Indians, to try to save
their lives, while, at the same time, they were trying
to kill the settlers.

Gov. B. Young, while speaking of the cutting of
the throats of women and children, as the Indians had
done south, said that it was heart rending.

Mr. Hennefer brought in word verbally that the
invading army would camp at night at Smith's Fork,
and that D. H. Wells had sent him to inform the captains of companies on the road, to urge all the men
that were ordered out to push forward.

Geo. Snow arrived at 4-45 P. M. , bringing a letter,
stating that Garland Hurt had left the valley with two
or three hundred Indians

At 9 P. M. , an express was sent out by Orlando
Ferrin and Jos. Foutz to Lieu. Genl. D. H. Wells,
stating that Major Blair was ordered out this day with
207 men, also S. S. Willis with 50 men; also giving
account of Hurt's stealthy departure. C. W. West was
also written to, to look out for the enemy that might
come in by different routes, as they had divided into
three different companies, it was thought for that purpose.

On the 30th, the California mail arrived.

L. E. Harrington reported that on Sunday last, (59)
Dr. G. Hurt started up Provo Canyon with 300 Indians;
it was supposed, to aid the soldiers.

On the 30th, at 6 a.m. , the drums beat and an
army of soldiers paraded our streets, numbering 400,
who were in readiness to march at a moment's warn-

ing, for the seat of war. We have about 800 men in
the mountains. It is a solemn time; the armies of the
Gentiles are making war upon us, because of our religion, and we have to defend ourselves against a nation
of twenty-five millions of people, and the war has just
commenced; we have to trust in God for the result.
We shall do what we can and leave the work in His
hands. There is a still solemnity resting over our
city. All are anxiously awaiting the arrival of the express. One of the letters by the Cal. mail states that
the Government had made arrangements to send light
draft boats up the Colorado River, with men and arms
against us, from that point.

In an interview between Gov. B. Young and
Captain Van Vliet, sometime this month, the following
conversation was had, as reported by W. Woodruff--

Captain Van Vliet said, "I think that Congress will
try to do all they can against you."

Gov. Young said, "If God inspires any man to
speak for us it will be well; we have got to trust in God.
(60) If you will speak in favor of us (and I think you
will) the Lord will bless you for so doing. He will require it of you. We have refuted lies so long we have
got tired of it, and we shall now trust in God for the
future. Congress could sent out an investigating committee to Kansas or any other place by to Utah; but
upon the mere rumor of liars they could send out 2000
armed Soldiers to Utah to destroy the people without
investigating the subject at all."

Captain Van Vliet said, "The Government may yet
send out one to Utah and consider it policy before they
get through with it."

Gov. B. Young said, "I do think that God has sent
you out here, and that good will grow out of it. I was
glad when I learned that you were coming."

Captain Van Vliet said "I am very anxious to get
back to Washington as soon as I can. I shall stop the
train on Ham's Fork on my own responsibility, and
leave them there."

Gov. B. Young said, "If we can keep the peace for
this winter, I do think there will be something turn up
that may save so much shedding of blood."

Capt. Van Vliet said, "I think so too; the troops will have to stop on Ham's Fork, for their provisions will be late coming up. I do not think there are more than a thousand troops coming. There is one regiment from (61) the Florida war, there are not more than 300 men; they have been reduced by the scurvy. That Florida war has cost many millions of money, and it is a speculating scheme. There are not more than 100 warriors and they have got hiding places which no man can find. It is seldom you can kill one; you may accidentally stumble on to one as you would a partridge; well this regiment are old men and the regiment is worn out."

October

On the 1st, an express arrived from Col. J. C. Little, giving an account of the number of soldiers with him and about Echo Canyon.

An express arrived from D. H. Wells, --Taylor and G. A. Smith, sent by Jos. A. Young and J. W. Cummings, saying that they had sent an express to the U. S. army, containing Gov. Young's orders for them to surrender all their arms and baggage to Lewis Robinson, Quarter Master General, at Fort Bridger, or to retreat to the States, or we should resist them. They were camped upon Ham's Fork and they were awaiting an answer to their message, and would send an express in as soon as they got it. They related an incident of their trying to stampede the army's animals, but found them not only hobbled but chained with a log chain. One bro. Simons was shot dead by another brother, accidentally.

At 7-30 P. M. Jas. W. Cummings, Jos. A. Young (62) and Geo. Dalton arrived from Bridger. They came in in 19 1/2 hours, in a wagon. Genl. Wells had deputed Lewis Robinson, J. D. McAllister and Lot Smith to visit the officer in command to leave them a copy of the laws of Utah Territory, the proclamation, and a letter from the Governor, informing them that they might either lay down their arms and stay there (at Ham's Fork) till spring, or they must start for the east immediately.

The Deseret State Fair commenced at the Deseret
Store. (See "Des. News," Vol. 7, pp. 248, -252.)

The following is from Joseph Taylor's Journal:--
"I organized under Genl. West in A. D. 1857,
into the 5th Battalion, and was placed as Major of the
company consisting of 100 men, and ordered to Echo
Canyon, on the 18th of Sept., taking up our line of
march, we arrived at Col. Little's camp being about
the 20th, staying one hour we then proceeded on to Col.
Jones' camp. 5th. Received orders to march to Genl.
Wells, where after our arrival we were dispatched to
the Big Bend of Bear River to join Col. Burton, remaining here two days. I was sorely afflicted with
biles, and although I found it very painful to ride, I
did not feel like giving up. There, in company with
Major McAllister, we were ordered to Black's Fork,
it being a distance of two days travel. Immediately
after camping this said evening (63) M^C. Allister struck
for Bridger. Next morning I struck for the same place.
While being here, my command was called upon to assist O. P. Rockwell. Stayed at Bridger two days
awaiting orders; then marched to cross Green River;
then countermanded to Black's Fork; but not finding
any of the command, we were ordered to march to
Major M^C. Allister's command. I then took the most
suitable route with four men and ten animals, one of
our command bearing westward, while some thought
I was making too much for the soldiers. I had very
peculiar feelings, such as I had not before experienced.
Marching along we then camped about 20 miles from
the soldiers. The next morning we took breakfast.
My mind still being for a westward course, while some
of the boys declined going my course, I called a vote,
some voting for and some against. However, marching on we came to Ham's Fork. Went on to the camp
grounds where the soldiers had been two nights before.
The boys thought I was crazy. I followed the soldiers'
trail about two or three miles, then turned round a
due west course up on to a little mountain; crossed a
small valley, and at the foot of the mountain we struck
a trail, while south of us we could see a smoke. Sup-

posing it to be M^c. Allister's command at the foot of the
mountain, Adjutant Stowell and myself being ahead, we
could see a company of soldiers nearly one mile before
us. (64) I told Adjutant Stowell that if he would stop
there, I would go and see who they were. I went down,
when all of a sudden, I was flanked by horsemen. I
drew my pistol and cocked it at them, when something
suggested me not to shoot. They seized my arms,
though my natural feelings were to die rather than
give them up. They dismounted me off my horse, and
seated me on an old mule, and leading the mule they
immediately marched, and seized Adjutant Stowell,
and dismounting him off his horse, and placing him on
a mule, they led us to their camp, where they manifested great rejoicing; while Captain Marcy thought
they had achieved great victory in capturing two Mormons and taking them as prisoners.

"Adjutant Stowell and myself were kept separate
all night, depriving us of the privilege of conversing
with each other, and, being kept in separate tents, it
was very cold, and they would not allow us any fire,
and but a very little to eat. I then asked them if that
was the way they treated their prisoners; they damned
me and told me to stop my talking. I told them I
wanted something to make us comfortable, but they
declined any conversation. I told the sentinel if he
would bring me part of my bed, he might take the other
part; I also inquired after the welfare of Adjutant
Stowell, but they would not tell me anything (65) about
him; so I sat there in the tent shivering and shaking
with cold, through the whole night.

"Morning came and great excitement prevailed
throughout the camp.

"I prayed earnestly that whatever I might say or
do, under these circumstances might be for good. At
this juncture Adjutant Stowell had been examined before
Col. Alexander, and I had a great anxiety to learn
what he had said; but not knowing, I then resolved to
say what ever might occur to my mind. I was then
marched to Col. Alexander's quarters; whereupon he
propounded the following questions

"Are you Major Taylor?"

"Yes sir."

"Where are you from?"

"Bridger sir."

"Where do you live?"

"In Salt Lake Valley."

"What is your business out here?"

"To fight a mob sir." "Where was you raised?"
"All over Sir."

"Where was you born?"

"In the State of Kentucky, a citizen of the United
States.

"Col. replied quite indignantly "You know a God
damned sight better-- You are some God damned
Englishman, or you would have known better."

(66) "Excuse me sir, I don't know any better."

"Guard, march him off, (which he did very dis-
gracefully.)

"In about three quarters of an hour the Colonel
sent for me again, not being fully satisfied, he addressed me thus-- "Major I have thought to ask you
a few more questions, (quite in a tone resembling soft
soap.) to which I rejoined, "Sir, any information I
can furnish you, I shall take a pleasure in doing so,
to the best of my ability."

"The Colonel asked, "What is the strength of the
Mormon troops?" I replied, "From 20 to 25 thousand
good warriors."

"At this broad statement, he stood aghast, while
I could have hung my hat on his eyes.

"They received my official orders at the time we
were taken prisoners. In those orders, I was, with
my command, to stay the progress of the expedition,
by stampeding their cattle, burning their grass, &c.,
and not to take life, only in case of self defence.

"Immediately after our examination, they held a
council of war among themselves.

"The decision of Col. Alexander was to go round
north, but was voted down by the other officers.

"They kept a trotting up and down Ham's Fork
day after day, keeping a strict guard over us, and (67)
issuing orders every two hours to shoot us dead if we
attempted to escape.

"Appearances were quite gloomy, but we did not feel ourselves whipped. We thought there would be an opening for us. At times, our boys were seen on the hill, and were fired at by the soldiers with their artillery and grape shot.

"On one occasion a company of our boys were in sight, whereupon the soldiers all mustered and started immediately after them, when two of the soldiers were taken prisoners, one of them a blacksmith, and the other steward of the hospital. In this affray, the Lieut. of their command, coming into camp, fell into the water and lost his arms in the creek, and being dreadfully scared, exclaimed, "The Mormons are close upon us and they have taken two of our men prisoners." By over hearing a conversation of the Colonel's, I learned that it was determined by them to liberate us, so that they might get the blacksmith back again. After this Sergeant Newman presented to Adjutant Stowell and myself, each a basin of vegetable soup, saying, at the same time that the soldiers were mostly fond of it. We shook our heads, while it occurred to our minds, as quick as thought, with infallible conviction that there was poison in the soup; we prayed that (68) if its contents were imbued with poison, it might not injure us; we tasted a little of it, after which we scratched a hole in the ground, and deposited the balance.

"In a few moments, Adjutant Stowell was taken very sick, and called on me to pray for him. I laid my hands upon his head, praying for him in the name of Jesus, after which he went to the rear of the camp, puking and purging very severely. He came back in a short time and found me similarly affected. I asked him to lay his hands upon my head and pray for me, which being done, I went to the rear of the camp also, puking and purging most heavily, so that I did not get over the effects of it for a week.

"Colonel Cunningham came into the camp with Mogaw's wife. We got down on the Emigration Road and there halted till Col. Johnson came up. The soldiers felt very much worn out and fatigued, owing to slow progress and the scarcity of provisions.

"They swore that the Mormons' Mustang ponies could run up hill and down as fast as they could on the level surface, and that the Mormons had invariably been in their camp ever since their leaving the Missouri River.

"Our expectations had been, up to this date, that when Colonel Johnson arrived we should be liberated, (69) but in this we were disappointed. The soldiers seemed to take courage, saying that the Colonel was a damned old tiger, and would put us through. Accordingly a court of inquiry was held, and a writ issued charging us with, the crime of treason. I asked the sheriff when the trial would come off; he answered, "At the first Judicial court to be held in Green River county by Judge Eckles," and it was reported to us by creditable witnesses that I should undoubtedly by hung at Bridger.

"The next day that held a council to make a forced march, leaving their heavy wagons, and take their light ones, and forthwith march to Echo in five days.

"We knew all they were doing, our ears being open to all they had to say. I thought this night we would go and leave them, notwithstanding our way seemed to be hedged up. After preparing and being ready to go, I finally gave it up. After praying I laid down to sleep, during which, a woman appeared to me, and she called me son; I called her grandmother. She ask me what I was doing there. I answered "a prisoner, madame." Addressing me again, she told me to get up and go home. At this I awoke, got up, cool and deliberate finding all quiet and still; the sentinel in the front seemed to be asleep. I took up my sack, where I had my clothes, and commenced to untie it, when brother Stowell asked me what I (70) was going to do. I said "Get up and let us go home;" but finding him unable to travel, I exclaimed, "Lord, Lord, can I leave him here?" "No, no," was the answer. I then laid down by his side, after which, the camp arose, took a light breakfast, and prepared for a march.

"The officers were all brought together, and General Johnson assumed the entire command, which placed us under a guard of 24 men. I felt as though it was a pretty strong force to be in the midst of 3000 soldiers.

"We soon took up the line of march for Fort Bridger, placing us near the front of the command, two men in the front and two in the rear, with their guns half-cocked, also two officers on our right, and two on our left, with their revolvers half-cocked by their sides.

"In the centre of the 24 men, they marched us along, when shortly Col. Alexander came to me and asked me, how I felt, to which I replied that I felt better, as I was great for home, while the fact of our wending our way homeward increased our hope. At the same time they seemed to have a despair corresponding.

"Captain Donovan said, We are bound for Salt Lake City if we have to tramp the snow, and Jesus Christ can not keep us out." The captain said, "We will place you in the front rank, to which we answered, "That was our rank when at home, especially when there (71) was any fighting to be done."

"After the above conversation came up a Mountaineer accosting me, said, "Good morning Major." Returning, I said, "Good morning sir." He continued, "You are in a bad fix." I replied, "I have seen whole families in a bad fix. We exchanged a few more words, and then the Col. told him to leave and not talk with me.

"Soon after this, the orders were, "Stop an hour and let the animals rest." I asked brother Stowell to spread his wrapper on the ground, as I was very tired; he then sat down, my head being towards his left thigh, and commenced conversation with me.

"I told him I felt powerful, more so than I was adequate to express. I said that if we had to get away we ought to exert ourselves, he being very anxious to go indeed; but from severe exposure had got the rheumatism so severely that he was unable to travel. In the afternoon I bid brother Stowell farewell, telling him that I was going to carry the express, and that I would remain there no longer. I felt as though I could say to the entire expedition, "shoot away and be damned." I told brother Stowell to be of good cheer,

for they should not have power to harm one hair of his
head, and that I was going away that evening. So I
commenced mimicking sickness (72) and was ailing
from this on, until I got within a mile of our place of
camping, taking a survey of the country

"It shortly commenced snowing and blowing. I
stood shivering and shaking with cold. I asked the
Officer of the Guard to bring me a cup of coffee, being
about used up. He said the baggage wagon had not arrived. I then asked him if he would be kind enough to
make me a fire, as I was very cold. He told the guard
to bring some sage and make me a fire. I stood there
till the fire was made and well surrounded. I told him
that I could not stand that, and that I would take a
brand and build another fire. I then built one, ten or
twelve feet from the one below, and shifted about from
one to the other, being in great distress. I took off my
comforter and placed it around my waist, untied my
garment strings and shirt neck, preparing for a race.
At the same time the sergeant had orders to shoot me
down like a beast, if I attempted to leave. I heard a
drove of cattle coming, pulled off my boots and held
them in my hand.

"It was evident, if I did not get better, I should
necessarily have to go to the hospital. In a few minutes the cattle came up; I kept piling on the sage, until
it fell down on one of the soldiers, which made him
curse like the Devil. I told him to please excuse (73)
me; I did not wish to burn him.

"While at Ham's Fork we went to Col. Alexander
and we asked him what he kept us there for, to which
he answered, we could go, so far as he was concerned.

"I stood with my boots in my hand till the cattle
came up, then made a spring; the third jump took me
behind an ox; I could have struck a man on a mule as
I went along. Being amongst the cattle, my buckskin
coat made a tremendous crackle; desiring, however,
that my coat might come off, so that I would not
frighten the cattle, and having a boot in each hand, my
coat came off, but which way, I could never tell. I ran
about three quarters of a mile in my stocking feet, and
by the time I got to the mountains, I lost my stockings.

I got up to the side of the mountain and put on my boots.
Upon the mountain I heard a tremendous pow-wowing.
After this I went down on my knees and thanked the
Lord for my deliverance.

"The snow was blowing and it was very cold,
which I felt the more sensibly being in my shirt sleeves.
Travelling about three miles, I supposed due East, I
thought to make for Fort Bridger, but shortly discovered my self on the brink of a precipice; thought I,
surely the Devil has hedged up my way (74) again, so
that I am never going to get out of it. At length, however, I succeeded in making my way out. I then travelled East, being cautious which way I proceeded,
fearing lest I should get on the back track, and become
bewildered. I rambled on the rocks, travelling all
night. Forded Smith and Black Forks. My clothes
were frozen to me, while I was almost frozen all over.
Just before daylight, a sleep came over me and it was
with a great deal of exertion that I could keep awake.
Daylight came, and I found myself within about three
miles of the Emigration Road.

"In a parallel course with the road, about sun rise,
as I went along, I found a bundle, which proved to be
an overcoat, and in the pockets were a pair of stockings. I travelled a little ways and came to a broken
down old ox. I tried to knock him down with some
rocks, but found myself unable to, being weak and very
hungry. Went on a little further, when I thought I saw
six men ahead of me, and I thought, is it possible that the
Devil has headed me again? I travelled as long as though
they didn't see me; went into the hollow and tried to
run, but could not do it; crawled into some greasewood.
When the parties came up, to my agreeable surprise, it
was John Thomson and five others. I rose up, and raising my hat, gave three cheers for joy. Bro. Thomson
told me to consider myself a prisoner, and (75) come to
him. I got up about three rods from them and we were
very glad to see each other.

"Thomson told me to get on him horse; I told them
I could not do it, being weak and worn out. Bro.
Thomson called on bro. Clark to assist him in putting
me on the horse. After being seated on the saddle I
could ride with some ease.

"We were then four miles from Bridger. After
reaching Bridger, we found the brethren just leaving.
Here they got me something to eat, and it was like
taking my life every swallow I took.

"The brethren furnished me with a good horse, and
I started for the place of Genl. Wells, overtaking him
at Muddy. I was very glad to see him and informed
him of what the soldiers calculated to do.

"The General stopped in the evening and camped
about an hour and a half; then brother Thomson and I
started over Big Mountain, which, by the time we got
on the summit, it seemed as though I would perish. I
told bro. Thomson to take me off my horse, to see if I
could walk a little, to warm up and aid the circulation.

"He took me off my horse and walking about two
rods, I felt myself unable to walk from weakness and
cold; not being able to keep up, I laid hold of the horse's
main, and called on bro. Thomson to put me on my
horse again.

"Being seated on the horse again, bro. Thomson
told me (76) to whip up the horse and follow him. The
horses being good ones, took us over to Bear River
quickly, where we found Captain Haight and company.

"They took me off my horse and folded me in some
buffalo robes, gave me warm drink and set me before
the fire, and administered to me by the laying on of
hands, after which I felt better.

"Early next morning, I started for Salt Lake City.
Travelling along I stayed invariably with the brethren
on the route, by whom I was kindly treated, and soon
arrived in Salt Lake City. I then went to see President
Young, and after talking with him for a while, he told
me to go and get me a gun, and go back again to the
mountains; so I arose early next morning & purchased
me a gun for the sum of $50.00 . I then went home,
reaching there about three o'clock in the morning.
Started away again about ten o'clock the same day for
Echo, with General West's command. The war being
over, we returned home in peace.

                                    "Joseph Taylor."
On the 6th, the semi-annual Conference of the
Church of Jesus Christ of Latter-day Saints, was held

in the Bowery, adjoining the north end of the Tabernacle, in the Temple Block, Great Salt Lake City.
(See "Des. News"--Vol. 7. P. 255.)

On the 7th, an express was sent to D. H. Wells,
at 10-45 A. M. (77)

A letter was sent to Jas. W. Denver, Commissioner of Indian Affairs, stating the abrupt departure
of Dr. Garland Hurt.

For "Expedition Against Utah" see "Des. News,"
Vol. 7, pp. 244--.)

On the 8th, in the evening an express arrived,
bringing news that it was expected General Harney had
arrived with 150 dragoons, many carriages and ladies.
The brethren had burned fifty-one provision wagons
and driven off the mules.

Governor B. Young directed certain brethren to
raise more men to go out to Echo Canyon. The number was 555 men.

On the afternoon of the 9th, an express arrived
from Box Elder, in six hours, stating that about 150
dragoons were on Bear River Lake.

On the 12th, an express went by Chas. Benson and
David Kimball, at 2-45 P. M., for D. H. Wells, with
letters and parcels for brethren, and letters from their
families.

About 700 of the brethren from Utah and Tooele
Counties, camped on the public square in the 16th Wd.
G. S. L. City ready to march at a moment's notice.

On the 13th, the brethren came in from the east,
and brought in about 150 head of cattle. Three teamsters and one deserter from the army helped drive
them in. The deserter reported that neither Johnson
nor (78) Harney, nor the Governor, nor judges, nor
any of the Territorial officers had arrived at the army;
neither any females. He said the soldiers were only
allowed three biscuits, two cups of coffee, and a small
piece of beef per day, that they were not half fed. They
had 76 wagons burned, and two wagons saved. The
captain of the company, who burned them, saved all the
private property of the teamsters, and when the wagons
were burned they gave back the teamsters all their
arms, & ammunition. One brother had his knee shat-

tered by the accidental discharge of a rifle; they had to
carry him a long distance on a litter; he suffered much
with it.

Jos. Woodmansee drove 152 head of cattle into the
city. He stated to Gov. B. Young that the cattle of the
enemy were guarded by men who had no interest for
them, and would be glad if our people would drive them
off, that they might be delivered from the task of attending them, that they might not suffer with the cold,
guarding them. The soldiers also complained of their
short allowance of biscuit and general rations.

On the 14th, in the afternoon, about one hundred
brethren and eleven baggage wagons from San Pete
passed in front of the Governor's office.

An express arrived at 5.35 P.M. Letters were
(79) sent to a few of the officers, for our army to send
a few men, equipped and rationed to march to Echo
Canyon.

The express sent to D. H. Wells gave instructions
to offer Perry a fair price for the goods, and take his
pay when we could pay, or he might go back to the
States and risk being burned, or he might choose what
course he pleased. Also to instruct Lewis Robinson to
see more of the teamsters and soldiers, and promise
them work and protection, and when they wanted, allow them to go to California, but disarm them without
an offer of retaining them, and to get soldiers to desert with as much ammunition as possible. Genl.
Wells was on Bear River, and the army had moved up
Ham's Fork.

An express arrived from General Wells, stating
that numbers of the army wished to desert and come
into the Valley if they had protection. The army was
weakening daily. The chief officers sent a very polite
note to Gov. Young, acknowledging the receipt of the
"Deseret News," which he had sent them.

Capt. Lot Smith has gone east to officiate in his
office in watching for the interest of Utah. The enemies were mostly hemmed in, but no disposition was
manifested to shed blood on either side. They are in a
close place; their provisions are fast diminishing (80)
and there is but little prospect of anything but starva-

tion before them. We have prayed that the Lord would
lead our enemies into the pit which they have dug for
the Saints, and the Lord has heard our prayers, and
our enemies are in the pit, and a fair prospect of their
being destroyed without our shedding their blood.

Colonel Rockwood informed us that there were
1100 men of our militia in the mountains and 700
camped on the public square and that we could raise
1500 men in this city and in 15 hours we could place
300 armed men in Echo Canyon.

On the 15th, Andrew Smith sent Henry Wheaten
with two kegs of powder, which were taken from the
soldiers.

On the 16th, Gov. B. Young received a letter from
Colonel Alexander, concerning the present state of affairs; also a letter from Genl. Wells. The brethren
had taken a herd of cattle of some 700 head and were
bringing them in.

Col. Alexander's letter was rather saucy, threatening us with extermination if we opposed him. He
considered himself able to come in and carry out the
commands of the Government. Gov. B. Young sent
him a strong answer, asking him why he stayed in
camp on Ham's Fork, for a month, if he considered he
had force enough to carry out his orders. He gave him
to understand that it was now the Kingdom of (81) God
and the kingdom of the Devil, and we trusted in God for
success and should go ahead.

The following is from the Journal of William R. R.
Stowell: --

"In the year of 1857, under the command of Genl.
West, I was appointed to act as Adjutant for Major
Joseph Taylor, who, with his command, was ordered
out to Echo on the 2nd of October 1857.

"I dreamed I was travelling home through the canyon, having been a prisoner among the soldiers with
another man, besides having made our escape without
any material injury.

"On the event of joining Col. Burton's camp, I lay
down for rest, fell asleep, during which I dreamed of
orders from General Wells for the removal of the entire command, which was verified in a few minutes by

receiving orders from the General above named, for
the command to move to Echo, with the exception of
Major Taylor's command, which was ordered to
Black's Fork. After Major Taylor left for Fort
Bridger, I received orders to forthwith repair to the
same place. After making an advance of two miles,
we were overtaken by Col. Rockwell, who requested
assistance in driving a large herd of cattle. I sent a
sufficient number of men, there being some left to
drive our pack animals to Fort Bridger. (82)

(M.ʳ Stowell was taken prisoner by the U. S.
troops at the same time Joseph Taylor was.)

"Stowell's Examination before Colonel Alexander--
"'Where do you live?.' I replied, 'Ogden City,
Utah County.' 'What is your business out here'? I replied; 'To repel a mob sir.' 'What are your reasons
for supposing us to be a mob'? 'Sir, the Mormons have
been harrassed by mobs from my first aquaintance with
them, while, to be consistent, I maintain that they are
a loyal, peaceable and an industrious people. It has
also been reported to us that there was an army coming from the States, under the name of 'Government
Troops', without any pretext or legal cause; hence we
regard it as vile mobocracy.'

"Col. Alexander seemed indignant. He then
asked, 'Are there many 'Mormons' in the Mountains'?
I replied, 'Yes sir, the mountains are full of them.'
'Are you acquainted with Echo?' 'Yes sir.' 'Are
there many companies in Echo?' 'Yes sir, a great many;
and more coming every day.' 'What is the strength of
the Mormon troops'? 'Probably from 25 to 30 thousand.' 'Have you much artillery?' 'Quite an amount of
it sir; I have seen peices in the different settlements.'

"Many more questions were put to me in a very
austere manner, after which I was marched off to the
guard house. After this I was examined by sargeant
(83) Newman, the one who afterwards attempted to
poison us, and who died a miserable death on Green
River while on his way back to the States; he it was who
found in my bosom our orders from General Wells,
which we had tried to conceal, or destroy, but all our
attempts failed. In a conversation with Col. Alexander,

I was asked if we were going to fulfil the orders we
had received; if so we might commence to kill them,
to which I answered that if they would go back and
mind their own business, we should not interfere with
them.

"On the 17th of Oct., Captain Donovan came to me
and asked me what I thought of Mormonism, to which
I replied that I would rather die than deny my religion.
He then said, 'Damn your religion; we don't care about
it if you will not fight the Government; we shall go to
Salt Lake City and Jesus Christ cannot keep us back.

At the time brother Taylor left, I had been very
bad with the rheumatism for about one week. On the
event of his escape, which, by the by, nobody seemed
to be conscious of for the space of about 15 minutes,
when the officer of the guard came, and on examination found Major Taylor among the missing, it created
great excitement throughout the camp, and a force was
immediately rallied and sent in pursuit of him, which
afterwards returned and reported that they had (84)
found him and killed him. I told them it was a falsehood and that they had not found him.

"After his escape they brought handcuffs to me,
but, being too small, they did not put them on me.

I asked the officer if he thought I was fool enough
to run away and freeze in the mountains. He said he
guessed he would not put them on.

"Almerin Grow, then a returning missionary from
Europe, was taken prisoner at Green River, a few days
before Major Taylor got away. Grow had an interview
with Col. Johnston, who said that they had nothing
against him and that he undoubtedly would soon be released. After some conversation he told the Colonel
that he thought he could give him some information that
would be of service to him, understanding that he was
purposing to go through to Salt Lake City with pack
animals which he (Grow) considered would be very un-
advisable, as he had been reliably informed that the
Mormons had some 3000 men well armed and equipped
in Echo and that if they should make the attempt they
would certainly be cut to pieces. This conversation
caused the Colonel to abandon the idea of going in that

winter.

"Before we got to Bridger their animals died like rotten sheep. On our arrival there I was placed in irons and hand-cuffed to another man. Shortly (85) afterwards I was shackled by the legs to another person, then the handcuffs were taken off. Passing along through some unpleasant circumstances until the Court was organized, when I was arraigned for trial. The clerk, in reading the indictment against me and 70 others, charged us all with the crime of treason against the United States Government, also a multitude of others whom they did not know, to the amount of 1,000 or more. After the indictments were read, I was asked "Guilty or not guilty?" Answer, "Not guilty." "Is the parties ready for trial?" Defendant answered, "Not ready. Time and opportunity were demanded to procure necessary witnesses, appealing for an adjournment till the next time of Court which the judge granted. Passing along until the month of February, when in compliance with previous arrangements, I, with Corporal Nicholson, who was a prisoner also, passed the guard and were shot at, then passed two pickets and two guards guarding the settlers' train, also the dragoons and Volunteers, and, travelling on, we passed Fort Supply. We then took into the mountains, aiming to go over the mountain into Provo Canyon, but on account of the deep snow and want of provisions, found it impossible to reach the summit; we then turned to the right to get into the Emigration Road near Bear River, but (86) finding our strength fast failing, owing to the severity of the weather, and no possible means of obtaining food, we were obliged to return to the soldiers' quarters or perish in the mountains. We therefore resolved to take the best course to save life which we did through much endurance, having froze our face, feet and hands, while our strength was almost exhausted.

"After our return I was again examined by Col. Alexander and placed in charge of the guard with ball and chain. I was visited by Judge Eckles shortly after, who said he would have froze to death in the mountains rather than to have come back; upon which I told him

that I was not ready to die yet. About this time I received a present of a pie from M.rs Wadsworth, who
had been living in Payson, apostatized and gone to the
soldiers. I immediately suspicioned that some trick
was about being played on me. In about a week Col.
Alexander, Judge Eckles and Wadsworth (husband of
M.rs Wadsworth), came to the guard house, and, calling me out asked me how I got along, and presented
me with another pie, Judge Eckles stating that the
weather was extremely cold. He then asked me if I had
any liquor to drink. I answered "No". Suspicion again
arose in my mind that they intended to poison me. I
said that I thought if I took a little it wouldn't (85a) hurt.
The Judge then said, "I have permitted Mr. Wadsworth
to bring you a small bottle of liquor." At the same
time Wadsworth drew the bottle out of his bosom and
handed it to me saying, "M.r Stowell there is some
chloroform in it" I took the bottle into the tent, and,
placing it on the ground drew the cork out and allowed
its contents to empty on the ground. A small portion
remained in it, when it was discovered by one of the
soldiers and drank, whereupon he was immediately
taken sick and conveyed to the hospital for medicine.
Another prisoner remarked, "They have tried to poison Stowell and you have got the dose." I had tasted
of the pie which made me sick; therefore I disposed
of the balance. When I received the bottle of liquor
I was charged by Judge Eckles not to let any of the
other prisoners taste it, and not be found drunk with
it myself.

"They continued to keep me very short of provisions until I saw Governor Cummings and had the
privilege of seeing and talking with him, and was by
him informed that I should not be tried by any jury of
that camp. Some in the camp wanted to have their own
way. He assured me that I should have an impartial
trial.

"Escort came; then the proclamation was issued,
pardoning the Mormons for all they had done, after
(86b) which I was released and came in with the Peace
Commissioners and the Governor, not feeling safe to
start alone, on account of the mobocrats which were

afloat.

"We travelled on till we got near the head of Echo
Canyon, then camped all night, when I was requested to
ride on horseback. After the camp had started and
passing down the canyon, Major MS. Cullough, one of
the Commissioners, left his carriage and changed with
the horsemen, and we together passed over the same
spot of ground, which I had previously dreamt about,
viewing the camp grounds, fortifications, &c, &c, of
the Mormons. In a few hours, I arrived safe at home,
finding that my family had removed to Utah County."

For Brigham Young's letter to Col. E. B.
Alexander, see "Mil Star", Vol. 20 P. 186)

On the 21st, a letter was received from Col. E. B.
Alexander, which closed saying, "He should not obey
the Governor's orders and his final disposal of the
troops would depend upon grave considerations which
I do not deem necessary to enumerate."

Robt. Burton said it was eighty miles from Col.
Alexander's command to the mouth of Echo Canyon.

Gov. B. Young said, "Here are the officers around
me. I will call a council of war. I think it is best for
Genl. Wells to call in all his forces to Echo and there,
rest, and not ride his horses to death un- (87) necessarily, but let the enemy alone now and they will soon
use themselves up. Keep a few to watch their movements and let them work and they will all soon be used
up." Dr. Hickman is with the Fifth Regiment who are
left, and Allen and his companions are with the Tenth
Regiment. Heber Kimball sent Col. Alexander a dozen
onions and the colonel said that if he had anything that
Heber wanted he would send it to him. He asked
Beatie why he tried to stampede their animals and
burn the grass. Beatie replied that he burned the
grass to get a better crop next year.

Some 700 or 800 head of cattle were driven in
about 12 o'clock, accompanied by some teamsters
and soldiers, who looked poor and hungry.

For the special correspondence of the N. Y.
"Tribune," regarding the movements of the U. S.
army &c. &c., see "Mil. Star," Vol. 20 P. 77.

On the 24th Gov. B. Young said, "I am satisfied

that we can live in this Valley and raise crops and keep
our enemies out. It is not in their power to overthrow
us, and by the help of God, we can remain here and
they cannot conquer us. I have reflected this thing
over in my mind, to see what way I could conquer this
people if I were they; and I cannot see, but one way,
and that they will not attempt to take. The United
States have spent three (88) millions of dollars this
season to fit out an army to destroy us and it has done
us no harm. But if I were going to attempt to destroy
this people I should have let them have their post office
and made one million of dollars of appropriation and
given them all they asked for; then spent another million
in carrying in Gentiles and merchandise and keep this
up yearly until I had filled the country with Gentiles;
but the Lord would not let them do this, but I should
know that I could not conquer them by force, and they
will find it out."

Gov. B. Young received word today that the enemy
have returned back on Ham's Fork, some 15 miles.

On the 25th, about 4 P. M., Genl. D. H. Wells,
G. A. Smith and John Taylor arrived. Gov. Young
spent the evening in council with them about the present
state of affairs and future prospects, etc. Gov. Young
said: "I mean to send word to the United States that if
they have sent troops here, the cattle which we have
taken I will give them credit for upon compound interest.
But I do not know that they have sent any; they have not
notified me officially anything about it, and I have no
right to know anything about it, but shall treat them
as a mob."

On the 26th, Peter W. Conover and Oliver Smith
arrived in this City this morning and called on (89)
Gov. Young. They brought news from our Carson
Valley company. Gave a rehearsal of all their travels
to Carson Valley and California and back again, which
was highly interesting. The Carson Valley saints and
they from California and Oregon were on the way to
this city and had 160 fighting men with 2,700 lbs of
ammunition belonging to the Church and a great deal
with private individuals, and a large amount of arms.
They left only two boxes of caps and one lb. of powder

in all Carson Valley.   It was sold to the brethren for
their places.

Gov. Young received a letter from Genl. Grant.
The army are still on Ham's Fork, not decided which
route they will yet take; they had got the chief wagon
masters in custody.

Gov. Young said he wanted San Bernardino,
Carson Valley, to remain and not be disturbed, "for
I want the people there to bring stock to supply us
from time to time as we need".   One young officer of
the army said "Jesus Christ could not keep them out
of Salt Lake City,' and another said, "The United
States would wipe us out another year, should they
send an army of 20,000 men. John Taylor said "Will
not the army go into Winter Quarters and remain there
until they get help from the United States?" Gov.
Young said "If an army comes to help (90) them in the
spring, we will use up this army first, then we will
use up the other before they get to the South Pass. In
the spring we must ask Alexander what he intends to
do; inform him he must not stay here until he gets
reinforcements, and if they will not leave in the spring
we will put 2,000 men around them, which would soon
use them up. I do not believe that they will have 500
fighting men in the spring. They are in a very critical
situation. They say they have no other way to get a
living for their families but to war. I think it is better
to let the army alone this winter. Many of them will
die, others desert and many be weakened with the
scurvy, and in the spring we will wipe them out if necessary, if they do not go away. We do all our business
in the name of Israel's God, and they in their own way.
The whole matter can be summed up in these few words,
'We are here at home by our own firesides, while they
are a great way from home.' I intend to send those
teamsters to the south, where they cannot get back to
the army."

For "Camp on Pacific Creek, Oregon Territory,"
see "Mil. Star," Vol. 20, P. 78.

November

On the 2nd, the California mail arrived, bringing news that the contract for the Eastern mail was let, and was to have started on Oct. 1st. (91)

Gov. B. Young sent a letter to Washakie, Chief of the Shoshones, requesting him not to fight, neither for nor against us; also a letter to Isaac C. Haight to procure an interpreter for Mr. Bell and company, who are about to start for San Bernardino.

Account of the return of the Carson Mission, given by Madison Daniel Hambleton:--

The express from Great Salt Lake City calling the mission home arrived in Wassau Valley (Washoe) Carson County, just after sun rise on Saturday, the 5th of September, 1857, requiring the mission to return to Salt Lake City en masse.

Three weeks from that day, 26th of Sept., the camp started with the exception of three families, viz., Moore, John Dilworth and John Hawkins. Moore and Dilworth went directly over the mountain, on the first arrival of the mission, and stayed there; Hawkins stayed in Wassau (Washoe) Valley.

Previous to our return home, we gathered some $800 in cash and sent to San Francisco, and laid it out for powder, lead and caps.

We had in the company 123 wagons, and about 450 souls. The men were divided into twelve companies, and the companies were divided into two divisions. Capt. William R. Smith over the first division; John Little over the second. Chester Loveland (92) Captain over the whole company. Madison D. Hambleton, Captain over the Guard.

We were 37 days on the road, reaching Salt Lake City Nov. 2nd. One man, Ralph Thompson, was run over by a wagon the morning we started and had his leg broken. He suffered considerable pain from the motion of the wagon, but was doing remarkably well when we arrived here. Three infant children died on the road. Had six births. Had some considerable sickness on the route from the distemper prevalent.

On the 3rd, an express arrived by Jos. A. Young,

with a letter from Col. E. B. Alexander, saying, "He thanked him for sending him his prisoners, and he would send back his prisoners, only he had a civil process against them."

Several California prisoners were taken today and brought into this city, they are supposed to be robbers from the mountains.

On the 8th, at 9 A. M., an express arrived from Gen. D. H. Wells, demanding help, as Col. Johnston seemed likely to want to push in. Letters were written to several militia officers, to muster men to send out.

Joseph Taylor had escaped from the enemy after being chased thirty miles barefoot.

On the 9th, John Taylor was sent to the assistance (93) of D. H. Wells, commanding.

Miner G. Attwood and Wm. H. Branch arrived about 4 P. M. They started from the States with hand carts in the spring.

On the 10th, 1300 men were ordered into the mountains, in addition to those already there, Cols. Phileman and C. Merrill commanding.

The Davis County militia passed the Governor's Office, for the mountains, with 242 men, 56 of whom were mounted; 17 officers of the line and 4 of the Colonel's staff. They had 23 baggage wagons. They continued their march towards the mountains of snow, as nearly 2,000 of their brethren had done before to meet the enemy. Many went with wet feet, poor shoes, and straw hats, without tents or fire at night, as they could not reach timber until next day. It was a very cold night. It was reported that there was eight feet of snow on top of the Big Mountain, over which the militia had to pass.

Very cold weather. Some of the men returned with frozen feet.

Under the unfavorable circumstances Gov. B. Young had maintained a steady and calm deportment, although his health at times was not good.

On the 11th, Geo. Chase, also G. W. Hickman and (94) Elijah Ward arrived with expresses from Gen. D. H. Wells. Hickman was detained for a time by the enemy. He said Capt. Marcy had used him very

well, and the army had concluded to come into G. S.
L. Valley on pack animals in twelve days.

Gov. B. Young sent J. M. Barlow and Henry
Brizzee with an express to Gen. D. H. Wells, with
instructions about returning jaded animals, wagons,
and thinly clad men. Some of the latter might cook
and be around about camp. Also not to attempt to run
off stock, owing to the inclement weather, but watch
the movements of the enemy.

On the 15th, Jerome Remington brought an express
from Gen. D. H. Wells, who recommended that the
Saints be united in their prayers, that the soldiers
might return and that we might not have to shed their
blood.

On the 21st, Gov. A. Cumming addressed a proclamation from near Fort Bridger, to the people of
Utah Territory, and wrote a letter to Gov. B. Young,
for which see "Millennial Star," Vol. 20 P. 125.

On the 26th, Benj. Simons called and had an interview with Gov. B. Young. He had been two days in the
camp of the enemy, gave information about the enemy's
movements and determinations. Said they were very
much in need of salt and their (95) animals were dying
fast. Also that they were cutting timber and digging
holes in the earth, which looks very much like their
going into Winter Quarters.

The merchants were suffering for want of food;
they ought to suffer, for they had been the means of
bringing on this war in a great measure.

On the 27th, Gov. B. Young sent out to the enemy
a load of salt, and also a letter to the commander.

On the 28th, Mr. Simons arrived with an express
saying that Gov. Cummings, Lieut. Col. Philip and
Lieut. Geo. Cook, 2nd Dragoons, the Ex-commander
of the Mormon Battalion in Mexico had arrived in the
enemy's camp, with other officers, on Saturday and
Sunday, last, with about 300 dragoons. They had
covered over the walls of Fort Bridger, and the corral
for storage, but their operations looked like a temporary work and not like winter quarters for the whole
army. It was still thought that they might attempt to
come into G. S. L. Valley.

On the 29th, an express arrived by the hands of Van Ettan and Terry; also a writing of A. Cummings to the people of Utah, which was read from the stand.

An express was sent out by Prest. Young to Gen. D. H. Wells at 1 P. M., principally to suggest that (96) Genl. D. H. Wells and the men return home, with the exception of a few to remain as scouts.

December

On the 1st, in the evening, Prest. Young was waited upon by Genl. C. C. Rich, and others who had returned from the Camp of Israel. The Genl. stated that with the exception of about fifty of the men, all the rest would return home in a few days. Genl. Wells would also return, and there was every probability of the mules and cattle of the enemy being frozen.

On the 2nd, the militia began to arrive early in the morning, having been dismissed by Genl. Wells, and they continued to pour into the city until a late hour.

Sometime during the day, A. Grow and H. S. Southworth arrived. They had been sometime detained as prisoners in the enemy's camp. A. Grow had been to Europe on a mission and H. S. Southworth went last spring to the States on a mission, and they were on their way home when they were taken. Mr. Southworth was taken prisoner on Green River by an officer in Capt. Cook's Horse company and put under guard with orders for the guard to shoot him, if he got five paces from him. He travelled under guard in this way until he got (97) to the main encampment, he was then put with the main prisoners of the camp and guarded with the mass. He came up with Howard Livingston; he wished Mr. Livingston to intercede with Col. Johnston to let him go home to his family, as they had nothing against him only that he was a Mormon. Mr. Livingston would do nothing for him. He reported that there was much of the spirit of desertion in the camp, as the officers treated the soldiers in a cruel manner. There were more ardent spirits than anything else in court.

On the 3rd, the California mail arrived in the
morning, and many of the militia returned to G. S. L.
City.

On the 7th, Capt. Clark's company of fifty returned home.

On the 11th, Mr. Holbrook said two men had been
killed in the south by the Indians and that W^m. M. Wall
and his company had hard work to get along amoung
them. Brother Wall had just returned from a mission
in Australia and had brought a company of Saints with
him to California. He there met Dr. Andrews and
other apostate Mormons, and they gathered a mob and
tried to kill him, but he boldly maintained his ground
and got away from them. He came on with the mail
and his (98) company was coming on behind him.

On the 14th, Gov. Young attended the Legislature.

On the 15th, the Assembly met in joint session at
10 A. M. Gov. Young presented his message which
was read. (See "Millennial Star," Vol. 20, P. 218.)

On the 16th, Ben. Simons arrived in the afternoon
and called upon Gov. B. Young with D. B. Huntington.
He said there were two or three classes of men now in
the army; one party the military and one was called
freeman. There was a fight between them, and seven
men were killed. Col. Johnston sent the military to
quell the mob, and Gov. Cummings told them to go
back, that when he wanted their assistance he would
call for it. The Superintendent of Indian Affairs said,
he had got a million of gold to give the Indians in this
Territory. One man gathered up one bag of salt, that
our men threw away, which was sent by the Governor,
but rejected by Col. Johnston. The man sold it to the
merchants for $20, and they sold it to the soldiers for
two or three dollars per lb. Ben Simons took out 900
lbs. of salt, and sold it for $2.50 per lb., making
$2,250, and $1.00 per lb. for service berries. Ben
Simons offered to give Gov. B. Young one half of the
money he made.

Gov. Young told him he didn't want any of his
money, he had enough of his own, but as he (99) wanted
to make some, he let him have the privilege.

Livingston said he would give $500 for the privilege of coming into the city if he did not stop but one day. M.Graw is the worst man in the army and has the most to say about us. There were 500 men who had left for the States, several of whom had frozen to death.

John Bigler, a great gambler, took out of the army in one day, by gambling $25,000 and carried it off in a buckskin sack. Ben Simons wanted to continue the trade and has another Cherokee to have a pass to go to him. Gov. Young asked him if he had not made money enough. He replied that he wished to make all he could. Gov. Young said that he must not take the enemy anything to eat; he might sell them salt and fur, but nothing to eat. They said there were plenty of potatoes and turnips at Fort Supply, but Gov. Cummings would not let them have them. Gov. Young said if they had powder they would make this city a perfect bedlam, and corrupt the people as far as they could.

For Resolutions expressive of the sense of the Legislative Assembly of the Territory of Utah, relative to the message and official course of his excellency Gov. Young, see "Des. News," Vol. 7, pp. 332-.

On the 26th, three prisoners who had been kept in custody in G. S. L. City some time, were (100) returned to the army, taking with them several copies of the Governor's Message and "Deseret News."

On the 31st, several persons came in from San Bernardino.

There was a very hostile spirit in California. They were driving out everything that ever smelt of Mormonism. The road from San Bernardino was lined with people on their way to G. S. L. Valley. (103)

INCIDENTS IN THE HISTORY OF UTAH

January 1858

On the 3rd, the California mail arrived, with news that O. Pratt, E. T. Benson, John Kay, John Scott and other missionaries, returning from England, had reached San Bernardino, on the 9th ult.

On the 4th, Gov. B. Young, by request of the Legislative Assembly, transmitted to that body, a copy of correspondence between himself and Cols. E. B. Alexander and A. S. Johnson. (See "Des. News," Jan. 13, p. 354.)

On the 6th, the Legislative Assembly adopted a memorial to the President and Congress (See "Des. News," Jan. 13, p. 357.)

John Taylor, speaker of the House of Representatives of the Legislative Assembly, on request of that body, furnished it with a copy of correspondence, between himself and Mr. W. J. A. Fuller, and Cap. R. B. Marcy, U. S. A. (See "Des. News," Jan. 13, p. 355.)

On the 7th, Geo. A. Smith forwarded to J. M. Bernhisel a copy of the Constitution of the State of Deseret, as Gov. B. Young had written him to present our petition for admission, hit or miss. Also mailed a "Deseret News" extra, and Gov. Young's message to members of Congress and others.

On, or about the 6th, John Taylor and Geo. A. Smith, delegates from the convention and people of Utah Territory presented the Legislative Assembly, a report of their labors. (See "Des. News," Jany. 20, p. 368.) (104)

On the 16th, at a mass meeting held in the Tabernacle, G. S. L. City, addresses and preamble and resolutions to the President and to Congress, were adopted.

On the 19th, O. Pratt, E. T. Benson, John Scott, and John Kay, arrived from Europe, accompanied from California by Geo. Q. Cannon, H. Mc. Ewan, Joseph

Bull, Samuel Miles, and Howard Egan. Many other persons also arrived from California during the winter.

The session of the Legislative Assembly closed on the 22nd. It established a weekly express mail to every part of the Territory.

The winter was a very mild one.

During this month and February, mass meetings were held at various other cities and settlements in the Territory, at which resolutions were adopted approving of the course of Gov. Young, and the action of the Legislature. (See "Deseret News," of the time.)

February

By the latter end of this month, the people of the Territory had voluntarily raised an armed force of a thousand mounted men, at an estimated expense of a million dollars, for the purpose of going into the mountains to defend the Territory.

On the 22nd, the Deseret Bank, Capital based on cattle, commenced issuing its bills, the plates of which had been engraved by David M^{c}. Kenzie.

On the 24th, Thos. L. Kane, of Philadelphia, Pa., (105) arrived in G. S. L. City. He had come from Washington, and left New York on the California mail steamer, Jan. 5, and travelled as Dr. Osborne.

On the 25th, he had an interview with Governor B. Young, and several other prominent gentlemen.

On Sunday, 28th, in the Tabernacle, Heber C. Kimball predicted the downfall of Stephen A. Douglas.

March

On the 8th, Col. Thos. L. Kane left G. S. L. City for Fort Bridger to visit the U. S. army. Gov. B. Young furnished him as escort.

The Indians in Rush Valley, westward, became troublesome at this time, stealing horses and cattle, threatening life, and shooting at the settlers. Gov. Young advised that the women and children and the live stock be removed to Tooele Valley. Segoet and Warahat were the Chiefs and leaders of the depredating

bands in those valleys. Warahat said he was opposed
to killing the Mormons, but an express arrived from
Rush Valley, stating that the Indians had driven off
cattle and fired upon the settlers.

On the 17th, at sunset, an express arrived, saying that thirty Indians had shot at the men in Rush
Valley and driven off all the cattle they could find.
They would have massacred all the families there, but
were kept off by eight armed men, who had just (106)
arrived in time to save them. Brigham Young ordered
fifty mounted men to start by daylight next morning;
his own wagons and teams to go and carry baggage.

On the 18th, three signal guns were fired in the
morning, for the armed men to gather. Sixty or
seventy men started on horseback and many baggage
wagons followed, with instructions to take the Indians,
bring them into G. S. L. City, and try them, shut
them up, and keep them as hostages for the good be-
havior of the others.

A council of war was called at the Historian's
Office at 2 p.m.: Present:-- Brigham Young, H. C.
Kimball, D. H. Wells, C. C. Rich, O. Hyde, O. Pratt,
W. Woodruff, G. A. Smith, F. D. Richards, E. T.
Benson, E. Snow, A. Carrington, and thirty military
officers. Speeches were made by the Presidency,
Twelve and other officers present. Brigham Young's
plan was to go into the desert and not war with the
people, but let them destroy themselves.

On the 22nd, the standing army of 1000 men had
been fitted up with a riding horse and pack animal to
each man, with revolvers and rifles, all fitted for active service.

On the 23rd, a friendly Indian told us, that their
chief had been to the soldiers' camp, and that Col.
Johnson, or Harney had told him that Brigham Young
had killed thousands of their children, and he would
kill them. The officers also told them that Joseph
Smith (107) was a good captain, and they had got his
head off easily; and Brigham Young was a small captain and they would soon cut off his head. In this way
they stirred up the Indians to war against us.

On the 29th, in the evening, the officers of the

Nauvoo Legion held council and determined to send out
six battalions into the mountains, as it was expected
that Gen. Johnson would attempt to push his way into
G. S. L. City, as soon as the mountains were passable,
and their animals able to travel.

On the 31st, companies of footmen started out into
the mountains to defend the passes, at Echo Cañon.

On the last days of this month, the books and papers
in the Church Historian's Office, were packed up and
sent to Provo. The cut rock for the Temple and the
foundation were covered with earth by plowing and
scraping the ground around. Many teams were in the
city, to carry people and church property to Provo.

April

On the 5th, Geo. A. Smith wrote to T. B. H.
Stenhouse, New York City, as follows--

"It is a general time of health, and everybody appears in good spirits. The people are vacating Salt
Lake City, and flying to the mountains. About three
hundred families left last week, as it is understood
here that the Government has ordered large reinforcements (108) to Utah, for the extermination of the
faithful, who will be found, probably, (if found at all,)
in rocks and deserets, or, like the ancient Saints, hid
in dens and caves of the earth.

"It has been the policy of Governor Young and our
people to keep the Indians neutral, should a contest.
ensue. I read in the last papers received from the
States loud boasts of having secured the Utah and other
Indians as allies against the Mormons. Strange as it
may seem to civilized persons, all the reckless and
unprincipled Indians of the mountains have been hired,
with new guns, blankets, clothing, ammunition, paint,
&c., to steal, rob, murder, and do anything else that
can be done to destroy the 'Mormons.' Indian agents
have sent messengers to all the peaceable Indians to
incite them to deeds of rapine and bloodshed. A number of scattering settlements have been attacked, and
innocent blood stains the skirts of the present administration, whose agents have procured the murders.

"I am an American, as you well know. I love my
country, and hate to see her rulers trample under foot
her glorious institutions, and re-enact barbarism
more cruel than that inflicted by the King of Great
Britain, through the hands of the red men upon the
scattered settlements of the colonies, in the war of
Independence. We wish 'life, liberty and the (109)
pursuit of happiness. '

"With 3,500 bayonets, rifles, revolvers and
ordinance pointed at us, and within three days' march
of our City, 4,500 more en route to reinforce them
carte blanche on the U. S. treasury, would seem
enough to satisfy our most bitter persecutors, without
hiring as allies, the savage hordes of the deserts and
mountains to murder, scalp, roast, and eat their fellow citizens, because they forsooth differed on the subject of religion.

"Who can believe it?-- the cause is rather odd.

"Men hate each other for the love of God!

"You are aware that all the Indian outrages in the
country, heretofore, have been caused by men who are
enemies to the inhabitants of this Territory--who have
passed through our borders and recklessly shot at and
otherwise abused the Indians.

"Experience shows that Indians, like congressmen
and government officials have their price.

"My new house is just ready to move into. Cost
about $12,000. I have sent my family away. I think
my buildings will make a good fire, should Johnson
advance on a sudden.

"I had hoped my family might have enjoyed a little
rest and eat the fruit of my little orchard, containing
one hundred and fifty assorted trees, many of which
are budded for fruit. (110)

"I have been driven from Missouri, where I left a
good property and planted fruit trees for somebody else
to eat. I passed through the same ordeal in Illinois. I
preferred leaving my homes to renouncing my religion.
The Government expelled me from Nebraska, although
they were well aware of my intention to leave in a few
months, for the mountains; and I can go again and a-
gain, until death shall furnish me a quiet resting place,

should our insane countrymen continue to trample the sacred rights of freemen, guaranteed by the institutions and blood of their fathers, under their feet with impunity.

"We have the pleasing reflection that our only crime is following the religion and practices of the Father of the Faithful, in whose bosom all Christians expect to rest."

On the 6th, the General Conference of the Church was held in the Tabernacle, G. S. L. City, and was adjourned, subject to the call of the President, Brigham Young.

On the same day, Brigham Young gave orders for all the people in G. S. L., Davis, and Tooele Counties to move into Utah County, and stop at the settlements of Dry Creek, (Lehi) American Fork, Pleasant Grove, Provo, Spanish Fork, Hobble Creek, (Springville) and Peteetneet. For the people of Ogden City to move to G. S. L. City, and the people north of Ogden to move to Ogden, (111) to send their inefficient men with the teams and keep their valiant men behind, with their guns always where they could lay their hands on them, and be prepared to fly at a moment's warning to meet the enemy. In this way to clear all the families, grain and property into Utah County, except such as were hauled away by the teams, which had come from the south, and such as were councelled to go.

After all the people had left G. S. L. City, it was the intention to leave an army to water the grain and take care of it, and if Johnson approached, to be ready to meet him.

For Proclamation of President James Buchanan, see public documents.

On the 7th, Brigham Young directed Orson Pratt to take his families to Fillmore, with their herds. He also wrote to C. C. Pendleton, of Parowan, to get his machine shop and water power for a public gun shop, machine shop, &c. He directed the press and types to be loaded for Fillmore, and George Q. Cannon to go in company. He wanted the next California mail to carry a paper from Fillmore to the States, He intended the other press to be taken to Parowan, so that the suc-

ceeding California mail would take a paper from that
point. He also directed Col. W^m. H. Dame to raise
sixty or seventy men in his district, to fit (112) them
out with tools, seed, grain and water barrels, and
explore the desert west and north of Parowan. They
were to take their departure from Pinto Creek and explore west and north across the desert, and take loads
of water and make deposits along, sending back wagons
as they were unloaded. They were directed to treat
the Indians in a friendly manner, learn their language,
and teach them how to work. W. Woodruff furnished
Dame with three pints of sugar cane seed and some
King Philip and White Flint corn.

Bishop Rowberry and the people of Tooele were
directed to settle at Dry Creek (Lehi).

On the 8th, A.M., a company from Ogden arrived.

An express from Echo Cañon arrived with the news
that Col. Thos. L. Kane and Gov. Cumming were
there, on their way to G. S. L. City. Gov. Cumming
met our outposts at Quaking Asp Hill. He was chal-
lenged by Howard Egan. Cummings saw one hundred
mounted men, while there. He remarked that they
were fine soldiers. He passed through Echo Canyon
in the night. The men had a number of camp fires
burning and a strong guard on duty. They formed two
lines, and as he passed down they presented arms. He
halted and made a speech. Said he hoped the day was
near when the peaceable inhabitants of Utah would be
allowed to follow their peaceful avocations, (113) without having to be in the mountains. His speech to a
great extent repudiated his last winter's proclamation.

Brigham Young Junr. and N. V. Jones came into
the Governor's Office, a little before dark. They had
just come from the mouth of Echo Canyon, where they
left Col. Kane and Gov. Cumming to take a day's
shooting. Gov. Cumming had a carriage and wagon,
two drivers, and Col. Kane in company.

Brigham Young sent serveral teams to Utah Co.;
many of them mired on the road. They had families
in them and the wagons were uncovered. Snow fell ten
inches deep where the men passed over the Big Mountain.

On the 9th, Col. Andrew Cunningham, who went
north with 200 men, to the relief of the settlers--from
Salmon River, returned. He had been absent one
month and travelled 800 miles. He left Thos. Smith,
with 22 teams and 70 men, at Spring Creek, and came
home with the balance of his command. It stormed
nearly all the time he was gone.

At Salmon River, Old Snagg and his band were
very sorry to have the settlers leave, and did their
best to have them recover their cattle. They found a
few of them, and gave Old Snagg and his band 200 bushels of wheat, and made him agent to dispose of 1,000
bushels of wheat, for the mission, which was left in
bins. (114) Snag was to change it for horses, fur, &c.
One Indian followed the company; he said he would
starve if the Mormons left. Many of the Indians cried
when the brethren left.

The murders of Miller, etc., at Salmon River,
and the robberies were committed at the instigation of
white men, Powell, the mountaineer, being with the
Indians that did it

Col. N. V. Jones said several of the brethren had
been to Ben Simond's camp on Bear River and were
told at three different times they were our friends; but
that Gen. Johnson had offered them 150\frac{00}{}$ for every
Mormon they would bring him, and $1,000$\frac{00}{}$ for Lot
Smith. Ben Simond said he would not accept offer,
for he was our friend; but that he expected an agent
there to distribute $15,000$\frac{00}{}$ of presents among the
Indians; there were one thousand Indian warriors on the
ground. Our brethren regarded them with suspicions,
although Simonds said, after he had got the presents,
he would tell what he would do.

At this time there were six hundred of our men in
the mountains, Col. Thos. Callister in command.

On the 10th, Gen. W. H. Kimball arrived with the
intelligence that A. Cumming and Col. Kane were at
Ben Simond's ranche on the Weber, to have another
day's shooting in that beautiful valley.

On the 12th, the city corporation, mayor, alderman, (115) and some councillors, went out to meet
Gov. Cumming, who had said that he did not want to

govern a people, if they did not want him. He was met
near the Hot Springs, four miles north, and escorted
to the city. The Governor put up with W^m. C. Staines.
The roads were lined with wagons, cattle, pigs, sheep,
and the brethren and sisters who were coming in from
the north. It was remarked that the brethren looked
fine. Gov. Cumming replied "Yes, but he was sorry
to see them used in that way, and the people fleeing
from their homes."

Gov. Cumming stated in his remarks, when he
was met by the city corporation, that he prided himself in presiding over a people, who knew their rights
and dared to maintain them. He also said, "I come to
enforce the law," which is no new thing to Mormon
ears. So said Gov. Ford to the citizens of Nauvoo,
while his confederates were murdering the prophets.
Not the first act of Gov. Cumming, since he entered
the Territory, had been in accordance with the laws
of the United States. He organized a temporary government, where a permanent one was already in exis-
tence. He located a seat of government in a military
camp, (one hundred miles from the settlements)
issuing a proclamation, declaring all the citizens of
the Territory traitors; proclaimed the organization of
a court in violation of the laws of Congress, which
declared that (116) a court should not be held until the
three supreme judges should meet at the capitol and
determine the times and places; and all this without
his being legally sworn into office, which rendered his
acts a farce. He sent two missionaries, who had been
picked up on the way, and detained as prisoners for
being Mormons in religion, in the snow and cold, without blankets or sufficient clothing, to bear his proclamation to the people of Utah; and as if in bitter
irony, he requested the receipt to be acknowledged by
return messengers. The above named messengers
were picked up about midnight, nearly perishing with
cold and fatigue, by some scouts, who were watching
the road.

The camp which formed his seat of government,
was strictly guarded, and no citizen of the Territory
was permitted to approach, for any purpose whatever,

except with a flag of truce, on pain of being fired upon.

Judge Eccles, in holding court, proved himself either entirely ignorant of the law or utterly regardless of its provisions.

Col. Kane told Gov. Cumming that he (Kane) had more friends here than in any other part of the world, or all the rest of the world.

Brigham Young remarked to Geo. A. Smith, that he did not feel the least gloom over the city, nor had he felt but what we should remain and finish the Temple. (117)

On the 13th, the men at the Public Works were making bins to hold 73 bushels of wheat, which were put in wagons, then the wheat was put into them. One empty bin was carried in a train and the wheat was emptied into the bin, and thus they did not need to empty the wheat, save in the bins.

Jesse N. Smith reported that he met the San Pete teams, on the divide south of Santaquin, in a severe snow storm. Snow eight inches deep and mud one foot; wagons not covered and women and children all exposed.

John Sharp took out a train of eleven wagons, averaging 3500 lbs. of flour or wheat.

Ben Simonds and Jim Cherokee, visited Brigham Young and expressed themselves as very friendly. Instead of the agents giving the Indians the presents promised, they gave some powder and lead, and 50 lbs. of tobacco to 500 Indians; but promised them big presents in a little while.

On the 13th, Col. Kane visited Brigham Young and said Gov. Cumming wished to see him. In the afternoon Brigham Young and Geo. A. Smith called on Gov. Cumming, at Wm C. Staines' (site of William Jennings' Devereux House) and were introduced by Col. Kane. Conversation ensued upon the weather, the valley, the improvements, his journey through the mountains, (118) and his surprise thereat, his reception and his satisfaction therewith.

On the 14th, Brigham Young sent a pack of sugar cane seed (sorghum) to be distributed among the Iron County farmers.

He also had an interview and exchange of sentiments with Gov. Cumming.

News came of Indian depredations at Lehi and in
Box Elder County.

Joseph Horne reported by letter, that they had
built a dam of rock, gravel and brush, 12 feet high,
across the Rio Virgen, and commenced clearing land
for the new cotton farm. They had grubbed six acres.
They dug and stoned a well, 12 feet deep, which afforded an abundant supply of water.

On the 15th, Gov. Cumming requested W. H.
Hooper, as secretary, to furnish him a schedule of the
property in his hands, belonging to the United States,
and an account of the Indian aggressions in the Territory.

In conversation, Gov. Cumming expressed himself as favorably impressed with the leading men of the
community.

On the 15th, eleven wagons with about seventy
bushels of wheat in each, and five yoke of cattle to each
wagon, started for Provo in charge of Edmund Ellswork.

For communications of Gov. Cumming to Col. A.
S. (119) Johnson, and Secretary Lewis Cass, see Public Documents.

On the 16th, eight wagons loaded with wheat, and
four with machinery, started for Provo, in charge of
Adam Sharp.

Brigham Young wrote to Gov. Cumming, offering
to furnish the army with provisions and such supplies
as were obtainable, until the army supplies from the
east arrived.

On the 18th, orders were issued for two-thirds of
the men in the mountains to return home.

John B. Kimball and Fay Worthen started to Col.
Johnson's camp, with dispatches from Gov. Cumming,
who sent copies of Sec'y. Hooper's reports of Indian
aggressions, and requested him, (Col. Johnson) to
secure the stock and punish the thieves, if they came
into his camp.

James Ferguson, Hosea Stout, and J. C. Little,
visited Gov. Cumming, who said he had examined the
court records and was astonished to see they were not
burned. He and Col. Kane visited the Utah Library and

he expressed his astonishment that it was not burned
up. He then went to Capt. Hooper's and enquired for
the safe belonging to the Secretary of the Territory.
Capt. Hooper took him into his barn. Gov. Cumming
asked him why he had the safe in such an out of the way
place. Capt. Hooper replied that we were going to
burn the city and did not want to burn any United States'
property. (120)

James W. Cummings showed Gov. Cumming the
records of the U. S. District Court. He gave James
W. Cummings an order, styling him Clerk of the U. S.
District Court, on W̄ᵐ̄ H. Hooper, Secy. pro tem, for
a safe to keep the district court papers and records;
thereby acknowledging Hooper and Cummings.

On the 20th, the memorial of Delegates of the convention, for a state constitution, and the Constitution,
were read in the U. S. Senate, and ordered to be
printed.

H. C. Kimball and D. H. Wells visited Gov.
Cumming, and spent four or five hours in conversation
with him.

On the 21st, Brigham Young, though in very feeble
health, started from G. S. L. City, accompanied by
G. A. Smith, Ed. D. Woolley and Samuel Sprague, M.
D., and a train of his own teams, loaded with lumber,
and arrived at American Fork in the evening. The
roads were lined with teams; they seemed to be passing through the fort all night.

A. Cumming, accompanied by Gen. W. H.
Kimball, Major H. Egan, and Surveyor General J. W.
Fox, started for Rush Valley, to take a look at the
military reserve in said Valley.

On the 22nd, Brigham Young and party arrived at
Provo. He selected a vacant block or public square to
lie east of the meeting house block, for a location for
temporary store houses. Eighteen loads of lumber
(121) which had been brought from the City, was unloaded and hands were immediately set to work to dig
post holes and commence the erection of a store house,
150 feet long, side posts to be 9 feet.

Geo. W. Bean returned from about 115 miles
west of Fillmore, 160 miles by the way the exploring

party of pioneers travelled. He reported that Bishop
Evans' report of that company was correct. The difficulty was to find soil, timber and water together.
They found a lake a quarter of a mile broad, and a
mile and a half long, at the outlet of which they were
going to farm. They had encountered severe storms
and consequently suffered much. The country was
desolate looking. Encountered 40 Indians.

On the 24th, Brigham Young and W. Woodruff returned to G. S. L. City.

A number of persons called on Gov. Cumming.
They generally wished to see him alone, and their
wants were, a little tobacco, sugar, coffee, tea, &c.
One man said he thought a thousand dollars would do to
get him away from Utah.

On the 28th, Brigham Young visited Gov. Cumming,
who said: "I can do nothing here without your influence."
He should require the U. S. Army to remain where it
was; should report to Washington that he had investigated, and found that the charges (122) against the people of Utah were false.

On the 30th, Brigham Young appointed 100 men to
remain in Box Elder County, and take care of the grain
on the ground, &c.; 300 in Weber Co.; 75 in Davis Co.;
30 in Tooele Co., and 300 in Salt Lake County, for the
same purpose.

In his last interview, Gov. Cumming enquired of
Brigham Young if there was not some way to stop the
moving. Brigham Young replied that if the troops
were withdrawn from the Territory, the people would
stop moving, but that 99 out of every hundred of the
people would rather live out their lives in the mountains than endure the oppression the Federal Government was now heaping upon them. Gov. Cumming said
he would do all he could to prevent the troops from
coming into the settlements, and more from coming
into the Territory, and, if they would come in he would
say to the people, "Take care of yourselves." And that
he would show Brigham Young his reports to the Gover-
ment.

May

On the 3rd, the California mail brought the news
that the Bill asking for an increase of the U. S. army,
was completely defeated, in the Senate, which caused
the enemies of the Latter-day Saints to howl.

On the 4th, Gov. Cumming told Ex Gov. Young
(123) that he was going to the army to fetch his wife,
and he should require the army to remain where they
were until he received returns from the dispatches he
had just sent, and if they refused to obey his orders,
he should call on the militia of the Territory to see
that they did.

Every man opposed to the Senate Bill to increase
the U. S. army, was characterized by the Administration as a "Mormon Sympathizer" and the Administration organs howled most piteously.

Copies of indictment of the court held in Johnson's
Camp had also been printed, and included the Presidency of the Church, Editor of the "Deseret News",
and a thousand others, whose names were unknown to
the jury. It also stated that on receiving the resolutions of the Legislative Assembly, a special term of
the Grand Jury was called, for the purpose of indicting
every member and officer, who signed them, for high
treason. Efforts had been made to indict Dr. Bernhisel.
They had   Howell, whom they styled a Mormon leader, before the Court, but put off his trial because he
had no witnesses. Cherokee Thompson had been arrested and put in irons. They represented him as a
leading Danite and murderer, and, according to their
reports, had performed feats that would throw Jack the
Giant Killer into the shade. (124)

On the 5th, Gov. Cumming, Col. Kane and Gen'l.
W. H. Kimball arrived in Provo and passed on to
Spanish Fork to visit the Indian farm. Gov. Cumming
requested Major Armstrong, Indian Agent, to meet
him at the farm in the evening.

The Administration evinced its fixed determination
to send 6,000 troops to Utah, and some of the papers
howled piteously at the defeat of the army bill, and
thought that should the army be withdrawn before its

close, Congress would authorize volunteers to supply their place.

Preparations were making to send Col. Kane by the eastern route to the States, as he wished to return. The death of Judge Kane, his father, would hurry him.

On the 6th, Col. Kane and Gov. Cumming arrived in G. S. L. City, having met 800 wagons in coming from Springville. It made Gov. Cumming feel bad to see the moving.

James Ferguson wrote a very cutting letter to Col. P. St. Geo. Cooke, of the 2nd Dragoons, in answer to Cooke's libellous letter, published in the "N. Y. Times", in which he denounced the Mormons as thieves, robbers, assassins, cowards, &c.

On the 10th, the messenger returned from the army. Col. Johnson said he should come in on the (125) 1st of June, and plant one post in G. S. L. City, and another on Provo Bench.

On the 11th, G. S. L. City was nearly vacated and the settlements north were entirely so. An average of about six hundred wagons had passed through the City daily, for two weeks.

On the 12th, Gov. Cumming wrote to Ex. Gov. B. Young, as follows:

"I regret to be obliged to answer your letter of the 8th, inst., in haste. I would thank you for the complimentary notice of myself, which it contains, but more for the tender you make of your continued exertions to advance the public good. I know the value of your services and exhort you patriotically to persevere.

"I trust particularly that you will succeed in persuading those who respect your opinion, and who are moving south, that there is no ground for the apprehension, which they appear to entertain. You may assure them that no effort on my part will be spared to restrain the troops at Bridger from a further advance, until a reply is received by me to dispatches which I have transmitted from this city to the Secretary of State at Washington."

On the 13th, Gov. Cumming and Col. Kane left G. S. L. City for Bridger, the latter on his way to Washington. (126)

On the 15th, E. M. Green, and his brother John Y., who had just arrived from Europe, called upon Brigham Young, with the information that the company left by S. W. Richards, viz: Jeter Clinton, L. H. Hatch, John W. Turner, and John M. Wakely had been arrested near Bridger, by the U. S. troops, but had been released on Wakely giving bonds in $5,000 to appear before the U. S. District court held in G. S. L. City, to answer to a charge of the murder of Long Bill, at Bridger.

One hundred and thirty men were detailed from Provo, to relieve the men at Echo Canyon Station.

On the 17th, Ex Gov. B. Young engaged the services of Jesse Fox, Surveyor General, to take a water level on the Provo Bench, to see if Provo River could not be taken upon the bench.

There was a great lack of clothing among the people at this time, which made it very hard for the militia in the mountains.

Many of the people in Utah County felt discouraged about putting in garden seeds, planting, etc., on account of a fear that they would be driven away and not reap the result of their labors.

Ex. Gov. B. Young said the greatest inducement to go back to G. S. L. City would be to build the Temple.

A Battalion of Infantry, under the command of Col. W^m. B. Pace, and thirty mounted men, under the command (127) of Capt. Abraham Conover, started for the stations in Echo Canyon to relieve the men there.

On the 18th, Dr. Clinton gave Ex. Gov. Young an account of his trip across the plains. He said he had formed some acquaintance with Col. Johnson, who appeared very friendly and said he would not detain him, and ordered him a posse. Met Judge Eccles, who was rotten hearted and as gross a man as ever he saw. Some person there remarked that Gov. Cumming ought to have gone to Salt Lake under the protection of the sword. Eccles said, the Mormons were trying to make a poor speculation out of Cumming; the military were the men to talk to. He said the people in the States were determined to put down the Mormons. Just before leaving, he could hear of companies being raised and

starting for Utah, every day. The rations of the army
were 13 oz. of flour and 1 lb. of bones, they could not
call it mear. Dr. Clinton asked a sargeant in Col.
Johnson's army, how many more they had in their
camp. He answered, "3,000 all told." He then asked
how many out of 1,000, if they were permitted to go
into G. S. L. City, would abstain from seducing the
women, if they had the chance. He said, "about fifteen." How many would abstain from getting drunk,
and how many would keep from taking the Lord's name
in vain? He answered, he thought not many. These
were the kind of men President Buchanan (128) sent to
put things to right in Utah. The common soldiers said
they did not feel like fighting white men, but would
rather go and fight the Indians. The officers were mad
because they could not come in when they pleased, but
had to stay out at Bridger and suffer a great many privations. He met about 50 men who were deserters
from the army. Some acknowledged they were deserters; others said they were expressmen.

On the 20th, Henry W. Lawrence, in conversation
with Ex. Gov. B. Young, said he thought Judge Eccles
was the meanest looking man he ever say. Ex. Gov.
Young said, he was the meanest man the Administration could find.

Ex. Gov. B. Young, George A. Smith, A.
Carrington, J. C. Snow, and J. W. Fox, rode on the
Provo Bench. A level was taken, and it was ascertained that the water of Provo River could be taken on
the bench, about a mile and a half, or two miles above
the State Road.

Friendly Indians from Tooele had been out and
brought in 18 horses. The Indians who had stolen them
said they were hungry and tired, and wished they had
not stolen them, for they were so wild they could do
nothing with them. (129)

Henry Lawrence enquired of Ex. Gov. Young what
he should do with Gilbert and Gerrish's cattle. He said
he might take them to their owners, as we had more

[The following paragraph should be inserted in
page 235, opposite, as the paragraph preceeding the (*).]

On the 27th, the Census of the population of G. S.
L. City was taken and found to be 1400. One thousand
of them were lodged there from the north.

cattle than we could take care of; and he had better hire
some of the brethren to help him drive them out, and
when they got to the Muddy, ride in himself and tell
Gilbert to come there and receive his cattle. He could
sell them to the army, and, thereby, raise means to
help himself, and it would be an act of charity to let the
troops have a little good beef, as they had been knawing
bones all winter, and would doubtless be very short before his supplies arrived.

On the 22nd, Amasa M. Lyman, who, with seventeen men, had been to the head of navigation on the
Colorado River, reported that they had passed track-
less deserts, and had visited the Mohave and other
Indians, the men and women of which tribes were of
large stature, and had many children. They farmed in
a rude way. The United States exploring parties, under Ives and Beal, had seduced many of their woman
and sown disease among them.

On the 24th, G. A. Smith, A. Lyman and several
others, visited Ex. Gov. Young, and discussed the
propriety of burning G. S. L. City and the settlements
north of it.

During this month, Ex. Gov. Young and others had
several interviews with John B. Cooper and (130)
James M. Harbin, who claimed to represent Col.
Kinney, of Central America.

Mr. Cooper wished to sell to Ex. Gov. Young and
the Mormons, Col. Kinney's claim to thirty million
acres of land in the Mosquito country, for ten cents an
acre. Ex. Gov. Young said if Mr. Kinney owned all
Central America and would give it him for nothing, he
would not go there; the climate was unhealthful. He
would not move from Utah. He was just where he
wanted to be and where he intended to stay.

(*) On the 29th, Ex. Gov. Young instructed the men in
Echo Canyon to return forthwith. The government officers stationed at Fort Bridger had collected about
1,000 Indians on Yellow Creek, and did not feed them,
and they were compelled to beg from our men, which
was very expensive for us. Ex. Gov. Young said he
had not been in favor of keeping the men there for the
last two months, only to satisfy some of the people.

O. P. Rockwell and a few others were sent out as
scouts. It was also proposed to send Nicholas
Groesbeck after his train of goods, that he left last
fall, at the Platte River, to try the pledge of Gov.
Cumming and Col. Johnson, that commerce would not
be intercepted. (131)

On the 30th, Messrs. Clarkson and Booky, of San
Francisco, in company with Jefferson Hunt and Robt.
Cliff, called upon Ex. Gov. Young. Mr. Clarkson said,
the proposition to sell Musquito Coast was known to
Prest. Buchanan, and all operations of the army were
suspended, until the result of Mr. Cooper's mission
was ascertained, as it was expected we would accede
to the proposition; he believed the government would
give us from ten to twelve million dollars and pay our
transportation, as they had spent eight million dollars
now, to no purpose, in the war against us.

Clarkson said it was the belief of the administration, if the authorities of the Church would leave this
country, that about one-third of the people would follow, the rest would settle down here and be good citizens.

June

On the 2nd, about 250 Utah Indian warriors, went
up and had a talk with Ex. Gov. Young at Provo. They
said they were hungry and wanted something to eat.
Ex. Gov Young gave them 1,000 lbs. of flour.
Peteetneet and White-eye were among them. A great
many of the Indians had on Infantry and Dragoon caps.

On the 4th, the guard from Echo Cañon, 150
strong, Major F. Wooley Commanding, returned to
Provo.

On the 6th, Gov. D. Grant arrived at Provo with
Prest. Buchanan's Proclamation to the people of Utah.
(132)

On the 7th, Ex. Gov. Powell and Major
M^{c}. Cullough, commissioners appointed by Prest.
Buchanan to visit Utah, and Dr. Forney, Superinten-
dent of Indian affairs for Utah, arrived in G. S. L.
City.

Geo. W. Bean gave a report of the exploration by himself and Company, of the South-western Deserts of Utah, generally spoken of as the White Mountain Country, from which he returned on the 5th, and on which they started from Provo, March 20th. They were joined at Cedar Springs March by an addition from Southern Utah to the company, making in all, 104 persons. Their route was by the Sevier River, Antelope Springs, Cache Cañon, Saleratus Valley, Long Valley, Snake Creek, were 45 men were left to farm, and the rest of the company divided into two parties, who explored the country considerably, north, south, and west. They met Col. Dame with an exploring company from Iron County, and returned by way of Beaver City, having travelled about 800 miles and crossed seven ranges of mountains and valleys, their general course being from north to south. A few scattered Indians were found on every range of mountains, in a most abject state of poverty, being almost naked, and living on roots, reptiles, and insects. They were at first very shy, as the White Knives, Pahvantes, and Utes robbed them of their squaws and children.

Various of the Indians of the Territory related (133) circumstances of the commerce of the soldiers and army attaches and followers with their squaws, some of such favors being bought with money, clothing, etc., and others being taken by force.

On the 9th, James Ferguson arrived at Provo, from the City, and stated that by agreement of the Commissioners with Col. Johnson, the army would not move until he had heard from them, and that if the people did not accept Prest. Buchanan's Proclamation, the government would send 50,000 men to Utah.

On the 10th, Ex. Gov. Young and others left Provo and arrived at G. S. L. City, meeting commissioners Powell and Mc. Cullough, Mr. Clarkson of the Central American Delegation, and others, in the evening at the Globe.

On the 11th, pursuant to appointment, Ex. Gov. Brigham Young, H. C. Kimball, D. H. Wells, W. Woodruff, G. A. Smith, John Taylor, Amasa Lyman, Ezra T. Benson, C. C. Rich, Lorenzo Snow, Erastus

Snow, F. D. Richards and several other invited citizens, met Commissioners Powell and M^C. Culloch, in
company with Gov. Cumming and Supt. Forney, who
were introduced to the assembly by Ex. Gov. Young.

Gov. Powell said the object of their mission was
to effect an amicable adjustment of the unfortunate difficulties existing between the general government and
Utah, in which Major M^C. Culloch concurred. (134)

Ex. Gov. Young inquired for the credentials of the
Commissioners, which were produced. He also spoke
on the settlement of the Territory, the reception and
treatment of the Federal officers for the territory, the
President's proclamation, the persecution of the people of the Territory.

The conference was continued in the afternoon, and
again in the evening. Remarks were made by Erastus
Snow, Gilbert Clements, Ex. Gov. Young, Gov.
Powell, and others.

On the 12th, the Eastern mail arrived with part of
the mail matter that had accumulated since 1857.

In the morning of the 12th, a similar meeting was
held in the lower room of the council house, when remarks were made by John Taylor, Geo. A. Smith,
James Ferguson, and Gilbert Clements.

In the evening, Gov. Powell addressed a crowded
audience in the council house.

On the 14th, Col. Johnson issued an address and
Gov. Cumming a proclamation, to the people of Utah,
assuring them that peace was restored and all peaceable persons would be protected, and also inviting the
citizens to return to their homes.

On the 15th, Gov. Powell and Major M^C. Cullough
arrived at Provo.

A party of about 90 Los Vegas Indians under
Patrarrump wanted to go and kill the U. S. mail party
at Los Vegas Springs, 3 1/2 miles from the Fort, because they (135) said one of the mail party had poisoned
an Indian. Benjamin R. Hulse, President of the Vegos
mission, opposed the killing, and persuaded the Indians
to wait until he found the Indian who was supposed to be
poisoned. Mr. Hulse travelled ten or twelve miles in
search of the missing Indian and found him very sick,

but administered to him and he was immediately restored to health, to the great joy of the other Indians,
some of whom, relatives of the lost one, had followed
Mr. Hulse, with the intention of killing had he not
found the missing man alive.

On the 16th, Ex. Gov. Young, H. C. Kimball,
Geo. A. Smith, W. Woodruff, John Taylor, A. Lyman,
A. Carrington, N. V. Jones, J. C. Snow, and
Dominicus Carter, had an interview with Gov. Powell
and Major M^C. Cullough in the Historian's Office, Provo.
Major M^C. Cullough thought it would be policy in Col.
Johnson not to take his whole army through the settlements, as there was such a large number of loose animals with it, and they might trespass on the growing
crops and thereby cause difficulty. If he had fruit
trees in the country, he would not have one of them
destroyed for the best animal in the army. Considerable conversation was had also upon the Indians, during
which Gov. Powell said they should cultivate the earth
and then they would not want so much of it, but acknowledged that they had been badly cheated by agents,
as he had seen it done. (136) Ex. Gov. Young said the
Indians ought to be paid for their land. Major
M^C. Cullough said that was right, but they should be
taught who were their masters; John Taylor said he
had found it cheaper to feed than to fight them. Geo.
A. Smith said if the emigrants had not killed Indians at
first, there would have been no trouble with them.

In conversation afterward, with Geo. A. Smith,
John Taylor, and others, Major M^C. Cullough said the
Mormons had better go and establish a republic, "For,"
said he, "the damned Christians will keep on persecut-
ing you." To which Geo. A. Smith replied that all
sects were persecuted at first, but when the Constitution of the United States was respected, the Mormons
would go to Jackson County, Missouri, and build their
Temple.

In the evening, Gov. Powell addressed an audience
of about 4000 in the Provo Bowery.

In the evening of the 17th, Gov. Powell addressed
the people of Lehi, in front of the house of Bishop
David Evans.

Ex. Gov. Young presented Gov. Powell with a number of Mormon books.

On the 18th, the militia officers received instructions to send as many men as would be necessary to take care of the property while the U. S. soldiers passed through the city. (137)

On the 19th, Col. Thos. L. Kane arrived in Washington and delivered to President Buchanan dispatches from Gov. Cumming.

On the 20th, the Eastern mail arrived by Gen. W. H. Kimball, who reported that Gov. Cumming had written a very sharp letter to Col. Johnson, accusing him of breaking his plighted faith, that he would not move his army until the 23rd, and that he would send in a Proclamation, before moving, to notify the people, but when said Proclamation arrived, it was dated at Bear River, June 14, forty miles on his way in. Also remonstrating against camping his army near G. S. L. City, stating that it would be an imposition upon the people.

On the 21st, D. B. Huntington reported that the Indians were very much disappointed, because peace was restored. They had expected to come in, and, while the Mormons and soldiers were fighting, would have a chance to rob and plunder.

On the 24th, Nephi Johnson and W. H. Dame arrived from their exploring tour in the south western deserts. The desert camp was located 147 miles due west from Parowan; Jesse N. Smith was left in charge. They had 40 acres of crops in, in a little cove, about two miles from the camp. He saw corn stalks that the Indians had raised last year, and (138) would measure about ten feet.

On the 26th, Col. Johnson and his army passed through G. S. L. City. The strictest order and discipline prevailed. They passed over the river Jordan and camped in the church pasture. A guard was placed at the bridge to keep the gamblers and blacklegs from following them. While the army was passing through the city there was not a lady to be seen.

Col. Cook passed through the city, with his head uncovered, as a token of his respect for the Mormon

Battalion. The army was supposed to number 1500 rank and file.

On the 27th, S. M. Blair visited Gen'l. Johnson at his tent. Gov. Powell and several officers and gentlemen were present. Lieut. Col. Smith made some remarks disrespectful about the Mormons. One of the company said, "Sir, you had better be aware how you talk about the Mormons, as they might hear you." He said he did not care a damn who heard him; he would like to see every damned Mormon hung by the neck. This same Smith was considered one of the flowers of the army.

On the 28th, Gov. A. Cumming, Col. W. H. Kimball, Adj. Gen'l. Ferguson, S. M. Blair, and others arrived in Provo. Ex. Gov. Young visited Gov. Cumming at the residence of Capt. W. H. Hooper. (139)

Maj. Ben. McCullough said to S. M. Blair that Gov. Young had the best material for composing an independent Government that he ever saw, and Brigham Young was hardly second to Christ or Mahomet.

S. M. Blair, when in G. S. L. City, asked Gov. Powell if any man of any grade or calling, on any occasion, offered to him an uncourteous word, while he had been in this Territory. He said, "No," but he had been treated with the greatest respect. Mr. Blair said he wished he would remember that when he got to Washington; and he was sorry to say he could not say as much for the officers of Col. Johnson's army, as he had been grossly insulted by Lieut. Col. Smith, and Capt. Reno.

The army moved from their camp on Jordan River, opposite G. S. L. City, to Bingham's Fort.

On the 30th, at 6 p.m., Prests. Young, Kimball and Wells, Geo. A. Smith, A. Lyman and A. Carrington started for G. S. L. City; they were escorted by thirty men from Provo, commanded by Wm Wall. Gov. Cumming accompanied the part from Provo.

It was announced that all who wished to return to their homes in G. S. L. City, were at liberty to do so. (140)

July

On the 1st, Ex. Gov. Young and party arrived in G. S. L. City at about 4 A. M., after a very pleasant night's drive.

Several gentlemen called upon Ex. Gov. Young and wished to deliver letters to him personally. All such interviews were denied. Some would not leave their letters because they could not deliver them personally.

On the 3rd, Commissioners Powell and M^c. Cullough started for the States about noon.

On the 4th, at 4 a. m., the Provo brass band commenced playing, and a flag was hoisted on Liberty Pole, in Provo, in celebration of the national Independence.

The streets were crowded with teams, loaded with families, household goods, &c., returning northward.

The army fired a national salute, at sunrise, noon and sunset.

On the 5th, the brass band played at 7 a. m.; then serrenaded Gov. Young, Gov. Cumming and other prominent citizens.

Cannons were fired morning, noon and night. Bro. Campbell supposed it was an effort to celebrate the 4th of July, but did not hear anything about it; he did not know what it was.

The doors were all locked and bolted round Ex. Gov. Young's premises. Admittance at the east entrance, where two brethren opened the door, admitted or took the names of (141) those who desired to go in.

Geo. A. Smith fastened his revolver to his comforter, around his shoulder, hanging at the left side.

On the 6th, Ex Gov. Young rented Livingston his old store for $2, 400⁰⁰. He talked to Livingston and Bell in a plain and forcible manner, in relation to the conduct of merchants towards the people. They would trade the people's blood for gold, and although residing in the community, and sustained by their custom and enriched by their traffic, were never heard in the public papers of the country contradicting the lies and misrepresentations perpetrated upon the people, nor even publishing one line in our behalf. The merchants sat and took it.

The army removed from their encampment on Bingham's Creek, and crossed over Jordan, then passed over the point of the mountain south by the dug way, and recrossed Jordan, soon after going into Utah Valley. They stopped our emigration most of the day.

A saw mill situated on Bingham's Creek, belonging to G. A. Smith, S. M. Blair, and Elijah Thomas, and worth $1,500, was burned up by the U. S. army, en route to Camp Floyd. The timbers were packed up the hill to the encampment of the army by hand and used to make camp fires; not a chip or stick was left on the ground two days after the army left. Mr. Thomas visited the mill about two weeks before the army camped there and (142) found it all right. Mr. Coon visited the encampment and saw the timbers belonging to the mill on the camp fires of the army.

Warren Snow reported that the murders in Salt Creek Canyon were perpetrated by the Utes, Sanpitches and Pe-ob-a-wats, who said they understood the Americans and Indians were going to use up the Mormons, and they thought they would pitch in.

On the 14th, Ex. Gov. Young received a letter from the asst. quartermaster of the army, refusing to pay for the fence, which the army burned up near Jordan Bridge, and also their pasturage.

The quartermaster had issued circulars, asking proposals for cutting hay, cord wood, lumber, and shingles, hay in Rush, Tintic and Cedar Valleys bordering on the lake, in all 4,000 cords of wood, 125,000 shingles, and several hundred thousand feet of lumber of various kinds.

People were rolling through G. S. L. City for the northern settlements, but in consequence of not having a sufficient number of teams, made slow progress.

On the 18th, the Board of Directors of the Deseret Agriculture and Manufacturing Society met and directed that the list of premiums for 1857, be reprinted for 1858.

On the 19th, (Monday) Judge Elias Smith administered the oath of office to Chief Justice Delano R. Eckles. (143)

August

County election on the 2nd; number of votes polled
1216, regular ticket; 37 opposition ticket.

Thos. S. Williams established an express line of
stages between Camp Floyd and G. S. L. City, fare
$5.00.

On the 5th, Hosea Stout reported the arrival of
Associate Justice Chas. E. Sinclair, by last Saturday's
mail. He said that Sinclair congratulated himself on
being absent from the Territory last winter, peradven-
ture he might have disgraced himself as Eckles had
done.

On the 8th, Ex. Gov. B. Young had an interview
with Col. Alexander. He told him, he had no doubt if
he had had half an hour's interview with him last fall,
the army might as well have come in then as this
spring. Col. Alexander was going back to the States.

On the 9th, Secretary John Hartnett was introduced to Ex. Gov. Young and others. In conversation,
he asked Ex. Gov. Young if the difficulty with the
United States was settled. Ex. Gov. Young answered,
"Yes," so far as he knew. He had been driven five
times from his home, without any just cause; this time
he did not wish to be driven. The President of the
United States had given us a good deal of trouble. Sent
an army to us and stopped all communication, by stopping the mail; then laid a plan for our destruction.
Hartnett said, he did not understand it so. Ex. Gov.
Young asked "What do you suppose he sent the army
for?" Hartnett said, "To protect the trains and people
against the Indians." Ex. Gov. Young asked, "Did you
not believe we (144) had burned the court records, and
broken the U. S. laws?" Hartnett answered, "I did."
Ex. Gov. Young said "This was all false; and we had
never opposed any good men, who were attending to
their business. But I have always taken the liberty to
speak my mind freely upon any subject, and the acts of
wicked men, who would act outrageously." Hartnett
said he did not think Prest. Buchanan intended the
army to fight. "He told me, when he found out there
was to be no war, that he was not willing to have any

blood shed until he had sent our Peace Commissioners
to try and make peace. Ex Gov. Young asked why he
stopped the mail without cause. They did it in Nauvoo.
Because of our religion, this army boasted all the
while that they would kill our Elders and take and do
what they pleased with the women. Hartnett said, "I
came here with the army, but did not hear them use
such language as your people say." Ex. Gov. Young
said "No, they would not say before you what they
would among themselves." He wanted the United
States to let us alone and let us mind our own business,
and keep the laws of God, and the Constitution of the
United States, as we had always done; then our difficulties would be settled as far as they could be, but the
people would not be driven from their homes in these
mountains; they would fight first. Ex Gov. Young said,
"We took the liberty to speak of the acts of men towards
the people, who hold the Constitution of the United
States sacred. Now, shall I speak of the acts of Judge
Eckles, who spent the winter in Green River Co., and
held court before he took the oath of office, (145) and
brought in bills of indictment against thousands of innocent citizens, and would accuse me of speaking
against the Constitution of the United States? They say
I was guilty of treason. No man can justly find any
fault with any of my official acts, except the stopping
of those trains, and that was to save the shedding of
blood."

Col. P. St George Cooke and Capt. Marcy called
upon Ex Gov. B. Young, and had a pleasant interview.

On the 15th, Ex. Gov. Young, in conversation with
some friends, said, "Both good and bad men acted out
what was in them, but God controlled all the acts of
men. When Col. Kane came to visit us he tried to point
out a line of policy for me to pursue, but I told him I
should not turn to the right nor the left nor pursue any
course, only as God dictated. I should do nothing but
what was right. When he found that I would not be directed, only as the Spirit of the Lord lead me, he felt
discouraged, and said he would not go to the army.
But, finally, he said if I would dictate he would execute.
I told him, as he had been inspired to come here, he

should go to the army and do as the Spirit led him to
do, and all would be right. He thought it very strange
that we were not afraid of the army. I told him we
were not afraid of all the world. If they made war
upon us, the Lord would deliver us out of their hands,
if we did right. God controlled all those matters.
When the army was coming here, there were many
Indians who came and wanted to fight the soldiers. I
would not employ them; this made many of them mad,
so they joined the soldiers, (146) and wanted them to
fight us. If they had commenced to war against us the
United States would have had a general war--they
would have destroyed the western cities." H. C.
Kimball said, Col. Kane asked him what would be the
result if he spoke against the Mormons. H. C.
Kimball answered him, and said his mind would become barren, and he could not do any good, but would
droop and die, but, as long as he would stand up for
the Church, he would be fruitful and feel well.

On the 17th, a portion of the U. S. troops arrived
in G. S. L. City from the east. They passed by Ex.
Gov. Young's mansion and the Temple Block, turning
north on the west side of the Temple Block, they halted
and rode under the Temple Wall a short time. There
were in all about 300 troops and about 50 wagons.

On the 19th, Jos. Young called and reported that
Capt. Marcy and Mr. Dickensen, asst. quartermaster,
who had surveyed with him the damages sustained by
him through the army camping on his land, over
Jordan, reported no damage done, although the army
demolished nearly 200 rods of Spanish wall fence and
ate up thirty acres of good grass land. The army said
they would back up damages done to private citizens.

On the 26th, Ex. Gov. Young and H. C. Kimball
started for Big Cottonwood Canyon, and, agreeable to
invitation by Ex. Gov. Young, his excellency, Gov.
Cumming, and several (147) other citizens, with ladies
and children rendezvoused at a romantic, shady location, at a distance above mill D, in Big Cottonwood
Canyon, and around a commodious bough covered
room, built by the Big Cottonwood Lumber Co., for
the accommodation of those who might wish to partici-

pate in the dance. Capt. Wm H. Hooper accompanied
the Governor there, and in returning, while M^{rs}
Cumming, on her spirited pony and escorted by Gen'l
James Ferguson, enjoyed a wider and more pictur-
esque view of the constantly shifting scenery, than
could those who occupied luxurious seats in carriages.
Music, dancing and the song enlivened the social gathering, in the enjoyment of which, none seemed to sur-
pass the Governor and his lady.

On the 28th, the picnic party returned, delighted
and refreshed by the pleasant drive, the pure canyon
breezes, and the two nights' and one day's encampment
amid leafy bowers by ice cold streams.

On the 29th, F. W. Lauder, Supt. of that section
of the Pacific wagon-road, between the South Pass and
City Rocks, called upon Ex. Gov. Young, and remained
three hours. Spoke liberally in relation to the people.
Ex. Gov. Young spoke upon some principles of Mormonism, which he said he had always believed. Mr.
Lauder acted last year as engineer in McGraw's Co.,
and made a report, not unfavorable to the Mormon
people.

Ex. Gov. Young read Fillmore's correspondence
to (148) the New York "Herald"--Many of his statements were clear lies.

September

On the 3rd, Dan Clark called and informed the
Historian that he passed Capt. or Lieut. Col. Smith
with 100 dragoons near Fillmore, four days ago. When
the command passed Round Valley, Young Cazier was
hunting stock and camped in Round Valley, with the
command. Col. Smith made him welcome and treated
him; but in the morning he interrogated him, whether
he would obey Gov. Young or Gov. Cumming, should
their instructions come in collision. Cazier replied,
he had known Gov. Young a long time and knew that his
counsel would be straight, and he presumed Gov.
Cumming's would be also. "Then", said Col. Smith,
"You would take Gov. Young's counsel first. -- Now,
leave this camp in five minutes." Cazier asked him

if he was in earnest. Smith said he was. Cazier put
off immediately, although his horse was tired, and
rode 25 miles to the nearest settlement.

On the 6th, 150 dragoons, under Capt. Haws,
with a train of wagons, came into G. S. L. City and
camped in the pastures south west of the City. They
were going out to Humboldt to chastize the Indians.

G. A. Smith and L. Hawkins visited Gov. Cumming,
who showed them a letter from Prest. Buchanan, sustaining and approving his course.

The following is extracted from a letter from
S. S. Smith:-- (149)

"Bro. Jesse (N. Smith) started with ten others,
today, to expore the head waters of the Rio Virgen.
Had a heavy rain, spiced with occasional flakes of
snow. The clouds cleared away during the night, and
the ground was white with frost, the next morning.
This continued for three successive days and nights.
The crops at Red Creek were much injured by this
frost, which made its appearance one month earlier
than last year. Corn, vines, leaves, &c., are entirely cut off."

On the 7th, Mr. Dodge, Indian Agent from Carson,
U. T., called on Ex. Gov. Young.

Kirk Anderson, of the "Missouri Republican" arrived in G. S. L. City. Some hinted that Prest.
Buchanan had a hand in sending him here. He came
here to edit a newspaper.

On the 8th, the company of dragoons for Humboldt
passed through G. S. L. City.

D. H. Wells instructed Geo. Q. Cannon in sending
for a button machine.

On the 9th, G. A. Smith, conversing with A.
Carrington and Mr. Cooper, said he had spent six
weeks in Provo this spring and had never seen a breach
of the peace. In G. S. L. City, within the last few
days, he had seen street fights, pistols drawn, &c.

On the 12th, Col. J. C. Little reported that the
brethren who had been selling timber to the army, had
been carrying their certificates to Asst. Quartermaster
Page, who was so drunk he could not attend to them.

On the 13th, G. A. Smith called on Ex. Gov. Young.

(150) A letter, in the handwriting of Judge Eckles, to
an officer in the army, (Lieut. Bennet) had been found
in the streets of G. S. L. City, which was read, in
which he informed Lieut. Bennet, that he had not as
yet been able to procure a bed fellow for him. He had
spoken to one lady on the subject, but she was not in
fit condition for his purpose; but there was another
that he thought he could get. "She is the second wife
of an old cuss, and if she can arrange to leave her
child, she could probably be induced to go, as it is
said, she is discontented."

The ermine must sit gravefully on the soldiers of
a chief justice who employed the influence of his high
position in performing (his) services as a pimp, to
provide gratification of lust to army lieutenants, and
that by the seduction of wives and mothers.

On the 14th, Col. Morrision, with four companies
of the Seventh Regiment, one company of recruits and
32 dragoons, to fill up the 5th and 10th regiments, arrived and passed through the city, by way of South
Temple Street to East Temple Street, thence south.

On the 15th, 200 policemen were selected and employed by the mayor.

At 4 p.m., the city police, mayor and city officers
met at Ex Gov. Young's new barn. Gov. Young addressed the meeting on the present and future prospects
of the people, and on the importance of the office of a
policeman. Also gave instruction on the duties of a
policeman. (151) About 75 new policemen were sworn
into office, and also eleven deputy city marshals.

A very large government train passed through the
city.

On the 19th, at 2 p.m., the new police force met
at the Council House and were organized into seven
guards of twenty men each. The Council House was
to be the police station. Each guard was to stand 24
hours.

On the 24th, Ex Gov. Young instructed Peter
Maughan, if his company numbered 35 or 40 men, to
return to Cache Valley, if they would build a good
strong fort, and keep up a guard of ten or fifteen men
to protect themselves, as the Indians in the north were

very hostile.   He wrote this letter on account of
Bro. Maughan's anxiety to go back to his place in that
Valley.

About the 27th, the City Hall was rented to the
marshal for the court

On the 29th, Mr. McNeal was taken out of the custody of the city marshal, by a writ of habeas corpus,
and tried before Judge Sinclair.   The Judge confirmed
the decision of the Mayor's court in assessing the fine,
but disallowed the costs, saying that the laws of Utah
would warrant the assessment of costs, but it was ar-
bitrary in the court.

On the 30th, a letter was received from Jacob
Hamlin, dated 10th inst., stating that the brethren and
Indians on (152) the Vegos, raised about 40 acres of
corn and wheat.   The mountain Indians came down and
stole the whole of it.   He also stated that there were
fifty missionaries connected with his mission, who
purposed visiting the Moquich, Navajo, Crabs and
other tribes, to try and find out if there were any white
children among them belonging to the emigrants, who
were massacred at the Mountain Meadows; by direction
of Dr. Forney, Supt. of Indian Affairs.

G. A. Smith received a letter from Jesse N.
Smith, dated 22nd inst., giving a description of the
exploration of the head waters of the Rio Virgin, by
himself and ten others.   He reported rather unfavor-
ably of that country for the culture of cotton, and said
there was very little land fit for farming purposes.

The following is from a letter to S. M. Blair by
Ben. M.C. Cullough, dated Washington, Aug. 27, 1858:

"I am glad to hear everything is getting on quietly
in Utah.   How long do you think it will last?   I must
confess I entertain fears regarding their long continuance.   The predjudices of mankind are so great against
each other, when they differ on religious subjects, that
there is no calculating on what they will do.   Consequently, if asked, I would express myself as I did in
Utah; viz, 'that it would be better for all parties, for
the Mormon people to remove to some other country.'
However, this is a matter that they alone must determine."

This was a fair admission, on the part of the
Peace Commissioners, that it was a religious war,
and that (153) the Mormon religion could not be protected by the government.

October

On the 4th, the Deseret Agricultural and Manufacturing Society, opened their fair for public inspection this morning at 10 a.m., in the City Hall.
     The Board of Directors had labored under many
disadvantages in getting up their fair this season, on
account of the late move of the citizens of the northern
counties. It was feared, at one time, that it would be
almost a failure; but by the untiring perseverance of
the Board, in collecting antiquities, arts and manufactures, and the kindness of Ex Gov. Young and Geo.
A. Smith, in furnishing articles of curiosity, &c., the
Board was enabled to get up quite a respectable exhibition. It would have done credit to a much older
country. The hall was crowded, not only by the citizens of the county, but by almost all the strangers,
who were staying in the city.
     At 2 p.m., Gov. Cumming and lady, Judge Sinclair,
Secy. Hartnett, and other gentlemen were invited to
visit the fair. Previous to their arrival the hall was
cleared of all other visitors. After the guests had examined the exhibition, they were invited to regale
themselves on apples, peaches, nectarines, grapes,
&c. They expressed themselves highly gratified and
much astonished at the specimens of horticulture and
art. Gov. Cumming and lady, and Judge Sinclair said
the fruit was as fine as any they had seen in the Eastern
States.
     The Nauvoo brass band was in attendance at the
(154) fair, all day.
     At 11 a.m., the U. S. Third Judicial District
court commenced its session at the City Hall, Associate
Justice Chas. E. Sinclair on the bench. U. S. marshal,
Peter K. Dotson; S. A. Gilbert, clerk, and attorneys
M℃. Cornick and Smith were present.
     S. M. Blair, H. Stout, John L. Smith and Kirk

Anderson were admitted to the Bar. W. C. Staines
was sworn in as Deputy marshal and crier of the
court. The clerk read the names of the Grand and
petit juries--who were adjourned until the first Monday
in November. The judge then read an address to the
Bar, in which he said he hoped they would sustain him
in enforcing the law, as he was determined that the
law should be executed, peaceably if he could, but forcibly if he must. S. M. Blair answered in behalf of
the gentlemen of the Bar.

On the 5th, the fair opened at 10 a. m., and was
crowded all day. On account of the rain, many of the
citizens were prevented from seeing the exhibition, and
it was agreed to open it another day.

On the 6th, the conference of the Church of Jesus
Christ of Latter-day Saints opened--(See "Des. News.")

On the 7th, Mr. Higbee described that part of the
Rio Virgin known as Toquerville Settlement, as being
a rough, barren, and inaccessible region, with but
little land fit for cultivation. (insert)

On the 9th, D. B. Huntington reported that Gov.
Cumming had ordered Gen'l. Johnston to station 100
men at Pondtown, and the same number at Springville
to protect the citizens from the Indians. The Governor
said he did not want any more Indians killed, but if
they did not stop their depredations, he would set fire
to the other end of the log, and smoke them out. (155)

On the 18th, Louis Vasques, of the firm of Bridger
and Vasques, executed a bill of sale of Fort Bridger,
to Ex Gov. Young, and acknowledged receipt of four
thousand dollars on Aug. 3, 1855, and four thousand
today. -- Also acknowledged before Samuel A. Gilbert,
Clerk of Third District Court, that Hiram F. Morrell,
was his lawfully appointed agent, and that he fully approved of the acts and doings of said Morrell in the
sale of said property.

On the 19th, Senator Broderick, of California, who
arrived by the Cal. Mail, the day before, on his way to
the U. S. Senate, Washington, called upon Ex. Gov.
Young and stated that the Mormon campaign, before it
was closed, would cost the Government forty millions
of dollars, and the Government was under the necessity

of borrowing that amount to carry on the business. He also stated that the politicians were all figuring for 1860, and no man dare offer an opinion in favor of the admission of Utah, for fear that it would blight his prospects. He said it was his opinion that the Union would not last long. (156)

On the 23rd, Senator Broderick started for Washington by the Eastern mail.

The troops that went on the Humboldt returned about noon, not having seen any hostile Indians.

On the 24th, David Evans informed W. Woodruff that when detachments of the army passed through Lehi, the officers generally turned their animals into the enclosures belonging to that settlement, without permission, and when he asked them for remuneration they damned him copiously; but, upon presenting the accounts to Gen'l. Johnson, he liquidated them freely, and assured the Bishop that it was his policy not to infringe, in the slightest, on the rights of the citizens, which policy he carried out independent of his subordinates.

On the 25th, D. H. Wells called on Secy. Hartnett and showed him a letter in the S. F. "Bulletin," containing a copy of an invitation to Judge Eckles, signed by Hartnett, Sinclair, Forney and others, congratulating Eckles on his anticipated return to a land of morality, and speaking of the necessity of his going to Washington to set matters right there.

Great Salt Lake City
October 25, 1858.

To those who are personally aquainted with me, no explanation relative to the "Bulletin" correspondent's charges would be required. For the information of the country at large, the following certificates and affidavit are published.

A. Cumming, Governor of U. T.

(157)

(From the San Francisco Evening Bulletin)
Letter from Great Salt Lake City.
(From our special correspondent in Utah Territory)

Great Salt Lake City, U. T.
Monday, September 13, 1858

Public Records in Utah all in Confusion.

The public records of this Territory are in a state of inglorious confusion, notwithstanding the assertion made by Gov. Cumming in his report to the Secretary of State that all the records, the Territorial Library and public property of the Territory, were in perfect order, and had not been injured or disturbed. The records of the U. S. District Court in this City, (Judge Sinclair's district) which have been lately delivered up to the newly appointed clerk, consist of a small record book containing about twenty packages, and a small bundle of papers, embracing those in no case prior to 1856, or later than the winter of 1857. There is no court docket; no clerk's docket; no fee docket; no order book; no copies of instructions from the Departments at Washington; no stationery; no furniture; nor no press for the Seal. How Gov. Cumming, in view of these facts, was able to reconcile his conscience to his report that these records are in a perfect state of preservation, I cannot tell you. I do not believe him capable of committing deliberate prevarication, and yet it is difficult to explain his report on any other theory.

The papers of the Territorial Secretary's office are equally imperfect. There is not an enrolled bill on file, nor any official evidence of a single legislative act (158) from the time of the organization of the Territory to the present day; so that it is doubtful whether we have any law at all in Utah. The papers of the Supreme Court Clerk's office were seized by Brigham Young during the rebellion, and have not yet been restored by him to their proper custodian. The records of the office of the Clerk of Judge Eckles' judicial district (the northern) are in the possession of Chauncey W. West, the Mormon Bishop of Ogden City, who has refused to respond to the demands which have been made for them. With regard to the law library of the judge of the Central District, Judge Sinclair has made every effort to discover whether there is a remnant of it, but has thus far not been able to find a single volume. Nor will he; for they are destroyed by fire, down to the last book, notwithstanding the Governor's instimation to the contrary.

No allusions were made by the Governor of this
Territory, in his report to the Secretary of State, in
relation to the destruction of the few books and papers
(whether borrowed or other) in the law office of
Williams and Styles. That act, so far as we have ever
heard, was a sudden, secret and lawless outbreak by
a very few persons, who, vigilance committee like,
took their own method for righting what they deemed to
be wrongs, and is an act for which the people of Utah
can in no wise be held responsible, further than that
responsibility which (159) would obtain in a local movement of disorderly persons in any other city or community.

The undersigned have examined the office books
of the First and Third Judicial District Courts of the
United States for Utah Territory and the office papers
of the same, from the organization of the Territory to
the present time, now in the custody of the Clerk of the
Third District. We find the following books:--
Record- Journal of 1st District Court commencing
Oct. 6, 1851, ending Feb. 22, 1856.
Court Docket, 1st District Court, commencing
Oct. 1855 to Feb. 1856.
Motion Book, 1st. District Court, com. Oct. 1856,
to Feb. 1859.
Register of Grand and Travers Juries--1852 to
Feb. 1856.
Journal 1st. District Court, com. Oct. 1852, to
Feb. 1856.
    Bar Docket   do   do   1854   "
 "   1856.
    Docket   do   do   1851   "
Dec. 1856.
    Journal   do   Feb. 1856   "
Apl. 1856
    Bar Docket 3rd Judicial Court, Nov. 4, 1856.
    Records   do   June 20, 1856.
    Docket Book   do
to Feb. 14, 1857

     do   do
to Nov. 1856

    We have arranged the papers in packeages corres-
ponding to each year since 1851 (when the court was
organized.). We find the books and papers well preserved, and the packages corresponding in size and
general (160) appearance to the entries on the records.

    We find the following entries on the Order Book of
the First District Court:--

    1st- "Be it remembered that on the night of the
11th October, 1855, the office of the clerk of the First
Judicial District Court in and for the Territory of
Utah, as also of the Supreme Court of said Territory
was forcibly entered and all the papers, complaints,
bills, notes and obligations including indictments were
feloniously taken and carried away, and the box in
which the same were kept under lock and key, was
carried away and was found out next morning at about
8 oclock in the bed of the River Jordan, cut open and
emptied of its contents."

    2nd. "Upon motion of A. W. Babbitt relative to
the stolen papers, the court made an order that the
parties in the cases before the court have the privilege
of making new papers. It is important that new papers
be filed nunce pro tunc." Oct. 15, 1855.

    3rd. "October 17, 1855. "The papers of the court
which had been abstracted on the 11th inst., were found
this morning on the floor of the Court room, having
been thrown in through the open window."

    We have examined the papers in several cases of
each year, and find them all correct, and we believe
that all the papers of the two Courts are now to be
found in the said office in a state of general integrity.
We find a single alteration only, in the paper filed in a
motion before the court to disbar an attorney, (161)
involving, as it appears, personal feelings; a spolia-
tion which is discoverable only by a minute examination,
or by one familiar with the facts. The general appearance of the books and papers indicate the completeness,
though they do not appear to have been kept in exact
system, with sufficient distinctness, however, to show
the course of proceedings.

We are satisfied that the fee book and motion book
are wanting from the Third District, which were at
one time in the possession of the clerk.

We are also perfectly convinced that the statements
made in the communication of His Excellency Gov.
Cumming, to the Honorable Secretary of State, are
fully borne out by the personal view and examination of
have had of the books and records in question.

If the personal or official veracity of His Excellency may, in any way, have been questioned in this
matter, we unhesitatingly pronounce it most unjust and
so certify to the country.

Great Salt Lake City, U. T.
October 25, 1858.

Henry Cabot.
Kirk Anderson.

We have read the foregoing statement of Messrs.
Cabot and Anderson, and having, by request, been
present at the examination to which they refer, concur
fully in said statement.

Charles E. Sinclair,
Associate Justice Supreme Court, Utah Territory, and
(162) ex-officio Judge 3rd Judicial District.

John Hartnett
Secretary of State for Utah Territory.
P. K. Dotson,
U. S. Marshal for Utah Territory.

Great Salt Lake City, U. T.
October 25, 1858.

We, the undersigned, having been requested to
examine into the condition of the Legislative Records
of this Territory, now in the hands of Hon. John
Hartnett, Secretary of Utah Territory, beg leave to
state as follows:--

On examination we find in the first place, the
Record of the Organic act, approved 9th September,
1850.

Secondly, we have found the Records of the Acts
passed at the sessions of the Legislatives of the years
1851-52, 1852-53, the adjourned session of June 1853,
1853-54, 1854-55-56, 1856-57, and 1857-58 to be com-

plete and in the possession of the Secretary of the Territory at the present time.

We also found, on examination, that there were at
the present time, in the possession of the Secretary of
this Territory, packages of the Enrolled Bills of each
session of the Legislature of this Territory, from
which we selected several from each session of the
Legislature, at random, and found them correct, and
we have no doubt and believe that they are all there.
(163)

We have also examined the Records of the Executive Documents, the Books of Accounts and the Letter
Book, all of which we found, to all appearance, to be
perfect.

We have not found any bound journal of the Legislature, but, at the same time, we are informed by a
person, in whom we place reliance in regard to his
means for information in regard to this point, that no
such record had been kept in book form.

We were, however, shown the slips of paper on
which were purported to be the Journal of the Legislature.

Henry Cabot.
Kirk Anderson.

I was present at the examination of the books, records, papers, &c., contained in the office of the
Secretary of State of Utah Territory by Messrs. Cabot
and Anderson on the day mentioned in their report, and
am fully satisfied that their examination was made with
care, and is correct as stated. I would furthermore
state that each item received by me as Secretary, was
receipted for by me to W. H. Hooper, and an inventory of the same forwarded to the proper Department
at Washington.

John Hartnett,
Secretary of Utah.

Great Salt Lake City
   U. T., 25 October, 1858.

   To His Excellency, A. Cumming,   (164)
Governor of the Territory of Utah.
Sir:--Having noticed a report in the public prints,

lately, setting forth that your statements in regard to the safety, and good condition of the records of the Courts of this Territory were not correct, I feel that it is due by me, both to your Excellency and the public generally, amongst whom those false statements are being circulated, to state what I know in relation to the Records of the Supreme Court of the United States for this Territory (said to be missed among the rest). Having been appointed on the 13th day of September, 1858, by the Honorables D. R. Eckles and Charles E. Sinclair, Justices of the Supreme Court of the United States for the Territory of Utah, to the office of clerk of said court, I received the records and papers belonging to said court, from my predecessor. I have examined those records and papers carefully and find them complete and in good condition, the records bearing date from the 22nd day of September, 1851, (the date of the first organization of said court by Judges Brandebury, Brocchus and Snow) to the 14th day of March, 1857, being the last term of said court held in this Territory, and which is signed by Judge George P. Styles.

{L. S.} In testimony thereof I hereunto set my hand and affix the seal of said court, at my office in G. S. L. City, U. T., the 25th day of October, A. D., 1858.

John G. Lynch,
Clerk Supreme Court, U. T.   (165)

Nathan Davis, with a company from Parowan, and the machinery belonging to the public machine shop, arrived, and the machinery was left at the Sugar House Ward.

A company of merchants and camp followers had gone to establish a city on the provo bench to be called Centre City. It was reported that they had invited Gen'l. Johnson to locate a military post there, and move in the spring with his troops.

On the 27th, O. Hyde and A. O. Smoot were at Ex Gov. Young's office. Mr. Smoot said that Gov. Cumming told him that he had made Secy. Hartnett, Kirk Anderson, Judge Sinclair, Mr. Dotson and S. A.

Gilbert acknowledge that the letter published in the San
Francisco "Bulletin," of Sept. 30th, was false, and
that our records were better than those of any other
young Territory that they ever knew anything about.

Mr. Miller, of the firm of Miller and Russell,
told Mayor Smoot that there would be 450 soldiers discharged next Monday. He said his information was
from an officer, who could be depended upon. He also
stated that 200 trains, to which were attached 600 men,
were bound to get in here, and be discharged. He had
paid off 35 teamsters, and anything they would not
steal he would not have as a gift, and the other 600
teamsters, who would be in soon, would be no better
than they.

Ex Gov. Young advised Mayor Smoot to see (166)
Gov. Cumming, and get him to use his utmost exertions to have those soldiers, above alluded to, marched
out of the Territory; and, if he refused, then have the
City Council get up a remonstrance.

Mayor Smoot said that Judge Sinclair was much
addicted to drinking, in consequence of which Gov.
Cumming was displeased with him.

G. S. L. City was very much crowded with
strangers today. Teamsters and gamblers drunk and
had a row with the police.

Instead of soldiers to be discharged on Monday
following, they were quarter master's men, who were
considered a great deal worse. Gov. Cumming was
trying to contract for their passage to California.
Dotson offered to take them for 50\frac{00}{}$ each if they
would walk, and 75\frac{00}{}$ if they had to ride. The Gover-
nor was going to see Gen'l. Johnson on the subject.

Lewis Robison reported that he had been to see
Gen'l. Johnson, in regard to the Bridger property.

Gen'l. Johnson said they were surveying a military
reserve at and around Bridger, 25 miles square and
taking in all the land that could be settled; but if the
Government acknowledged his (Robison's) claim there,
he would give him 600\frac{00}{}$ a year for the use of it; but
he thought it would take higher authority than there was
in this Territory to establish his claim. He said he
thought 600\frac{00}{}$ a great deal of rent for the ranche. (167)

Robison told him that if he could not have more than that, he would just as soon have nothing.

On the 30th, D. H. Wells visited Dr. Forney, Supt. of Indian Affairs, who had just returned from the Humboldt. He said he had talked with 1500 Indians on the route, made them presents, and they had promised him to stop killing the whites.

Mr. Wells asked Dr. Forney if he found any evidence among the Indians that we had ever incited them to hostilities against the people of the United States.

He replied that he knew there was not a word of truth in it, and he had contradicted that report more than twenty times.

Mr. Wells asked if he had any objections to contradict it in the place where it was made.

The Doctor said he had not and would do it in his next report to the Department; and he would show the report to Mr. Wells before he sent it.

On the 31st, Ex Gov. Young had a visit from Jeremiah Hatch, Indian farmer at San Pete, who reported as follows:--

"The Indians had taken all the stock from the Indian farm, and were gathering at Fish Lake, three days' travel from Manti. Josiah Call and Sam Brown were killed by Tamock, Uinta's son, and one of them after he was wounded, shot and killed Tamock. They say they did not know they were Mormons. (168) But Mr. Hatch thought they did know it. Tamock was a bad Indian. Arropeen has been among the Navajoes, and is now gathering all the Indians at Fish Lake; he is mad at the Americans. All the Utes, Sanpitches, Peobawats, Parvantes, and Piedes acknowledged Arropeen the Great Chief. He says the Navajoes will assist him. He is in correspondence with the Snakes, Shoshones and Bannocks, and they are also ready to join him, making sixteen nations, and if the Mormons will join them, seventeen nations can wipe out the Americans. He is determined on war, unless Brigham says not, and he will obey him. If the Mormons won't fight now, they will pretty soon, for the Americans told them, that as soon as snow covers the mountains, the blood of the Mormon captains will flow. The President directed Gen'l. Wells that it was not good to shed blood. Arropeen says Dr. Forney has a little heart and it is dark as night. Brigham Young has a big heart and it is white and clean as the sun. The Indians say that three men came out of the ground into their midst, when they were in Grand Council, and told them they must not fight the Mormons."

Ex Gov. Young told Capt. Hunt to get up trains and carry the discharged soldiers to California. Hunt said he met 500 discharged soldiers, on their way to California, in a state of starvation. Dr. Forney was more afraid of them than of the Indians.

Isaac Bullock reported he had been with Capt. (169) Simpson, exploring the road from Provo to Fort Bridger. The Captain felt very sore at not destroying Brigham Young; as he came out here to do it.

November

On the 1st, Jeremiah Hatch, Indian farmer from San Pete, called upon Dr. Forney, who told him he wanted to settle his accounts with him, and he would allow them; and told the clerk to make out the bills, upon which he left the room. When he returned he took the bills and tore them, saying the Mormons at San Pete were a set of damned robbers, to charge such prices. Hatch told him they had sold to him cheaper than to the army. Forney said he would settle with Mr. Hatch at the farm, as he was going there in a few days.

Some of the discharged teamsters and quarter master's men had bought some large freight wagons and poor cattle, that had just come in from the States, and had started for California by the south route.

On the 2nd, Kirk Anderson had established his printing office in Theodore Johnson's building, south of the Historian's Office. The title of his paper was to be "Kirk Anderson's Valley Tan." The first number was to be issued on next Saturday, price 8\frac{00}{}$ per year.

On the 4th, D. H. Wells called upon Gov. Cumming and expressed to him his fears, that if he left G. S. L. City, to go to Fillmore, evil and designing men would take advantage of his absence, and get up a fuss. The

Governor expressed some fears of that kind himself.
(170)

The teamsters were reported to be stealing about
80 mules per day, from Government. Large numbers
of them were starting for California.

On the 5th, Mr. Wilson, U. S. Dist. Atty., arrived in G. S. L. City, with his wife, to whom he had
been married eight months.

Gen'l. Wilson had letters of introduction from
Atty. General Black and Secy. Cobb to Gov. Cumming,
and from Col. Kane to ex Gov. Young.

Marshal Dotson served a writ on Mayor Smoot,
commanding the City Corporation to appear in court on
the 15th inst., to answer to a complaint of trespass, at
the instance of T. S. Williams, for the destruction of
his library of 480 volumes, valued at 10\underline{\underline{00}}$ each.

(6th) Kirk Anderson issued his first number of
"Kirk Anderson's Valley Tan." The leading article
was a long communication copied from the "National
Intelligencer" against polygamy in Utah.

Mr. Anderson was furnished with hands, and some
type and fixtures for his paper, by the "Deseret News"
office.

"Valley Tan" was the name of a poor kind of
whiskey made in the Valley.

The army stopped buying grain, supplies having
arrived from the States.

Isaac C. Haight said the State Road was lined with
teamsters and deserters. About 200 had passed Cedar
City before he left; a great many on foot, and some
(171) companies with as many as 14 men to one wagon,
and six or seven men to one pack animal, and others
carrying their own baggage.

Two thirds of the people at Cedar City were leaving, some for California; some for the lower settlements, but the greater portion for Beaver.

W^{m}. M. Hall said that about 100 teamsters had
started to the States, by way of Provo Canyon.

M^{C}. Cormick and Williams applied to Gov. Cumming
for a license to make whiskey in Mill Creek Ward. The
Governor informed them that there was so much rowdy-
ism, he thought it useless to increase the quantity of

whiskey. M^C. Cormick said he had invested every dollar he had in the world, in the distillery, and unless he
could get a license he would be ruined. The Governor
said he was sorry, but could not help him, as it was
not best. M^C. Cormick and Williams then examined the
law and found it to be the Governor's perogative to
grant licenses.

On the 13th, for Special Conference Minutes, see
"Deseret News."

David Evans went to Camp Floyd and was treated
courteously by Gen'l. Johnson, who ordered the
quartermaster to pay him for pasturage, furnished detachments of the army, which the officers had refused
to pay.

Gen'l. Johnson was discharging a great number of
men, and paying them in drafts instead of cash. (172)
These men asserted that they were hired until next
Spring, to be discharged at Fort Leavenworth. Many
of them were stealing mules to pay themselves for being discharged in this region without rations or transportation home.

Mr. Majors, of the firm of Miller, Russell and
Co., called upon ex Gov. Young yesterday, and wished
to trade some poor mules for fat ones. He had withdrawn from the above named firm, because they would
bring liquor to the Territory.

At 5 p.m., Peter Dotson, U.S. Marshal, came to
ex Gov. Young's Office, to serve a summons on him, to
appear and answer to a charge, by D. H. Burr, for un-
lawfully taking possession of instruments belonging to
the United States. Gov. Young sent word for him to
leave a copy and he would acknowledge the service--
Dotson left. In about a quarter of an hour Frank
Gilbert came and wished to see Gov. Young, who sent
D. O. Calder to inform him that he was authorized to
receive any papers that he might have for Mr. Young.
Gilbert said he had a summons, and he wished to serve
it on Mr. Young in person. He was then informed that
he could not see him. He then asked for Jas. Ferguson,
Jos. A. Young and Brigham Young Jr.--Jas. Ferguson
went out and spoke to him. Gilbert left, but soon came
back and left copies of summons for Brigham Young Sr.,

Brigham Young Jr., Jos. A. Young and Jas. Ferguson.

On the 22nd, theives were getting strong hold in
G. S. L. City, stealing horses in the streets, through
the day, (173) and wagons out of yards by night.

W. C. Staines said that Attorney Wilson was insulted at the way in which Judge Sinclair kept his court.
He said he had introduced articles into the charge to
the grand jury that he had no business with. The conversation was upon the ruling of the Court, and the
state of affairs in general.

On the 27th, the Church Historian, Geo. A. Smith,
was presented with a personal card, being the first
printing done with the Deseret type.

On the 29th, in reply to the question propounded by
the Grand jury, the Judge informed them that they were
not in enquire into acts committed in Green River Co.,
and also that the U. S. Dist. Atty., Mr. Wilson, would
explain to them why he had withheld bills upon the subject mentioned in their vote to the court. Mr. Wilson
then assigned the following reasons for the course he
had taken in the matter: (For speech of Dist. Atty.
Wilson, see "Des. News," Dec. 1, 1858.)

On the 30th, at 3 p.m., Marshal Dotson came to
the gate opposite ex Gov. Young's office, and asked the
gate keeper if Mr. Young was in. The gate keeper said
he did not know, but if he had any papers would see if
Mr. Young was in. Dotson said he would first have to
go and get a copy. Just then, H. B. Clawson came out,
and told the marshal to wait and he would see if Mr.
Young was in his room. Ex Gov. Young told Clawson
to show the marshal in. The marshal served a subpoena on Brigham Young, Sr., to appear in court as a
witness on the 1st of December, in the case of Burr
vs. Ferguson. (174)

December

On the 1st, H. C. Kimball, D. H. Wells, O. Hyde,
O. Pratt, G. A. Smith, and John Taylor met at Ex
Gov. Young's room, armed with pistols and knives,
ready to accompany him to court. He had his coat and
boots on, to be ready when called for.

Gov. Cumming called and said he would accompany Gov. Young to court. Gov. Young said he had addressed a note to the Judge, informing him that he was
rather unwell, and asked the privilege of staying in his
room until his presence was wanted, which the Judge
agreed to. The Governor said he would go to court and
tell the Judge, when he wanted Mr. Young, he would
introduce him to the court.

On the 3rd, Gov. Cumming and ex Gov. Young
were present at the Dist. Court. Gov. Young attended
as a witness. (See "Des. News." Vol. 8 p. 170.)

H. C. Kimball, D. H. Wells, O. Pratt, G. A.
Smith, W. Woodruff, J. Taylor, F. D. Richards and
several other brethren accompanied ex Gov. Young to
court. Judge Cradlebaugh, Gov. Cumming, the President's clerks and the Historian's Office clerks, and
about 300 other people were present. The brethren
were well armed, in the event of any disturbance. The
Judge appeared rather embarrassed.

On the 9th, an alias subpoena was served upon D.
H. Wells by Deputy Marshal Brookis on the M̥. Neal
case, suing for $25,000 damages.

Ex Gov. Young received a letter from Warren
Snow, (175) who said that "Sanpitch" was very mad at
Gen'l. Johnson and his soldiers. Arrapene informed
Mr. Snow that Messrs. Call and Brown were attacked
by six Indians, who thought they were "Americats."
Brown was shot and fell dead. Call fought desperately
and killed an Indian. Dr. Forney, Supt., had recently
visited the Indians, but had made no inquiry into the
murder of Brown. Arrapene said he was willing to
obey Brigham's counsel, which was to let the soldiers
alone; but he could not understand why Brigham should
give him such counsel; but he should have pitched into
them anyhow, if he had not received a letter from
Brigham telling him not to. Many of his Indians were
mad at the time, because he would not go and let them
kill the Americans. He also said the Indian farm had
gone to wreck; the grain was wasted, and the Indians
had to be fed by the citizens. The citizens of San
Pete were herding and corralling their animals, to
pervent the Indians from stealing them.

[The following paragraph should be inserted in page 267, opposite, as the paragraph preceeding the (*).]

On the 17th, Judge Sinclair held a court of examination, on the body of a deaf and dumb boy, who was killed by a policeman in self-defence. The judge had the body disinterred to hold the examination.

(*) On the 18th, Mr. Livingston called upon ex Gov.
Young and wanted to know if he would furnish the grain
to fill the government contract of 150,000 bushels of
wheat, oats or barley; if he bade and got the contract.
He thought (176) of bidding to furnish it at $2.50, and
would give $2.00.

The court of examination of the dead body of the
deaf and dumb boy, continued. Drs. Garland Hurt's,
Darwin Richardson's, and Jeter Clinton's statement of
the marks on the body corroborated the testimony of
the witnesses. This made a change in the feelings of
the court.

This affair manifested the malicious and vindictive
spirit of Judge Sinclair, and was an insult to the whole
of the civil officers of the City, and an outrage on the
community. It was evident from the course Judge
Sinclair had taken since he had occupied the judicial
bench in the Territory, that he was determined to rake
up something to excite the public mind against the citizens, and produce a collision between the U. S. authorities and the people. He had not done one hour's real
business since he commenced his court in October, to
the present time. The time to hold the District Court
was limited by law to 60 days, which time had long
since expired; but he still continued the term without
doing any business, and the "lock-ups" were full of
prisoners, who were awaiting their trials; but the
Judge, deaf to the call of justice, instead of giving
every man a speedy trial, as pronounced by the Constitution of the United States, continued to search after
some cause of quarrel with the Mormons, but, so far,
in vain. The Lord had frustrated all his plans, and he
had become a perfect stink to the people. Many of the
Gentiles had remarked that they could dis- (177)
tinguish a marked difference in the proceedings of the
Judge, when a Mormon happened to be so unfortunate
as to be brought before his honor.

During the present examination, in which Judge
Sinclair acted as a precinct magistrate, there was
scarcely one Mormon witness examined, without being
abused. It was easy to discern an entire difference in
the demeanor of the court, when a Gentile came to the

stand.

The Legislature met at the State House, Fillmore and organized both Houses of the Legislature and elected officers; then met in joint session and received the Governor's message through the secretary. It was read by the clerk. The joint session then dissolved, and each house met by itself and passed a Resolution, adjourning the Legislative Assembly to meet at the Social Hall, G. S. L. City at ten a. m., on Monday, 27th of Dec., 1858. The Legislators left Fillmore in the evening, for G. S. L. City.

On the 20th, Gov. Cumming told Gen'l. Wells that the deputy marshal had had a writ in his possession for Christensen, for killing the dumb man, 14 days before he served it on him. The deputy told the Governor, he could not find the man. The Governor laughed at him and told him he had seen him in the street every day.

On the 21st, W. A. Hickman called on ex Gov. Young, and told him he had had a private conversation with Judge Sinclair. The Judge remarked to him that the Mormons were unwilling to admit that (178) they were guilty of treason or any other crime, with which they have been charged; but before he was through with them, he would show them that they had done a great deal. He said that he had seen some Mormons that he liked, but the leading men and the public generally he despised, and would make them know he was after them.

Ex Gov. Young, H. C. Kimball, D. H. Wells, G. A. Smith, Jos. A. Young, and B. Young Junr., visited Gov. Cumming. In conversation, Gov. Cumming said --he had letters from several persons in Carson, and they all agreed that their best man was "Lucky Bill," whom they hung. One man there said he believed every man, self excepted, deserved to be hung. They are a desperate set. One hundred and eleven of them are entitled to vote. They were a good deal more numerous when the Honey Lake boys were with them; they were divided into two parties, about equal in strength, and when one got weaker than the other, the Honey Lake boys would come over and help the weaker. So they had hell all the time.

On the 25th, Judge Sinclair got drunk, fell into the

gutter and drew a pistol on Craig, and Craig drew a
knife on the Judge; they were both too drunk to do any
hurt.

An express arrived in the City, from the States,
(11 days, from St Joseph, Mo.) bearing Prest.
Buchanan's message to Congress. The postmaster refused to distribute the message. (179) Mr. Chorpin
also refused to allow the message to be read, except
to his own friends. It was read to Gov. Cumming and
then taken to the "Valley Tan" office.

Gov. Cumming had written to Prest. Buchanan,
requesting him to send him the message by the express,
which was a trial of speed from the States to California,
between the northern and southern mail routes. Gov.
Cumming said that if he had known it would have been a
party affair he would not have done it.

J. G. Bigler, of Nephi, reported that about 200 soldiers and attaches, and upwards of 2,000 animals were
camped west of the field at Nephi. Captain Turnley,
who staid over night with Geo. W. Bradley, on his way
to Sanpete, used very abusive language toward the people of the Territory, and accused the Mormons of general immorality. He said he would rather shoot
Brigham Young than a wolf. He told Lewis Bruce that
if he would procure the wife of George Henry Bradley,
for him to cohabit with, he would give him fifty dollars
and the woman a hundred dollars for one night.

Judge Sinclair, Associate Justice of the Supreme
Court of the United States for the Territory of Utah,
(and committing magistrate for Salt Lake County) got
so drunk that he had to be led out of the house, by two
of his friends, to spew; he was so drunk he could not
stand; his friends laid him on the snow, and put snow
on his head and face; in this situation he laid and
spewed until his stomach was emptied, he was then led
back to the house; they had to go through a small gate,
which would only admit of one person at a time; consequently his honor had to stand by his own merit; but his
understanding, being so much weakened by the late (180)
bacchanals, refused to perform their office, and his
honor pitched upon his head, into the snow.

A few night's previous, the Judge attended a ball,

and got pretty mellow; and, in conversation with one
of his friends, he remarked that he had come here to
do the Mormons good; the people had been abused; but
he intended to change his policy towards them. His
friend said he knew the Mormons had been abused and
misrepresented, and he intended to stand up for them
until death. At the close of the dance, the Judge asked
Miss Kesler to let him accompany her home, but she
refused.

On the 27th, the Legislature met at 10 a.m., according to adjournment, and completed its organization.

On the 30th, Dr. Forney returned from Sanpete as
mad as could be. Arropeen was mad and would not go
and see the Doctor; this made the Doctor mad because
he had to go and see Arropeen. Arropeen asked him
why he did not bring an interpreter that the Indians
knew, and could feel at home with. Told him his talk
was like bawling, would go in one ear and out the other,
but Brigham's went into his ear and sank into his heart,
and stopped there. This enraged the Doctor. (181)

INCIDENTS IN THE HISTORY OF UTAH

January 1859

The emigration from Europe, which had been stopped for the time being, on account of the "Utah War," was again opened in the commencement of the year. Those who could come were advised to cross the plains with hand carts, if they could not procure teams. (See "Mil. Star," Vol. 21, pp. 8 and 9.)

The Indian farm at Spanish Fork was abandoned after the killing of Pintels.

Gov. Cumming, notwithstanding his intemperate habits, proved to be the most generous, whole hearted and upright man of all the officers, recently sent to Utah.

Gen. A. S. Johnson, since he located in Cedar Valley, manifested a disposition to observe the promises of the Peace Commissioners, and not interfere with the people; but nearly all his subaltern officers, in their conversation and business dealings with the citizens of the Territory, evinced a hostile, bloodthirsty and revengeful disposition, and it was really a miracle that a collision was avoided, when it is considered that all the officers, almost without exception, under Gen. Johnson, heartily desired to shed the blood of the Mormon leaders. They were stung by the reflection that the Saints considered the army was in the Territory on suffrage and by a compromise made between Brigham Young and the Peace Commissioners, and they wished to avenge themselves upon the "Mormons" for stopping the army and hedging it up in the mountains, and keeping it there until the Peace Commissioners (182) negotiated for its passage through the Wasatch range. A large portion of the officers were men of intemperate and grossly licentious habits, and the soldiery were largely enlisted from the dregs of the foreign emigration. There were several hundred men, who had been discharged by the government, after their arrival in Utah, and had no means of subsistence except by stealing. They had gambled away, and otherwise squandered their earnings, and were therefore ready to rob, or commit any other crime to obtain subsistence.

During these unsafe times, Brigham Young kept Wm Derr and M. G. Atwood keeping his gates, and no persons were permitted to enter his office except by permission. He also had five brethren sleep in his office at night, in case of surprise. The gate opposite the door of his office had a bell attached to it, which gave an alarm when opened.

On the 2nd, meeting was held in the Tabernacle, which had not been open for public meetings since the preceeding June.

Alderman Raleigh fined the late Indian agent $32.00 for drunkenness and threatening the lives of the police.

On the 4th, the District Court met at 11 a.m. Although the U. S. marshal had to adjourn the court the day before, on account of the absence of the judge, on the reading of the minutes they showed that the judge adjourned the court.

When Judge Sinclair came into court he had the (183) appearance of having been drunk for several days.

Mr. Wilson, U. S. Attorney, had drawn up an indictment containing two counts, --one for murder, and the other for manslaughter. At 3 p.m., the grand jury came into court and reported the bill of indictment against Christensen ignored.

Capt. Tyler told Mr. Candland that there were 24 commissioned officers coming from Camp Floyd to sit as a court martial upon all crimes committed in the Territory, and said he (Tyler) was to be one of that Court, and then lots of men would be hung, as martial law would be the rule of action.

On the 5th, the District Court met at 11 a.m. Judge Sinclair issued an order for the release of Christensen.

Dr. Forney, Supt. of Indian Affairs, recieved by last mail, official notice that Dr. Hurt was removed from the Indian agency and a Mr. Morgan appointed in his stead.

On the 6th, the Legislative Assembly met.

On the 14th, the Legislature met and passed a memorial to Congress, asking for the admission of Utah, under the name of "Deseret," into the Union. Gov. Cumming refused to sign it; his signiture, however, was not necessary to a territorial memorial. The memorial was sent to Congress.

Isaac Bullock waited on ex Gov. Young, in relation to the settlements in Green Co. ex Gov Young said he was anxious to have the settlements re-established to shelter our emigration in case they were caught out late in the season.

Mr. Bullock wrote a letter to Gov. Cumming in relation to the military reserve being established over the (184) farms of the citizens of Green River Co., and asking him to direct the military not to obstruct the settlements.

On the 21st, the Legislature met and after transacting some business and offering resolutions of thanks to Gov. Cumming for his wise policy in keeping the peace and maintaining the laws in the Territory, it adjourned to meet on the second Monday of December.

On the 29th, Geo. A. Smith delivered an address to the Utah branch of Deseret Agricultural and Manufacturing Society in Provo. A company was formed to engage in raising sugar cane and tobacco on a large scale.

On the 31st, the Board of Regency met in the President's office. A committee was appointed to translate a chapter of the Bible into the Deseret system of orthography to be printed in the "Deseret News."

February

On the 7th, Orson Hyde was appointed to get out slates for the use of schools from a quarry at or near Provo.

On the 8th, the committee of the regency commenced work on a dictionary of the Deseret character.

On the 14th, G. A. Smith wrote as follows--

"The mail arrived this morning from the States. The tone of the papers is rather conciliatory toward Utah. They take no notice of the 'Tan', but extract from the 'Deseret News'. L. N. Scovil has been appointed clerk of the 2nd Judicial District by Judge Cradlebaugh. This shows a little different spirit from Judge Sinclair. (185) The court is to be held at Provo on the 8th of March.

"Secy. Hartnett has paid some of the members of the Legislature in part, and some he will not pay. The Governor signed all the bills that passed the Assembly, that were of any general importance."

On the 17th, a large spread eagle was placed over the gate east of ex Gov. Young's Bee Hive house. The eagle stands of a bee hive, and is made of wood bound together with iron, carved by Ralph Ramsay.

Thos. Fox arrived from Rush Valley, and said that some of the soldiers had been killing some cattle not belonging to them, and insulting the people there.

On the 23rd, Thos. Fox stated that the officers of the army said that the only way to get along with Mormonism was to form a vigilance committee and kill Brigham Young.

March

On the 2nd, the Eastern mail arrived. Upon its arrival Mr. Morrell, Post master, was crossing the street to his breakfast, when he was called upon to come back and receive the mail; whereupon he replied, "D--n the mail, let it go to hell," and went on his way.

On the 8th, the 2nd Judicial District court commenced its session at Provo. The judge delivered his charge to the grand jury. The judge had a company of U. S. soldiers attending on his court. He said that (186) if the laws could be carried out there would be a great many prisoners, and, as there was no jail it would be a great expense to keep them, so he thought best to have a company of soldiers to guard them. The soldiers pitched one of their tents at the back door of Mr. Robins' house. Mr. Robins politely requested the lieutenant to have it moved. The lieutenant told him to make as little noise about it as possible, as the soldiers had authority to knock down, kill, and drag out.

B. K. Bullock, Mayor of Provo, called on Judge

Cradlebaugh, and asked him if he was afraid of the
people of Provo, that he considered it necessary to
bring a military guard with him. The judge replied,
"No," though he had been in places that he was afraid.

The City Council of Provo found it necessary to
double the police force, to take charge of drunken soldiers, who were attempting to break into houses.
Mayor Bullock informed Judge Cradlebaugh that the
civil authorities could take care of all prisoners, that
the soldiers were drunk and very abusive, and that the
citizens were annoyed and felt themselves imposed
upon by the presence of the military, and it was difficult to prevent a collision, and he offered to protect
the Judge himself. The Judge said he was sorry, but
he only wanted the soldiers while he was doing U. S.
business, and to save expense.

On the 10th, citizens of Provo memoralized the
Mayor and City council against the use of troops (187)
around the court.

Judge Cradlebaugh was very vindictive towards
the Mormons, and Judge Sinclair was there drunk much
of the time, and damning the Mormons freely.

The troops were taken to Provo without the request, consent, or knowledge of Gov. Cumming, and
even against his wishes, evidently with the intention of
raising a disturbance, as many of the soldiers and officers thought it inglorious for them to come to Utah
and not have a chance to kill a few Mormons. Some
officers of the army had declared that if they could not
succeed through the courts they were in favor of catch-
ing certain prominent Mormons, taking them to Camp
Floyd, and lynching them.

A company of about 40 dragoons visited Manti,
Sanpete County, with two persons who claimed to be
deputy marshals. These two men rode through the
streets, yelling, cursing, etc. They halted a young
man on horseback, threatening with drawn revolver, to
shoot him. With abundant oaths they denounced the
citizens as murderers, cut throats, thieves, etc, and
declared that they had come to the Territory to hang
every God damned Mormon president and bishop, and
they would do it before they left, with much more of

the same kind. These two men were named Joseph
Allen and George Crossman Junr., son of Col.
Crossman, deputy quartermaster general, U. S. A.
Allen drew his revolver on Mayor Whiting, and fired
it, the bullet narrowly missing the Mayor. The two
then rode up and (188) down the streets, with drawn
revolvers, aiming at different persons, and firing several
shots, but fortunately hitting no one. They wound
up their performance with three cheers for Judge
Cradlebaugh and three groans for Gov. Cumming, "The
God damned old Jack-Mormon."

The Grand jury of the 2nd Judicial court addressed
the following memorial:--

"To Hon. John Cradlebaugh, Associate Justice of
the Supreme Court, and ex officio Judge of the 2nd
Judicial District, Utah Territory.

"We, the Grand Jurors in and for the body of the
Second Judicial District, in and for the Territory of
Utah, in which your Honor is now holding court, and of
which court we are Grand Jurors, respectfully represent to your Honor that we are not aware of any law by
which armed bodies of men are authorized to be quartered around said court nor in nor around this city;
neither are we severally or collectively cognizant of
any reason for armed troops being quartered as aforesaid. --Should any legitimate order, or valid reason
for the presence of said troops be known to your Honor,
we hereby respectfully request you to be so kind as to
communicate those facts to us for our better information, and, in the absence of such facts, further respectfully request your Honor to order the removal of
said (189) troops to their proper location, since we
deem their presence as leading directly to the hin-
drance of the free action, and due supremacy of the
civil law, and the proper conduct of business in the
court, over which your Honor is presiding, and of
which we are the Grand Jurors.

"We apprehend no difficulty in sustaining your
court, and in safely keeping any and all prisoners that
may be ordered by your Honor into the custody of the
civil officers."

Gov. Cumming told Judge Cradlebaugh that the

Government was about to distribute a large amount of arms to the Mormons. Judge Cradlebaugh thought that was very bad policy for the Government. The Governor replied that he did not make the policy for the government, and that he should give out the arms when they arrived, as the Mormons had never had their quota of public arms.

On the 17th, while the court was trying to do all the mischief it could, Gov. Cumming was at Provo, trying to have the troops removed.

On the 18th, subpoenas were served upon Johnson, McDonald, Farren, Mc. Ghee, and Stewart. Their names were called; they stood up and were arrested for murder, and placed in charge of a detachment of soldiers, who were guarding the court houses. About the same time, Benj. K. Bullock was arrested by the U. S. marshal, charged with the murder of the Parishes and was placed (190) in the prison tent and guarded by soldiers.

Geo. A. Smith called on Mr. Wilson, U. S. Attorney and asked him if the subpoenas were made out at his request. He said he had not been notified in relation to the arrests at all, and if the Judge thought by pursuing such a course to cause him to resign, he was mistaken. He considered that it was wrong for the Judge to subpoena men and then arrest and detain them as prisoners, under the false color of calling upon them as witnesses. Geo. A. Smith asked the attorney if there was any evidence adduced before the Grand jury calculated to criminate Bullock. He replied that there was not a shadow of evidence against Bullock.

On the 19th, B. K. Bullock, H. H. Kearns and A. C. Mc. Donald were before the court. After hearing all the testimony they could muster against them, the Judge released B. K. Bullock, stating that there was nothing against him. The other two were remanded to prison and their case continued until the 21st.

On the 20th, word was received from Provo that 800 U. S. troops were then en route from Camp Floyd to that place with a light battery. The officers assured the brethren that the presence of the troops were only required to overawe the lawless, and enforce the civil

law. It was learned from a reliable source that the
troops were sent at the request of Judge Cradlebaugh.

On the 21st, a council was called, and a petition
to Gov. Alfred Cumming to vindicate the cause of the
United States (191) and this Territory, and prevent the
civil officers from being trampled under foot by the
military, was drafted. It was elaborately got up, showing that the court at Provo was illegal. Arrangements
were made to have men on hand to protect the citizens.

The court met at Provo at 9 a.m. Judge Cradlebaugh
called in the grand jury, and informed them that he had
done everything in his power to assist them in discharging their duties, and, as they had done nothing, they
were discharged.

In his closing remarks he said the Legislature had
legislated to tie up the courts, and to keep things out of
their proper channel; but the court had the power to
turn the savages (Indians) loose upon the community and
should do so, but that it would magnify the law.

John Daley, of Springville, after being subpoenaed
as a witness, was arrested by one of the deputy U. S.
marshals, charged with being accessory to the Parish
murder.

The Judge ordered Marshal Dotson to pay off the
traverse jury and dismiss them, as the court would
have no more business for juries.

On the 22nd, two of the deputy marshals subpoenaed
Alfred N. Nethercot as a witness in the Parish case,
after which he was arrested upon a bench warrant.

On the testimony of Leonard Philips, a warrant
was issued for the apprehension of James C. Snow, also
one for Aaron Johnson.

The Judge spent most of the day in examining witnesses, trying to find something against several of the
leading men (192) of Provo and Springville.

There was a meeting in each district of G. S. L.
City to get signatures to a petition to Gov. Cumming to
have the troops removed from Provo and to report to
Congress or to the President, affairs as they were;
and the course the judges had pursued. Thousands
signed the petition.

John Kay and W^m. Horner arrived from Provo with

an express. Wall, the marshal and sheriff of the
county, had gone by order of the court, with the marshal of the court, to arrest James C. Snow, and Aaron
Johnson, as the court wished to secure all the leading
men he could, but they did not arrest them. Wall reported to the court that he could not find them. Judge
Cradlebaugh told him he was a damned liar, and that
he had helped them to get away. He had 800 soldiers
around and would not let a Mormon go into Court, except the lawyers, and such men as they arrested.
They subpoenaed men as witnesses, and, as soon as
they came into Court, arrested them with bench war-
rants, and put them under military guard, without
food, or blankets on them at night.

Soon another messenger arrived from Rush Valley,
bringing news that Howard Spencer, the son of Orson
Spencer, was nearly or quite killed, by a soldier at
Spencer's place, under the following circumstances,
as related by Alfred Cliff:

Alfred Cliff went to Rush Valley with Howard
Spencer (193) to see about their cattle. When they
arrived at the house of Daniel Spencer they met five
soldiers. They told Spencer he could not stay there
overnight. This appeared to be an officer. Howard
told him that the house belonged to him, and he should
stay there overnight. The soldiers then went away,
and returned with about a dozen men in all. The officer
again told Spencer he should not stay there overnight.
Spencer said he would, and got off his horse and went
from the first corral into another corral, where his
food was. The man who seemed to command the soldiers, rode up to him on horseback and took his gun by
the breech, and struck him over the head by the barrel
with all his might across the side of the head, and he
fell, to all appearance, dead. He straightened himself
out as he fell. Soon after, Luke Johnson came up to
him to take care of him, but Cliff then left for G. S. L.
City, and reported, not knowing what followed, or whether or not Spencer was dead. Daniel Spencer and some
others started to get him, whether dead or alive.

At Provo, Judge Cradlebaugh dismissed the Grand
jury, making a hostile speech to them, filled with
falsehood and levelled directly at Ex Gov. Young.

On the 24th, D. H. Wells had an interview with
Gov. Cumming, who returned to the City the night before. D. H. Wells asked him what he was going to do
in relation to the disturbance. He seemed somewhat
troubled about it, and said he had reported to Government that he could (194) not be responsible for the
peace of the country unless he had control of the military, and they out of the control of the judges; and that
he would make the same report by the next mail. He
said there was no necessity for calling out the military
at Provo. He was told the circumstances of the attack
on Howard Spencer, and said he would immediately
have that subject investigated. Gov. Cumming told
Gen. Wells that there appeared to be shrinking on the
part of Judge Cradlebaugh as he wished to shift the
responsibility of sending the 800 troops to Provo, to
Gen. Johnston. The Judge denied making a requisition
for them.

A messenger arrived from Rush Valley with word
that after Spencer was knocked down, they sent for an
army surgeon, who examined his head and found his
skull broken, one part having lapped over another.
The surgeon sawed a piece of the skull out and put it
together, and they thought there was a chance for him
to do well.

Ex Gov. Young received a letter from Camp Floyd,
stating that Gen. Johnston was disarming every person
who left the camp, who had been there on business.

Ex Gov. Young said that if Gov. Cumming did not
protect the people they would have to protect themselves.

On the 25th, a copy of a petition, containing 3455
signatures, which had been procured in G. S. L. City,
Tooele and the north, was presented to Gov. Cumming.
His Excellency seemed alive to the responsibility of
his (195) position. He was engaged preparing a report
to the Department at Washington.

Howard Spencer was brought into G. S. L. City in
the morning. It was thought he would recover, though
his case was a critical one.

Gov. Cumming told D. H. Wells, in presence of
M̃ͬͤ Cumming, that Marshal Dotson told him that there
was no excitement at Springville, as the people were

nearly all gone from home. Wells replied that it was
very strong evidence of excitement at Springville if the
people had all fled for their lives from an army which
was menacing them. Mrs Cumming said she thought
so too.

On the 26th, a dispatch was recieved from Provo,
stating that Judge Cradlebaugh continued his court in
Star Chambers. He had issued twenty five subpoenas
for witnesses, not one of which could be found. Attempts were made to buy witnesses with an outfit for
California. The seventh Infantry and a battery of artillery were posted on the Provo Bench, and a detachment of the Tenth in charge of the court house. Prisoners were guarded by them out of doors.

For Proclamation by Gov. Cumming and Protest
of the Grand jury at Provo, see "Des. News," Vol. 9,
p. 28.

John Kay arrived from Provo with news that the
troops, supposed to number 1200, had moved down to
the road a mile and a half north of Provo, in range with
State Street, so as to cannonade the town. Many of the
people in Springville and other places in the country
had fled to (196) the mountains. It was considered reliable that 1000 more soldiers had been sent for from
Camp Floyd, for what object was unknown.

Daniel H. Wells, George A. Smith and John Kay
went to see the Governor, and presented a petition that
had been got up in Utah County, asking him to reproduce his proclamation of pardon, pardoning all offences
committed before a certain date.

The Governor doubted his authority, but was willing to reproduce it. Gen. Wells asked the Governor
what should be done if that army moved in this City,
as, from threats made by military officers and others,
it was evidently their intention to try and harass and
arrest Brigham Young, and it was also evident that
were he in their hands he would be massacred, and the
people would not submit to have Ex Gov. Young dragged
into a military court and murdered. The Governor replied that he was not prepared to give an answer to that
question, but if such an emergency occurred he would
then decide what to do. Wells told him that the emer-

gency was likely to occur before tomorrow morning,
and we would be obliged to decide, and may as well do
so at once, and that the people had submitted to have
Joseph and Hyrum Smith treacherously murdered in
the same way as they were trying to get up now.   He
also told the Governor that Capt. Turnley and Col.
Crossman had declared (197) that Brigham Young
should be hung, and many other officers had made similar declarations.   He further said that Mr. Miner
heard the lieutenant, who was in command at Rush
Valley at the time Mr. Spencer's head was broken,
state at the dinner table in Provo, that when he started
to Rush Valley, Col. Smith, the commander of the post
at Camp Floyd, ordered him not to take any prisoners,
as it was cheaper to bury men than to feed them; but he
could assure him that Brigham Young was not going into that camp to be murdered, as he was innocent of
any crime, but he would be willing to submit to an investigation before the proper civil tribunal, but the
people could not be induced to allow him to go into that
military court to be butchered, even if he were willing.

The Governor said his instructions gave him the
control of the army, but it appeared that his instructions, and the instructions of Gen. Johnston clashed.
He regretted very much that he was so far from the
capital.   He would give a great sum if he could telegraph to Washington.   He gave assurance that he
would do all in his power to secure the safety of the
people.

On the 28th, Gov. Cumming allowed Col. Little to
take a copy of his last dispatch to Gen. Cass, wherein
he reported the condition of affairs at Provo, stating
that the use of the troops there was unnecessary and
calculated (198) to make trouble, that no disorder had
occurred there among the people, and the course pursued was more from hatred towards the Mormons than
a love of justice.

Jacob Houtz arrived from Provo with dispatches.
There was no change in the state of affairs there.
Blair and Stout felt that it was getting rather hot arround
there.   Houtz brought a Copy of the protest of the Grand
jury.

On the 30th, at about 3 a.m., the town of Springville was surrounded by a company of U. S. dragoons,
with Marshal Dotson at their head, who searched the
town, but found no men at home. They surrounded
Bishop Aaron Johnson's building, but found no man.
In the big house they found 23 children and an old
crippled woman at work fixing a plow.

Marshal Dotson said there must be an air telegraph to Springville, as no man knew their intention
to search the town.

Judge Cradlebaugh delivered an address on the
bench in relation to Gov. Cumming's Proclamation, in
which he accused the Governor of falsehood, and of
frustrating the ends of justice and insinuated that he
intended to have the old man arrested. The judge also
stated that he intended to hold court all summer, and
that he should remove to his residence in a few days.

The Judge made the most vigorous attempts to
draw something out of witnesses to criminate Brigham
Young in the Parish affair.

The merchants of G. S. L. City said at this time
that if they could not get up a collision between the
Mormons (199) and the army they would all become
bankrupt, which was an acknowledgement that they were
at the bottom of the outrage upon the people.

Gov. Cumming recieved a communication from
Gen. Johnston in regard to the Spencer affair, in
which he stated that Howard Spencer resisted an officer
in the discharge of his duty with a pitch fork and the
officer broke his head in self defense. Gen. Johnson
denied giving Spencer permission to occupy the premises, although Spencer held Johnson's letter giving
that permission.

April

On the 1st, an express arrived from Provo bringing word that the Court there had adjourned sine die,
and the army was to return to Camp Floyd.

It was reported that the Judge had dismissed
Mr. Netherwart, saying that he was a damned fool and
did not know enough to tell the truth; but McDonald,

Kearns and Dailey were held in custody.

Judge Cradlebaugh said he would sit as a committing magistrate for the next six months, or until the Chief Justice came on, and he would ferret out everything connected with the outrages committed in his district.

A. Miner stated that he head Judge Cradlebaugh say in the bar room of his hotel at Provo that if he could get a Mormon convicted he would have him executed so quickly that there would not be time to get a reprieve from Gov. Cumming.

For Court procedings, &c., in Provo, see "Des. News" Extra, of April 2nd, 1859. (200)

The prisoners in the tents, guarded by the soldiers, were treated with great severity, and threats were made of shooting them on slight pretexts, and orders were given accordingly. One soldier said he feared there would be no hanging job for him, before leaving Camp Floyd, though Judge Cradlebaugh had promised him that he should have considerable.

Judge Cradlebaugh said if he could get Kanosh, the Indian chief, he would hang him whether guilty or not.

On the 4th, Judge Cradlebaugh adjourned his court for the 2nd district. The troops marched into the City of Provo, down Main Street, and returned to opposite the courthouse, opened their column at the centre and took the prisoners, A. F. McDonald and H. Kearns into their charge.

The attempt of A. Durfee and J. Bartholomew to turn states evidence, had, so far, resulted in their being illtreated more than the other prisoners. The Judge took their testimony in secret, and, as they had not succeeded in criminating any dignitary high enough in authority, he had no doubt concluded that by rough treatment he could frighten them to swear to anything he might suggest to them. They were also taken in charge by the troops and marched to Camp Floyd. (201)

The attempt of Judge Cradlebaugh to criminate Church authorities was a total failure, and it was very clear that his whole effort was to get hold of something to criminate ex Gov. Young.

The Judge issued a subpoena for Alfred Bill Esq.

He enquired of Mr. Bell if he knew anything of the killing of Lance. Bell told him the name of the person who made the affidavit that Lance committed a rape. The Judge then went to American Fork and commenced hunting up witnesses himself, but without success.

On the 4th, an election for city officers was held in G. S. L. City.

On the 6th, the annual Conference of the Church of Jesus Christ of Latter-day Saints, convened in the Tabernacle, G. S. L. City.

Ex Gov. Young had an interview with Mr. Wilson, Attorney General for Utah. Mr. Wilson said that he could now understand how the late war and military demonstration against the Mormons had been got up. He was satisfied it had been brought about by misrepresentation of speculators, contractors, merchants and political demagogues.

Mr. Wilson had sent to Judge Black, Washington, a full and true report of the court procedings. He also informed them that the grand jury was as good a jury as he could wish in any country, and (202) that he was satisfied that all persons who ought to have been indicted would have been, had not the Judge dismissed them.

Secy. Hartnett and Marshal Dotson entered the Historian's Office. Mr. Hartnett said he wanted to find Gen. Wells. He was informed that that was not Gen. Well's office. He then took up the journal of the Legislative Council and told the marshal to lay the writ of replevin on that book. The marshal took out his writ and took possession of the journal. Geo. A. Smith told Mr. Hartnett that on account of sickness Mr. Hawkins had not been able to fully finish the journal and return it to the secretary's office. Geo. A. Smith wished to have the writ read, which was done by Robt. L. Campbell. The writ was issued by the clerk of the 3rd Judicial District Court. The secretary appeared very much excited.

On the 15th, Marshal Dotson again called at the Historian's Office and left a copy of the writ of replevin served on Leo Hawkins, the previous day. Secretary Hartnett was reported to be very angry because Leo

Hawkins had not been able to finsh copying the Legislative minutes in the journal, and D. H. Wells had not
signed them.

On the 18th, an express arrived in the city stating
that a battery of artillery and two regiments of infantry
were calculating to start for G. S. L. City last night.
The rumor spread through the city and produced some
little excitement. Gov. Young remarked he guessed
they would not come, though it would be well to be on
the look out. (203)

Marshal Dotson and some of his deputies went to
Nephi with writs for the bishop and others, but, not
finding them at home, they employed some Indians to
go into the mountains to hunt them up. An Indian informed Andrew Love that Dr. Forney had promised to
give them horses, cattle, blankets and other articles
if they would hunt up the bishop and others who were
supposed to be with him.

On the 19th, Seth M. Blair returned from Camp
Floyd. He reported that McDonald was confined in a
room 6 x 9 feet with a man accused of horse stealing,
and Kearns was in another regiment in the same condition. When the detachment reached Camp Floyd
from Provo with the prisoners they were surrounded by
about 3000 soldiers, camp followers, &c., who shouted
for ropes to hang the "damned Mormons". McDonald
took off his hat, bowed to the mob and remarked to
Capt. Heath that he supposed this was an introduction
to civilization.

S. M. Blair had considerable conversation with
Gen. Johnston. The General said he expected Major
Prince by way of California by the south, with a train
of specie to pay off the soldiers. He said he was sending from three to five hundred soldiers to meet him.
Judge Cradlebaugh was to accompany them. It was
supposed that the main object of the troops going south
was to make arrests.

For several days past men with stripes on their
pants were noticed at different points around the city
and particularly just above Ex Gov. Young's mansion
and apparently looking out locations for batteries.

Since the commencement of the persecutions of

the (204) bishops, presidents, counsellors and teachers
of the Church in the southern judicial district by Judge
Cradlebaugh and the U. S. Army, a number of those
pursued who fled to the mountains, found it cold lying
on the snow and difficult to avoid being tracked by the
Indians that Judge Cradlebaugh had turned loose upon
them. To avoid further exposure, a considerable number had taken shelter among their friends in G. S. L.
City, keeping close doors during the day and taking a
little exercise during the night. Several of those gentlemen met in the evening and concluded to return
home secretly, gather together their persecuted
friends, who were also hunted, and conceal themselves
in the mountains in parties sufficiently large to prevent
the attack of the Indian allies of their pursuers and
move often enough to elude the pursuit of the army and
pursue this course until military terrorism should
cease to be used to crush the civil rights of American
citizens in the Territory on account of their religion,
and that as soon as courts could be held and law and
justice administered in a manner that was customary
in other states and territories, which were not op-
pressed by priestcraft, speculative greediness and
political intrigue, they would present themselves before the courts and have a full and free investigation
of all charges published against them by the Hon. John
Cradlebaugh, who was acting as a judge, prosecuting
attorney, jury, marshal, sheriff, jailor, committing
(205) magistrate, and ex officio commander in chief
of the army, &c., driving hundreds from their homes,
leaving their fields uncultivated, and keeping others
incarcerated in military dungeons for months without
trial, in direct violation of both Territorial and Federal
laws and the constitution of the United States, and the
instructions of the Department to the executive of the
Territory and Gov. Cumming's official protest. Among
the gentlemen present at this meeting were Jacob G.
Bigler, Aaron Johnson, Elias H. Blackburn, and
William Miller.

On the 24th, ex Gov. Young, D. H. Wells, and
Geo. A. Smith visited Gov. Cumming. The conversation turned upon the threatened move of the army upon

G. S. L. City. Gov. Cumming said he had understood
for some time that such was their intention, but he was
in hopes they had given it up. Mr. Wells asked Gov.
Cumming by what law prisoners for civil offences were
detained in military custody by the army. The Governor replied, "Violence." The Governor said his report
to the State Department, in which he testified of the
good order and peaceful disposition of the people, of
the unnecessary use of the military at Provo, that such
use of the military, in his opinion, was more from
hatred to the Mormons than love of justice, and, if
continued, would result in much bloodshed. Ex. Gov.
Young said the course pursued was driving hundred of
men into the mountains and laying the foundation for a
famine, for thousands of acres must be (206) idle because of the interference of the military with the people, and it must be done to favor contractors for grain
and other supplies. He was willing to have any of his
acts scanned before any court of justice or civil tribunal as he had never committed nor sanctioned any
criminal act, but he would not be nosed about by the
military, and he would not go into their camp alive.
Yet he believed there would be no collision, and he
would do all he could to avoid one.

Gov. Cumming requested D. H. Wells, if the army
started for the City, to let him know as soon as possible. He hoped to get instructions from Washington before the judiciary or the army forced any issue.

(See Letter in "Millennial Star," Vol. 21, p. 407.)

About this time there were hundreds of men riding
on the ranges stealing cattle and horses, and as Judges
Sinclair and Cradlebaugh had refused to punish thieves,
they were allowed to steal with impunity.

The present U. S. Judges in the Territory had,
so far, refused to punish petit larceny, grand larceny,
robbery, rapes, murder, &c., unless the offenders
were men of influence among the Mormons. As con-
clusive evidence of this statement, Judge Sinclair refused to try, during a term of court of 90 days, half a
score of prisoners in G. S. L. City, who were indicted
by the grand jury, but adjourned his court without making any order concerning the prisoners, who were in

jail, thereby legally entitling them to their liberty.

Judge Cradlebaugh dismissed Mose and Looking Glass, (207) Indians, turning them loose upon the community without trial, though indicted for ravishing a woman and her daughter, and endangering the life of the girl by enlarging her passage with a knife. The murders of Call, Brown and a dozen others, not Mormons, the Judge refused to inquire into.

In all the settlements throughout the Territory the principal men left their homes and took refuge wherever they thought most advantageous, the reason of which was that Judge Cradlebaugh had decreed to arrest all presidents and bishops, whether charged with crime or not, and Sinclair had determined to bring an army to G. S. L. City and hold a court for the arrest of the Mormon leaders.

May

On the 1st, ex Gov. Young instructed that the machinary of the Bucket factory at Parowan be brought to G. S. L. City.

Judge Sinclair returned to G. S. L. City without an army, and with no signs of his holding court at present.

Dr. Forney returned to the city, bringing three children with him. He left the residue of the children rescued by the brethren from the Indians, after the massacre at Mountain Meadows, at the Indian farm.

(See letter from J. Jaques to A. Calkin, "Mil. Star," Vol. 21, p. 476.

For Proclamation of Gov. Cumming, see "Des. News," Vol. 9, p. 80.

On the 9th, Silas Smith, Jesse Fuller, Deputy (208) Surveyor and W. M. Wall, went up to Provo Valley to lay out a town. Several men were at work on the road in Provo Canyon. A large settlement was commenced in the Provo Valley.

On the 17th, a letter from the Attorney General of the United States, containing the instructions of the President, to Alex. Wilson Esq., District Attorney for Utah, was published in the "Washington Constitution".

The President had carefully considered the condition of
Utah, and expressed himself as being satisfied with the
conduct of Mr. Wilson. He wished the law to be impartially administered, and every officer to confine
himself to his own duties. Said that he was to make no
distinction between the Gentile and Mormon, or between Indian and white men, and to prosecute the rich
and the poor, the influential and the humble with equal
rigor, and thus entitle himself to the confidence of all.
     An important and interesting letter from the
Attorney General of the United States, (Judge Black)
under the instruction of the Presdient, to the Judges of
Utah was published in the "Weekly Constitution."
     Judge Black said that the President had recieved
a letter from the Judges on the subject of the military
force, in which the court of the 2nd District of Utah
was attended during the term held at Provo. He had
carefully considered it, as well as other advices relating (209) to the same affair, and had directed the
Judge to give his answer. He wanted the Judges appointed for the Territory to confine themselves strictly
within their own official spheres. Said the Government
had a district attorney who was charged with the duties
of a public accuser, and a marshal who was responsible for the arrest and safe keeping of criminals, and
there was nothing left for the Judges to do, except to
hear patiently the cases brought before them, and to
determine them impartially, according to the evidence
adduced on both sides. In referring to the orders of the
Governor for the removal of the troops being wholly
disregarded, the Judge said-- The Governor is the
supreme executive of the Territory. He is responsible
for the public peace. From the general law of the land,
the value of his office, and the instructions he received
through the State department, it ought to have been
understood that he alone had power to issue a requisition for the movement of the troops from one part of
the Territory to another, that he alone could put the
military forces of the Union and the people of the
Territory into relations of general hostility with one
another. The instructions given to the commanding
General by the war department, were to the same ef-

fect. In that paper a requisition was not spoken of as
a thing, which anybody except the Governor could make.
Besides, the matter upon which Judge (210) Cradlebaugh's
requisition based itself was one with which the Judge
had no sort of official connection. It was the duty of
the marshal to see that the prisoners were safely kept
and forthcoming at the proper time.

On the whole the President was very decidedly of
the opinion--

First- That the Governor of the Territory alone
had power to issue a requisition upon the commanding
General for the whole, or part of the army.

Second- That there was no apparent occasion for
the presence of troops at Provo.

Third- That if a rescue of the prisoners in custody had been attempted, it was the duty of the marshal,
and not of the Judge, to summon the force, which
might be necessary to prevent it.

Fourth- That the troops ought not to have been
sent to Provo without the concurrence of the Governor,
nor kept there against his remonstrance.

Fifth- That the disregard of these principles, and
rules of action, had been in many ways extremely unfortunate.

About this time, the New York "Herald" reported
Judge Cradlebaugh removed and Gov. Cumming sustained.

On the 23rd, Seth M. Blair reported that he had
petitioned Judge Sinclair for a writ of habeas corpus to
take A. F. McDonald and - Kearns from the custody of
the army and give them a hearing as to the legality of
their imprisonment. Sinclair refused to grant the
writ upon the ground that he was aquainted with the circumstances of their (211) imprisonment.

Mr. King told J. W. Cummings that Judge Sinclair
had got an invitation to return home and resign his
judgeship, and save the disgrace of being removed.

June

See letter from Geo. A. Smith to Asa Calkin in
"Mil. Star," Vol. 21, p. 495.

On the 3rd, Hon. John Cradlebaugh wrote to Prest.
Buchanan charging the Church with the perpretation of
the Mountain Meadow massacre and other atrocious
crimes.

On the 13th, Capt. Anderson's command returned
from Fort Hall, and camped in the Big Field on a piece
of wheat belonging to John Van Cott. Mr. Van Cott
rode down to the camp and called Capt. Anderson in
question for taking this liberty, whereupon Capt.
Anderson gave him all manner of abusive language and
ordered the soldiers to arrest him. As soon as Gov.
Cumming heard of his arrest, he sent Secy. Hartnett,
and Col. J. C. Little to request Capt. Anderson to release him, which the Captain refused to do. (For details, see "Des. News.")

On the 16th, Jacob Hamblin made affidavit, in
which he said that he heard Major Lyons say in the office of Dr. Jacob Forney, Superintendent of Indian affairs, in G. S. L. City, in presence of Dr. Forney,
that he believed Brigham Young had ordered every one
of the murders which had been committed in the (212)
Territory; that he would like to have the first shot at
him, and that they meant to have started the shooting
through camping on the wheat fields the other night
(referring to Capt. Anderson's detachment camping in
the Big Field, G. S. L. City on the 13th, and Major
Lyon's detachment camping in Samuel Snyder's meadow, near G. S. L. City on the same day and without
leave.).

M. J. Shelton also made affidavit that on the 16th
of June he heard U. S. marshal Dotson remark to Secy.
Hartnett, in the store of J. M. Hockaday and Co., that
he would be damned if he was not in hopes of a row, the
night on which the U. S. troops camped on the field of
John Van Cott. Secy. Hartnett also remarked, upon
the same occasion, that he was in hopes that it might
end in a row.

On the 18th, the Judges of the Supreme Court were
in session. They decided that G. S. L. City was the
seat of government de facto. The court appointed a
court to be held at G. S. L. City on the first Monday in
August, and one at Carson Valley on the first Monday

in September.

On the 28th, Capt. Anderson of the 2nd dragoons and his command passed through G. S. L. City on their way east.

Capt. Reynolds, with his siege battery, passed through G. S. L. City on their way to Fort Van conver, Oregon Territory. The battery consisted of six pieces (213) of cannon, with an extra carriage to each gun.

Messrs. Blair and Stout, who had written to Judge Eccles at Camp Floyd, requesting that the prisoners McDonald and Kearns be placed under the care of the civil authorities, received an answer to their letter, in which Judge Eccles stated that he was informed that the prisoners there were in the custody of P. K. Dotson, marshal for the Territory, guarded by the soldiers as a civil posse, and that the general commanding had notified the marshal by letter of this date. that he would keep them no longer, and that, unless removed soon, he would order them to be released.

July

On the 1st, Capt. A. B. Miller, of the firm of Miller, Russell and Co., called upon ex Gov. Young and said that a few hours before he started from Fort Leavenworth, a telegraphic dispatch was recieved by Mr. Russell from the war department, stopping the fitting out of 1500 wagons that were fitting out for Mexico and Utah. Mr. Russell reported back that they had a thousand men employed and about 1500 wagons ready and all organized for starting. He then started for Washington to ascertain what the matter was.

Mr. Miller further said that there were 1100 murchant wagons, besides the settlers' trains on the road to G. S. L. City, and more than half of them were three ton wagons. Two million dollars' worth of goods at cost and (214) carriage, were on the way for Utah.

Mr. Miller said that Russell and Co. had had the entire control of the mail from G. S. L. City to the States.

On the 16th, Horace Greely Esq., Editor of the New York "Tribune," delivered as address before a

meeting of the G. S. L. Typographical Association,
held in the Council House.

On the 24th, Pioneers' Day was celebrated. The
ladies and gentlemen turned out en mass dressed in
home made cloth.

On the 28th, the district court met in the Council
House. The Grand jury was empannelled and sworn,
after which the Judge gave them his charge. (See
"Des News.")

The emigration to California continued to throng
the streets. They were selling their surplus outfit at
auction.

August

On the 1st, the election went off very peaceably,
whithout any opposition.

On the 11th, a U. S. soldier was shot on Main
Street G. S. L. City. The circumstances were as
follows-- The Grand jury found an indictment against
Pike of the U. S. army, for assault and battery on the
person of Howard Spencer. Pike was arrested at
Camp Floyd and brought to G. S. L. City by deputy
marshal John Bigler, and when going down Main Street
with four other non-commissioned officers a person
stepped up to him and shot him, the ball passing
through his right side. The person who shot him
walked across the street, (215) then commenced his
retreat at full speed across lots to Jordan River, and
made his escape. The wounded man made affidavit
that it was Howard Spencer who shot him.

On the 14th, Sergeant Pike, the soldier who was
shot on the 11th, died of his wound.

On the 15th, Judge Sinclair adjourned court, out
of respect to Sergeant Pike, as he said, but it was supposed that the true cause was that he was so debilitated
with intoxicants that he was unable to do business.

On the 16th, Joel Terry came in from Cedar
Valley with a letter from Bishop Allen Weeks, which
stated that last night about 11 oclock 22 soldiers came
to the settlement, six miles north from Camp Floyd,
and set fire to a stack of hay. Three young men saw

them set it on fire and rallied the settlement, and attempted to put out the fire, upon which the soldiers fired upon the citizens about 60 rounds, and thereby prevented them from extinquishing the flames. The stack and yard around it were consumed. Three of the settlers went to Camp Floyd and informed Gen'l. Johnson of what was going on. He said he would send a guard, but that he could not control the soldiers while Spencer was at large.

On the 19th, a number of mule trains, loaded with provisions, started out to meet the hand cart company.

On the 20th, Edwin D. Wooley came in from Provo and reported that he had seen Mr. Miller of Springville, who told him that on Thursday night, the 18th inst., a company of twenty men, supposed to be (216) soldiers, surrounded the house of Bishop Aaron Johnson to arrest him, but he did not know what success they had, as he had to leave in the night.

Families were leaving Cedar Valley on account of the hostile disposition of the soldiers.

On the 22nd, the U. S. District Court commenced its session at Nephi, Judge Eccles presiding.

Among the articles seized by Marshal Dotson in McKenzie's office or shop, was the plates belonging to the Deseret Currency Association. They had been hauled around from place to place until rendered useless. Dotson took them to ex Gov. Young and wished to return them, but as they were injured so much he refused to take them.

On the 27th, the "Mountaineer," a new paper was issued, and was recieved by the public in a very welcome manner. It was published and edited by Blair, Ferguson and Stout, weekly, thereafter.

The Grand jury in the Court at Nephi was composed of gamblers and Camp followers from Camp Floyd.

Word was received by ex Gov. Young from Cache Valley that the Indians had stolen sixteen horses and killed six others in retaliation for Cutler piloting Lt. Gay's company to the Indian camp in Box Elder canyon --One Indian and one squaw were wounded.

Ex Gov. Young wrote in reply that he wished (217) the people to make themselves secure in forts, and stack their hay so that the Indians could not burn it.

September

Ex Gov. Young imported, this season, with other machinery, three sugar mills, two nail machines, and a button machine, which were much needed in the Territory.

For arrival of hand cart companies see "Des. News," Vol. 9, p 212.

For minutes of a meeting of the Deseret Agricultural and Manufacturing Society, see "Des. News", Vol. 9, page 213.

For important comments in relation to the McKenzie case before the court at Nephi, see the "Mountaineer, page 10.

For "More Indian Difficulties," see "Mountaineer," page 11.

For items on emigration, see "Mil. Star," Vol. 21, p. 727.

For "Massacre near Fort Hall," see "Des. News," Vol. 9, page 227.

For "Difficulties North," see "Des. News," Vol. 9, p. 220.

On the 30th, the first annual fair of the Provo branch of the Deseret Agricultural and Manufacturing Society was held at Provo in the Store House in the Tithing Office Yard. A very respectable display of Agriculture, art and manufactures.

October

On the 3rd, the annual fair of the D. A. and M. Society (218) opened. The productions of the Territory exhibited would have done justice to any state in the Union. (For particulars, see "Mil. Star," Vol. 21, p. 800.)

For historical items, see letter from Ex Gov. Young to A. Calkin, "Mil. Star," Vol. 21, p. 816.

On the 15th, Andrew Smith was arrested for disorderly conduct. He had been living for some time in Camp Floyd and had just returned to G. S. L. City.

He got drunk and said he had come to kill Brigham
Young, but if he could not kill him he would kill Mayor
Smoot or the first Mormon he met, as he meant to
shed Mormon blood. A. O. Smoot, Mayor of G. S. L.
City, directed the police to arrest him, which was done,
and he was taken before Justice Clinton, who ordered
him to be detained until the 17th for trial.

On the 16th, a portion of the troops stationed on
Bear River passed through G. S. L. City on their way
to Camp Floyd.

On the 17th, Marshal P. K. Dotson served a writ
of habeas corpus on A. O. Smoot, issued by Judge
Eccles at Campt Floyd, directing him to bring the body
of Andrew Smith before him at Camp Floyd. Mayor
Smoot informed Mr. Dotson that Smith was not in his
custody and never was, and handed the writ back to
him, but the marshal refused to take it, saying it was
directed to A. O. Smoot and he had done with it.
Mayor Smoot sent the writ back to Judge Eccles by
express stage, informing him that Smith was not in
his charge, but he had understood he had been arrested
(219) by the police for breaking a city ordinance. He
had been tried before Justice Clinton, fined and set at
liberty.

On the 22nd, J. C. Little reported that himself,
S. M. Blair and James Ferguson had called on Gov.
Cumming in regard to a writ that had been issued at
Camp Floyd by Chief Justice Eccles for A. O. Smoot,
on a charge of contempt in not complying with a writ
of habeas corpus for the body of Andrew M. Smith.
The Governor said they must make their complaint in
writing, and then he would take the subject into consideration.

On Friday the 28th, Thos. H. Ferguson, who was
found guilty of murder at the late session of the Third
District Court for the Territory was executed. (For
particulars, see "Des. News," Vol. 9, p. 280.)

On the 29th, ex Gov. Young called on G. A. Smith
and stated that he had had several interviews with a
gentleman by the name of Capt. Gibson, who had been
for some time on the Island of New Guinea or Papua.
He had his ship seized and was imprisoned for two

years by the Dutch East Indian Company, on a charge
of exciting the natives to rebellion against the company.
Capt. Gibson's object in visiting Utah was to use his
influence with ex Gov. Young to get the Saints to move
to New Guinea or Papua. He said the climate was
very temperate, ranging from 72° to 91°.

Mr. Gibson said that the only object he had in
view in wishing to induce the Mormons to go to New
Guinea was to do good to the natives of the island, as
he believed them to be descendants of the house of (220)
Israel. Ex Gov. Young told him to investigate the
latter day work, and if he found it to be true he could
be baptized, and he would ordain him an Elder and send
him and a few other Elders to that people, and he could
do them more good that way than any other that he
knew of.

November

On the 23rd, Zerubbabel Snow, Judge of Probate
Court for Cedar County, furnished Gov. Cumming with
affidavits in regard to the outrage committed at Cedar
Fort on the 15th of August last by the soldiers of Camp
Floyd; also a schedule of property destroyed and damages sustained by the citizens of Cedar Fort, amounting to $5,188.

For "Organization of Cache Valley settlement,"
see "Des. News," Vol. 9, p 309.

On the 30th, Elder Jas. Horne and company arrived from Hebersville. Elder Horne, with six others,
started from G. S. L. City on the 18th of March last,
for the purpose of raising a crop of cotton on the Rio
Virgin. The result of their labor had produced 3,700
lbs. of cotton, which they brought with them. They
also raised about 15 gal. of molasses.

December

On the evening of the 4th, the thermometer stood
at 21° below Zero, the coldest night ever known in the
Valley prior to that time.

On the 12th, the Legislative Assembly convened at

the Social Hall in G. S. L. City. (See "Des. News,"
Vol. 9, p. 324)
    For Governor's message, see "Des. News,"
Vol. 9, p. 325.   (221)

INCIDENTS IN HISTORY OF UTAH, 1860.

January

For Memorial from Gt. Salt Lake County court
to the Territorial Legislature, on support of prisoners,
--see Deseret News, Jan. 11.

On the 15th at a party at Wilford Woodruff's,
Capt. Walter M. Gibson said that when in the States he
labored hard to have peace commissioners sent to
Utah, and, though at first unsuccessful, he eventually
was successful.

February

13th. --Election to elect city officers under the
new city charter was held to-day which resulted in the
election of the following officers:--

A. O. Smoot,	Mayor
J. C. Little,	Marshal
H. B. Clawson,	Treasurer
R. Campbell,	Recorder.

18th. --On the evening of the 18th Jacob Hamblin
arrived from Washington County. He has just returned
from an excursion to the Moquis Indians. He brought
from the Moquis' country 1 1/2 bushels of peach pips,
also some dried peaches, which Mr. Dodge, the great
horticulturist of San Bernardino, said were the best
peaches in the country. The Moquis Indians told
Mr. Hamblin that since his previous visit, some U.
S. Soldiers had been to visit them and had given them
spades, hoes and other tools, and told them to kill the
Mormons if they came (222) there again. They received Mr. Hamblin and company very kindly, but
would not trade for nor buy any of the tools he had
taken to trade to them. They thought he should give
them the tools, as the U. S. Soldiers did. The Moquis
raise a considerable quantity of peaches, which they
dry; the pips they preserve for a time of scarcity.
Mr. Hamblin states that ten families had settled at a

big spring, near the Santa Clara, six miles below
Hamblin's Fort. It was thought to be a good place to
raise cotton.

19th. --H. Lunt, Bishop of Cedar City, wrote
Feb. 5th, 1860:--

"We held a conference to-day with the Indians and
had a 'big talk.' The Piedes' Captain has lately died,
and I was chosen by them to be their 'Nehal' (captain).
We made them a present of some flour, potatoes,
wheat, &c. Many of the old Indians were dying off.

On the 20th the Regency of the University met in
G. S. L. City. Brigham Young announced his intention
to have a Free High School kept in the Wilkin House on
Union Square, and to be called the Union Academy.
Proposed Orson Pratt, Jun., and James Cobb as
teachers, and Orson Pratt, sen. as Superintendent.
Said he would lay the matter before the conference,
April next, for sanction. Also, if the conference ap-
proved of it, the Academy would be sustained from the
tithing funds. (223)

Chancellor Pratt concurred in Brigham Young's
remarks, and spoke at length of the utility of high
schools.

Brigham Young desired the Regency to visit the
schools throughout the Territory--lecture on education,
law, the sciences, &c., and call on others to lecture.

21st. --For letter from Chas. C. Rich and Erastus
Snow to the Editor "Deseret News"--headed--Tour
Through Utah County. --see "Des. News," Vol. 9,
p. 411.

29th. --On the evening of the 29th Brigham Young
called at the Historian's Office and remarked that
Genl. Johnston was about to leave for Washington, and
the rest of the army would soon leave. There were
only five companies then at Camp Floyd.

March

1st. --Geo. D. Watt called at the Historian's
Office and exhibited a box of cigars--the tobacco from
which they were made was grown by himself and manufactured in this city. The cigars looked very fine.

Prof. Orson Pratt delivered a lecture on "The
first principles of Philosophy" in the Social Hall,
G. S. L. City, which was crowded.

2nd. --Brigham Young, while in conversation with
Geo. A. Smith, said the army was all called away, except three or four companies.

Prof. Orson Pratt lectured in the 14th Ward,
G. S. L. City, upon "Natural Philosophy." At its
close Wilford Woodruff recommended that family reading (224) books, should treat on the subject of science,
&c., and not novels.

5th. --In the evening Prof. Orson Pratt delivered
a lecture in the Tabernacle on "Philosophy."

12th. --Probate Court commenced its session.
Grand Jury called and impanneled.

19th. --Prof. Orson Pratt lectured in the evening
on "Astronomy."

April

6th. --Annual Conference Minutes--see "Des.
News," Vol. 10, p. 45.

8th. --Col. Cook had been appointed to the command of the army to be left in Utah (10 companies.).

9th. --Jesse W. Fox, Surveyor General, reports
that he had surveyed 4 town sites in Cache Valley and
from 50 to 100 lots of farming lands of 20 acres each.

10th. --Bishop Henry Lunt of Cedar City, called
on Governor Cumming. The Governor enquired about
Brigham Young and said he would go and see him often,
but if he did, it would be the hue and cry that the
damned old Governor could do nothing without going to
consult Brigham Young. Said, this was an abused
people and if he could do them good he would.

16th. --The Indians have committed several outrages in the northern counties the last week. A man
named Thomas Miles was shot with (225) ten arrows
and beat with a war club.

An Indian was brutally murdered on the Sevier
River near the bridge, by Deputy Marshal Kirk and a
man from Camp Floyd named Johnston. The body was
found in the river by Bp. Branson and others.

21st. --California mail arrived and brought papers confirming the intelligence of the death of T. S. Williams, by Indians, near San Bernardino.

For particulars of the murder of a young Indian on the Sevier, see "Mountaineer" April 21.

23rd. --John Spriggs called at Historian's and presented specimens of coal dug from the coal mines on the Weber. The samples were as fine as any found in almost any country. Mr. Spriggs has also discovered a vein of black band iron stone, and a fine vein of Potter's clay two feet thick.

May

4th. --A young man, John Parkinson, stated that the Indians in Cache Valley were very hostile. They had stolen $1500.00 worth of horses from the Inhabitants of Cache Valley.

A letter from Capt. W. H. Hooper dated Washington, May 8th, said that Mr. A. Wilson was appointed Chief Justice of Utah, Mr. Hardy of Georgia, and Robt. P. Flenniken of Pittsburg, Associate Justices. Mr. Wootten was confirmed as Secretary. (226)

24th. --Pony express from California reported the Pah-Ute Indians hostile. Two express riders were reported killed and another missing. The boys at all the stations between Diamond Springs and Carson Valley were driven in. In a battle on the Truckee about 60 persons from Carson were reported killed.

Howard Egan obtained from Governor Cumming a requisition for a detachment of troops from Camp Floyd to protect the Western Mail and Express.

26th. --B. Young went to look at the road for hauling granite from Little Cottonwood Cañon. He had given a contract to John Sharp to haul 500 cords granite for the foundation of the Temple.

27th. --The "Mountaineer" published an extra concerning the Indian difficulties on the route to California.

28th. --The crickets had been so numerous at Battle Creek, Utah Co., that they made the earth look black. The people with cattle and chickens turned out to fight them by stamping and thrashing. Straw was

also put on the ground and burned. In three days the
crickets took flight to the mountains.

31st. --Word was recieved from Carson Valley
confirming the reports of the Indian difficulties and the
killing of about 60 men, including Major Orms- (227)
by the Commander, on the Truckee river, in a battle
with the Indians. Judge Cradlebaugh went out at the
head of a party from Carson, but got frightened and
returned to Carson. The war was the effect solely of
the disgraceful treatment of the Indians by the whites.
The women and children were being sent away from
Carson Valley to California. Fifteen hundred persons
left in one day.

June

1st. --Eastern pony express arrived about 1 p.m.
with word that the Senate had confirmed the appointment of Harding of Ga. and Flanniken of Pittsburgh,
Pa., Associate Justices of Utah. Judge Black had
assured Capt. Hooper that the Senate would not reject
Alexander Wilson for Chief Justice, and Mr. Grice of
Pa., had been appointed Marshal for Utah.

4th. -- Excursion Through the Northern Counties
--see "Des. News." Vol. 10, p. 124.

5th. --Pony Express arrived about 10 a.m. from
Diamond Springs and Rush Valley. Communication
with California was suspended through the Indian difficulties.

12th. --The Express from Ruby Valley arrived at
7.15 p.m. Indians still hostile. No communication
with California.

19th. --Pony express came in from California at
10.15 a.m. Indians still troublesome. Route open.

Company of emigrants for California arrived from
(228) the States.

21st. --California mail arrived to-day. The
California people believed the Carson Indian war was
immediately caused by abuse of the Indians, and that
the Mormons instigated and drilled the Indians also
furnished them with arms, ammunition and supplies.

25th. --Pony express arrived in the evening from

Robert's Creek. Indians had again attacked Schell
Creek Station, which was ultimately abandoned to them.

26th. --Pony express arrived at 8 p. m. from Ruby
Valley. Indians had burned Butte Valley Station. Sub-
Indian agent, Wm. Rodgers, was distributing blankets
and shirts to the Indians. He and his associates had
shot two Indians and were defending themselves.

July

4th. --Celebration of Our National Birthday--see
"Des. News," Vol. 10, p. 148.

Emigration. --see "Des. News," Vol. 10, p. 172.

6th. --The pony express arrived from the West in
the evening. The Indians still very hostile. They felt
determined that the whites should not pass through
their country.

19th. --A large company of emigrants from the
Eastern States passed through G. S. L. City for
California; with good horse teams and loose horses.

20th. --"The Companies on the Plains."--see
"Des. News," Vol. 10, p. 188.

24th. --Excursion to the Headwaters of Big
Cottonwood. --see "Des. News," Vol. 10, p. 165. (229)

"The Twenty-fourth of July."--see "Des. News,"
Vol. 10, p. 176.

August

3rd. --1300 acres of grain are sown in Beaver
settlement.

4th. --President and Directors of the Deseret
Agricultural and Manufacturing Society met in G. S. L.
City.

In Minersville 500 acres were in cultivation and
the settlers expected a crop of about 5000 bushels of
wheat.

9th. --A train of 30 wagons, emigrants under
Capt. Walling, arrived in the afternoon. Ten wagons
of Gentiles came in with them, all from the States.
The bulk of the company camped on the Eighth Ward
Public Square

15th. --Amusing Visit to the White House.

Geo. A. Smith went over to B. Young's Office,
and Capt. Hooper showed a daguerrotype of the members of the House of Representatives, and told several
amusing anecdotes of several of them. He stated that
when the Japanese Embassy were entertained at the
White House, Mr. Buchanan instructed the door-keeper
to permit the members of Congress to enter with not
more than one lady each. The Honorable Isaac N.
Morris of Illinois took with him five ladies. The door-
keeper told him that he could not be admitted with more
than one lady. Said Mr. Morris "Well, I am in a devil
of a fix! Here I am the Delegate (230) from Utah, with
my five wives!" "Well," said the doorkeeper, "if you
really are the Delegate from Utah, you may pass in."
Mr. Morris afterwards apologized to Capt. Hooper for
making use of his name to procure the admittance of
the four ladies into the White House.

24th. --Brigham Young exhibited some nails made
at D. H. Wells' factory, where 600 lbs. could be made
per day. They were of good quality.

26th. --For "Arrivals from the East.--see "Des.
News," Aug. 29.

27th. --Capt. D. Robinson's Hand Cart Company
of emigrants from the States arrived about 5 p.m.,
consisting of about 230 souls, with six wagons, 39
handcarts and ten tents. They camped on the Eighth
Ward Square, and were serenaded by Capt. Ballos'
Band. The Bishops of G. S. L. City sent from their
various wards an abundance of vegetables and other
eatables.

28th. --For arrival of companies.--see "Des.
News," Vol. 10, p. 212.

September

On the 1st Capt. John Smith's company of emigrants arrived, and on the 4th Capt. J. D. Ross' company.

8th. --Probate Court met. Case B. Young v.
Ex-Marshal P. K. Dotson. Decided for Plaintiff.
Dotson to pay $1668.00 damage to plates of Deseret

Association, and $648.66 costs. (231)

October

3rd. --Territorial Fair commenced this morning, Pitt's brass band in attendance, at the Deseret Store, G. S. L. City.

Frank Wooton, Secretary of Utah, in a state of intoxication, went to the President's Office, G. S. L. City, and desired gatekeeper Attwood to let him in. Attwood informed him that he was not in a condition to go in. Wooton said he was Secretary of State and it was a damned pretty thing if he could not go in. Wished Attwood to make a minute of it, and, if he would not, he would do so himself. Wooton enquired for H. B. Clawson, and on being told he was not there he still insisted on going in. Atwood informed him that if he desired to see Brigham Young he would have to call again. He replied that he should not call again and went off cursing and saying that the Federal Officers were insulted and the dignity of the United States trampled on in the person of the Secretary of Utah.

John Kalapsye, (a Hungarian) in the U. S. employ at Camp Floyd, called on Geo. A. Smith, and afterwards on Brigham Young with whom he conversed for a long time. Mr. Young said he had only one favor to ask of him--that when he left Utah he would tell the truth about the people.

3rd. --"Weber County Fair."--see "Des. News," Vol. 10, p. 249.

4th. --Fair continued in G. S. L. City. Very good exhibition of home industry. At the cattle (232) show at the Territorial Fair, Mr. Murphy said--one of the bulls was better than the one that took the prize at Dresdon, Weikly Co., and Paris, Benton Co., West Tennessee.

Judge Kinney arrived.

5th. --Capt. Budge's emigrant company arrived.

6th. --For Minutes of "Semi-Annual Conference.--see "Des. News," Vol. 10, p. 253.

Daniel W. Jones started May 1st, 1860, with four companies 5th Infantry, three companies 10th Infantry

and piloted them to New Mexico. On returning he was
attacked by Indians and robbed of $600 in wagon, mules,
and merchandise.

12th. --"Arrival of emigrants from the West."--
see "Des, News," Vol. 10, p. 261.

16th. --John Sharp reported that the men were still
digging into the new coal beds near the Weber. They
made a fire on Saturday with a few shovels full which
they excavated, and on returning Monday, it was still
burning and a good fire. Thirty-five men were at work
in the Cañons on this side, making a good road, but
there were some difficult places and the work progressed slowly.

17th. --Gov. Cumming sent for Brigham Young to
come and see him, and B. Young called on him this
morning. The Governor consulted with him in relation
to the expediency of calling a spe- (233) cial Session of
the Legislature in consequence of judges Kinney and
Crosby ruling that the judges could not do anything in
the way of holding courts until the Legislature had met
and assigned them to their districts by name. Governor Cumming wished to know if there was any impropriety in calling the Legislature together. Should the
Supreme Court sustain this Rule, it will completely
invalidate the Acts of the Judiciary in Utah during the
last four years, soon after Governor Cumming came
into the Valley.

For "Report of the Board of Directors of the
Deseret Agricultural and Manufacturing Society on the
Exhibition of 1860."--see "Des. News," Vol. 10,
p. 261.

18th. --A. R. Wright arrived with his train consisting of eleven wagons and sixty-three head of cattle.
He had performed the journey from the States in sixty
travelling days.

For Proclamation of Gov. Cumming, calling
Legislature together, Dec. 10, see "Mountaineer,"
Dec. 20, also "Mil. Star," Vol. 22, p. 796.

November

2nd. --Murder of George A. Smith, Jun.[r] by

Indians. --See "Des. News," Vol. 10, p. 317.

12th. --Convening of the Extra Session of the Legislature. --see "Des. News," Vol. 10, p. 292.

Governors Message to the Legislative Assembly. --see "Des. News," Vol. 10, p. 296.

On the 19th, thirteen teams, from Parowan, arrived bringing back the bucket factory, staves, &c.

21st. --Capt. Walter M. Gibson started for Japan, (234) &c., to-day, south via San Francisco. He took his daughter with him, but his two sons remained.

24th. --Secession of the Southern States. "The Mountaineer" to-day contain the news, by pony express, concerning the withdrawing of the Southern States from the Union. It commenced in South Carolina in fulfilment of the prophecy of Joseph Smith, the Prophet, or the revelation of the Lord through him, which had been published in the "Pearl of Great Price" and other books.

December

10th. --The Legislative Assembly met at the Social Hall at 10 a.m., organized and adjourned to meet at 11 o'clock next day in the Court House.

For communication to the Legislative Assembly of Utah annexed to the Governor's Message. --See "Des. News," Vol. 10, p. 320.

On Christmas night, Secretary Wooton happened on "a Bender" with a double barreled shot gun in his hand. He gave hot chase to Mr. James, Representative from Carson County, Mr. Broadhead, a lawyer of eastern recent importation, and several others who took the matter up seriously, and made off at a 2. - 40 pace, amid the vociferous threatenings to shoot of the elated Secretary. He was kindly taken and locked up till he got sober and felt "elevated a little lower." (235)

INCIDENTS IN THE HISTORY OF UTAH.

January, 1861

On the 1st, the new Assembly Rooms in the 13th Ward, G. S. L. City, were dedicated. (See "Des. News," Vol. 10, p. 357)

On the 3rd, W. Woodruff, Chairman of the Committee on Revenue, to whom had been referred that portion of the Governor's message relating to the subject of Taxation at Fairfield and Camp Floyd, gave his report, for which see "Des. News," Vol. 10, p. 362.

In a letter from Geo. A. Smith to John L. Smith, the following account of the murder of G. A. Smith Jun[r], by the Navahoe Indians, was given, as related by Thales Haskell:--

"George A. was shot on horseback. In bending his head down to dodge a ball aimed thereat, he fell, and the Indians took off his buckskin shirt, but disturbed him no further. George pulled three arrows out of his body before the brethren arrived. Bros. Haskell, M[c] Connell and Hamblin hazarded their lives in bringing George into camp. The Navahoe Indians, with whom Bro. Haskell was aquainted informed him that George was killed by Indians who had some of their relations killed by U. S. soldiers. George was so paralyzed by the shot in the hip, that he seemed to have little feeling in his lower extremities, consequently he did not suffer a great deal of pain. The party had no idea whatever, that the Indians would kill any of them, though aware they would steal. It appeared (236) that two-thirds of the Navahoes were anxious to destroy the whole party. Their escape was rather miraculous. The Moquitch mission is broken up for the present."

On the 14th, a meeting of Bishops and members of the Legislature was held in Brigham Young's new School House, for the purpose of having a conversation over the measures contemplated for the guidance of the future emigration from the Missouri River to G. S. L. City. Brigham Young, H. C. Kimball and several apostles were present. (See "Des. News," Vol. 10, p. 372.)

On the 17th, the members of the Legislative Assembly had a social party in the Social Hall, G. S. L. City. (See "Des. News," Vol. 10, p 373.)

February

For an article on Emigration, see "Mil. Star," Vol. 23, p. 72.

For particulars of an Indian outbreak at Grantsville, see "Des. News," Vol. 10, p. 400.

On the 11th, at a meeting of the Church of Jesus Christ of Latter-day Saints, held at South Weber, Davis Co., by Wilford Woodruff and John Taylor, the following named persons were cut off from the Church of Jesus Christ of Latter-day Saints for believing in the claims of one Joseph Morris to be a prophet, seer and revelator in place of Brigham Young:-- Richard Cook, Bishop of South Weber; John Cook, John Firth, William Kendall, (237) Robert Farley, John Parson, Nels Morrison, Nathan Brooks, John Frolsom, Mrs Margaret Cook, Mrs Helen Cook, Mrs Sarah Cook, Mrs Mary Cook, Mrs Anne Cook, Mrs Joanna Kendall, Mrs Adelia Smith Frolsom.

On the 19th, Orson Hyde delivered a political lecture in the 13th Ward Assembly Rooms, G. S. L. City, for which see "Des. News," Vol. 10, p. 408.

For letter from R. L. Campbell to Geo. Q. Cannon, relative to the erection of the Seventies' Hall of Science, &c., see "Mil. Star," Vol. 23, p. 271.

A circular was forwarded by the presidency of the Church to the various settlements, recommending the sending of ox teams from the Territory to the Missouri River to fetch emigrants and their baggage, and such other things as might be procured.

March

On the 4th, the annual election of the Deseret

Agricultural and Manufacturing Society was held at the
City Hall, G. S. L. City. (See "Des. News," Vol. 11,
p. 1.

For "Indians in Tooele," see "Des. News," Vol.
11, p. 5.

For "Encampment of Indians in Mill Creek," see
"Des. News," Vol. 11, p. 8.

For "Indian Troubles in Prospective," see "Des.
News," Vol. 11, p. 16.

On the 28th, George A. Smith returned from a
trip south. He said the lead mines worked by N. V.
Jones had turned in silver worth $1700 a ton. (238)

April

On the 1st, Delegate Capt. Hooper presented to
the U. S. Senate a list of names of inhabitants of Utah
to fill the government offices in Utah Territory. He
presented Brigham Young for Governor.

A circular from the President and Directors of
the Deseret Agricultural and Manufacturing Society, to
the inhabitants of the Territory of Utah, was issued,
from which the following is extracted:--

"We desire to place before you our position and
propects, that, understanding these, you may not only
associate with us willingly, but also realize something
of the results to be attained by that harmonious co-
operation. The Legislation having made no appropriations to the Society this year, it is presumed that our
future operations will have to be self sustaining. We
must do without the support of our infancy and child-
hood, and rely upon ourselves; hence, we wish to urge
upon you the propriety of organizing auxiliary branches
in every district and settlement of our Territory. ***.

"We, therefore respectfully, yet earnestly, invite
all citizens to become members of the parent society,
and announce that we shall accept of all such on payment of one dollar annually. ***.

"The Board has had in contemplation, for some
time, the establishment of an experimental farm, nursery, &c. Late debate, proving the necessity and (239)
advantages of such farm, (even though on a limited

scale) has determined them to make the attempt. The
Mayor and Common Council of G. S. L. City, with a
like appreciation, nobly offered a choice piece of suitable land on a five years' lease, for a nominal consideration, and we are now preparing to raise choice
grains, grasses, roots, fruits, shrubs, trees, plants,
flowers, &c.; of course this is a labor of time and consequent expense. From the many communications addressed to us, from the manifest interest felt for us by
the Agricultural Department at Washington and in many
sections of the States, we hope to be able to remit to
branch societies, for distribution, some of the products
of this enterprise, together with the results of our experiments; for this we need your assistance, your
funds to put them out to usury for our common benefit.

"From this fund will arise also the premiums
given at our State Fair, to compete in which all members are eligible. ** We have determined to award
diplomas, periodicals, magazines, and standard works
on subjects interesting to us as agriculturists, mechanics, &c. ** Thus we may treasure up knowledge
and intelligence, which will be its own exceeding great
reward, constituting, it may be some inducement to
our rising generation to spend their idle hours in study,
and (240) around their father's fireside.

"It is also in contemplation to form a library in
connection with the Society, to consist of Standard
works on agriculture, mechanics, science, &c., for
general reference and consultation. Several of our
most prominent citizence have cordially proffered their
influence and assistance here, and in the States.

"** The importance of stock, of new grains, useful roots and fruits, labor saving machinery, &c., are
some of the first things which will demand our attention. **

"Is there one man identified with us who will stand
aloof? We believe not; hence we feel assured now is
the time for action, that we may keep pace with the
general spirit of our community."

On the 5th, the Utah Chief, Peteetneet, accompanied by Sanpitch and some twenty other Indians of
their tribe, came into G. S. L. City to see the super-

intendent, get some presents, &c. (See "Des. News,"
Vol. 11, p. 40)

On the 6th, the General Conference of the Church
of Jesus Christ of Latter-day Saints convened in the
Tabernacle, G. S. L. City. (See "Des. News," Vol.
11, p. 44.)

On the 8th, George A. Smith and Wilford Woodruff
ordained A. Vanderwoode to the office of a Seventy,
blessed him and set him apart as the first missionary
ever sent to Holland. He was a native of Holland. (241)

May

On the 15th, Brigham Young and a number of
other citizens of distinction left G. S. L. City to pay a
visit to the south. (See "Des. News," Vol. 11, p 116.)

For historical items, see letter from H. C.
Kimball to the Presidency of the European Mission, in
"Mil. Star," Vol. 23, p. 477.

On the 17th, Gov. Cummings, accompanied by his
wife, left G. S. L. City, on his return to the States,
having as understood, asked for and obtained from the
Department leave of absence for six or eight months,
and it was presumed that he did not expect or intend to
return and resume his official duties. (See "Des.
News," Vol. 11 p. 96)

For account of the new settlement on the Sevier,
see "Des. News," Vol. 11, p. 123.

June

On the 8th, Brigham Young and company arrived
in G. S. L. City from their trip south.

For account of Brigham Young's & Co's trip south,
and other historical facts, see letter from him to A. M.
Lyman and C. C. Rich, in "Mil. Star," Vol. 23, p. 509.

July

On the 4th, the anniversary of American independence was celebrated. (See "Des. News," Vol. 11, p. 148.
For description of G. S. L. City Theatre, &c.,

see "Mil. Star," Vol. 23, p 538.

For historical information, see extract of a letter from Wm Clayton to Geo. Q. Cannon, in "Mil Star," Vol. 23, p. 566. (242)

August

On the 16th, Mr. Carpenter, President of the Salt Lake and California Telegraph Line, called on Brigham Young to secure his interest in protection of said line.

For Resignations and appointment in the Nauvoo Legion of the Territory of Utah, see "Des. News," Vol. 11, p. 191.

September

On the 2nd, a company left G. S. L. City for the purpose of selecting a suitable location and making surveys for a new settlement in Uintah, before the main company which had been selected to go thither, and which would start, according to arrangements, on or about the 23rd inst., should arrive.

On the 4th, a wooden font, 9 1/2 x 12 feet, erected by Brigham Young, a few rods east of his school-house, G. S. L. City, with two dressing rooms attached, made by boarding the large car or wagon used in a celebration in 1852 or 1853, was dedicated and Brigham Young placed it in the hands of the Bishops for their use.

On the 6th, Brigham Young and company left G. S. L. City for Cache Valley.

On the 9th, John M. Lytle, Mosiah L. Hancock, Wm P. Lytle, Joseph Harmon, Joseph M^c. Rae and John Fay started for Uintah Valley. They were volunteers to make the road thither.

The authorities of G. S. L. City, having hauled the frame work of a market place to South Temple Street near East Temple Street, west side, the joiners (243) were framing it together.

On the 12th, Brigham Young and company returned to G. S. L. City. The Indians at Box Elder were disaffected and in the northern settlements of Cache had stolen sixty horses.

On the 13th, Elisha Jones brought some few specimens of seven headed wheat, grown at North Bend, about 6,000 feet above the level of the sea.

On the 15th, Levi Stewart and E. W. Van Etten arrived with express from Uintah Company, saying they had not found the good country anticipated. Brigham Young directed to John Lytle to recall the road makers.

On the 18th, the pony express arrived. New arrangements were entered into to increase the members of the pony express club. Hitherto Brigham Young, the "Des. News," and a few others, paid the whole expense of the messages received. The design was to increase the members of the club to 100, which would reduce the expense to 20 cents per week to each member.

On the 19th, the Uintah road party returned. Surveyor General Fox arrived the previous evening, he and party having explored extensively Uintah Valley.

For "Evacuation of Camp Floyd, by the U. S. Army," see "Mill. Star," Vol. 23, p 612.

For report of the exploring and surveying party that started for Uintah Valley on the 2nd, see "Des. News," Vol. 11, p. 172. (244)

On the 23rd, the Hon. J. M. Bernhisel, Delegate to Congress, left for Washington in the Overland Mail coach.

On the 25th, the pony express arrived. Express read by Wm Clayton in the school house. So many had joined the club, that the President's Office, in which the express had hitherto been read, was too small to convene the club comfortably.

The "News" reappeared to the satisfaction of many who were hungering and thirsting for news. The pony express not being published, and the complete suspension of the "Deseret News" and "Mountaineer" for months back, had created a dearth for news.

On the 28th, Capt. Hooper received a letter from Governor Cummings from Boston, from which it was easily inferred that he would like the people to petition for him to be Governor again.

During this month, several companies of emigrants arrived in G. S. L. City, from the East.

October

On the 6th, the Semi-Annual Conference of the Church of Jesus Christ of Latter-day Saints convened in the Bowery in G. S. L. City. (See "Des. News," Vol. 11, p. 185)

On the 11th, Mr. Street, Agent for the Western Telegraph Line, commenced at Livingston, Bell and Co's store, G. S. L. City, and put up insulators and wire, nearly to the south part of the City. (245)

On the 13th, Brigham Young wrote to Orson Hyde, requesting him to raise and organize, in Sanpete County, thirty to fifty families to settle in the southern part of the Territory, with a view to the cultivation of cotton.

On the 14th, M^r. Creighton and Telegraph Constructors brought the insulators and wire into G. S. L. City, and finished putting it up in the afternoon, by drawing it into the store lately occupied by Hooper, Eldridge and Co. The wire was up, to the States, except a small connection which needed to be made between Echo Canyon and Fort Bridger.

For letter from Supt. of Indian affairs, on Indian Affairs, see "Deseret News," Vol. 11, p. 192.

The telegraph dispatch from the East, which came in by mail on the 15th, from "Outer Station at Pacific Springs," brought the following paragraph, dated, Washington, October 9th. :--

"Brigham Young has lost Uintah Valley--one of the most fertile in Utah, after having announced his intention to settle it with the Saints. The President, by an order dated October, has directed an Indian reservation to be made there."

On Sunday, August 25th, a company of about 200 efficient men were called to go and make a settlement in the Uintah Valley, which had always been represented the finest valley in the Territory. (246)

Surveyor General Fox and several pioneers were sent ahead to explore the country, and in a week after a few road makers followed after them, and the bulk of the company made preparations to follow. Soon an express arrived from the explorers, stating that the

Valley had been misrepresented, and was not adapted
to sustain large settlements, which statement was confirmed by the party on their return. On receiving the
express, Brigham Young had it read to the meeting in
the Bowery, when he publicly announced the abandon-
ment of the project. Mr. Martin, Superintendent of
Indian Affairs for the Territory, on hearing of the proposed enterprise, immediately wrote to the Commissioner of Indian Affairs, informing him of the same,
and recommending the setting apart of the Valley and
vicinity for an Indian reservation, in order to prevent
the Mormons from settling there.

The paragraph quoted above shows that President
Lincoln had acted upon the recommendation of
Mr. Martin, with the expectation of breaking up a newly
formed settlement of 200 or 300 families, and probably
raising a quarrel between the Government and the
Mormons.

The following history of the settling of Southern
Utah was given in an extemporary address in the Historian's Office, G. S. L. City, Thursday, Oct. 17,
1861, by Elder George A. Smith, and reported by I.
V. Long:--

"In the year 1854, a number of brethren, including (247) Jacob Hamlin, Rufus Allen and others, having
been selected and appointed, and having been previously
engaged in missionary labors and exertions among the
Indians of Harmony, Santa Clara and Rio Virgen, located a place for a fort on the Santa Clara stream,
about nine miles above its juction with the Rio Virgen.
They selected a small fertile spot, overshadowed with
large cottonwood trees of very luxuriant growth, on
the north side of which was a high mountain, apparently
of red sandstone, forming a semi circle, like a half
moon. The heat of the southern sun rendered the place
very warm, and, perhaps, aided in the luxuriant
growth of the vegetation along the stream, where the
trees could gather moisture.

"They built a few small log cabins, after which,
they sent to Parowan and Cedar City, a distance of
from 70 to 90 miles, to obtain mechanics to assist
them in building a stone fort, inclosing those cabins.

They planted a few cotton seeds, a little indigo, some corn and garden vegetables. The band of Indians who occupy the land on those two rivers were naked, and they were denominated Pi-edes. They cultivated small patches of corn and melons, which they did almost entirely without implements, and, of course, their manner of cultivation was exceedingly rude. They irrigated the land by just simply turning on the water, and letting it run to great excess, washing away and wasting a great deal of soil, (248) and rendering it unfit for use. In time of scarcity they lived upon seeds of wild cymling made into cake; it is a very bitter sort of squash, with a hard shell, and these seeds were ground up for bread in times of great hunger, but only eaten at those times.

"The missionaries built a number of cabins of small cottonwood logs, which they cut along the stream, covering them with willows and dirt. These cabins they erected in a square, and soon after surrounded it with a stone wall about nine feet high, two feet thick and 120 feet square.

"Very little farming was done, and that in a very rude way, until 1857. I visited that country in the summer of 1857; there were then thirteen Indian dams across the stream, above the Santa Clara Fort, and there was not water enough came down to the Fort to furnish palatable drink to the inhabitants there at that time. The settlers had good specimens of cotton; they had the first growth of peach trees, a few, not numbering more than 25 or 30 in the whole place. They had cultivated about 30 or 40 acres of land.

"While there I should have suffered severely for the want of wholesome water, --the thermometer being 105° in the shade--had it not been for the abundance of water melons brought in by the Indians. In consequence of the heat and the haste I was in, I travelled in the (249) night, came down the canyon known as Jacob's Twist, fifteen miles from the Fort, and proceeded up the river over a road that is scarcely passable even in the day time, till I was surrounded by a large number of Indians, who invited me to stay over night. I thought proper to accept. They brought us corn and water

melons, and, in fact, treated us very kindly. They
had then indigo growing, but it was from seed brought
from India and did not seem suitable for this country,
and did not yield seed for several years, and they finally lost the seed.

"A little cotton has been raised in this settlement
every year from then till the present time, and it has
invariably produced well and been of a good quality.
The arrangement with the Indians in relation to their
manner of irrigation, was made by getting them together and aiding them to perform with the plow what
they had been accustomed to do with sticks, and to
teach them to irrigate in a way to avoid the waste of
water occasioned by irrigating in their slovenly manner.

"Fourteen miles easterly, from this point on the
Rio Virgen, a settlement was formed for the raising of
cotton, in 1857. The site selected was known as
Washington City. The persons forming this settlement were mostly southern men, who had lived in
Texas and other southern States, where they were in
the habit of raising cotton by negro labor and with very
little culture. When they arrived in (250) this desert
region, they were terribly home sick and disconted,
and out of about 100 that settled there, probably not
twenty remain to the present time. The settlement
now numbers only about thirty families. They planted
their cotton seed which they had brought from the
States, and which was several years old. They also
planted corn and several kinds of vegetables. They
raised a good crop of corn, but not over one third of
the cotton seed came up. They did not know how to
irrigate it; hence they had to learn that by experiments.
The experiments amounted to failure in many instances,
at the same time almost every man who planted cotton
was enabled to gather a little. It was generally planted
in patches of quarter acres scattered over a field of
400 acres.

"Robert D. Covington, who was appointed Bishop
of this place, has cultivated cotton every year since,
and he has preserved specimens from each year's
crop up to 1860, and, doubtless, will save some this

year too. Every year the staple has improved and the
seed is becoming more natural to the climate, and the
improvements thus made appear to give manifest evidence of success, as well as encouragement for the
continuance of the enterprise.

"In the year 1857 there was a quantity of peach
stones planted, but as very few had fenced to any great
extent, there was little or no protection against the
ravages of cattle, and consequently the peach trees
were considerably (251) browsed down; however, the
culture of peaches took its start from that very year,
and many very fine bearing trees exist now.

"In the fall of 1858, a considerable amount of
grape cuttings, imported from California, were scattered through the country, but few, however, were
taken care of, and those men living on the Santa Clara,
had but little time to fence, devoting their exertions to
the instruction of the Indians. The culture of the sor-
gum sucre, or chinese sugar cane, commenced in
1858 and has been successfully and profitably prose-
cuted up to the present time.

"The people of this settlement have worked under
the greatest disadvantages--they had to go from 50 to
90 miles to get their wheat ground; all the way up hill,
over the rim of the basin, and they had frequently to go
that distance to get a little job of blacksmithing done.
Many Southern men, who had been cotton raisers, declared that cotton nevered could be raised there, and
that it was only a hoax to think of it. Many of the early
settlers who have remained there are acquiring considerable herds of cattle, goats and sheep, which they
keep at the Mountain Meadows and other places found
along the rim of the Great Basin and other grassy
places within forty miles of the settlements.

"A location was made at a place, since called
Toquerville in the spring of 1858, by T. I. Willis, and
(252) the soil soon proved to be not as productive as at
other places, but the climate more healthy.

"In the spring of 1859, settlements were made in
the Upper Vergin by Nephi and Sixtus E. Johnson and
others. To get to this point they had to pass through
the canyons and other mountains that had generally

been considered impassable. The same health and
prosperity has attended the settlements in those upper
valleys, that has attended that of Toquerville, and the
soil being richer almost to an excess.

"Aided by appropriations from the Territorial
Legislature, the roads considered so very difficult
heretofore, have been rendered quite passable. In
1857, in my journey from old Harmony to the present
seat of Washington, I thought it was the most desperate
piece of road that I ever travelled in my life, the whole
ground for miles being covered with stones, volcanic
rock, cobble heads and so forth; and, in places, deep
sand. Our slow progress caused us to suffer for want
of water. When we reached the "Grape Vine" Springs,
it was regarded by me as one of the pleastaness spots
upon the earth--a little cool water in a desert!

"The Indians inhabiting these springs are among
the most degraded specimens of humanity. When
General Fremont passed through this country in 1844,
his party unmercifully killed a number of those Indians,
and emigrants and travellors have considered it lawful
(253) to shoot them whenever they approached their
camp, whether friendly or otherwise; the saying being
frequently made, "It does the rascals good to bleed
them." This course of treatment had rendered it both
difficult and dangerous for the missionaries to go
among them, and it required a good deal of patience,
time and perseverance to prevent their murdering the
emigration, or any straggler that came along, or that
might leave the company when passing through.

"The natives then cultivated water melons, which
were, however, of an inferior kind; they also cultivated
a certain weed resembling the red root or green
amaranth, for the sake of the seed it yielded. When I
went down there and stepped into their corn patch, I
pulled up one of these red roots, and they were offended
about it, observing that they raised them for the seed.

"Among their regulations or domestic institutions,
was one, not altogether favorable to old maids and vir-
gins of mature age, who, refusing to marry after five
applications, were ravished by the disappointed suitors,
four of them holding her in turn. The Chief was re-

monstrated with, by Jacob Hamblin, for allowing such a thing, but he, (Tutsegabbots), said it was right and according to the custom of his fathers, that a squaw who refused to marry and bear children, should be compelled to become a mother; then as it was done in this way, nobody could tell who was the father of the child." (254)

For account of the completion of the telegraph line between Utah and the States, and first messages passed over it, see "Des. News," Vol. 11, p. 189.

D. H. Wells spent several hundred dollars lately in experimenting on iron ore in Big Cottonwood Canyon, which turned out to be copper, quite a large vein of it.

On the 28th, Geo. A. Smith called on Brigham Young in his office. The Petition for a post office at the central city, about to be located in Washington County, was read, and Brigham Young was asked to name the city. He told Geo. A. Smith he would name it if he would be satisfied, which he said he would. Brigham Young then named it "St. George."

On the 29th, a petition for post office at St George, Washington County, with signatures, was mailed to Hon. J. M. Bernhisel.

November

The teams which were hauling blocks of granite for the Temple, were bringing in their heavy loads every day, generally three and four yokes of cattle, and a load consisted of one large block. About 40 or 50 stone cutters were on the Temple Block, at work on the granite blocks.

For article on the training of the Latter-day Saints, see "Mil. Star," Vol. 23, p. 739.

For letter on "Utah Affairs," see "Mil. Star," Vol. 24, p. 42. (255)

December

For historical letter on the Southern mission (the cotton country), see "Mil. Star," Vol. 24, p. 41.

On the 9th, the Legislative Assembly met at the

court house, G. S. L. City, and organized. (See "Des. News," Vol. 11, p. 194.)

For Governor John W. Dawson's message, see "Des. News," Vol. 11, p. 197.

On the 12th, George A. Smith dictated a memorial for the admission of the State of Deseret (Utah) into the Union.

On the 15th, George A. Smith presented to Brigham Young an act, to provide for calling a convention, who said, --"That is right, and let the convention ask the general government to admit us as a State."

On the 18th, George A. Smith dictated a memorial to Congress for Lands to Settlers, and for educational purposes.

The foundation walls of the Temple, which had been temporarily covered up, when the work thereon was suspended in 1858, to prevent injury while the war cloud, then approaching from the East, was passing over, were recently uncovered and the rubbish cleared away, preparatory to the recommencement of the work of building early in the coming spring.

There had been a large quantity of granite blocks hauled from the Little Cottonwood Quarry during the last two months, most of which were squared and fitted for the places they were to occupy in the walls.

On the 19th, Geo. A. Smith dictated a memorial to (256) Congress for Semi-Weekly Mail from Fillmore to San-Bernardino.

For an act to provide for a Convention of Delegates for the formation of a Constitution and state government, which Governor Dawson vetoed, see "Des. News," Vol. 11, p. 208.

For "Executive Communications," see "Des. News," Vol. 11, p. 208.

On the 24th, the new meeting and school house in the 14th Ward was dedicated. (For description of same, see "Des. News," Vol. 11, p. 216.)

On the 31st, Gov. Dawson resigned his office, and left for the East. (See "Des. News," Vol. 11, p. 212.) (259)

INDICENTS IN HISTORY OF UTAH, 1862

January

On the 4th, Mr. Rockwood, from the special committee appointed to enquire into the reasons that induced Gov. Dawson to leave the Terriroty during the session of the Legislative Assembly, reported that they had applied to the Hon. Secretary for such information as he might have in his possession, and had received the following communication:--

Executive Department
G. S. L. City, Jan. 4, 1862.

Gentlemen:

In answer to your letter of inquiry concerning the cause of Gov. Dawson's early withdrawal from the Territory, I present the following extract from a note received by me from that gentleman on the day of his departure:

"My health is such that my return to Indiana, for the time being, is imperatively demanded; hence, I start this day."

Gov. Dawson announced to me, on the day of his arrival, his intention to return to Indiana at the close of the Legislative session, but I am not aware that any reason was assigned by him for his departure at an earlier day, other than the one above given.

Respectfully
Frank Fuller
Secretary and acting Governor.

(260)

On the 6th, a mass meeting was held at Great Salt Lake City to consider the election of delegates to a constitutional convention. (See "Des. News," Vol. 11, p 220.)

On the 14th, the Legislative Assembly elected certain territorial officers. (See "Des. News," Vol. 11, p 232.)

On the 20th, a constitutional convention was held in the county Court House, Great Salt Lake City.

(See "Des. News," Vol. 11, p. 237 and succeeding numbers.)

On the 23rd, the constitutional convention adjourned.

On the 27th, the "Jordan Irrigation Company" was formed, Wilford Woodruff, president, Geo. A. Smith treasurer, R. L. Campbell secretary.

A great sensation was created by the arrest of "John the Baptist," a native of Venice, Europe, but a grave digger at G. S. L. City, on account of his having opened the graves and robbed many of the dead of their clothing. Hundreds of sorrowful people visited the County Court House to endeavor to identify the clothing recovered.

On the 31st, C. W. Waite, of Chicago, was appointed Justice for Utah.

February

On the 10th, a municipal election was held in G. S. L. City. (See "Des. News," Feb. 12.)

For items concerning Ex Gov. Dawson, see "Des. News," Vol. 11, p. 261.

For account of destructive flood in Washington County, see "Des. News," Vol. 11, p. 260. (261)

Lectures were delivered frequently during the winter in the Seventies' Hall, G. S. L. City. (See "Des. News," Vol. 11, p. 264.)

March

On the 1st, C. B. Waite, of Illinois, and Thos. B. Drake, of Michigan, were confirmed associate justices for Utah.

On the 3rd, a general election for the "State of Deseret" was held. (See "Des. News," Vol. 11, p. 300.)

On the 6th, the Theatre was dedicated. (See "Des. News," Vol. 11, p. 290.)

On the 17th, Gov. B. Young issued a proclamation, convening the Legislature of the State of Deseret. (See "Des. News," Vol. 11, p. 300.)

April

On the 6th, the annual general church conference convened. (See "Des. News," Vol. 11, p. 332.)

On the 14th, the first session of the Legislature of the State of Deseret commenced. (See "Des. News," Vol. 11, p 332. For Governor's Message, see p. 329.)

On the 26th, news came that Indians had killed about a dozen whites near the mail station at Devil's Gate.

On the 26th, Capt. W. H. Hooper, with an escort of twenty men, under R. T. Burton, started for the States. The escort was designed to accompany Capt. Hooper to beyond danger of Indian depredations.

On the 28th, Prest. Lincoln telegraphed to Ex Gov. Young for ninety men for service on the plains, in consequence of Indian hostilities. (See "Des. News," Vol. 11, p. 348.) (262)

On the 30th, Captain Lot Smith's company mustered at the Council House, G. S. L. City.

May

On the 1st, Capt. Lot Smith's cavalry company left for the plains. (See "Des. News," Vol. 11, p. 357.)

Unusually high waters in the creeks this month. (See "Des. News," Vol. 11, p. 356.)

For article on meeting houses, see "Des. News," Vol. 11, p. 356.

A large number of teams left for the States this month, to assist the emigration.

For treatment of the Indians see "Des. News," Vol. 11, p. 372.

June

For silk culture in Utah, see "Des. News," Vol. 11, p 388.

Waters in G. S. L. City still very high and doing

considerable damage

On the 9th, Hon. J. M. Bernhisel presented the constitution of the State of Deseret, with accompanying memorial, in the House of Representatives, and on the 10th, the Vice President presented the same in the Senate.

On the 11th, a requisition from the Governor for several hundred militia to execute a writ of Judge Kinney's on Joseph Morris, the Weber River prophet, caused a stir in the city.

For Indians on the Western route, see "Des. News," (263) Vol. 11, p. 400.

On the 12th, the militia, about 300 in all, under command of Robt. Burton and T. McKean, started to arrest Joseph Morris. (For account of expedition, see "Des. News, June 18 and 25.)

The waters of City Creek this month, were unusually high, tearing away a ravine down the upper part of North Temple Street a number of feet wide and deep, and filling up the road four or five feet high further down. The inhabitants on each side of the street were busy day and night, trying to save their houses and lots from being destroyed by the flood.

The waters were also very high in other valleys, destroying many bridges, and doing much other damage.

An epistle of Brigham Young was read to the Morrisites, wherein the Bishops were advised to employ and feed any of them that were disposed to work.

About this time large companies of emigrants were passing through G. S. L. City en route for the gold mines. They would assemble on the 8th Ward Square and send requests to Ex Gov. Young to go and preach to them. He did so several times, much to their gratification (264)

The hostilities of the Indians along the mail route annoyed the citizens materially, and the discharge of Potter, the horse and cattle thief, and the confederate of Indians and thieves, was considered at attempt on the part of the Judge and those in his interest, to involve the settlers in bloodshed with the Indians.

On the 25th, Ex Gov. Young sent Dr. Clinton to

dress the wounds of the Morrisites; also sent up flour
to feed the destitute among them.

July

For account of observances of the 4th, see "Des.
News," July 9.

On the 7th, Stephen S. Harding, of Indiana, the
newly appointed Governor, arrived.

On the 11th, Associate Justices Waite and Drake
arrived. Judge Waite was accompanied by his family
--Judge Drake was a bachelor, or a widower.

For statistics of teams, etc., set from G. S. L.
City to meet and aid the emigration on the plains, see
"Millennial Star," Vol. 24, p. 458.

For anniversary of 24th, arrival of pioneers, see
"Des. News," Vol. 12, p. 33.

August

On the 2nd, a portion of Lot Smith's command,
consisting of 36 horsemen, and about (265) a dozen
wagons, with mostly four horses each arrived from
the plains.

For address of Deseret Agricultural and Manufacturing society officers to the people, see "Des. News,"
Vol. 12, p. 48.

On the 4th, a general election was held. For result of same, see "Des. News" of 13th.

For expedition after Indians, see "Des. News,"
Vol. 12, p. 52.

On the 12th, Ex Gov. Young sent teams to take
flour to Col. Connor's command of volunteers coming
from California.

On the 18th, Col. Connor, commanding Department of Utah and Nevada, had issued an imperial order
from Fort Churchill enjoining loyalty upon the citizens
of the Department, and intimating that he would arrest
any guilty of uttering disloyal sentiments.

On the 29th, Capt. Lewis Brunson and emigrant
company of 48 wagons, arrived in G. S. L. City. The
company consisted of half Americans and half foreign-

ers.

September

On the 1st, Ex Gov, Young and several others left
G. S. L. City on a tour to the southern part of the
Territory. (See "Des. News," Vol. 12, p 77. For
progress of the company, see subsequent issues.)

For Indian attacks on emigrants, see "Des. News"
(266) of September 24. For arrival of emigrants, see
same number.

On the 14th, Captain W. H. Hooper returned from
Washington, D. C.

On the 24th, Captain Homer Duncan's company of
emigrants arrived in G. S. L. City.

On the 25th, Ex Gov. Young and company returned
from their southern tour. (See "Des. News," Oct. 1.)

October

On the 1st, Capt. Horn's emigrant train arrived.
It left Florence on the 29th of July and consisted of
about 570 persons, with fifty-two wagons. It had a
very prosperous journey, but little sickness and no
serious accidents.

For murder of emigrants in the Humboldt Country,
see "Des. News," Vol. 12, p. 112.

On the 2nd, Capt. James S. Brown's company of
emigrants arrived. (See "Des. News," Vol. 12, p.
113.)

For Indian Depredations in Cache Valley, see
"Des. News," Vol. 12, p. 116.

On the 5th, Capt. Ansel Harmon's company of
emigrants arrived. (See "Des. News," Vol. 12, p.
113.)

On the 6th, the Semi-annual Conference was held
in G. S. L. City. (See "Des. News," Vol. 12, p. 124.

For report of the annual State Fair, held in the
State House, G. S. L. City Oct. 2, 3 and 4, see "Des.
News," Vol. 12, p. 116. (267)

On the 16th, Capt. Canfield's emigrant company
arrived. (See "Des. News," Vol. 12, p. 132.)

On the 17th, Capt. W. H. Miller's emigrant company arrived. (See "Des. News," Vol. 12, p. 132 and 136.)

Ex Gov. Young and company started on a tour northward. (See "Des. News" of subsequent dates for further particulars.

For arrival of Col. Connor's command of California Volunteers, see "Des. News," Vol. 12, p. 133.

On the 19th, H. D. Haight's emigrant train arrived. (See "Des. News," Vol. 12, p. 132.)

On the 25th, Ex Gov. Young and company returned from their northern trip. (See "Des. News," Oct. 29.)

On the 28th, two campanies of cavalry of Col. Connor's command arrived.

About this time a large number of settlers went to live in Washington County, on the southern border of the Territory, principally with a view to raise cotton.

November

On the 19th, Judge J. F. Kinney arrived from the States.

For Indian difficulties westward, see "Des. News," Vol, 12, p. 164.

Col. Connor sent word, about this time, by an Indian named Jack, that unless the Cache Valley Indians returned the white boy they had as (268) prisoner, he would wipe every one of them out.

On the 27th, soldiers returned from Cache Valley with the white boy they went after.

December

For an expedition to Bear River, after Indians, see "Des. News," Dec. 10.

On the 8th, the Legislature met in the County court House, G. S. L. City, and adjourned to the State House. (Council House).

On the 10th, Gov. Harding delivered his message to the Legislature.

For the first time since spring, the Theatre was opened and a large social party was held therein on christmas eve. (269)

INCIDENTS IN HISTORY OF UTAH 1863

January

For Indian outrages in the northern part of the Territory, see "Des. News," Vol. 12, p. 237.

On the 13th, a joint session election was held in the Council Chamber, G. S. L. City, for the election of the several Territorial, county, and other officers made elective by the joint vote of the Legislative Assembly. (See Des News, Vol. 12, p. 233 for result.)

On the 14th word was received in G. S. L. City that George Clayton and Henry Bean, who left Bannock City on the 25th of November (1862) with the express for G. S. L. City, were murdered by Indians just beyond Bear River. (See "Des. News," Vol. 12, p. 232.)

For report of the Superintendent of common schools, see "Des. News," Vol. 12, p. 243.

For items on emigration, &c, see letter from Jos. W. Young to Geo. Q. Cannon in "Mil. Star," Vol. 25, p. 157.

On the 19th, a meeting of the General Assembly of the State of Deseret, was held in the State House, G. S. L. City. (See "Des. News," Vol. 12, p. 236.)

For message of Governor Harding to the General Assembly of the State of Deseret, see "Des. News," Vol. 12, p. 233.

On the 22nd, a detachment of infantry and baggage wagons (Cal. Volunteers) started for Cache Valley after Indians.

For historical items, see letter from Geo. A. Smith to George Q. Cannon in "Mil. Star," Vol. 25, p. 187.

On the 28th, on the affidavit of W$^{\underline{m}}$ Bevans, a miner, (270) made before His Honor Chief Justice Kinney, on the 19th inst., a warrant was issued and placed in the hands of Marshal Isaac L. Gibbs, for the arrest of Bear Hunter, Sandpitch and Sagwitch, chiefs of several hundred warriors of Snake Indians, now inhabiting Cache Valley (See "Des. News," Vol. 12,

p. 244.)

For announcement of Ex Gov. Young concerning
his relations towards the "Des. News," see "Des.
News," Vol. 12, p. 244.

February

On the 3rd, Jacob Hamblin arrived in G. S. L.
City with three Moquich Indians, the first of that tribe
who had visited the City.

For account of Col. Connor's and Volunteers' expedition to the Indians on Bear River, see "Des. News,"
Vol. 12, p. 253.

On the 7th, Jas. H. Martineau reported that the
soldiers, (Connor's command) in the late engagement
with the Indians, killed 90 squaws and children. Many
squaws were wounded--40 or 50 Indians escaped. Several squaws were killed because they would not submit
quietly to be ravished. Other squaws were ravished in
the agonies of death. From 200 to 250 were killed in
all.

For announcement of the sale of the arms, mules,
horses, ponies and other property taken from the
Indians at the recent battle of Bear River, see "Des.
News," Vol. 12, p. 260.

On the 14th, W^m. E. Maxwell and the three
Moquich (271) Indians left for their home. Presents of
sheep shears, hoes, axes, dyestuff, &c., were given
to them.

For article on the Literary and Scientific Institute
in Ogden, see "Des. News," Vol. 12, p. 277.

March

On the 3rd, a mass meeting was held in the
Tabernacle, G. S. L. City, for the purpose of considering the hostile feelings of Gov. Harding to the people
and their religion, as exhibited in his insulting message to the Legislative Assembly, as also the actions
of other federal officers. A Petition to the President
of the United States for the removal of Gov. Harding
and Judges Waite and Drake was read and accepted.

(See "Des. News," Vol. 12, p. 284.)

On the 4th, John Taylor, Orson Pratt, Senr., and Jeter Clinton, according to appointment, waited upon Gov. Harding, Judges Waite and Drake, requesting them to resign their offices. (For report, see "Des. News," Vol. 12, p. 292.)

On the 9th, the citizens of Fillmore assembled at the City Hall to give expression to the feelings entertained towards Gov. Harding and Judges Waite and Drake for attempting to subvert the rights of the people of Utah and to bring evil upon them. (See "Des. News," Vol. 12, p. 301.) The citizens of Springville and Spanish Fork also met for the same purpose.

In the afternoon, the U. S. flag was unfurled from the top of ex Gov. Young's Bee Hive House. The City soon presented a busy scene, all the citizens with their arms wending their way to ex. Gov. Young's, in obedience to the signal during the day for the (272) men to gather, while the discharge of the cannon was to be the signal at night.

In the evening, ex. Gov. Young's offices and premises, Daniel H. Well's premises, Historian's office, Tithing office, &c., were all full of armed volunteers. This was in consequence of the report that Gov. Harding and Judges Waite and Drake had issued a warrant to arrest Brigham Young for polygamy, and had put it into Col. Conner's hands to serve the writ through military force, and the citizens were resolved that it should not be done in that way.

Ex Gov. Young was taken before Judge Kinney, on complaint of J. A. Thompson, for violation of the Polygamy Bill. Marshall Gibbs served the writ on ex Gov. Young, who went down to Judge Kinney's chamber, north-west room of Council House, and was examined. Gave bonds in the sum of $5,500$\frac{00}{}$, L. D. Young, Enoch Reese, Theodore M^C. Kean and O. P. Rockwell being bondsmen. (See "Des. News," Vol. 12, p. 292.)

See article on the mass meetings in "Des. News," Vol. 12, p. 292.

On the 13th, the recognizances of twenty Morrisites engaged in resisting process last June, were declared forfeited.

On the 14th, the meeting house at Bountiful, Davis
Co., was dedicated. (See "Des. News," Vol. 12,
p. 300.)

A mass meeting was held at Ephraim, Sanpete Co.,
(273) to protest against the unjust conduct of federal
officers towards the people. (See "Des. News,"
Vol. 12, p. 312.)

On the 19th, several Morrisites were indicted.
(See "Des. News," Vol. 12, p. 309.

On the 22nd, news reached G. S. L. City that the
stage driver was shot in Deep Creek (200 miles west)
by Indians. A passenger was also mortally wounded.

On the 23rd, news arrived in G. S. L. City that
two other men were killed by the Indians at Eight Mile
Creek. (See "Des. News," Vol. 12, p. 312.)

See article of Judge Waite assuming the preroga-
tive of holding court in the Third District, when the
Legislature had assigned him to the Second, in "Des.
News," Vol. 12, p. 309.

For "More Indian Difficulties," see "Des. News."
Vol. 12, p. 312.

For trial of the Morrisites, conviction, and sen-
tence, see "Des. News," Vol. 12, p. 316.

For the Judge's charge to the Jury in the Brigham
Young Polygamy case, see "Des. News," Vol. 12,
p. 317.

On the 31st, Gov. Harding pardoned a number of
persons convicted of murder and resisting the officers.
See "Des. News," Vol. 12, p. 317)

April

See "Mil. Star," Vol. 25, p. 217; also "Des.
News," Vol. 12, p. 324, for career of Gov. Harding,
&c.

On the 6th, the Annual Conference of the Church
convened in the Bowery, G. S. L. City. (See "Des.
News," Vol. 12, p. 337.)(274)

For "Executive Enormities," See Des. News,
Vol. 12, page 324.

For information regarding the expedition after the
Indians in the mountains east of Utah Lake, see "Des.

News," Vol. 12, p. 336.

For historical items, see letter from Geo. A. Smith to Geo. Q. Cannon, "Mil. Star," Vol. 25, p. 332.

For letter, giving full particulars of the Indian attack at Battle Creek, see "Des. News," Vol. 12, p. 341.

On the 15th, the Seventies established a library and reading room at G. S. L. City, containing the principal newspapers in the United States, also the principal monthly magazines, pictorials, &c., as well as a few British newspapers. The reading room was a free institution.

Early in the morning, two companies or more of troops, marched into Spanish Fork canyon and came upon a body of Indians between the two bridges, one mile above the mouth of the canyon on the south side of the river, evidently unexpected. A battle ensued, resulting in the death of from ten to twenty persons. (See "Des. News," Vol. 12, p. 341.)

On the 20th, ex Gov. Young, accompanied by H. C. Kimball and several other gentlemen, left G. S. L. City on a tour through the central and southern counties. (See "Des. News," Vol. 12, p. 340.)

On the 22nd, Mr. A. H. Conover arrived in G. S. L. City from Bannock City with the express, bringing about 500 letters. He was accompanied by Mr. House, (275) a member of the express company, ex postmaster Morrell and another individual who came in the capacity of Indian interpreter. (See "Des. News," Vol. 12, p. 341.)

For "Incidents of Travel-Progress of Prest. Young and Company," containing historical items, see "Des. News" Vol. 12 pp. 352, 353, 368, 371, 373, 379.

About this time, a new military post at, or near Soda Springs, Idaho, was to be established, in order to hold the Indians in check in that vicinity. (See "Des. News," Vol. 12, p. 345.)

On the 29th, a villainous attempt to kidnap a young woman was perpetrated at Bountiful, about ten miles north of G. S. L. City, by a band of soldiers from Camp Douglass. (See "Des. News," Vol. 12, p. 349.)

For "Immigration Movements," see "Des. News,"
Vol. 12, p. 352.

May

For historical items, see "Mil. Star," Vol. 25,
p. 280.

On the 4th, according to report, Capt. Smith,
2nd cavalry, C. V., who had marched, with his company from Camp Douglass soon after the late Indian
attacks on the western mail route in the vicinity of
Shell Creek, for that point, by order of Gen'l. Connor,
taking the northern route via the Humboldt, had a fight
with Indians, fifty miles south of Shell Creek, in which
29 aborigines were killed and considerable stock captured. (See "Des. News," Vol. 12, p. 364.)

On the 5th, company H., 3rd Infantry, C. V.,
Capt. Black, left Camp Douglass to establish a post at
or near Soda Springs, as formerly announced, and
company E., of the same regiment left for the west to
establish a post at Reese River. (See "Des. News,"
Vol. 12, p. 357.) (276)

On the 6th, Gen. Connor left Camp Douglass with
a company of cavalry for Soda Springs, Idaho, for the
purpose of selecting a site for the new military post in
that vicinity, &c. (See "Des. News," Vol. 12, p. 364.)

On the 8th, as reported by Mr. Burt of Brigham
City, six or eight Indians of Sagwitch's band, as supposed, made their appearance in Box Elder Canyon or
Valley, about four miles from Brigham City, at a herd
house, and made inquiry of a boy who was there alone
relative to the whereabouts of the soldiers. The boy
replied that he did not know, but supposed that they
were in Salt Lake City. They told him he was a liar,
and then took the lad's hat and two horses that were
near by, and went to the herd some distance away,
where they got eight or nine more, which they succeeded in driving off. (See "Des. News," Vol. 12,
p. 364.)

For historical incidents of Goshen, see "Des.
News," Vol. 12, p. 371.

For Indian hostilities, see letter from J. C.

Wright in "Des. News," Vol. 12, p. 371.

On the 16th, Kanosh, head chief of the Pahvan Indians, accompanied by chief Mo-sho-quop and eight others, came to visit Ex Gov. Young and company at Fillmore. Kanosh stated that his fears of the soldiers (Col. Connor's Volunteers at Camp Douglass) had been very great for the last month, and he knew not where to go for safety; that the agents and superintendents had paid no (277) attention to him of late years; neither giving instructions nor presents, that he was getting to be very poor; his tribe was diminishing, &c. Gov. Young told him not to fear, but stay at home, and if the soldiers came flee to the mountains and keep out of their way. Kanosh and the rest expressed great love for and confidence in Gov. Young and the people, but the little love they had for the "Americans" had left them.

On the 19th, ex Gov. Young and company returned from their southern trip.

On the 20th, the men who went in search of the Indians and to recover, if possible, the horses stolen by them from the citizens of Weber, Box Elder and Cache Counties, on or about the 9th inst., overtook the Indians in a canyon near Bear River Lake. A few shots were exchanged when the red thieves fled, leaving behind 108 of the stolen animals, which were recovered and brought back (See "Des. News," Vol. 12, p. 369.)

For article on the reprehensible course of Federal officers in Utah, see "Mil. Star," Vol. 25, p. 328.

See "Brief History of the Federal Courts and Judges in and for Utah, previous to the crusade," in "Des. News," Vol. 12, p. 380.

On the 30th, Gen. Connor returned from him expedition. (See "Des. News," Vol. 12, p. 388, for his report.)

June

For plan of the new Tabernacle, &c., see "Des. News," Vol. 12, p. 387.

See "History of the Federal Courts and Judges

since the (278) Crusade," in "Des. News," Vol. 12,
p. 388.

See "Gov. Harding Superseded" in "Des. News,"
Vol. 12, p. 388.

For Gen. Connor's treaty with the Indians, at or
near Fort Bridger, see "Des. News," Vol. 12, p. 396.

See article on Judges Eckles and Sinclair, &c.,
in "Des. News," Vol. 12, p. 396.

On the 11th, Gov. Harding left Utah Territory.

See article on "Federal courts and Judges" in
"Des. News," Vol. 12, p. 404.

See account of "Another Horrid Indian Massacre"
in "Des. News," Vol. 12, p. 404.

For article on "Our New Governor--J. Duane
Doty," see "Des. News," Vol. 12, p. 412.

See "Des. News", Vol. 12, p. 416 for article entitled "Judge Drake and his Judicial Blunders."

See "Overland Emigration" in Des. News, Vol.
12, p. 416.

On the 24th, Geo. A. Smith wrote:-- "Large companies of emigrants have passed through the city en
route for the gold fields. They assemble on the 8th
Ward square and send requests to Prest. Young to
come and preach to them. He has done so, at least
three times, much to their gratification.***

"The hostility of the Indians along the mail route
has annoyed the citizens materially, and the discharge
of Potter the horse and cattle thief, and the confederate
of Indians, thieves. &c., is considered an attempt on
the part of the Judge and those in his interest to involve the settlers in bloodshed with the Indians.

This morning's paper brings out Judge Kinney as
(279) the candidate for delegate to Congress.

"There is considerable scarcity of water for irrigation, as the warm weather in the early part of the
season disposed of the snow in the mountains before
we were ready for it ***

"The abutments to sustain the Tabernacle are
raising and some of them are already up to their
height.

"I received, today, my pay for services as one of
the Grand jury, the principal business of which was to

present Gov. S. S. Harding as a nuisance against the
peace and dignity of the United States.

"S. S. Harding has been removed to Valparaiso,
S. America, the government thereby, no doubt, hoping
to get rid of his noise. Gov. Doty has qualified and
entered upon the duties of Territorial Governor."

On the 25th, a respectable number of those interested in the political welfare of the people of G. S. L.
County, met to confirm the people's nomination of the
next delegate to congress, and also to nominate such
officers as the voters of G. S. L. County were authorized by law to elect. (See "Des. News," Vol. 13,
p. 5.)

July

See communication from Geo. W. Bean,
Charlestown, Wasatch Co., giving an account of the
soldiers fighting the Indians in that locality, in "Des.
News," Vol. 13, p. 20.

The 4th was celebrated in almost every town and
settlement in the Territory, processions, firing arms
and cannon, flags flying, bands playing, singing,
dancing and speech making being the order of the day.

On the 6th, the annual sitting of the Supreme
court (280) commenced and closed. For minutes See
"Des. News," Vol. 13, p. 13.

For communication on the construction of a road
through Goshen Canyon, at the head of Goshen Valley,
leading into Juab Valley, by which the travelling distance between the southern portions of the Territory
and G. S. L. City would be shortened some 25 miles,
&c., see "Des. News," Vol. 13, p. 27.

See article on Federal Courts and Judges, in
"Des. News," Vol. 13, p. 10.

On the 8th, Prest. B. Young addressed a company
of emigrants on the 8th Ward Square, G. S. L. City.
(See address in "Des. News," Vol. 13, p. 18.

On the 9th, Geo. A. Smith and Chief Justice
Kinney started south on a political canvas, returning
on the 29th.

On the 10th, a letter was received from a telegraphic operator at Deep Creek, by Major Egan, giving particulars of an attack made by Indians on what was known as Canyon Station, near Deep Creek, which resulted in the killing of four soldiers and the station keeper, Wm Riley, and also in the burning of the station house and barn with their contents, including five horses. (See "Des. News," Vol. 13, p. 20.)

See article on "The Emigration to Utah," in "Des. News," Vol. 13, p. 21.

See "Des. News," Vol. 13, p. 27 for synopsis of Judge Kinney's speech to the citizens of Manti, Sanpete County, while on a tour through the southern counties in company with Geo. A. Smith. (281)

On the 15th, Judge Kinney addressed the people of Nephi, and was well received as the nominee for Delegate to Congress.

On the 16th, in response to a general invitation, given by Ex Gov. Young, about the 19th of last May, to those who served in the Mormon Battalion, and to those who were of the pioneers of 1847, a grand festival was held at the theatre in G. S. L. City, in commemoration of the organization of the Battalion on the banks of the Missouri in 1846. (See "Des. News," Vol. 13, p. 29.)

On the 17th, Iron and Washington Counties were visited by a flood, whereby four children were drowned and much property destroyed. (See "Des. News," Vol. 13, p. 31.)

For an article on "Federal Courts and Judges," see "Des. News," Vol. 13, p. 28.

On the 24th, the 16th anniversary of the entrance of the pioneers into G. S. L. City, was celebrated throughout the Territory. (See "Des. News," Vol. 13, p. 40.)

See "Prospectus of the Deseret Academy of Arts-- Public School, Romney's, Hall East Temple Street, G. S. L. City," in "Des. News," Vol. 13, p. 34.

On the 26th, Sagwitch, one of the Shoshone chiefs, was shot while in the custody of a detachment of C. Vs. (See Des. News," Vol. 13, p. 37.)

On the 29th, Hon. G. A. Smith and Judge Kinney returned to G. S. L. City from their flying tour south. ("Des. News," Vol. 13, p. 37.) (282)

On the 30th, Gov. Doty and Gen. Connor, pursuant to previous arrangement, held a treaty with Pocatello, Sanpitch and other chiefs of the late hostile bands of Shoshones at Brigham City, which resulted in a peace arrangement between those bands and the government, the military and the citizens, &c. (See "Des. News," Vol. 13, p. 37.)

On the 31st, Mr. Jacob Meeks arrived in G. S. L. City from his ferry on Snake River, accompanied by four Indian Chiefs, or principal warriors. They had an interview with Gov. Doty. (See "Des. News," Vol. 13, p. 37.)

August

On the 3rd, the annual election was held.

See article on Judge Kinney's speech in "Des. News," Vol. 13, p. 28.

On the 4th, by a dispatch from Schell Creek, it was learned that Capt. Smith, in command of the troops in that vicinity, had discovered a nest of Gosh-Utes about 20 miles north of Schell Creek Station, and killed twelve of them, only two escaping.

On the 7th, the Hon. John Titus, of Penn., arrived in G. S. L. City, to succeed the Hon. John F. Kinney, as Chief Justice of the Supreme Court for Utah Territory, and was inducted into office on the 12th by taking the prescribed oath, administered by Gov. Doty.

On the 19th, ex Gov. Young and company started north on a preaching excursion. (283)

See article on the proposed Spanish Fork Road in "Des. News," Vol. 13, p. 42.

On the 29th, Hon. J. F. Kinney, Delegate to Congress from Utah, took his departure Eastward by the overland Stage Coach, on his way to the Federal City, accompanied by Isaac L. Gibbs Esq., U. S. Marshal for Utah. (See "Des. News," Vol. 13, p. 48.)

For arrival of emigrant companies see "Des. News," Vol. 15, p. 52.

See letter from Geo. A. to John L. Smith in "Mil. Star," Vol. 25, p. 651.

September

See "Des. News," Vol. 13, p. 45, for ex Gov. Young's trip north.

On the 4th, Capt. Patterson's company of emigrants arrived.

For "New Woollen Factory," see "Des. News," Vol. 13, p. 56.

For arrival of emigration companies see "Des. News," Vol. 13, p. 64.

See account of a mountain storm in G. S. L. Valley, in Des. News, Vol. 13, p. 64.

On the 17th, Major P. A. Gallagher and command passed through G. S. L. City, on their way to Camp Douglass. (See "Des. News," Vol. 13, p. 72.)

On the 18th, C. C. Rich and company arrived in Bear Lake Valley to make settlements there. (284)

About this time, owing to the scarcity of mill appliances and the great amount of bread stuffs sent north, flour had greatly risen in price in G. S. L. City.

On the morning of the 25th, a party of mounted men from Fort Bridger calling themselves U. S. soldiers committed an outrage on a company of emigrants.

Capt. Peter Nebeker's train of emigrants arrived.

On the 27th, the meeting house in Kay's Ward was dedicated (See "Des. News," Vol. 13, p. 81.)

October

On the 1st, Gov. Doty, in concert with Gov. Nye, of Neveda Territory, made a treaty with the Indians in Ruby Valley. (See "Des. News," Vol. 13, p. 97.)

For arrival of emigrant companies, see "Des. News," Vol. 13, p. 88.

See account of the annual State fair, held in G. S. L. City on the 2nd and 3rd, in "Des. News," Vol. 13, p. 88.

On the 6th, the semi-annual conference convened in the Bowery, G. S. L. City. (See "Des. News," Vol. 13, p. 96.)

On the 9th, Capt. Hyde's train of emigrants arrived.

On the 15th, Capt. White's company of emigrants arrived (See "Des. News," Vol. 13, p. 105.)

See Proclamation by Gov. Duane Doty in "Des. News", Vol. 13, p. 124. (285)

November

See article on cotton in Utah in "Des. News," Vol. 13, p. 128.

On the 16th, ex Gov. Young and company started on a tour through the settlements in Sanpete County, returning on the 25th.

On the 22nd, Gov. Doty left G. S. L. City by the mail stage for the east, on a visit to Washington. (See "Des. News," Vol. 13, p. 144.)

See letter from ex Gov. Young, on Utah affairs in "Mil. Star," Vol. 26, p. 61.

December

See account of ex Gov. Young's visit to Sanpete County in "Des. News," Vol. 13, p. 152.

See letter from Geo. A. Smith, on Utah affairs in "Mil. Star," Vol. 26, p. 107.

On the 14th, the Legislature met in the State House. (See "Des. News," Vol. 13, p. 168; also acting Governor's message in same issue.)

While Arza E. Hinkley and a lad of 14 years of age, named Smith, were returning from East Weber with a flock of sheep, they were met and brutally assaulted on the dugway, near the mouth of Parley's Canyon, by nine or ten soldiers, most of them under the influence of liquor. (See "Des. News," Vol. 13, p. 169.)

See letter on Utah affairs from E. L. Sloan in "Mil. Star," Vol. 26, p. 122; also one from B. Young Junr. page 109.)

On the 21st, Gen'l. Connor's troops were on their last 15 days' rations. They had applied to Bishop John Sharp to feed them. A vote was taken in the (286) Council that they should be fed, and, at the suggestion of ex Gov. Young, wheat was to be sold to them at

3\underline{^{00}}$ per bushel.

See letter from W. Woodruff in "Mil. Star," Vol. 26, page 140. (287)

INCIDENTS IN HISTORY OF UTAH, 1864

January

On the 5th, the first number of the "Daily Union Vedette" appeared.

On the 9th, the new meeting house at Farmington, Davis County, was dedicated. It was built of rock, 40 by 60 feet, and would seat 400 persons.

The Legislative Assembly memorialized Secretary Stanton to remove the troops from Camp Douglass and the Territory, they being an unnecessary expense to the government.

On the 22nd, the Legislative Assembly adjourned.

February

In consequence of the light snowfall and the anticipated consequent small amount of water for irrigation, a number of the inhabitants of Iron County concluded to make one or more settlements at the head of the Sevier River.

March

Ex Gov. Young desired the Regency of the Deseret University to consider the subject of introducing the system of phonotypy instead of the Deseret Alphabet.

On the 31st, Judge Titus stated in court that he had been instructed to ask, as part of the moral test, of applicants for naturalization if they had broken the law of 1862 against polygamy or bigamy.

April

On the 6th, the general conference of the Church of Jesus Christ of Latter-day Saints, met in the Tabernacle. (See "Des. News," of April 13.) (288)

On the 11th, the second cavalry, California

Volunteers, left the City on their homeward journey,
to be mustered out of service, being unwilling to re-
enlist.

The point of outfit for emigrants to Salt Lake was
this season changed from Florence to Wyoming, both
on the Missouri River.

On the 30th, D. H. Wells and Brigham Young,
Junr. started on a mission to England.

May

On the 7th, Orson Pratt started for California, on
a mission to Austria.

On the 16th, Ex Gov. Young, H. C. Kimball, Geo.
A. Smith, W. Woodruff, and others started on a visit
to the Bear Lake Settlements, returning on the 26th.

Several new settlements on the Sevier were
formed this season. (See "Des. News," Vol. 13, p.
264.)

June

For expulsion of Walter M. Gibson from the
church, in the Sandwich Islands, see "Des. News,"
June 1, p. 280.

On the 4th, the new baptismal font in the Endowment House, G. S. L. City, was dedicated by Brigham
Young.

On the 12th, ex Gov. Young and others visited
Ogden. (See "Des. News," June 15, p. 297.)

In the morning of the 19th, Rev. Dr. Sheepshanks,
English Episcopal missionary from British Columbia,
read the Church of England service, and preached in
the Tabernacle.

On the 22nd, Gov. Young and others started on a
(289) visit to Cache Valley, returning on the 29th.
(See "Des. News," Vol. 13, p. 321.)

July

The 4th was celebrated in G. S. L. City and the
settlements generally. (See "Des. News," Vol. 13,

pp. 320, 328.)

The "Daily Telegraph" started on the morning of the 4th, T. B. H. Stenhouse, Editor and proprietor.

On the 8th, Gov. B. Young and others started for Provo, returning on the 11th. (See "Des. News," Vol. 13, p. 329.)

The "Vedette," published at Camp Douglass, two separate days declared that the government would take provisions where and when it needed them, and at such prices as it pleased.

Early this month, Captain Stover, quartermaster, rented a store across the street from the south side of the Temple Block, for a store house. On Sunday the 10th, Captain Brown's company of 76 dragoons went and occupied the store. General Connor ordered Captain Stover to remove his quarters to Camp, as he (Connor) would use the store for a provost marshal's guard, Captain Chas. H. Hempstead being appointed provost marshal. Captain Stover remonstrated, as he had hired the premises for a storehouse, but Gen. Connor was inexorable. This palpable breach of faith produced a general feeling of excitement and distrust, which was aggravated by rumors that a proclamation of martial law was intended. Petitions to Gov. Doty and the City Council for the removal of the troops (290) were circulated, but it was concluded that the proper authority to apply to was the Secretary of War. It was decided to build up the south entrance to the Temple Block with an adobie wall.

On the 15th, the Mormon Battalion had a social party and supper at the Social Hall. (See "Des. News," July 20, p. 337.)

On the 16th, a circular was issued on the care of breadstuffs. (See "Des. News," Vol. 13, p. 336.)

For article on Cotton culture in Utah, see "Daily Telegraph, No. 18.

On the 22nd, Gov. Young and others visited Tooele, returning on the 24th. (See "Des. News," July 27, p. 345.)

The 24th passed without any public demonstration in the City, though such were indulged in at various of the settlements.

August

On the 4th, Gov. B. Young and others started on a visit to Morgan County, returning on the 8th. (See "Des. News," Aug. 17, p. 366.)

On the 8th and 9th, a convention was held in the Tabernacle, G. S. L. City, in regard to prices of bread stuffs. (See "Des. News," Vol 13, pp. 360, 366.)

On the 17th, a mass meeting was held in the Bowery, G. S. L. City, to consider the feasibility of making a canal from the Jordan, at the south end of G. S. L. Valley, to bring water to G. S. L. City, and also of boring Artesian Wells in G. S. L. City. (See "Des, News," Aug. 24, p. 376.)

On the 18th, Gov. Young and others started on (291) a visit to Heber City, returning on the 22nd. (See "Des. News," Aug. 31, p. 382.)

For article on cotton manufacture in Utah, see "Daily Telegraph," No. 51.

September

On the 1st, Gov. B. Young and others started on a visit to the Southern part of the Territory; returning on the 29th. (See "Des. News," Sept. 14, p. 401, and Oct. 5, p. 4.)

On the 25th, three companies of California Volunteers passed up to Camp Douglass, preceded by a military brass band.

October

About this time, trains of emigrants to Utah were arriving frequently.

On the 4th, the breadstuffs' convention met again and established a scale of prices. (See "Des. News," Oct. 19, p. 18.)

On the 6th, the semi-annual Conference of the Church of Jesus Christ of Latter-day Saints commenced in the Bowery, G. S. L. City. (See "Des. News," Oct. 12, p. 12)

About this time, between one and two hundred men

were making arrangements to settle in the southern
part of the Territory, with a view to raising Cotton and
making settlement at the head of navigation on the
Colorado river.

On the 10th, Zion's Camp (Kirtland and Missouri)
(292) had a festival re-union at the Social Hall, G. S.
L. City. (See "Des. News," Oct. 12, pp. 13 and 20.)

On the 11th, digging was commenced for an artesian well, north of the 20th Ward school house, just
outside the old city wall, G. S. L. City

November

On the 11th, Gov. B. Young and others started on
a visit to Kaysville and Ogden, returning on the 17th.
(See "Des. News," Vol. 14, p. 64.)

About this time the subject of making of a canal
from the east side of the Jordan, south, for irrigating
and for boating rock from Cottonwood for building purposes, was agitated. (See "Des. News," Vol. 14, p.
61.)

On the 26th, a mass meeting was held for the same
purpose (See "Des. News," Nov. 30, p. 69.)

December

On the 12th, the Legislative Assembly met in the
State House, G. S. L. City. (292)

INCIDENTS IN HISTORY OF UTAH
1865

January

For Brigham Young's views on theatres and theatrical performances, see "Des. News," Jan. 11, p. 116.

W. W. Drummond, formerly of Oquawka, Ill., and appointed by President Pierce as one of the United States district judges of Utah, in 1855, was recently convicted by the San Francisco courts, upon two indictments of fraud, in drawing bills of exchange upon parties in the East, and selling them to persons in that city. He drew one on a bank in Buffalo, New York, where he averred he had large sums of money, but in every instance the bills were returned protested. (For further particulars, see "Daily Telegraph," Vol. 1, No. 166.)

For items concerning Utah affairs, see letter From B. Young, "Mill. Star," Vol. 27, p. 205.

For a "Gentile's" views on leaving G. S. L. City, see "Daily Telegraph," Jan. 14.

About this time, owing to Indian difficulties, eastward mail matter for the States was forwarded via California.

A correspondent of the St Louis "Republican" gives the following extract of a letter from Judge Drummond's wife:

"The last letter we had from Drummond, he was in Sacramento, California; he left the woman he had with him in Utah, in Chicago." (See "Daily Telegraph" Jan. 20.)

For return of Oliver Cowdery to the Church, and incidents of his death, see "Mill. Star," Vol. 27, p. 57.

February

On the 4th, a mass meeting was held in the (294) Tabernacle, G. S. L. City, on the subject of making a canal on the east side of the Jordan River to the City. (See "Des. News," Vol. 14, p. 148.)

For account of Jacob Hamblin's boat trip down the Rio Virgen from St George to the Colorado, see "Des. News," Vol. 14, p. 173.

For notice of Judge (Gov.) Harding and his concubine, see "Daily Telegraph," Vol. 1, no. 195.

On the 16th, Mayor A. O. Smoot directed the City Marshal to remove certain fencing which unauthorized parties had erected around the Warm Springs.

March

On the 4th, the re-inauguration of President Lincoln was celebrated by military procession, speeches, etc., in G. S. L. City. (See "Des. News" and "Daily Telegraph."

On the evening of the 7th, the City Council of G. S. L. City gave a social ball to the civil and military officers in the Social Hall.

April

On the 6th, the General Conference of the Church of Jesus Christ of Latter-day Saints commemced in the Tabernacle, G. S. L. City. (See "Des. News," Apl. 12, p. 220.)

On the 10th, the Breadstuffs convention met again in G. S. L. City and agreed to sustain the previous prices. The subject of erecting a telegraphic line through the Territory was also discussed.

For Indian depredations in Paradise Valley and vicinity, see "Des. News," Vol. 14, p. 238. (295)

On the 15th, the stores were closed, and flags were hung at half mast and draped with mourning, on receipt of the news of the assassination of President Lincoln, and supposedly of Secretary Seward.

About this time there were some Indian troubles in Sanpete Valley and parts adjacent. Brigham Young exerted himself, sending his son Joseph A., and advising the people to do all they could to bring the difficulties to a peaceful adjustment.

On the 19th, in the Tabernacle, G. S. L. City, Amasa M. Lyman and Rev. Norman Mc. Leod addressed a large and mixed audience on the occasion of the funeral of President Lincoln.

May

On the 3rd, Brigham Young and others started on a visit to Cache Valley, returning to G. S. L. City on the 11th. (See "Des. News," Vol. 14, pp. 244, 252, 260 and 269.)

On the 17th, Sheriff Golding served an attachment on Mr. Putney, who was going east; upon which a military officer served a notice on him, that the said Mr. Putney was to be exempted from civil process. This took place near the foot of the Little Mountain, Emigration Cañon.

On the 18th, Brigham Young, writing to D. H. Wells and B. Young, jun., in England, said, "There has been considerable feeling manifested of late in certain quarters, because measures are being taken to check the increase of iniquity, and to cleanse all (296) nuisances from our city and streets. The corrupt and all the workers of iniquity are disturbed and uneasy, and they raise an outcry through their organ, the 'Vedette' about my teachings and reproofs. They would really like, now the war east appears to be off the hands of the Government, to have attention drawn to us here, and troops to be sent out to break us up. They openly avow their intention to break the power of the Priesthood, and to destroy our organization, and since the receipt of the news of the surrender of Generals Lee and Johnston, and the capture of Jeff Davis, they have been very exultant and their tone is more arrogant and defiant than it has been. But the Lord Almighty has not surrendered, if Lee and Johnston have; and they who think that they have but to bring sufficient human force to bear against us, to destroy us and the kingdom of God, will find out, to their confusion and ultimate shame and misery, that He still reigns, and that He has the power in heaven and on the earth to accomplish His purposes and to fulfil His word."

About this time a considerable number of missionaries left G. S. L. City to preach the Gospel, some in
Europe, and others in the Sandwich Islands.

The Chicago "Tribune" of the 25th contained an
account of the granting of a divorce to Mrs Ella P. (297)
Drummond, from Judge Wm W. Drummond, better
known as "Judge Utah Drummond." The charge
against him was adultery, which had been fully proved.
Mrs Drummond was adjudged five hundred dollars a
year alimony. (see Daily Telegraph.)

On the 25th and 26th, Indians, supposed to be part
of Black Hawk's band, murdered seven persons in
Sanpete Valley, making about a dozen slain by Indians
in that part of the Territory that spring. see "Daily
Telegraph." Another man was killed on the 29th.
Indians were committing depredations on the mail
routes east and west, also.

June

On the 5th, Brigham Young and others started on
a visit to Utah County, returning on the 12th. During
the visit a conference was had with Indians at Spanish
Fork, when a treaty was made with them by Col. O.
H. Irish, Superintendent, and a number of presents
were distributed among them. (See "Des. News,"
Vol. 14, pp. 292, 293, 301.)

On the 10th, Hon. John F. Kinney, delegate from
Utah to Congress, returned to the city, accompanied
by his brother, E. M. Kinney.

On the 11th, Hons. Schuyler Colfax, and W^m
Bross, and Messrs Albert D. Richardson and Samuel
Bowes (Bowles) visited G. S. L. City, and were hos-
pitably entertained. (See "Des. News," Vol. 14, p.
292. Also "Daily Telegraph.") (298)

On the 13th, Gov. James Duane Doty died. He
was buried on the 15th. (See "Des. News," June 21,
p. 300, also "Daily Telegraph.")

On Sunday evening, 18th, Speaker Colfax delivered,
to a large audience in the Bowery, G. S. L. City, an
oration on "The Life and Principles of President

Lincoln. "

While Speaker Colfax was in G. S. L. City, a petition was got up to President Johnson, asking him to appoint O. H. Irish Governor of Utah. The petition was presented through Speaker Colfax.

On the 21st, Brigham Young and others left G. S. L. City on a visit to Utah and Juab Counties, returning on the 27th.

On the 24th, the new meeting house at Nephi, was dedicated (See "Des. News", Vol. 14, p. 309, 314; also "Daily Telegraph.")

July

The 4th was celebrated in G. S. L. City by procession, speeches, etc. (See "Des. News," July 5, p. 316.)

Hon. J. M. Ashley, chairman of committee on Territories in Congress, arrived in G. S. L. City.

On the 7th, Brigham Young and others started on a trip to Sanpete County, returning on the 19th. (See "Des. News," July 19, pp. 329, 330, 338.)

On the 20th, the Mormon Battalion had a picnic ball at the Social Hall, G. S. L. City. (See "Des. News," July 26, p. 341) (299)

On the 22nd, Hon. Amos Reed, Secretary and acting Governor, returned from the East.

The 24th passed off quietly in the city, with no public celebration.

More rain fell this summer than in any previous one since the settlement of Utah.

On the 31st, the Provost Guard were vacating the store south of Temple Block, which Gen. Connor had deceitfully obtained for that purpose.

August

On the 1st, Brigham Young and others started on a trip to Cache Valley, returning on the 11th. (See "Des. News," Vol. 14, pp. 358, 353, 361.)

On the 15th, George A. Smith returned from a tour in the Southern part of the Territory, during

which he had travelled upwards of seven hundred miles
and preached about thirty-seven discourses. (See
"Des. News," Vol. 14, p. 369)

In the "Deseret News," Vol. 14, p. 372, is an article by Brigham Young and others, stating that a book
entitled "Joseph Smith, the Prophet," written by his
mother Lucy Smith, was inaccurate in some particulars, and that some of the doctrines taught by Orson
Pratt in the "Seer" were incorrect.

On the 25th, Brigham Young and others visited
Tooele County, returning on the 27th.

This month the provost guard was located at the
8th (300) Ward Square, and the south entrance to the
Temple Block was reopened.

September

On the 4th, Brigham Young and others started on a
visit to the Southern portion of Utah, returning on the
29th. (See "Des. News," Vol. 14, pp. 394, 402, 410;
Vol. 15, pp. 2, 10.)

For prospectus of the "Juvenile Instructor," an
illustrated semi-monthly magazine, edited by George
Q. Cannon, see "Des. News," Vol. 14, p. 396.

For article on the Bowes (Bowles)--Richardson
correspondence from Utah, see "Des. News," Vol. 14,
p. 396.

For "Indian Treaty," between Col. O. H. Irish
and Southern Indians, see "Des. News," Vol. 15 p. 5.

On the 30th, Charles Durkee, the newly appointed
Governor, arrived in G. S. L. City.

October

On the 6th, the General Conference of the Church
of Jesus Christ of Latter-day Saints assembled in the
Bowery, G. S. L. City. (See "Des. News," Vol. 15,
p. 4.)

On the 10th, the breadstuffs' convention met in the
Tabernacle, G. S. L. City, and agreed to sustain the
prices previously established. (See "Des. News," Vol.
15, p. 5.)

On the same day, the members of Zion's Camp
(Kirtland and Missouri) held their anniversary festival
in the Social Hall.

Brigham Young, when last on the scales, weighed
199 lbs., and when measured, with his feet bare, stood
five (301) feet, eight and a half inches high.

The Indians were still troublesome in Sanpete
Valley. On the 17th, under the leadership of Black
Hawk, they made a sudden descent at Ephraim, killing
seven persons and drove off about a hundred animals.

November

For account of a three days' general muster of the
militia of Great Salt Lake County, the first week in
November, see "Des. News," Vol. 15, p. 36.

Brigham Young issued a circular, urging the construction of a telegraph line through the Territory.
(See "Des. News," Vol. 15, p. 37.)

On the 22nd, Brigham Young was taken sick with
pleurisy, from which, however, he soon recovered.

December

The art of telegraphy was extensively taught in
G. S. L. City, about this time. (See "Des. News,"
Vol. 15, p. 68.)

On the 11th, the Legislative Assembly met in the
State House, G. S. L. City. (303)

INCIDENTS IN HISTORY OF UTAH, 1866

January

On the 2nd, the G. S. L. City Council met for the first time in the new City Hall. The building was dedicated on the 8th.

The military were dispersed around the Territory by General Connor, just at the beginning of winter, and generally they had a cold time of it, building quarters. There were, all told, less than 1500 of them.

Snow was deeper this winter than known for years, and there was excellent sleighing from Cache Valley to Parowan, where the road was broken. In G. S. Lake and Utah Valleys it was estimated at from fifteen to twenty inches deep on the level. In the northern part of the Territory it was nearly a foot deeper. Several people were frozen.

The Rev. Norman M^C. Leod went to California to raise money to build a church; collected $1500 in greenbacks, and, with the aid of a few friends in Utah, built a hall for religious worship, and known as Independence Hall.

Brigham Young, hearing that there were many poor strangers in Salt Lake City and environs, advised the Bishops to hunt them up, and obtain employment for them, and see that they were fed.

This winter, the Navajoes and other Indians committed serious depredations in Southern Utah, and, on the 8th, committed two murders and stole a large (304) number of live stock. Expeditions were sent out after the Indians, and one company killed seven Indians.

February

On the 3rd, Col. George A. Smith was appointed aid-de-camp in the Lieut. General's staff, with the rank of Brigadier General of Cavalry. The order making the appointment, was dated, Head Quarters, Nauvoo Legion, Adjutant General's Office, Great Salt

Lake City, Feb. 3rd, 1866, and signed by Daniel H. Wells, Lieutant General, N. L., and Militia of Utah Territory. Col. Smith was given special orders to organize the military forces of the Iron Military District, to include Iron, Washington, Kane and Beaver Counties, and to act in concert with adjoining counties for the purpose of suppressing Indian depredations.

See "Deseret News," Vol. 15, p. 118, for settlement in Arizona.

In the City Election on the 12th, 2433 votes were polled for Mayor, Daniel H. Wells, also other officers.

On the 26th, a meeting was held in the Council House, G. S. L. City, in order to start a company to regulate the price of flour and supply the Northern Mining regions.

March

A meeting was held on the 3rd, in the G. S. L. City Tabernacle, when a company was (305) organized, under the name of "Utah Produce Company," with Edward Hunter as Chairman, and A. O. Smoot, H. S. Eldridge, H. W. Lawrence, W. S. Godbe, and William Jennings as Directors.

On the 11th, Brigham Young, in meeting, said as the Indians were hostile, let us exercise faith about them, and learn what the will of the Lord was. Let us send our Interpreters to them and make presents and tell them they must stop fighting. It was better to give them $5,000 than have to fight and kill them.

At Independence Hall, Great Salt Lake City, on the evening of the 18th, at 6 p. m., Major (late Captain) Hempstead officiated in place of Rev. N. McLeod, who, by a telegram read at the meeting, was ordered by the Secretary of War, through Gen'l. Pope, to report at Washington, showing that McLeod was attached to the army here. Major Hempstead exhorted the flock not to scatter in the absence of McLeod, and to be assured that his absence would be as short as possible. The Major said that he was willing to lecture on week nights; but respectfully declined taking any part in the services on Sunday nights. At the close, being too bashful to pray, he arose and said, so far as he was concerned, the meeting was dismissed.

About this time, many of the troops in the Territory were being discharged, without much means to take them back to their homes, and many dissatisfied thereat. Those who were stationed in Sanpete and Utah Counties were marched up to G. S. L. City to make (306) up for deficiencies.

April

Indians were still troublesome, killing persons, and running off live stock from Sanpete, through Sevier County, down to the Muddy settlements south of St George.

The general Conference of the Church of Jesus Christ of Latter-day Saints commenced on the 6th, preceeded by meetings on the 4th and 5th, in the Tabernacle, G. S. L. City. (See "Des. News," Apl. 12, p. 148.)

For letter of Erastus Snow concerning improvements in Southern Utah, and Indian troubles there, see "Daily Telegraph," April 7.

In the District Court held at Provo, commencing on the 24th, Judge Drake scored most of the judges who had preceeded him, and had a high time generally.

On the evening of the 27th, some soldiers from Camp Douglass committed a number of outrages in G. S. L. City, shooting at, and barely missing several persons. (See "Des News," Vol. 15, p. 173.)

This spring there were sent from Utah to the Missouri River to assist the emigration to this Territory, 397 wagons, 3042 oxen, 89 horses, 134 mules, 49 mounted guard, 456 teamsters, and 10 captains. (307)

May

On the 1st, Brigham Young wrote to the people in San Pete, Piute and Sevier Counties to collect together in bodies of not less than 150 men, arm themselves well, and take such measures as would effec-

tually secure their lives and property from any further
depredations by the Indians; to guard their cattle by
large bodies of armed men, in going to mill or the
Canyons, or even in going to work in their fields to
adopt the same precautions; and to build strong forts.

Fifty men under the command of Col. H. P.
Kimball left G. S. L. City, and were to be augmented
by other 50 men at Provo, to proceed to Sanpete to aid
the settlers to protect themselves.

For particulars concerning Indian and other affairs
in Southern Utah, see "Des. News," May 24, p. 197.

On the 8th, Col. Potter, and Captains Grimes and
Price, of Camp Douglass, called on Brigham Young,
wishing to know if he would guarantee the protection of
property of certain saloon keepers, who were afraid of
being abated as nuisances under the late city ordinance.
Brigham Young informed them he would do as he had
done, use all his influence for the protection of property. They read a dispatch from Gen. Sherman, which
said, "The Mormons ought to know that the United
States only wanted a pretext to destroy them." (308)

The Militia of Utah County, had a muster on the
8th. (See "Des. News," Vol. 15, p. 189.

On the 10th, two soldiers brutally attacked a man
on the west side of Jordan River, with a slung shot,
knocking him off his horse, but, some men approaching, the soldiers made off. (See "Des. News," May
17, p. 189.)

About this time, Christian Larson, of Spanish
Fork, was shot and killed by a party of ten Indians,
while herding cows on the bench near that city. James
Atkin and Michael Christenson narrowly escaped. The
Indians then returned to the canyon, taking ten head of
horses. Six head of horses since were found killed,
half a mile up the canyon, and it was ascertained that
150 horses in all had been run off in that vicinity

The troops and camp followers came to Utah for
the alleged purpose of the regeneration of its people,
and hence those new comers were popularly known as
"Regenerators," and many very curious scenes in this
"regeneration" business occurred from time to time.
A lady at Springville, whose husband was gone to the

wars (Indian difficulties), was attacked by one of these "regenerators," who endeavored to force her to his wishes, and afterward declared that it was on her invitation. This maddened her still more, and she took a pistol and, on his refusal to retract, she shot and killed him before witnesses. (See "Daily Telegraph," No. 277, May 20. See also Vol. 2, no. 282.) (309)

For historical items, see letter of George A. Smith, "Millennial Star," Vol. 28, p. 412.

June

On the 11th, Gen'l. D. H. Wells left G. S. L. City for San Pete, the scene of Indian troubles, with 25 men.

One hundred militia were preparing to leave the next day, as a relief to those who went some time ago; this relief going for 40 days.

Considerable midnight marauding in the city by parties of soldiers about this time. (See "Daily Telegraph," No. 294.)

The Indians made a raid on Round Valley near the middle of this month, driving off about 300 head of stock and killing two men.

On the 24th, Indians killed one man, wounded another, and ran off some horses at Thistle Valley, Sanpete.

On the 26th, Indians killed one man, wounded another, and ran off some animals near Spanish Fork. (See "Des. News," Vol. 15, p. 245, 255. See also letter of Brigham Young's, "Millennial Star," Vol. 28, p. 523.)

July

The 4th was celebrated in G. S. L. City with great enthusiasm. (See "Des. News," Vol. 15, p. 253.)

On the 9th, Gen. Babcock, of Gen. Grant's staff, who was on a tour of inspection, called on Brigham Young.

For "The Colorado Route" for the transportation of goods from San Franciso to Utah and Montana, See

"Des. News," Vol. 15, p. 253 (310)

On the 13th, Brigham Young and others left G. S. L. City for Grantsville, Tooele Co., returning on the 16th. The new meeting house at Grantsville, 60 x 38 feet, with ante-room 16 x 16 feet, was dedicated on the 15th. (See "Des. News," July 19, p. 260.)

The Mormon Battalion had a social party in the Social Hall, G. S. L. City, on the 16th. (See "Des. News," July 19, p. 260.)

The 24th was observed quietly in G. S. L. City, no public precession, but a liberal display of flags.

On the 26th, the police of G. S. L. City visited three "gambling hells" and destroyed their furniture, etc. (See "Des. News," Vol. 15, p. 277.)

On the 26th, Brigham Young and others left G. S. L. City on a visit to Springville, Utah County, returning on the 29th. (See "Des. News," Vol. 15, p. 276.)

August

On the 6th, Gen. D. H. Wells returned from his southern campaign.

On the 9th, Brigham Young had a visit from Washakick, and a number of Indians. He gave them two beeves and some tobacco.

For various incidents, see letter of B. Young in "Mill. Star," Vol. 28, p. 604.

On the 12th, Hon. W. H. Hooper, Delegate to Congress, arrived in G. S. L. City from Washington. Also John E. Smith, the new Assessor of Internal Revenue for Utah. (311)

On the 17th, Major W^m. Casper and five platoons of his command returned from San Pete, to G. S. L. City, after a campaign of over 65 days. They were addressed by Gen. Wells in front of his residence. Major Casper returned his thanks for their good conduct and behaviour during the whole campaign, after which they were discharged. They gave three cheers for the Major, and quickly dispersed, pleased to get home.

On the 21st, the Gardener's Club of St George, Washington County, had an interesting fruit and vegetable exhibition in the St George Hall. (See "Des. News," Vol. 15, p. 321.)

On the same day Washakee and his tribe, to the number of about 1000, visited Ogden Valley, stayed several days, had a feast, a dance, and a good time generally, received some presents, and left in a very good humor. (See "Des. News," Vol. 15, p. 309.)

On the 30th, Alexander Smith, son of the Prophet Joseph Smith, arrived in G. S. L. City. He was on his way as a missionary to California to preach the claims of his brother Joseph to lead the Church, two other missionaries accompanying him.

September

The surplus water from City Creek, the few last years, having torn out a deep and wide gully in the centre of the upper part of North Temple Street, the City Council were now making an aqueduct or water way, paved with large rocks, at a cost of $25,000. (312) (See "Des. News," Vol. 15, p. 325.)

On the 3rd, Brigham Young and others left G. S. L. City on a visit to Cache Valley, returning on the 12th. (See "Des. News," Vol. 15, pp. 332, 333.)

For account of Southern Utah Agricultural Society Fair, held in the early part of this month at St George, see "Des. News," Vol. 15, p. 349.

The G. S. L. City council, having authorized the city marshal and police to abate certain nuisances where gambling and liquor dealing were going on contrary to the city ordinances, some establishments of that kind were entered and abated, the apparatus being destroyed and the liquor spilt.

More of the militia, who went to Sanpete to assist in protecting the settlers from Indian depredations, returned home this month, and next. (See "Des. News," Vol. 15, pp. 349, 357.)

About this time, a number of unprincipled persons endeavored to squat upon the public squares, parade ground, race course, etc., in G. S. L. City, and considerable excitement ensued in consequence. (See letter of Brigham Young in "Mill. Star," Vol. 28, p. 733;

also "Des. News," Vol. 15, p. 348.)

October

The General Conference of the Church of Jesus Christ of Latter-day Saints, commenced on the 6th in the Bowery, G. S. L. City. (See "Des. News," Vol. 15, p. 356.)

On the 10th, Zion's camp held a re-union festival in the Social Hall, G. S. L. City. (See "Des. News," Vol. 15, p. 365.)

On the 15th, Capt. Haight's train of 65 wagons arrived in G. S. L. City, bringing the wire for the (313) Deseret telegraph.

On the 22nd, Capt. Abner Lowry's train of 60 wagons and about 100 passengers, entered G. S. L. City. This was the last emigration train of the season.

On the 22nd, Dr. J. K. Robinson was decoyed from his house and murdered by some unknown person or persons. (See "Des. News," Vol. 15, pp. 381, 394, 396.)

For Indian raid at South Creek, near Beaver, on the 23rd, see "Des. News," Vol. 15, p. 392.

On the 31st, the Militia of G. S. L. County assembled on the west side of the Jordan at G. S. L. City, for muster and drill, for several days. (See "Des. News," Vol. 15, p. 388.)

November

The first week in November, the telegraphic wire was up between G. S. L. City and Montana.

Men were busy this month in putting up the Deseret Telegraph throughout Utah, from Logan to St. George.

December

For current historical items, see letter of Samuel W. Richards in "Millennial Star," Vol. 29, p. 75.

On the 10th, the Legislative Assembly of the Territory assembled, and the next day Gov. Chas. Durkee presented his message.

On the 20th, a number of merchants of G. S. L. City made a proposition to Brigham Young to sell out to him. (For correspondence on this subject, see "Des. News," Vol. 16, p. 1.)

For sentiments of Brigham Young concerning the murder of Dr. Robinson and similar crimes, see "Des. News," Vol. 16, p. 11. (315)

INCIDENTS IN HISTORY OF UTAH, 1867

January

By the beginning of the year the stone aqueduct, a water way, for the surplus waters of City Creek, was finished, the holes in the street caused by the floods were filled up, and the street brought to a satisfactory grade.

About this time Captain Andrus of St George, and a company, followed a party of marauding Indians, supposed to be Navajoes, who had stolen stock from Pine Valley, and were going south, killed eleven of the Indians and re-captured the stock.

In the "Deseret News" of the 9th, Brigham Young, Heber C. Kimball, and Daniel H. Wells published a circular, advising the people of the Territory, the capitalists particularly, to purchase machinery for manufactruing purposes and establish useful manufactures.

On the 10th, the G. S. L. City Hall clock was first put in fair running and striking order. Weight of clock, 400 lbs., pendulum weight and compensation 60 lbs., diameter of dial three feet, length of pendulum fourteen feet, weight of bell and mounting 875 lbs.

For efforts to create difficulties between the Federal Government and Utah, by Rev. McLeod, Judge S. P. McCurdy, and others, see "Des. News", Vol. 16, p. 12. (316)

On the 15th, the Deseret Telegraph was opened between G. S. L. City and St George. On the 1st of December, 1866, the first message was sent from G. S. L. City to Ogden. (See "Des. News," Vol. 16, p. 28.)

The session of the Legislative Assembly terminated on the 19th. The Legislature memorialized Congress to repeal the Anti-polygamy act of 1862, and to admit Utah into the Union as a State.

In "Des. News," Vol. 16, p. 36, Jan. 30, Amasa M. Lyman, one of the Twelve Apostles, published his

confession that he had taught false doctrine in denying
the atonement of Jesus Christ.

For character of John B. Weller, see "Des.
News," Vol. 16, p. 28.

On the 23rd, the new meeting house, 50 by 30 feet,
in the 8th Ward, G. S. L. City, was dedicated. (See
"Des. News," Vol. 16, p. 37.)

February

On the 4th, Wm H. Hooper was elected Delegate
to Congress for the Territory, and Representative to
Congress on the Union State ticket. The election was
also for the "Amended Constitution" of the State of
Deseret.

On the 12th, Brigham Young had a social party at
the Lion House, Gov. Durkee and many (317) of the
influential men of the city being present.

About this time, Nevada State Legislature passed
a resolution to petition Congress to annex Utah to
Nevada, or Nevada to Utah.

For letter of a Mormon woman in regard to marriage, etc., see "Des. News," Vol. 16, p. 57.

For a Frenchman's Views of the Mormons, see
"Des. News," Vol. 16, p. 262.

On the 24th, Brighton, a few miles west of G. S.
L. City, was organized, by Geo. A. Smith and A. M.
Musser, as an eccleseastical ward, with Andrew W.
Cooley bishop. (See "Des. News," Vol. 16, p. 69.)

On the 25th, Hon. John Bidwell presented a resolution in the House of Representatives for a larger
military force in Utah.

For article on proposed annexation of Utah to
Nevada, and on Nevada, --its Government and Finances,
see "Des. News," Vol. 16, p. 68.

March

On the 7th, Orson Hyde wrote concerning the
Indian troubles in Sanpete. He said in 1866 the settlers
had kept from 300 to 500 men constantly on duty to op-
erate against the Indians, expense and charges borne

by the settlements; that in 1865 about 200 were on similar duty; that about a hundred Indians and 60 whites
had been killed in all. (See "Des. News," Vol. 16, p.
94.) (318)

During the winter just passed, the people of the
Territory built 432 miles of electric telegraph line,
connecting the principal settlements north and south,
with a branch line of 65 miles, making 497 miles in
all.

On the 21st, the Deseret State company was organized, with Brigham Young as president. (See "Des.
News," Vol. 16, p. 109.)

On the 20th, Indians made a raid on the stock of
Glenwood and Richfield. Part of the stock was recovered, and one man was wounded. Three persons were
found killed and horribly mutilated near Richfield.

On the 23rd, Brigham Young and D. H. Wells
went on a visit to Grantsville, where a company had
preceded them, returning on the 25th.

On the 23rd, Daniel H. Wells,' Secretary of State
for the State of Deseret, certified that the constitution
of the State of Deseret, as proposed to be amended by
the act passed by the State Legislative Assembly, had
been adopted and ratified by the people of the State at
the election, and that the proposed amendments had
become constituent parts of said Constitution. At the
general Election, held on the 4th of February, 1867,
fourteen thousand and five votes were cast for, and
thirty votes against said amendments. (319)

April

(*) For article on explorations on the Colorado River,
by Henry W. Miller, Jacob Hamblin, and Jesse W.
Crosby, see "Des. News," Vol. 16, p. 209.

On the 14th, John B. Meredith arrived near the
bridge on the Jordan River, with the schooner "Star of
the West," having a cargo of salt from Great Salt Lake,
he claiming it as the first voyage up the river from the
lake, thus proving the river navigable. (See "Des.
News," Vol. 16, p. 133.)

On the 22nd, Brigham Young and company started

[The following paragraph should be inserted in page 370, opposite, as the paragraph preceeding the (*).]

On the 6th, the General Conference of the Church of Jesus Christ of Latter-day Saints commenced in the Tabernacle, G. S. L. City. (See "Des. News," Vol. 16, p. 116.)

from G. S. L. City on a visit to St. George, returning
May 15. (See "Des. News," Vol. 16, pp. 141, 144,
148, 161, 165.

On the 30th, it was decided to silence Amasa M.
Lyman from preaching, because of his persistent denial of the atonement of Jesus Christ.

May

Concerning the Indian troubles in Sanpete County,
see "Des. News," Vol. 16, p. 148.

On the 15th, Brigham Young and company arrived
in G. S. L. City, on their return from a visit to St
George, and were very heartily welcomed by the people. (See "Des. News," Vol. 16, p. 161.) (320)

June

On the 1st, Indians made a raid on Fountain Green,
Sanpete Co., and ran off some stock, killing one man
and wounding two others. Being closely pursued, they
shot most of the stock. On the 2nd, they killed two
men at Twelve Mile Creek, in that county. On the 7th,
they attacked a merchant train, killed two men, and
ran off some stock near Washakie Station, about 300
miles east. (See "Des. News, Vol. 16, pp. 181, 189,
192, 197, 201.)

On the 22nd, Indians ran off stock from near
Paragoonah, Iron County.

Provo Bridge floated away on the 23rd, the river
was spreading wide and the water doing considerable
damage.

On the 24th, a detachment of militia left G. S. L.
City for the Sanpete and Sevier country, to assist in
protecting the settlers from Indian depredations.
About a hundred volunteers were assisting in the above
object. The settlements in Sevier and Piute counties
had been abandoned, in consequence of Indian attacks.

July

The 4th was celebrated in G. S. L. City, with

procession, oration, speeches, etc. (See "Des. News,"
Vol. 16, p. 220.)

On the 16th, a grand anniversary ball was given in
the theatre, in commemoration of (321) the enrollment
of the Mormon Battalion. (See "Des. News," Vol. 16,
pp. 225, 236.)

About this time, much of the eastern mail matter
came in very irregularly, and some of it robbed or
purposely mutilated.

The 24th was observed in G. S. L. City by a grand
pioneer ball in the theatre, and in the settlements in
various ways. (See "Des. News," Vol. 16, pp. 244,
245.)

On the 27th, the juveniles of G. S. L. City had a
social party in the theatre.

On the same day, clouds of grasshoppers were in
the air, many of them alighting and feeding in and near
the city.

Brigham Young and others visited South Willow
Creek (Draper) returning the next day.

August

On the 1st and 2nd, grasshoppers innumerable
were eating up the vegetation in G. S. L. Valley and
parts adjacent. These insects had been troublesome,
more or less, for about a week previously, and continued a week or more longer. (See "Des. News,"
Vol. 16, pp. 248, 260, 284.)

On the 11th, the West Jordan Ward Meeting
House was dedicated, Brigham Young being present.
(See "Des. News," Vol. 16, p. 261.)

On the 12th, Indians made a raid on the teams of
Springtown, Sanpete County; also killing (322) one man
and mortally wounding another. (See "Des. News,"
Vol. 16, pp. 268, 274.)

On the 16th, Brigham Young and others started on
a visit to Tooele, returning on the 18th. (See "Des.
News," Vol. 16, p. 269.)

On the 23rd, Brigham Young and others started on
a visit to Utah County, returning on the 28th, attending
the dedication of the new meeting house at Provo on

the 24th. (See "Des. News," Vol. 16, p. 282.)

Indian Supt. Head had a talk with Black Hawk, chief of the raiding bands, at the Uintah reservation, who expressed a desire for peace. (See "Des. News," Vol. 16, p. 277.)

September

On the 2nd, Brigham Young and others started from G. S. L. City on a visit to Bear Lake Valley returning on the 17th. (See "Des. News, Vol. 16, pp. 293, 300, 306, 309, 319.)

Orson Hyde spoke of the increase of water in various streams and places. (See "Des. News," Vol. 16, p. 281.)

On the 4th, Indians killed a man near Warm Creek, Sanpete. (See "Des. News," Vol. 16, pp. 293, 301.)

On the 4th and 5th, the Gardeners' Club had a very interesting and successful fair at St George. (See "Mill. Star," Vol. 29, p. 685.)

For articles concerning "Federal Judges in Utah," (323) see "Des. News," Vol. 16, pp. 292, 308.

This month, Elbert Eastam and Ben Hampton, having built a yacht at Bear River bridge, sailed down Bear River to G. S. Lake, 75 miles, thence up the Jordan River to G. S. L. City, making the journey in two days.

October

On the 6th, the general conference of the Church of Jesus Christ of Latter-day Saints commenced in the new but unfinished Tabernacle. (See "Des. News," Vol. 16, p. 313.

About this time the "Deseret News" was not issued with perfect regularity, owing to Indians running off a freight train near Plum Creek and burning the stock of printing paper on the way to G. S. L. City in August. (See "Des. News," Vol. 16, p. 316.)

On the 10th, about 40 members of Zion's Camp (Kirtland and Missouri) had a social party in G. S. L. City.

November

On the 4th, a meeting of superintendents and teachers was held in the 13th Ward Assembly Rooms, to organize a Sunday School Union. Geo. Q. Cannon was elected President. (See "Des. News," Vol. 16, p. 325.)

The "Des. News" of the 20th contains the valedictory (324) of Albert Carrington as Editor, and the salutatory of George Q. Cannon as his successor.

On the 21st, the first number of the "Deseret Evening News," daily, appeared. The Semi-Weekly "Deseret News" was commenced Oct. 8.

In "Deseret News" of the 27th appears the prospectus of the "Utah Magazine," a literary journal, edited by E. L. T. Harrison.

In October and November militia musters and drills were held in the various counties. (See "Des. News," Vol. 16, pp. 321, 325.)

December

On the 1st, a new meeting house 34 by 24 feet, with a gallery 14 by 24 feet, was dedicated. (See "Des. News," weekly, Vol. 16, p. 355.)

On the 2nd, a meeting was held at the Council House to inaugurate the opening of classes under the name of the "School of the Prophets." (See "Des. News," weekly, Vol. 16, p. 337.)

Hon. W. H. Hooper, in the House of Representatives, introduced a bill for the admission of Deseret as a State into the Union.

On the 29th, Mill Creek Ward Meeting House, G. S. L. County, was dedicated. The building was 40 by 62 feet, with a vestry 18 by 25 feet and two stories high.

INDEX

384

bury's Island).

Donovan, Capt. ---, 197, 206.

Dotson, Peter K. , 251, 257, 259-60, 263-5, 278, 280, 283, 285-6, 292-3, 295, 297, 306.

Doty, J. Duane, 340-1,343 -5, 349, 355.

Douglas, Stephen A. , 54, 143, 219.

Dowry, ---, 154.

Drake, Thos. B. , 326, 329, 334-5, 340.

Draper, ---, 372.

Driggs, Starling, 8.

Drummond, Mrs. Ella P. , 355.

Drummond, Wm. W. , 162, 166, 169, 181, 352, 355.

Duffin, Isaac, 135.

Duncan, Capt. Homer, 330.

Durfee, A. , 284.

Durkee, Gov. Charles, 357, 366, 369.

Dutch East India Co. , 298.

Dunyon, John L. , 82, 86.

Eagle Gate, 274.

Earl, Jacob, 21.

Earl, Jesse, 187, 188.

Earthquake, 138.

Eastam, Elbert, 373.

Echo Canyon, 192-3, 197, 202-5, 209, 221, 224,233, 235-6, 317.

Eccles, Delano, 197, 207- 8, 227, 234-5, 245, 249, 253-4, 259, 293, 295,297.

Eckles, Judge (see Eccles, Delano).

Edelman, James, 59.

Edwards, Edward, 164.

Egan, Howard, 25, 110, 179, 219, 224, 229, 303, 342.

Egar, John, 58.

Eldredge, Alanson, 29.

Eldredge, Horace S. , 33, 55, 64.

Eldredge, Ira, 12, 29, 32, 55, 78, 171.

Eldredge, John, 57-8.

Eldridge, H. S. , 46, 360.

Ellswork, Edmund, 228.

Ellsworth, Edmund, 35, 57, 175, 228.

Elk Mountain, 162, 164.

Emigration, 94, 123, 156, 163, 175-6, 182-3, 185, 271, 294, 304-5, 307-8, 311, 316, 328-31, 340-4, 348, 350, 361, 366.

Emigration Canyon, 5, 354.

Emigration Road, 200, 207.

Endowment House, 348.

England, 67, 218, 348.

Ensign Peak, 3.

Ensign, Samuel, 71.

Ephraim, 336, 358.

Epistle, First General, 48.

Epistle, Second General, 68.

Epistle, Fifth General,86.

Epistle, Sixth General, 101.

Epistle, Seventh General, 120.

Epistle, Ninth General,

392

343.

Smith, Lt. Col. ---, 241, 247-8, 282.

Smith, Alex, 365.

Smith, Andrew, 204, 296.

Smith, Elias, 170, 243.

Smith, George A., 1-5, 68, 71, 73, 76-7, 94, 109-10, 112, 121, 127-8, 133-4, 136-7, 142-4, 149-50, 154-6, 158, 162, 168-71, 182-4, 192, 210, 218, 220 -1, 227, 234, 237-9, 242-3, 248, 250-1, 265-6, 268, 273, 277, 281, 285-7, 291, 297, 302, 306-7, 312, 314, 318, 323-4, 326, 333, 337, 341-3, 348, 356, 359, 363, 369.

Smith, Geo. A., Jr., 308, 310.

Smith, Hyrum, 282.

Smith, J. C. L., 56-8, 133, 157.

Smith, Jesse N., 168, 227, 240, 248, 250.

Smith, Job, 67, 94.

Smith, John E., 364.

Smith, John L., 131, 310, 343.

Smith, John, 20, 21, 25, 251, 306.

Smith, Joseph, 220, 282, 365.

Smith, Lot, 192, 203, 327, 329.

Smith, Lucy, 357.

Smith, Oliver, 210.

Smith, S. S., 248.

Smith, Silas, 289.

Smith, Col. Thomas L., 156, 225.

Smith, Wm. R., 212.

Smoot, A. O., 22, 33, 46, 170, 259-60, 263, 296-7, 300, 353, 360.

Snake Indians, 34, 261.

Snow, ---, 126.

Snow, Erastus, 1, 25, 35, 66-8, 128, 137-40, 143, 163, 170, 220, 237, 301, 361.

Snow, Geo., 190.

Snow, J. C., 239, 278-9.

Snow, Lorenzo, 22, 66-8, 137, 237.

Snow, Warren, 173, 243, 266.

Snow, Willard, 31, 55, 60, 66-7, 76, 89, 90.

Snow, William, 82.

Snow, Zerubbabel, 90, 101, 104, 109-10, 112, 149, 259, 298.

Snyder's Mill, 135.

Society Islands, 24-5, 67.

Soda Springs, Ida., 337-8.

Social Hall, 153-5, 177-8, 268, 299, 302, 309, 311, 349, 351-2, 356-7, 364, 366.

South Carolina, 309.

South Cottonwood, 179.

South Fork, 4.

South Fort Valley (Beaver), 169.

South Pass, 126, 141, 171, 211, 247.

South Weber, 311.

Southern Exploring Co., 69.

Southworth, H. S., 149, 215.